University of Washington Publications on Asia

Sponsored by the Far Eastern and Russian Institute

THIS BOOK is a product of the Modern Chinese History Project carried on by the Far Eastern and Russian Institute of the University of Washington. Members of the group represent various disciplines in the social sciences and humanities. The work of the project is of a cooperative nature with each member assisting the others through critical discussion and the contribution of ideas and material. The responsibility for each study rests with the author.

LI HUNG-CHANG
and the HUAI ARMY

A Study in Nineteenth-Century Chinese Regionalism

By Stanley Spector

Introduction

Regionalism in Nineteenth-Century China

BY FRANZ MICHAEL

University of Washington Press   Seattle

Copyright © 1964 by the University of Washington Press
Library of Congress Catalog Card Number 64-11052
Printed in the United States of America

IN MEMORY OF LYNN

Preface

THE dissolution of the Manchu Empire in the late nineteenth and early twentieth century, followed by the rise of the Republic of China and later the Communist Chinese People's Republic, were events that have compelled the ever increasing attention of the world. After centuries of self-enforced seclusion, China has gained for herself a place in world affairs that brings her into the current of modern history. The movements that brought contemporary China into being, like all historical developments, arose from forces deep within the society, but it requires relevant experience, such as the decades of conflict and revolution witnessed in China, to illuminate them.

The theoretical foundations of this study were laid to a great extent by Professor Franz Michael, in his work on Chinese regionalism and its effect on the development of modern Chinese institutions and political power. I have placed this theory in a smaller framework, organized around a personality, Li Hung-chang, following him through the sets of conflicts that appear to me to have been the major interacting forces dominating the Chinese scene in the fifty or sixty years that ushered in the Chinese Revolution of 1911.

Li Hung-chang was one of the outstanding figures in modern Chinese history. In him one sees a meeting point, a representation of conflicts, thus a true historical personality. When Li entered upon his long and remarkable career in the middle of the nineteenth century, China had already experienced her first defeat at the hands of the Western nations. As a result of the Opium War the Manchu rulers of China had been forced to open five ports (Shanghai, Amoy, Foochow, Ningpo, and Canton) for foreign trade and residence of Western merchants, missionaries, and diplomatic representatives. Hong Kong was ceded to

Great Britain and became a naval base for the British. These were small beginnings; the West.touched only small portions of China's vast coastline, and her interior was still unaffected by foreign influence. In the years following the first Treaty Settlement of 1842-44 foreign trade grew, and foreign steamships began to ply China's coast and rivers; gradually China was being drawn into the world market and reshaped by alien cultures.

The process of acculturation was long and painful; eventually every aspect of Chinese social organization was affected. Old ideas had to be reformulated and even abandoned, and institutions proven satisfactory in the past had to be reformed if they were to survive at all. Such changes point up the relationships among the various institutions within a society. A stable society is a delicate balance of forces, a continuum of equilibria in which the variables have been brought into temporary balance. To alter one factor is to set in motion a series of changes and readjustments that depend upon alterations all along the line. When such changes are occurring perceptibly, the future is uncertain and security is undermined. For this reason those who are content with their lot in society are often reluctant to accept any changes. But conservatism of this kind is only possible in a society with few outside contacts, where strong controls exist and where levels of expectation can be kept constant through various forms of social and ideological manipulation.

Such was the condition of conservatism in traditional China, particularly during the Manchu period before the Western incursions (1644-1838). The Manchus had effected a coalition with the Chinese gentry class which secured the positions of both parties. The gentry were set apart from the commoners and given exclusive career privileges in the government bureaucracy. This bureaucracy served the Manchu-dominated state and upheld the system which kept the Manchus on the throne and in occupation of China, and the gentry class as a whole (though not as individual families) at the upper level of the social structure. The system worked remarkably well. China remained a distinct empire with sufficient co-ordination on a national scale, effected through the bureaucracy and the standardization of gentry values and efforts, to carry on the essential functions of any large centralized governmental organization, particularly defense, taxation, and the protection of basic industry and trade. On the local level, tradition, manifested through custom, ritual, education, and the countless forms of activity that constitute social behavior, bolstered stability and discouraged tendencies toward change. During the very period when Europe and America were experiencing the profound series of social, political, and economic changes that we call the Industrial Revolution, China was bound in a conservatism that was to leave her dangerously weak in the face of the technology and science maturing outside the Great Wall.

The most profound of the conflicts in which Li Hung-chang played his role was centered around the problem of westernization. Li was one of the few great Chinese officials of his period who clearly perceived that China's survival as a nation depended upon her ability to absorb Western culture. To be sure, his view was limited. The aspects of Western culture that interested him most had to do with military tech-nology and organization and with economic development. But these are fundamental matters. Theory and science are nurtured in material environments, and application is a powerful spur to thought. In this respect Li Hung-chang was a great planter of ideas. Against the will of an entrenched opposition he built armies, shipyards, factories, and railroads which depended on Western techniques, and he accustomed a whole generation of Chinese to these important aspects of modern culture. The importance of Li as a modernizer of the nineteenth cen-tury makes him worth observing. His efforts illuminate the problems that overwhelmed China and the considerations that guided the choices made by Chinese leaders as they took steps to meet these problems. A study of Li's career affords a view of the chain of developments that brought China into the modern age.

The second great conflict in which Li was caught up was the conflict within the Chinese ruling group itself. All political movement takes place against a background of interest conflicts, whether on the class, group, or individual level. In nineteenth-century China repression and exploitation of the great mass of common people were carried on through the Manchu-gentry coalition. Large-scale rebellions, such as the Taiping, Nien, and Hui rebellions of the late nineteenth century, were indications of very deep and widespread conflicts between the people and their ruling coalition. But these rebellions were ruthlessly suppressed. Li first became famous as one of the greatest and most ruthless of the suppressors. As a member of the ruling group, how-ever, Li was also involved in a struggle for power for his own interests. This conflict, viewed broadly, took the shape of a running battle between the central government, directly under the Manchus, and the regional officialdom dominated by members of the gentry class who had turned to militarism during the long years of rebellion after 1850. Opportunities for military leadership placed in the hands of these regional leaders weapons which they employed to bulwark them in their quest for security and greater power within the bureaucracy. Li Hung-chang rose to be the most powerful of these nineteenth-century regional leaders, achieving an almost unique position in the political hierarchy. An examination of the stages of his rise, the methods he employed to strengthen himself, and the institutional reforms he effected in order to maintain his power helps us weigh the factors and dynamics of power within a bureaucratically dominated society.

Closely related to the struggle between the central government and regional leaders were the conflicts among the regional leaders themselves. Li's activities, followed in detail, provide interesting insights into official behavior and the manner in which officials used governmental, military, and economic machinery to extend their influence and carve out for themselves bases of power within various regions of China and particular segments of the bureaucracy. The methods through which they built up and maintained personal followings and the outlooks which accompanied such activity likewise became important precedents for modern Chinese political behavior.

During Li's long career he employed hundreds of men, reflecting their interests, directing their careers, and placing them in position for the roles they were to play later. The study of Li Hung-chang must of necessity furnish glimpses of these men, two of whom were to serve as presidents of the Republic of China. While I have tried to avoid the obvious temptation of making history revolve around my central character and do not want to credit or blame Li for the doings of his successors, I found it instructive to compare Li and the contemporaries of his early life with the men he later patronized. The difference between these types of leaders was more than a difference in years. There was a vast cultural gulf between the traditional leaders like Li, who responded in a novel way to new situations, and the later transitional generation of militarists, specialists, and bureaucratic merchants.

No one familiar with Chinese history, or for that matter with Chinese opera, will be surprised to find that the main theme of this work is a military one. Despite the popular belief that China was a land of peace where the pen was more powerful than the sword, force was an important determinant of power. In China no means for the peaceful transfer of power or assertion of interests existed. The great civil bureaucracy which, it is apparent, did encourage a literary orientation among the upper class, was tied to military power and held down by the ultimate threat of force. By building up and jealously guarding his own military forces, Li gained sufficient strength to escape bureaucratic bondage. The power organization he developed on this basis introduced China to the modern world and fatally challenged the power of the imperial government.

S.S.

Acknowledgments

I WISH to thank the members of the Modern Chinese History Project, University of Washington, for their group efforts, extending over a period of years, which have been the primary influence on this work. While it is hardly possible to acknowledge adequately all the individual contributions, I wish to express my particular debt to Franz H. Michael and George E. Taylor, who have given the manuscript their attention from its inception as the draft of a doctoral dissertation. Chung-li Chang, Chang-tu Hu, Siang-tseh Chiang, and James Liu provided great help in checking translations, suggesting sources, and helping me to understand many of the complicated features of Chinese administration and practice. Hellmut Wilhelm, Kung-chuan Hsiao, Vincent Shih, and Lawrence Krader offered penetrating criticism and many constructive suggestions. Chao-ying Fang, formerly of the Chinese History Project, Columbia University and University of Washington, provided helpful guidance in the early stages of the work and brought to my attention the poem by Li Hung-chang quoted in Chapter I.

In London I had the advantage of the scholarly judgments of Professors O. B. van der Sprenkel, Edwin G. Pulleyblank, and R. H. Tawney, whose interest in the manuscript provided great encouragement.

My original concern with Li Hung-chang's role in the bureaucracy was shaped by my contact with Karl August Wittfogel, who helped me toward a better understanding of the nature of the bureaucracy in imperial China.

I wish also to draw the attention of the reader to Professor Albert Feuerwerker's fine study of early Chinese industrial enterprises and the role of Sheng Hsüan-huai, a leading industrial promoter, entitled *China's Early Industrialization*, which was published by Harvard University Press in 1958. Professor Feuerwerker's book came to hand too late for reference within the body of my text, but its contribution to an understanding of the general field, and indeed, of Li Hung-chang himself, warrants this special mention.

Dr. Ruth Krader, Curator of the Far Eastern Library, University of Washington, furnished unfailingly courteous and efficient bibliographic service. Invaluable editorial criticism, advice, and assistance from Miss Gladys Greenwood brought the manuscript close to completion. In the final stages I had the additional help of Mrs. Beverly Plank, also of the Far Eastern and Russian Institute, University of Washington.

I am grateful also to Professor Kuo T'ing-i for his reading of the final manuscript and to Dr. J. P. Lo for help in checking certain points. My secretary, the late Miss Lynn Kauffman, carefully checked the entire manuscript and was of invaluable aid in the organization of the statistical material and tables of personnel. To all of them I owe my special thanks. For her general readings and encouragement, Juanita Spector has my deepest appreciation.

Finally I wish to express my gratitude to the Social Science Research Council which provided me a Research and Training Grant enabling me to carry out important parts of my research in this country and England.

ABBREVIATIONS

Chinkiang Consular Despatches	United States Department of State. *Despatches from United States Consuls in Chinkiang, 1865-1902.*
CSK	*Ch'ing-shih kao.*
Lu-chou chih	*Hsü-hsiu Lu-chou fu-chih.*
LWCK Collected Works	*Li Wen-chung kung ch'üan-chi.*
LWCK Foreign Office Letters	"I-shu han-kao," in *Li-Wen-chung kung ch'üan-chi.*
LWCK Letters	"P'eng-liao han-kao," in *Li Wen-chung kung ch'üan-chi.*
LWCK Memorials	"Tsou-kao," in *Li Wen-chung kung ch'üan-chi.*
LWCK Naval Board Letters	"Hai-chün han-kao," in *Li Wen-chung kung ch'üan-chi.*
LWCK Telegrams	"Tien-kao," in *Li Wen-chung kung ch'üan-chi.*
NCH	*The North China Herald and Supreme Court and Consular Gazette.*
Shanghai Consular Despatches	United States Department of State. *Despatches from United States Consuls in Shanghai, 1847-1906.*
Tientsin Consular Despatches	United States Department of State. *Despatches from United States Consuls in Tientsin, 1868-1906.*
Tso, *Shih tzu-liao*	Tso Shun-sheng, *Chung-kuo chin-pai-nien shih tzu-liao ch'u-pien.*
TWCK Letters	*Tseng Wen-cheng kung shu-cha.*
TWCK Memorials	"Tsou-kao," in *Tseng Wen-cheng kung ch'üan-chi.*
TWCK nien-p'u	"Nien-p'u," in *Tseng Wen-cheng kung ch'üan-chi.*

Contents

INTRODUCTION, *by Franz Michael*   xxi

I   EARLY CAREER   3

II   THE RISE OF THE HUAI-CHÜN   25

III   LI HUNG-CHANG TAKES OVER KIANGSU   51

IV   THE HUAI-CHÜN AND THE NIEN REBELLION   102

V   THE HUAI-CHÜN IN TRANSITION   128

VI   LI HUNG-CHANG AND THE PROBLEM OF "SELF-STRENGTHENING"   152

VII   PROBLEMS OF MILITARY FINANCING   195

VIII   LI HUNG-CHANG'S QUEST FOR "WEALTH AND STRENGTH"   234

IX   THE DISINTEGRATION OF LI HUNG-CHANG'S POWER   259

X   THE MAN AND HIS INFLUENCE   270

REIGN PERIODS OF THE CH'ING DYNASTY   321

GLOSSARY OF CHARACTERS   323

BIBLIOGRAPHY   333

INDEX   341

Tables

1. Hsiang-chün Officers by Origin and Career   21
2. Huai-chün Company and Personal Guard Organizations   43
3. Huai-chün Components in 1865   99
4. Revenue Sources for the Suppression of the Nien   125
5. Huai-chün Accounts, 1871-93   202
6. Huai-chün Income, Expenditures, and Balances, 1871-92   206
7. Huai-chün Income by Region   208
8. Huai-chün Income Bases   214
9. Annual Quota for Huai-chün Revenue, 1885   216
10. Tientsin Coastal Defense Reports   221
11. Pei-yang Defense Accounts, 1875-91   222
12. Sources of Income for Pei-yang Defense, 1875-91   223
13. Sources of Pei-yang Revenue in Percentages   224
14. Regional Sources of Pei-yang Income   225
15. Total Reported Huai-chün and Pei-yang Income, 1873-93   231
16. Huai-chün and Tientsin Coastal Defense (Lien-chün) Combined Income   232
17. Western-oriented Functionaries under Li   288
18. Li's Military Officers   301

Maps

Shanghai–Nanking Area   26
Huai-chün Campaigns in Kiangsu, 1862-64   85
Location of the Huai-chün: 1870-92   140-41

Introduction

Regionalism in Nineteenth-Century China

By Franz Michael

REGIONALISM has been one of the most important phenomena in Chinese imperial history. By "regionalism" is meant the emergence in key areas of China of military and political power centers that assumed some of the important functions of the state but still remained within its framework. The emergence of such regional power centers occurred in periods of crisis, when the authority of the dynasty's central government had been weakened and the dynasty's political decline invited the establishment of such regional governmental machines.

The nineteenth century was a time of such internal crisis: the Ch'ing dynasty, weakened by the decline of its administrative and military organization, was shaken by a number of large rebellions that threatened the survival of the dynasty. During this period of chaos and rebellion, regional armies were formed by outstanding gentry leaders—men like Tseng Kuo-fan, who established the pattern followed by others and who became the mentor and senior colleague of Li Hung-chang, one of the leading figures in the China of his time. These regional leaders organized their own military forces in their home regions, combined this locally-based military power with political organizations loyal to them, and drew their financial support from the regions they occupied. These regional organizations provided their leaders with bases of autonomous power.

Yet they did not challenge the final authority of the dynasty itself. The powers they exercised were indeed invasions into the central field of authority which a strong dynastic government would never permit, but the incapacity of the weakened Ch'ing government to carry out successfully its administrative and military responsibilities left a power void, which was then filled by these regional leaders. In assuming military, administrative, and financial authority, the regionalists still recognized the ideological authority of the dynastic center of the state based on the mandate of heaven. And for that reason their assumption of authority and their organization of regional bureaucratic machines remained within the framework of the dynastic state, even while undermining its authority and contributing to its eventual downfall.

What made possible the emergence of such regional organizations and what determined their nature? The answer lies in the bureaucratic nature of Chinese society; the relation between the Chinese society and state; the character of the educated elite, the gentry, and its functions in society and state; and in the central government's problem of maintaining control over its own local administration and preserving an appropriate balance between the power of the state and the autonomy of the sphere of the Confucian social order. Indeed, an examination of the phenomenon of regionalism, which emerged when the whole imperial system was out of balance, provides a clearer view of the complex system of balances and tensions that was maintained when the Confucian society and state were functioning successfully.

The Dual Role of the Gentry

The emergence of regional organizations that cut into the power of the dynastic government was made possible by the dual role played by the educated elite of imperial China, the gentry, which provided the social leadership that managed the affairs of Chinese society and also formed the stratum from which the government selected its official staff and on which it had therefore to depend.

Whenever the central authority declined, regional political organizations could be formed and assume some functions of government because the stratum of educated elite from which the state staffed its organization remained intact; the members of this educated elite continued to act as social functionaries and were always ready to lead or to transfer their service to the newly emerging political organizations. It was the gentry's role in state and society that formed the link between social continuity and political reorganization.

The gentry's role in imperial society and state was based on their acknowledged superiority in the knowledge of the rules of human conduct and management of human affairs accepted in this society. Their authority was based on their education—an education through which they gained not only the skills needed for the management of people and affairs, skill in the writing of the official language, knowledge of the history and practice of government, and proficiency in the handling of affairs within the existing social order, but, most of all, an inculcation in the ethical precepts of Confucianism, which were the heart of the Chinese cultural tradition. The Confucian order, of which the gentry were the guardians and representatives, assigned to them functions of arbiter and of organizer, which they were assumed to carry out by applying in practice the ethical tenets of the Confucian teachings that made up the principles of operation of both the society and state. Through their knowledge of the accepted rules of human conduct, this educated elite had become a professional group that provided the managers of affairs indispensable for the functioning of the Confucian order. Their qualifications were individually gained through education in the Confucian classics, and recognized and guaranteed by the dynastic government through the examination system.

The relationship between the dynastic governments and the educated stratum, the Confucian gentry, originated in early imperial time when the Han rulers made their peace with the Confucian scholars and accepted their services for the state. In doing this the dynasty recognized the Confucian interpretation of the social order and gained at the same time the sanction for its government that Confucianism provided. In Sung time this relationship between the educated elite and the state became formalized through the full development of the examination system, which gave the state's confirmation of the gentry's academic qualification as the necessary prerequisite for official service. By Ch'ing time this system had reached further sophistication, and the gentry's leading position and privileges were entirely based on the academic degrees that verified the gentry's qualification. The qualification thus ascertained gave the gentry not only a monopoly of state service but also the state's assent to their autonomous role as public functionaries in society.

The government's acceptance of the gentry's role as public functionaries in society was a major factor that worked for the stability of the Chinese system. Chinese imperial history is famous for the length of its unbroken tradition of over 2,000 years. However, it was the social institutional tradition and its intellectual basis rather than the political order that provided the continuity of Chinese imperial history. The instability of the dynastic history with its cyclical crises and new beginnings stands in marked contrast to the relative stability of the social institutional order in imperial times. The survival of the Chinese tradition therefore depended on the strength of its social order.

The importance of the social order in the continuity of Chinese history was all the greater because the area of the activity of the dynastic state was far more limited than is usually recognized. The dynastic government concerned itself in the main with what it regarded as the decisive spheres of political authority—the areas of supreme importance for power and control. Military force was in principle a government prerogative; the people were forbidden by law to carry arms,[1] and only the emperor's officers and officials had the right to lead troops. The dynastic government reserved to itself the right to impose and collect taxes, and the government had the monopoly of appointment of civil and military officials, who were solely responsible to the head of the government, the emperor. The government had also the law-making power, though its code was a criminal code only and therefore limited in its sphere of application.[2] It was meant to support the Confucian moral code, which was basic for all human relations. These were the major areas in which the government tried to maintain a monopoly, and although in other spheres officials might become active, there was no attempt to monopolize; and much of the official activity shaded over and was connected with the autonomous power of the local leadership of the gentry.

The limited scope of state functions can also be readily deduced from

---

[1] There was always a conflict between the government's inclination to prohibit the possession of all weapons by anyone except its own military forces and the necessity to tolerate private possession by the civilian population of some weapons for self-defense against banditry and in times of unrest. The distinction is quite clearly drawn in many of the government regulations that deal with this problem. See, for instance, *Ta-Ch'ing hui-tien shih-li,* compiled by K'un-kang *et al.* (Shanghai, 1908), 772:3a-14b. The control of men and horses and the possession of armor, shields, guns and cannons, or of banners and signal flags were strongly prohibited under threat of severe punishment. The use of bows and arrows, spears, swords, and crossbows, and of pitchforks and tridents was, however, permitted. There were periods when even these weapons were forbidden. See *Ch'ing-ch'ao wen-hsien t'ung-k'ao* (Wan-yu wen-k'u ed.; Shanghai, 1936), 195:6599: "In the fifth year [of Shun-chih (1648)], the prohibition on private possession of weapons was tightened. The Board of Punishment, after a meeting, secured an imperial decree that henceforth no one, excepting civil and military officers on duty and soldiers, might privately have possession of muskets, guns, armor, spears, swords, bows and arrows, and other weapons. The penalty for violation was death to the violator, confiscation of his property, and enslavement of his wife and children by the state. The heads of ten households residing adjacent to him were to be beaten and banished."

However, one year later this strict regulation was modified again: "In the sixth year, because the people had no weapons and could not defend themselves against bandits and this was to the bandits' benefit, it was decreed that except for guns and armor, which were as before strictly forbidden, the people might possess muskets, fowling pieces, bows and arrows, swords, spears, horses, etc."

[2] See Franz Michael, "The Role of Law in Traditional, Nationalist, and Communist China," *The China Quarterly,* January-March, 1962.

the small size of the government's official staff. During Ch'ing time there were only some 40,000 civil and military officials—most of whom were in the capital—to manage, with the help of their secretaries and underlings, all those affairs that the government reserved for itself or tried to handle. This small number of officials is in sharp contrast to the large size of the whole group of degree-holding gentry, from which this staff was selected. In Ch'ing time some 1,000,000 to 1,500,000 gentry provided the social leadership that could carry on the affairs that the government did not handle.[3]

The large majority of the gentry thus never became officials but carried on in their home districts and provinces a great variety of functions on which the well-being of society and the safety of the government depended. The services the gentry were expected to render ranged from arbitration, welfare activities, and the management or co-management of the vital public works to the education of the future gentry generation and the maintenance of the Confucian system itself. In the services they rendered, the gentry acted on their own and not under the orders of the government or under the discipline of the administrative organization. Their responsibility was not—like that of the officials—toward the emperor. To them, their education had given them an obligation to serve society, to "carry the burden of the world on their shoulders," and while their responsibility included a loyalty to the Confucian state as well as to the society, this loyalty was not necessarily focused on the ruling house if it had lost its "mandate."

Though not under government authority, the gentry services were, however, linked to the political divisions of the state. The members of the gentry carried on their functions within the jurisdictional areas of their home districts and provinces. The area of their gentry services was not that of any landed property of their own.[4] The gentry's social responsibility was that of a professional group whose position and power depended on the certification of educational qualification by state examination degrees. These degrees were allocated to the districts

---

[3] Chang Chung-li, *The Chinese Gentry* (Seattle: University of Washington Press, 1955), p. 111.

[4] Landownership was not the basis of power, nor in fact was it the major source of gentry income. The gentry as a whole had neither a large income from land nor a permanent hold on large landed estates. Some of the gentry owned no land at all. The majority, while investing some of their money in land, derived their main income from public services. Large landed estates, the exception rather than the rule in China, could not be easily held together for any length of time because there was no rule of primogeniture but rather a division of property through inheritance. Land was not the basis of political power. See Franz Michael, Introduction to *The Income of the Chinese Gentry*, by Chang Chung-li (Seattle: University of Washington Press, 1962).

and provinces—the political areas in which the gentry played a functional role. The social autonomy of the gentry was therefore placed in the framework of the political divisions of the state, a system that enhanced the importance of the gentry's role of social leadership and facilitated its transition to a role of political authority within the state structure.

Within these areas, the gentry handled a vast number of widely divergent responsibilities. They acted as arbitrators in local conflicts between individuals, families, villages, and even districts and provinces. They had to care for the poor and weak; they organized the rice kitchens and the charity granaries, and collected and administered the funds used to alleviate the difficulties of the poorest elements of the population. They organized and managed local public works: the building of roads, bridges, dikes for flood protection, and irrigation and drainage canals so vital for the agricultural economy. The arbitration, the charity, the public works could be small matters or very large ones. The large ones were of obvious importance, and the small ones were not isolated activities that occurred occasionally, but were a systematic handling of all the many problems that concerned the people of the area. Taken together the activities of the gentry determined the well-being and the peace and order of their areas.

For the society as a whole the gentry were thus a group of social functionaries who were professional managers who handled judicial, economic, welfare, and a host of other problems. The gentry were qualified for such work through their Confucian education, which gave them the knowledge of the moral code which was the operating system of regulations for the management of human affairs in the Confucian society.[5] This code provided them with uniform standards for decisions in their large area of management of affairs in what had become a bureaucratic society.

State and Society

The work of the officials in government and the activities of the gentry in society were, however, not sharply delineated and kept apart. In the important area of public works, for instance, there was a close link between official and gentry management and responsibilities. While smaller works were often undertaken by the gentry themselves, with or without formal official approval and participation, the larger works

---

[5] See Franz Michael, "The Role of Law in Traditional, Nationalist, and Communist China," *The China Quarterly,* January-March, 1962.

were initiated and frequently directed and financed by the government, but with the help of the gentry. Even when the officials took a most active part in organizing public works, they depended on the gentry for cooperation in bringing in the local population and frequently providing funds from the area concerned. For the Ch'ing period, it may be safe to say that practically all the public works undertaken were done with gentry participation, if not by the gentry on their own. This cooperation between government and gentry could be observed in many other fields. No local official could manage his district without the practical cooperation of the local gentry.

Since the gentry already managed important public functions in the districts and in the provinces, their responsibilities could be expanded if need and opportunity arose. Even those services which were in time of strong government a monopoly of the administration could be taken over by this local leadership if the government's internal decay and corruption paralyzed official action or made it ineffective. The power that slipped from the hands of the official administrators could be taken up by local leaders, who, backed by local military force, could rebuild from local and regional roots the political organization and power which the government was not able to retain. For the gentry maintained, in times of such crisis, its status, prestige, and monopoly of training, which enabled some of its leading members to move up from their social base and assume a new official role in the newly formed regional governmental organizations. The very existence of this large educated elite of the gentry and its autonomous role of managing the vast area of public affairs was therefore not only the basis of the survival of the traditional order in times of crisis but also a potential threat to the central government's control of the state administrative system and therefore an element of constant concern to the dynasty.

One may indeed wonder about this role of the gentry. Why had, even at the end of the imperial time, the Ch'ing dynasty, as highly sophisticated in its administrative system and methods as it was, limited its official staff and its administrative activities to the most essential aspects of government? Why did it rely so heavily on the gentry to manage local affairs under their own initiative? The Ch'ing government certainly had the power to prevent any real local autonomy of the common people and had initiated subadministrative systems of control, such as the *pao-chia* and *li-chia*, which were meant to prevent any such local autonomy. Why did the government not manage all public affairs through appointed officials or subofficials under its direct con-

trol? Why did it leave so much leeway, privilege, and responsibility
to the gentry? The answer, we hold, lay essentially in the ideological
authority of the gentry, which no emperor could take away from them.

Their Confucian learning gave the gentry not only the knowledge
of the accepted code of human relations necessary for their professional
activities but also the authority to interpret these rules in a society
whose order was based on the Confucian tenets. The Confucian principles were based on an interpretation of the social order which, by its
very nature, limited the jurisdictional activity of the state and left a
large sphere of human relations to the working of a moral code in
society which was to be applied by those who were believed to be
versed in it. This whole tradition remained in the hands of the gentry,
whose services to the state depended on the dynasty's acceptance of
the Confucian system as a whole. The gentry themselves carried on
and transmitted the Confucian traditions in their role as teachers outside state control. Any attempt to limit or undermine their functions
as teachers and leaders of society would have touched at the heart of
the Confucian system.

This position gave the ruling stratum a special status in relation to
the head of the government, the emperor, the holder of the heavenly
mandate, who was in theory all powerful but who depended on the
gentry to carry out his will. His problem was to maintain a central
control over a bureaucracy which was only in part in his government
administration and which, outside it, carried on the education in, and
propagation of, a system of ethical values, beliefs, and ideas which
remained outside imperial control and was believed to be a part of an
absolute truth, to be accepted by the emperor as much as by its
guardians, the educated elite, and by all the people who believed in it.

The dynastic government could only attempt to relate this intellectual sphere to its own system of authority. To do this, the government
established its system of examinations through which the results of
Confucian education were given formal recognition. This system of
examinations not only gave government approval to the educated but
in practice also enabled the government to have a say in the selection
of the social leadership. During the Ch'ing dynasty, only those who
had gained an examination degree were formally recognized as members of the privileged educated group. By setting quotas for the examinations, the government succeeded in limiting the gentry and in gaining
some control over admission to this group.

The interests of the government and of the gentry largely coincided, but they could be at variance; and it was the government's concern to prevent this ruling stratum from organizing an opposition and becoming dangerous, as it was the gentry's concern to maintain its prerogatives and defend community and group interests against overbearing central power. Conflicts between the interests of the central government and the gentry, if kept within bounds, could provide a useful check on abuses by either side, but they could also lead to a stifling conformity or a breakdown of government.

The Ch'ing Policy of Control as a Self-defeating System

There was no clear line of authority between the functions of officials and those of the gentry, and the official who represented the interests of the government of the state was at the same time a member of the gentry in his home area. The danger that the central government sought to avoid was an invasion of state power and assumption of official authority by members of the gentry and, most of all, a joining of forces between local officials and gentry in the establishment of centers of local bureaucratic power which the central government could no longer control. To prevent this threat, the imperial governments of successive dynasties devised a number of measures to divide and check the authority of the officials of their administration and to supervise and control the gentry. The measures became more sophisticated in time and reached a high degree of development under the Ch'ing dynasty. But then, as earlier, they did not prevent the eventual disintegration of central control, and in fact may have contributed to dynastic decline.

To check the power of the gentry and the bureaucracy, the Ch'ing dynasty, like earlier imperial governments, widely applied the system of playing one group against another and one official against another. An alien dynasty could rely on its own group as a special source of power, and the Manchus are a most revealing example of the way in which a foreign group could build its own authority into the Chinese administrative system.[6]

More important still may have been the checks established within the officialdom itself. In Ch'ing times, one can discern two distinct types of official careers: service in the central government and in local and regional administrations. The inner corps of officials at the court and in the central government offices can be differentiated from the

---

[6] Franz Michael, *The Origin of Manchu Rule* (Baltimore, Md.: Johns Hopkins Press, 1942), chaps. vi and vii.

men who made their careers in the districts, prefectures, and provinces.[7] The offices of the provincial and local administrators themselves were divided in a system in which no one had full authority and each official could be used to check another. The division and overlapping of authority among officials at the provincial level was obviously a major security measure. The governors, the financial commissioners, the judicial commissioners, the salt intendants, the educational commissioners, and the provincial commanders-in-chief of Ch'ing time were all responsible to higher central authority, but there was no clear definition of their respective spheres of function. They were dependent on cooperation, and yet were rivals. They were appointed by the central government, on which their career depended. In some cases they were to report on each other, and none of them, not even the governor-general, was in full control within a geographical area of jurisdiction.[8] None was therefore able to organize his bureaucratic organization against the government, but also none was able to act quickly and show initiative to solve an urgent problem or to introduce new measures and changes for general improvement.

In the central government there was an equal lack of authority for any given position. Everything indeed depended on the emperor. It was a system which placed all premium on security and none on initiative. To prevent a link between officials and gentry, no official was permitted to serve in his home district or province, and each term of office was too short to allow for acquaintance and connection with the

---

[7] For a specific example, see Alfred Kuo-liang Ho, "The Grand Council of the Ch'ing Dynasty," *Far Eastern Quarterly*, XI (1952), 167-82.

[8] A short summary of the practice of officials reporting on each other is given in *Ch'ing-kuo hsing-cheng-fa, fan-lun* (Tokyo, 1918), Vol. II. This is a condensed Chinese version of a seven-volume work in Japanese under the same title (*Shinkoku Gyōseihō*) which appeared in Tokyo in 1915. "Since, according to practice, the governors-general (*tsung-tu*) assumed, ex officio, the title of junior president of the Censorate and thus had the function of taking charge of the hundreds of officials in the capital and the provinces to determine their success or failure, their righteousness or their depravity, their supervisory power therefore extended beyond their subordinate officials. They could censure civil and military officials of equal rank or even of rank above their own. This power of censure was actually applied to governors, departmental directors of schools, imperial commissioners, Tartar generals of Manchu garrisons, commanders-in-chief of the Army of the Green Banner, and other high officials" (p. 54).

"The circuit intendant traveled through the prefectures, subprefectures and departments to find out the industry or laziness [of the officials] and to study their ability or lack of ability, and then to report to the provincial judge, who would communicate with the governors-general or governors" (p. 79).

"The good or bad characteristics, the industry or laziness [of the officials] of the departments and districts should be known to the prefect, who would then promote or censure them" (p. 90).

local social leadership.⁹ This measure was meant to keep gentry and officials apart but worked to the disadvantage of efficient government.

The main means for preserving the power of the imperial government, however, was the monopoly (or near monopoly) maintained in the three decisive areas of authority: appointment of officials, control of taxation, and control of the army. A strong imperial government would have full authority in these fields. Corrosion of government control in these areas was a sign of dynastic decline.

The Ch'ing government's loss of control resulted from a growing ineffectiveness of the whole bureaucratic machine, as had occurred before in the dynastic cycles. Such decline has been ascribed to corruption, so often mentioned in Chinese sources; and this factor, in the view of most historians, has been the main cause of the downfall of Chinese dynasties. But corruption itself is a phenomenon caused by some deeper factors; it is not an explanation in itself. Some corruption may exist in almost all government systems and existed probably in China at almost all times. It is only when corruption reaches such a degree that the whole administrative organization becomes ineffective that it leads to the breakdown of government. Why did this occur ever again in Chinese history and when was the crisis point reached? The answer may be that the system of control itself caused its own decline. The system of checks, division of authority, and the use of terror, at times against individuals and families, at others against whole groups to prevent independence or autonomy, was, in a sense, self-defeating. It discouraged all initiative, all resourceful action, and stifled the administrative machine to such a degree that only routine measures could be carried out and officials could not easily deal with emergencies. It handicapped all energetic, ambitious, and enterprising members of the whole administrative organization. There was little leeway for new ventures, and the only way to get ahead was by getting a greater share of the existing government revenue. To move up or even to hold their own, officials had to build up their connections and

⁹ *Ta-Ch'ing hui-tien shih-li,* 47:1a-7a; also *Ch'ing-kuo hsing-cheng-fa, fan-lun,* II, 52 ff., 64 ff., 382 ff. The whole question is summarized by H. B. Morse, *International Relations of the Chinese Empire* (London and New York: Longmans, Green, 1910-18), I, 9-10. "All officials in the provinces ... are appointed from Peking. ... Appointment to one post is made usually for a term of three years. For officials low in rank, the rule is almost universally followed; they may be reappointed once, but at the end of their second triennial term at latest, they must strike root afresh in new surroundings, and, incidentally, must again contribute to the maintenance of their superiors. ... To some especially lucrative posts appointments are ordinarily made for one year only. Another restriction is peculiar to China and is never relaxed: no civilian official is ever appointed to a post in the province of his birth."

secure their positions and actions against the bad will and denunciations of competitors or rivals. The system itself therefore made
necessary a regulated giving of gifts and contributions in an atmosphere of intrigue and influence-peddling which no one could escape.
The very safety measures of the system led to its undoing.

The last resort of government authority was the army. Military
victory was the basis for the establishment of new dynasties. A cen-
trally controlled military force was the guarantee of their continuation
in power. But the army was a part of the administrative organization,
and it too was prone to corruption. When the officers pocketed the pay
of their soldiers and the ranks were depleted by desertion, the central
army became useless as a fighting force and even an additional cause
of unrest.

The Ch'ing Military and its Decline

As a conquest dynasty, the Manchus started their rule with a mixture of military forces—their own banner troops and a Chinese professional army, the *lü-ying*. In the organization of these forces the stress
on central control and security was brought to an extreme.

Already in Manchuria when the banner forces were established, they
were organized in such a way that no military commander could have
full authority.[10] The banners were administrative as well as military
units; each banner had its agricultural land assigned to it, but the land
consisted of scattered plots intermingled with land belonging to other
banners, so that no territorial unit was created. Each banner had a
bureaucratic administration handled by an appointed staff. The commanders for military campaigns were appointed for each occasion, and
each force was made up of small units from different banners.

After the conquest of China the banner troops became a special
imperial guard, a sort of security force, garrisoned at the capital and
in a few key strategic locations around the country; a part of the
banners remained in Manchuria. Each garrison was made up of a
mixture of units from different banners, served by their respective banner administrations. Even the Manchus' own security force was thus
held down by administrative safeguards that could not but hamper its
military effectiveness.

The *lü-ying* were scattered around the country in smaller garrisons,
none large enough to resist the concentrated force of the nearest
Manchu garrison. The *lü-ying* soldiers were professionals, dependent
on their pay and usually natives of the region of their garrison. Their

---

[10] Franz Michael, *The Origin of Manchu Rule*, chap. vi.

officers were members of the official bureaucracy, appointed to their positions and not permitted to serve in their home districts or provinces; they were rotated at frequent intervals and were dependent for their careers on the central government.[11] No central command over the *lü-ying* forces existed; the emperor alone remained the supreme military authority. Brigade generals and provincial commanders-in-chief had command over several garrisons, but their power was limited by an intricate system of checks and balances. Some units were under the command of governors and governors-general, and there was no clear division of authority or chain of command between the governors-general, governors, commanders-in-chief, and brigade generals. Even lower administrators had command over military forces for the defense of their administrative areas. The administration of the *lü-ying* was in the hands of the Ministry of Defense, one of the six administrative agencies.

Whenever a campaign was to be undertaken, the commander-in-chief had to be specially appointed, and his force was to be made up of a mixture of banner and *lü-ying* troops drawn from several garrisons. It can readily be seen how clumsy the administration and deployment of these military forces became, and how inevitably they would share the ills of the whole administrative organization.

The decline of the banners and *lü-ying* forces was already apparent in the eighteenth century and had become most serious by the middle of the nineteenth century.[12] The banners were the first to deteriorate. Their forces labored under special handicaps. The banner soldiers were prohibited from leaving their units to become farmers or to follow any other profession. They were to remain a privileged, salaried group, isolated from the general Chinese life. The pay of the garrisons was set at the beginning of the dynasty and remained the same. When the banner families increased, there were no additional funds to add a corresponding number of positions to the ranks, and the pay became insufficient. The pay had been fixed in relation to the prices of the middle of the seventeenth century, prices which had gone up four to ten times during the eighteenth and nineteenth centuries.[13] What had been a comfortable salary in the beginning became an insufficient dole for a force whose morale was broken by lack of training and long years of inactivity. On several occasions a special sum was given by the

---

[11] *Ta-Ch'ing hui-tien, chüan* 35; Lo Erh-kang, *Lü-ying ping-chih,* esp. pp. 177-82.
[12] *Ibid.*
[13] Lo Erh-kang, *Hsiang-chün hsin-chih,* chap. i; Wang Ch'ing-yün, *Hsi-ch'ao chi-cheng,* 4:48b-56a.

emperor for distribution to the banner garrisons to alleviate their economic hardships. But when this money was spent—and it was spent rather quickly—nothing had changed. The Manchus had the choice either of permitting the banner population to enter professions and to merge with the Chinese population or of continuing to keep them as a group apart in a sort of privileged decay. They chose the latter course and hoped that in this way they would retain the loyalty of a group that had no way out. And indeed from the period of the Taiping Rebellion down to the Chinese Revolution of 1911, the Manchu garrisons, though no longer a serious military factor, remained loyal. Whole garrisons were wiped out, and, as the reports put it, "died loyally."

The decline of the *lü-ying* forces started somewhat later and was brought about by slightly different causes. Though individual examples of evil practices are described as early as the seventeenth century, the *lü-ying* retained their fighting value until the end of the eighteenth century and still played the major part in the campaigns under Ch'ien-lung. With the turn of the nineteenth century, however, the *lü-ying* shared in the general decline of the administration. Comments in many sources began to indicate the prevailing corruption and malpractice.[14] The officers quite generally followed the practice of pocketing the pay of the soldiers, and those who were not handling such funds were bribed into complicity by large gifts. Indeed, the embezzlement of pay by the officers was a very close parallel to the embezzlement of tax money by the local administrators, except that one was taken on the way from the source to the government, the other on the way from the government to the recipient. Since the soldiers did not receive enough to live on, there were large-scale desertions from the forces. The actual strength of the units at the beginning of the nineteenth century has been estimated at one-half to one-sixth of the nominal units recorded on the books.[15] These desertions were not hindered by the officers, who continued to pocket the money of soldiers no longer

---

[14] Examples are given in *Ch'ing shih-lu, chih* 59, Chia-ch'ing, 4th year, 44:4a ff.; 47:16a ff., 29b ff.; and 74:20b ff. For a general description, see Hsiao I-shan, *Ch'ing-tai t'ung-shih,* II, 210-12, 250-51.

[15] Lo Erh-kang, *loc, cit.; Chinese Repository,* VI (1838), 593-605; Despatches from U.S. Ministers to China, National Archives, Microcopy 92, Roll 6, *Canton Mail,* June 14, 1849. For a special example provided by the Taipings' capture of Nanking, see Hsüeh Fu-ch'eng, "Shu Mien-yang Lu shuai Shih-hsien Chiang-ning shih" (An Account of the Loss of Chiang-ning by Marshal Lu from Mien-yang) in *Chung-kuo chin-pai-nien shih tzu-liao, ch'u-pien,* 1:116-22.

present. Those that remained in the garrisons had to look for other income, which they found as peddlers, small-scale traders, or as thieves and robbers. The soldiers' main compensation in lean times came during campaigns, when they looted and ravaged the areas in which they were supposed to fight. Since campaigns also meant that the officers would receive government funds for supplies, they became profitable economic enterprises for officers and men, and were drawn out as long as feasible at the expense of the government. Officers and headquarters got rich, and military appointments were highly valued and paid for.[16]

In the famous corruption case of Ho Shen, who had become fabulously rich as the leading official under Ch'ien-lung, a major accusation was the corruption of the military organization which he had fostered and from which he had profited. The seriousness of the decline of this aspect of government was fully realized by the court, but little effective action could be taken. At several times an attempt was made to reduce the size of the *lü-ying* army and use the funds saved for better pay. Since the actual size of units was so much smaller than the nominal number of soldiers, such reduction would have cut into the amount of graft of the officers and administrators. These imperial orders were sabotaged in the military organization, and in the first half of the nineteenth century most of the *lü-ying* army became worse than useless.

With the weakening of the army the Chinese government lost its ability to maintain order and prevent the unrest that resulted from the discontent with maladministration. The decline of the imperial government's administration and its military force invited an extension of authority by nonofficial local leaders. The power abdicated by the imperial government was taken over by local officials and gentry, and the second phase of the cycle began with the build-up of local power.

The Build-up of Local Power

Of the three elements that were the keys to power in the battle between central and local power—administrative appointment, taxation, and control of the army—the last was the decisive factor in such times of crisis and change. The establishment of a bureaucratic administration and a system of taxation was made possible by military control. Even early in its rule, the Ch'ing government accepted the forces of local leaders into its service as auxiliaries when rebellions

---

[16] Hsiao I-shan, *op. cit.*

occurred. As long as the regular central armies of the banners and the *lü-ying* were strong and reliable, these local organizations were no threat to central control, and their leaders could be either eliminated or paid off with rank and position in the administration. Whenever possible, such local forces were incorporated into the *lü-ying* army after the emergencies or local disturbances were over. The rest were officially "disbanded," a procedure that took them off the official records but did not necessarily remove them as political and military factors from the districts where they had been organized. With the decline of the administration and armies it was, however, no longer possible for the government to eliminate or incorporate local forces. The retreat of government activity increased the gentry's responsibility in local defense. Their local military activities were sometimes undertaken with the knowledge and approval of officials, but sometimes without such approval or even in open opposition to the officials, as for example, in defense of an area against high taxation or in resistance against government measures or government favoritism in the conflict between different communities. In the official reports there is an increase of examples of so-called "bad gentry," gentry leaders who for one reason or another led forces in opposition to the government.

Military organizational and command ability did not, however, require the administrative qualifications of the gentry. Local upstarts, so-called bullies, and "bandit leaders," could use the time of political chaos and popular despair and discontent to organize a military force and establish their own local authority. Local leadership was frequently provided by the heads of secret societies, which existed at all times during the last centuries of imperial history but grew more important during periods of political chaos and discontent, when they could become the organizational framework of military uprisings.

In reporting the development of local military organizations of the time, the officials judged the forces according to their relationship to the government. If they were approved of, they were counted as government forces; if not, they were "bad gentry," "bandits," or "rebels" according to the size and political purpose of the force. The actual story was much more complex, and the line between "good" and "bad" gentry, or between "bandit" and officially recognized local corps was rather fluid. A military leader could change sides two or three times, as for example Miao P'ei-lin, one of the best known military organizers in Anhwei province during the time of the Taiping and Nien rebellions.[17] Much of the fighting was carried out on a local level, and the officials often remained neutral as long as possible. When they sided with one of the contestants, the other automatically became a bandit. In the official terminology the accepted military organizations were approved *t'uan-lien,* local corps; those in opposition were *fei,* or bandits. Sometimes there was even a distinction drawn between "good" and "bad" *t'uan,* just as a distinction was drawn between "good" and "bad" gentry.

Toward the middle of the nineteenth century, the conditions created by the decline of government and local unrest had reached crisis proportions. These were the conditions that could be exploited by ambitious leaders to organize the discontented and armed local people for a general uprising in rebellion against the government. The rebellions of that time, the Taiping, the Nien, and the Moslem rebellions, all originated from small-scale warfare among armed groups and from local battles, in which the government took sides only when a local disturbance became serious enough to pose a threat against its own authority.

The rank and file of these rebel forces were mostly peasants; for that reason these, like earlier rebellions in Chinese history, have sometimes been characterized as "peasant rebellions." True, peasants made up the manpower of the rebel armies—discontented peasants who had left their fields because conditions had become intolerable—but these were not peasants joining rebel armies to fight for peasants' rights. Becoming a soldier was a way out of misery and an opportunity for better things, and peasants also went into the armies that declining dynasties raised to defend themselves. But the leaders of the rebellious armies did not fight for a peasant revolution, and those among them who had been peasants left, like the rank and file, their land and their peasant life to profit from the conquest of empire. They wanted to move up into the bureaucratic elite, become emperor or official, and escape the misery of their previous life. This had been the tradition of rebellions. The heroes of Chinese history were not social revolu-

---

[17] For a short account of Miao P'ei-lin's life and titles, see Hsü K'o, *Ch'ing-pai lei-ch'ao* (Shanghai, 1928), VII, 158-65. For his activities, see Chiang Siang-tseh, *The Nien Rebellion* (Seattle: University of Washington Press, 1954), *passim,* esp. pp. 93-96; and Fan Wen-lan, Chien Po-tsan, *et al., Nien-chün* (6 vols.; Peking, 1953), *passim.* For an account of his capture and execution, see Hsüeh Fu-ch'eng, "An Account of the Execution of the Two Rebels Ch'en Yü-ch'eng and Miao P'ei-lin," in *Nien-chün,* I, 359-62. His letter to Sheng Pao may be found in *Wen-hsien ts'ung-pien* (Peking, 1930-43), 22:6b-8a.

tionaries but military commanders and high officials, heroic in their fighting and skillful in their politics. This kind of traditional rebellion was not an attempt to change the system, and when there was a promise of military success the gentry could join the rebellious force or offer their services to the victor to re-establish the political system on the same social base, or they might themselves organize the rebellious uprising.

The Defense of the Social Order

The situation in the nineteenth century, however, differed from the past in one crucial point. Of the three major rebellions of that time, the Taiping Rebellion was the only one whose openly expressed purpose was the conquest of the empire and the establishment of an imperial government. The Taiping Rebellion differed from the others, and from earlier rebellions, in the role that a religious ideology played in its organization and the sanctioning of its leadership, and in the new political and social structure it attempted to establish. Its leaders wanted not only to overthrow and replace the imperial government but to establish a new religious ideological system as the foundation for the new state and the training of its new elite. In this sense the Taipings were revolutionary. They attacked not only the dynasty but also the ideology and with it the ruling stratum itself.[18]

The Taipings might very well have succeeded in destroying the dynasty, but their attempt to overthrow the ruling elite required as its first condition for any chance of success the ability to build up a counter-elite of their own for their government and administration. Of great interest are the Taiping attempts to create such an elite. Two of their most important leaders, Yang Hsiu-ch'ing, the first main military organizer and actual head of the Taiping administration, and Hung Jen-kan, the cousin of the Heavenly King, who joined the rebellion in its last stage, attempted this and failed. The Taipings were destroyed partly because of their inability to create a government of their own based on a new bureaucratic elite which they never succeeded in producing.

The attack against the Confucian order forced the gentry to fight the Taipings in order to preserve the system itself. Tseng Kuo-fan, who became the defender of the Ch'ing government against the Taiping attack, appealed to his fellow gentry to come to the support of the

---

[18] These points are fully developed in the forthcoming study by Michael, Chang, et al ., The Taiping Rebellion: A Documentary History.

Confucian system instead of calling on them to save the dynasty. Speaking of the Taiping ideological attack against tradition, he said:

How could that be a change that concerns only our Ch'ing dynasty? No, it is a serious change that concerns our entire moral tradition (*ming-chiao*) from its very beginnings, and makes our Confucius and our Mencius weep in the netherworld. How can anyone who can read and write remain quietly seated, hands in sleeves, without thinking of doing something about it?[19]

The defeat of the Taipings came then not from the government forces but from the new regional armies that had been formed in the provinces the Taipings had overrun—mainly Hunan and Anhwei—the armies of Tseng Kuo-fan, Li Hung-chang, Tso Tsung-tang, and others. The first successful resistance against the Taiping forces had been carried on by local corps led by gentry. When the imperial government realized this, it encouraged the gentry to organize on a large scale what it expected would be such local corps. To tolerate and encourage such a development was not new. It had already been done during the Opium War a decade earlier. Now with the growing threat of the Taiping armies, the government not only permitted such organization to be carried on by gentry on the spot but encouraged some of its trusted officials to resign from government service to form the desired defensive force as gentry at home.

The New Regionalism

Tseng Kuo-fan, the creator of the so-called Hunan army, which became the model for other provincial armies, had, however, a larger program in mind. Instead of establishing a number of local corps which could be valuable for local defense but too weak and small and too hard to move to be useful in campaigns against the large Taiping armies, Tseng Kuo-fan organized a regional army which could be used outside its home area as a force for regular military campaigns.[20] In establishing such an army he made use of the existing local corps and combined them into a larger force. The organizational pattern of this regional army also followed the model of the local corps. Its commanders selected their own officers, and each officer in charge of a unit picked his own men and remained responsible for their pay and welfare. There was a personal loyalty between men and officers and between the offi-

---

[19] From Tseng's "Proclamation regarding a Punitive Campaign against the Yüeh Bandits," 1854, in *Tseng Wen-cheng kung wen-chi,* 3:1b, in *tse* 92 of his *Complete Works.*

[20] Lo Erh-kang, *op. cit.*

cers and their commanders. The army units wer under the personal authority of their officers and carried their names. The whole regional force was loyal to Tseng Kuo-fan, who controlled it. It was Tseng Kuo-fan who appointed and dismissed officers, thus forming and dissolving units at will. Officers' promotions depended on him, although they were still formally approved by the court on Tseng's proposal. The soldiers and the officers came from the province in which the army was formed —Hunan, the home province of Tseng Kuo-fan. Financial support came from the Hunan gentry, who also provided the officers of the force.

Tseng Kuo-fan soon realized, however, that to finance his army and its campaigns he needed larger resources than the contributions collected by the gentry. What he needed was regular appointment as an official governing the area so that he could control its tax. The dualism between regular administration and the new military organization was bound to lead to conflict and rivalry, which handicapped the effort of defense by the new army. The government resisted for a long time the acceptance of the inevitable, and only when its own armies were destroyed by the Taipings did it appoint Tseng Kuo-fan and later other regional army commanders such as Li Hung-chang and Tso Tsung-t'ang as governors of the provinces their armies defended. The Ch'ing government had to disregard its own rules on division of authority both in the administration and in the military system and on the maintenance of central control over the army, and had to permit a combination of loyal local forces into regional armies under commanders who established their own military and administrative organizations. It had to permit the violation and abrogation of all the principles of divided authority and central control on which its political system and security depended. The appointments of Tseng, Li, and others added to the military power of these regional commanders the power of civil administration in their own provinces. What they had done with their armies they now did with their administrative organizations: they selected and appointed their own men, thus creating their own bureaucratic organizations. In contrast to their military organizations, their administrative staffs were not selected primarily from their own provinces, an indication that it was personal and organizational loyalty rather than attachment to a geographic area on which the new bureaucratic units were founded. Regionalism, as we like to call this development, must therefore not be interpreted narrowly as a provincialism with a local patriotism hostile to outsiders. The leaders of these new bureaucratic organizations that grew within the imperial bureaucracy could be shifted from one province to another without losing control of their organizations, which they took with them, and without even losing their military power, since their armies remained loyal to them.

Even when the head of a regional organization and some of his staff and forces were transferred to the capital, this transfer did not mean a merger with the central government. Li Hung-chang, and later Yüan Shih-k'ai, still based their power on the personal loyalty of their organization and their control of funds and military forces, even when they had been transferred to Peking as governor-general of the capital province or high officials of the central government. Such moves did not transform their regional organizations into the basis of a new central government power.

Only after the revolution did Yüan Shih-k'ai attempt to rebuild a central government from his own organization, adding to his own military and administrative power the claim to central authority, which had become vacant since the dynasty had lost the heavenly mandate and which Yüan Shih-k'ai attempted to assert for himself in a mingling of traditional and modern sanctions of government. But he failed. At this time, of course, Confucianism, which had provided the unity between state and society and had maintained the concept of the state even in times of rebellion and regional decline, had lost all support. Without it and without the gentry, whose dual role had been based on it, the regional organizations deteriorated into warlordism. With the end of Confucianism, new guiding principles would be needed to reintegrate both state and society.

In its origins, however, nineteenth-century regionalism had, as in earlier times, been made possible by the traditional relationship of state and society. The new regional leadership had emerged from the local gentry, who extended their area of function to include what had been the prerogative of the government—the defense of their home districts and provinces and, indeed, of the whole society. The new administrative organizations that were established maintained close contact with the local gentry, from whom they continued to derive their support. The regional leaders owed their power to the control of their own armed forces, their own administrative staff, and their own funds. But the government had to add its official blessing and recognition through the formality of appointing these leaders and members of their staffs to provincial or other office within the official hierarchy. The regional machine remained therefore a part of the official bureaucracy, undermining its central control. This development tended to dissolve central authority and create new regional nuclei of power, as dangerous to the dynasty as open rebellion.

When the emergency was over and the main danger seemed to have passed, the imperial government attempted to reduce or break the new autonomous power of the new leaders. But the regional power, once established, eventually held its own. The organizations of Tseng Kuo-fan, Li Hung-chang, and other regional leaders of the nineteenth century marked the beginning of the disintegration of dynastic power that finally led to the collapse of the dynasty and to the system of war-lordism that replaced it.

When in the nineteenth century the power of the Ch'ing dynasty declined because of the corruption of the administration and the dis-integration of the central armies followed by rebellions, it was the gentry leadership that rebuilt local government through military and administrative organizations under its control. Once more, when the political structure was at the point of collapse, the gentry leaders acted to preserve the continuum of the social order. And in this they suc-ceeded at the time.

The new gentry leadership remained loyal to the Ch'ing dynasty because the Taiping uprising had been directed not merely against the dynasty but against the social system itself. Once victory over the Taipings was secured, the new leaders did not dissolve their political and military organizations in spite of the imperial government's at-tempt to reduce or break their autonomous power. There was no real T'ung-chih Restoration, since the regional power, once established, carried on; and the central government failed to regain that crucial part of its military, administrative, and financial authority that it had lost. The problem of the political decline was not resolved. And before it could be resolved through a new centralization of dynastic power under a new mandate, the intellectual crisis of the Confucian beliefs brought on by the impact of the West undermined the social order itself, which was made more vulnerable by the disintegration of its political institu-tions. Whether under other political conditions this system itself could have been transformed to survive in the world of the twentieth century, whether for instance reforms like those of K'ang Yu-wei might have had a chance for success, is a matter of speculation that cannot concern us here.

The crisis of the decline of the gentry itself, however, came only after the early crisis in which the gentry preserved the system. In this earlier crisis the elements of decline and continuity of traditional state and society were still at work. The special role of an educated stratum, the gentry, in state and society; the reliance of the Ch'ing government on the services of the gentry in the official bureaucracy; the complex of stratagems developed to maintain central control over the bureaucracy and to neutralize the gentry; the breakdown of this system of control in inefficiency and corruption; the build-up of local and regional military power; and the role of the educated in preserving social and intellectual continuity—these appear as the main factors in the Ch'ing dynastic crisis of the middle nineteenth century, factors that we believe to be of importance, with variations, for earlier periods as well.

Li Hung-chang's career characterizes the history of this crisis. Following the example of Tseng Kuo-fan, the founder and organizer of the first regional army of the time, and under Tseng's patronage, Li Hung-chang organized his own regional force and created his own administrative organization, which remained the basis of his power within the system of the Ch'ing dynasty. But he also represented a development that went beyond the traditional regional leadership. The history of Li's career took its special course because it occurred at the end of imperial times, when institutional problems of traditional Chinese history became merged with new elements brought in by the impact of the West. Li's establishment of a base at Shanghai and his use of the financial resources of the new economic development were an application of traditional methods of organization and control to the new world of trade and industry introduced to China through the treaty ports. Li's application of the traditional gentry-official system for managing the Chinese agricultural economy to the new aspects of the economy remained characteristic of the system of political control that continued to stifle private enterprise and prevented the Chinese revolution from running its full course.

February, 1963

LI HUNG-CHANG
and the HUAI ARMY

A Study in
Nineteenth-Century
Chinese Regionalism

I. Early Career

The hero takes in hand a mighty sword,
Ambition soaring o'er the Hundred Foot Tower.
In ten thousand years gone by
Who else has shaped history?
Though I must serve one thousand miles from home
It is the means of achieving title and rank.
I must quicken my pace
If I would know the success of a thoroughbred.
No time for me to chase wild seagulls.
I smile as I head for the road to Lu-kou-ch'iao
Over which shall pass a man to the Isle of Immortality.

Li Hung-chang (1844)

Proceeding to Peking in 1844 to prepare for his final government examination, Li Hung-chang recorded his thoughts in an optimistic and almost prophetic poem.[1] Only twenty-one years old at the time, he already exhibited the intense aspiration and political ambition that were to be driving forces in his phenomenal rise to power in the years that followed. His career, which at the outset unfolded along traditional scholarly lines, was favored by personal and family circumstances and given direction by opportunities which arose as a result of the political crises of mid-nineteenth-century China. For Li Hung-chang the most decisive of the opportunities were those that opened the way for him to participate in military affairs and take in hand "the mighty sword" of his youthful ambition. In turn, his military orientation came about as a direct consequence of his gentry status.

Li Hung-chang was born in Ho-fei, in the province of Anhwei, in 1823. He was the son of a vice-president of the Board of Punishments,

---

[1] Li Hung-chang, "Ju tu," or "Entering the Capital," in *Li Wen-chung kung i-chi,* 6:1b, in *Ho-fei Li-shih san-shih i-chi,* compiled by Li Kuo-chieh (1904).

3

Li Wen-an, holder of the highest academic degree—the *chin-shih*.[2] The Li family had produced scholars and government officials for several generations, and enjoyed a position of prominence among the gentry families of the region.[3] Although Li Hung-chang did not automatically acquire personal gentry status by reason of birth, his membership in a gentry family made it almost a matter of course that he would be given the education necessary to enable him to compete in the government examinations and, if successful, become a member of the gentry in his own right.

For centuries the gentry had dominated Chinese society, serving as leaders in their local communities and holding a monopoly of official positions.[4] During the Ch'ing period (1644-1912), regulation of the size and qualifications of the gentry group was achieved through an examination system, which measured the fitness of the individual candidate as a potential bureaucrat and local leader. The qualities demanded by the government were of a practical, moral, and ethical nature, the objective being to perpetuate Confucian traditions which were instrumental in maintaining stability and sanctioning the imperial rule.

The course of scholastic preparation was arduous, requiring the systematic passing of successive examinations. Success in the examinations resulted in the bestowal of academic degrees. These degrees were treasured as the surest source of wealth and power in China. Because educational qualification was the distinguishing mark of those who had thus earned privileged status, these men have been called the scholar-gentry. While public office was largely reserved for the scholar-gentry, the qualified candidates for office exceeded by many times the number of offices to be filled. In fact, only a small minority of the scholar-gentry ever had the opportunity to serve in public office. Those who were fortunate enough to receive appointments were not permitted to serve in their native localities. To Li Hung-chang this prospect apparently was not an undue sacrifice, for in the poem quoted above he saw service far from home as the means of advancement. But even those who failed to receive public appointments, and therefore re-

---

[2] *Ch'ing-shih kao,* compiled by Chao Erh-sun and others (Mukden, 1937), 411:1a, hereafter cited *CSK.*

[3] *Hsü-hsiu Lu-chou fu-chih* (1885), 58:1b-6b, hereafter cited *Lu-chou chih.*

[4] The following description of the gentry is based almost entirely on the section on gentry in Franz Michael and George E. Taylor, *The Far East in the Modern World* (New York, 1956), pp. 23-28, and follows the concepts and research findings of Chang Chung-li, *The Chinese Gentry: Studies on Their Role in Nineteenth-Century Chinese Society* (Seattle, 1955).

mained at home, had important and frequently rewarding services to perform.

The functions of the gentry in their home localities covered a wide variety of essential activities. Wherever government officials did not or could not handle public tasks, the gentry were there to carry on. In large undertakings they worked in co-operation with the officials. In some areas of activity the gentry had a monopoly by tradition. They served as local arbiters in individual and community disputes. They sponsored and organized charitable and welfare activities, and took responsibility for the upkeep of temples and schools. They provided teachers for the young and participated in the village "exhortations," where they preached Confucianism to the people. The great public works systems which lay at the basis of the Chinese economy were of special concern to the local gentry. They assisted the officials in organizing projects, took responsibility for their maintenance, and attended to the countless details involved in the organization, direction, and sustenance of masses of laborers. In times of civil strife, when the government failed to offer protection to localities, it was the gentry who most often stepped in to preserve order in the communities for which they felt responsible. When this involved the raising of armed forces, a dangerous usurpation of government authority, the stake of the gentry in their communities was so great that they ran the risk of conflict with the state itself. When such occasions arose and gentry military activity of this sort became widespread, the very foundations of the government were threatened. Such crises are familiar to all students of Chinese history.

Because Chinese social tradition emphasized the attachment of the individual to his birthplace and family, those gentry who served in public office were discouraged from concerning themselves with their native localities. They were expected to confine their attention to the areas to which they were assigned as officials. Only thus could the government hope to check the growth of dangerous local and regional cliques of gentry and officials.

Whether in office as government officials, or out of office and serving as leaders in their local communities, the scholar-gentry enjoyed privileges of rank and opportunities for wealth through service denied to the common people. Moreover they had the satisfaction of receiving the homage and respect of the common people whom they patronized.[5]

---

[5] Chang Chung-li, *The Chinese Gentry*. This comprehensive survey of the role of the gentry in nineteenth-century China brings to light the significance of their func-

In 1847 at the age of twenty-four Li Huang-chang entered the highest rank of the gentry by successfully passing the *chin-shih* examination. Although it is frequently said that any farmer's son had an equal opportunity to compete in the examinations, there can be no doubt that the leisure and wealth afforded by gentry family membership were decisive factors in Li's success. He appears, however, to have been gifted with a good deal of intellectual capacity and literary talent, since he was appointed a member of the Han-lin Academy, a privilege reserved for the top competitors.[6] In this capacity he served for several years at Peking, rising to the position of *pien-hsiu*, or compiler. Although his duties were of little political importance, his membership in this small scholastic elite placed him in an excellent position for a future high appointment. During his years at Peking Li was fortunate to have as his mentor Tseng Kuo-fan, a scholar of excellent reputation in the highest academic and political circles of the capital. Tseng Kuo-fan and Li's father had received their *chin-shih* degrees in the same year, 1838, and thus were bound by a traditional sentiment, somewhat like a feeling of kinship, known in Chinese as *t'ung-nien* ("same year").[7] The young Li was therefore "adopted" by Tseng, who, although not a major political figure at the time, within a few years was to carve out for himself an extraordinary position of power.

Under ordinary circumstances Li Hung-chang probably would have continued to serve in Peking, rising in one of the many government bureaus. Or perhaps he would have been sent out to serve in some important position in one of the provinces. Instead a crisis arose which took him from office in Peking and returned him to his home to serve as a member of the gentry in defense of his native region.

In 1850 a rebellion had flared up in Kwangsi province and spread to the Yangtze valley. By 1853 the rebels, who became known as the Taipings, had taken Nanking and established their capital at this site of former imperial courts. Their armies, moving north and west, overran Hupeh, Hunan, and Anhwei provinces and took control of central China. The central government was forced to recognize the weakness of its standing armies and found itself compelled to rely upon local resistance corps under the leadership of local gentry. In calling upon

---

tions on both the local and national levels. I am indebted to Dr. Chang for his courtesy in permitting me to consult his preliminary data as well as early drafts of his work as it was in progress.

[6] *Lu-chou chih*, 58:1b-6b.

[7] Arthur W. Hummel, *Eminent Chinese of the Ch'ing Period* (Washington, D.C., 1943), p. 751, hereafter cited Hummel, *Eminent Chinese*.

the gentry to furnish such leadership, the court was merely acknowledging what in fact had already begun.[8] For while the Manchus had a throne to lose, the gentry too were in danger of losing their prestige, power, wealth and privilege. In self-defense they rallied to resist the Taipings.

The Rise of Local Corps in Anhwei

Always suspicious of gentry power and distrustful of local military forces, the government had made it a policy to keep arms from the people except under the gravest emergencies. But by 1852 the rich ricelands of the Yangtze valley, from which the court's chief revenues were drawn, were seriously threatened by the Taiping armies. In that year an imperial edict, noting a precedent in the use of local corps to suppress outbreaks during the Chia-ch'ing reign (1796-1820), called upon the high officials of Hunan and Hupeh to encourage gentry organization of similar corps at once.[9]

Li Hung-chang stepped from his orderly official career to the uncertainties of gentry-military leadership in 1853. Early that year, the central government, alarmed at the situation in Anhwei province, had ordered Lü Hsien-chi, vice-president of the Board of Works, to return to his home province of Anhwei to organize local corps.[10] Among the officials whom Lü requested to assist him was the *han-lin* compiler of the second class, Li Hung-chang.[11] It is not difficult to see why Li should have been selected for the task. His family was well known in Lu-chou district, where Ho-fei is located, and his father, as vice-president of the Board of Punishments, was one of the hundred top government officials in China. The luster of family name, added to Li Hung-chang's personal qualifications, gave him the prestige now needed to muster the villages to gentry command. But greater rank and experience than Li Hung-chang's were needed, and shortly after his own return his father, Li Wen-an, was dispatched to supervise the organization of the forces in Lu-chou district. At Peking, Li Wen-an had already earned a reputation as an expert on military affairs; now his

---

[8] *Ch'ing-ch'ao hsü-wen-hsien t'ung-k'ao*, compiled by Liu Chin-tsao (Shanghai, 1936), 215:9618-19.) See also Lo Erh-kang, *Hsiang-chün hsin-chih*, pp. 1-2. I have used a handwritten copy of this work made by Professor Lo and presented to the Modern Chinese History Project, University of Washington. Unfortunately the page numbers of the published edition are not indicated.

[9] *Ch'ing-ch'ao hsü-wen-hsien t'ung-k'ao*, 215:9618-19.

[10] *Ta-Ch'ing li-ch'ao shih-lu*, compiled by Man-chou ti-kuo kuo-wu-yüan (Tokyo, 1937), Hsien-feng reign, 81:18a, hereafter cited *Ch'ing-shih-lu*.

[11] *Lu-chou chih*, 22:2b.

presence at the center of the struggle spurred on his neighbors and
local followers to exert greater efforts at self-defense.

While Taiping armies threatened the Huai valley, a second group of
rebels, who came to be known as the Nien, rose to take advantage of
the collapse of law and order brought on by the civil war. In many
instances these Nien bands had originated as local forces formed for
defense against the Taipings, but they sometimes found the government armies an equal threat to their security, and offered resistance to
both.[12] Soon they were in open revolt. On the other hand, there were
numerous forces formed for local defense which did not actively oppose
the government but balked at offering full support. It was toward
these relatively neutral local corps that Li Hung-chang and Li Wen-an
turned their attention, and Lu-chou became a center where local corps
were mustered and trained for service to the government.

Most of the partisan leaders who rallied to Li Wen-an were members of the local gentry. One of his earliest followers was a man named
Chang Shao-k'an, who undertook to manage local corps and contributed several hundred hu of rice to support the forces (1 hu = 5 tou, or
pecks). There is no mention of Chang's social rank in the records, but
it is noted that he was a native of Ho-fei, Li's own district.[13] A *sheng-
yüan*[14] by the name of Chang Chih-mou and his brother organized local
forces and solicited funds for that purpose. The two brothers themselves contributed 3,000 tan of rice (1 tan = 133⅓ lbs.). A third
brother contributed 2,000 tan of rice and 1,000 taels of silver (about
330 pounds in the English currency of the period). In the following
year, 1854, the three brothers sold over 6,000 acres of land and contributed the proceeds, a sum of 10,000 taels, to local defense.[15] Several

---

[12] See Siang-tseh Chiang, *The Nien Rebellion* (Seattle, 1954). Dr. Chiang carefully analyzes the basic structure of the Nien organization and depicts its development into a regional amalgamation. In the course of research Dr. Chiang and I often
discussed our materials and conclusions. Since we were in basic agreement on most
issues with which our monographs were concerned, we agreed on a division of subject matter. Consequently, whereas Dr. Chiang has placed considerable emphasis on
the actual course of the Nien campaign and the organizational features of the Nien
and of the various government armies, I have omitted detailed references to the
strictly military aspects of the campaign and have concentrated rather on the development of the Huai-chün and on the financial and technological factors which gave the
Huai-chün its ultimate superiority over the Nien forces.

[13] *Lu-chou chih,* 36:34a.

[14] An official designation for those who have received the first, or *hsiu-ts-ai,* literary
degree. See William F. Mayers, *The Chinese Government* (2d ed.; Shanghai, 1886),
pp. 69-70. A more extensive discussion of the *sheng-yüan* is found in Chung-li Chang,
The Chinese Gentry, passim.

[15] *Lu-chou chih,* 36:33b-34a.

of the contributors were men who had purchased titles, such as Chang Chih-yin and Sun Yu-ch'eng, both *chien-sheng*, who had given rice and money for defense and war relief.[16]

Men who distinguished themselves as collectors of contributions were often officially requested to lead and organize local corps, but such requests may merely have been recognition of activity previously begun. One such case was that of Wang Kan-ping, of whom the Lu-chou local history notes: "Wang Kan-ping was a rich man of Ho-fei. He used his money to associate friends [for defense]. Thereupon Chiang Chung-yüan requested him to lead local corps and manage provisions and rations."[17] A *chien-sheng* from Ho-fei is described as having "ruined his family in supplying military rations and raising trained volunteers to ease the difficulty of that city."[18] Ch'ien Hung-pin, the son of a Ho-fei *chien-sheng*, was also noted for his efforts to raise contributions.[19] Shih Ming-k'ang of Ho-fei and the *chien-sheng* Liu Li-pin proposed and assisted in the "beating of earth into walls."[20] These earthwalls proved to be an effective deterrent to would-be attackers, and were similar to the defenses later used by the Nien rebels.

Li Hung-chang Leads Local Corps

Li Hung-chang's first important military action was to root out local corps which had affiliated themselves with the Nien rebels. In 1853, a large clan by the name of Hsieh extended its influence over more than ten villages in the Ho-fei district. Under the leadership of a man called "the Fourth Tiger Hsieh," its members engaged in bullying their neighbors. These bullies appear to have also been associated with a Nien leader whose forces were centered around the town of Yin-chou. Troops had been sent several times to arrest the leader and suppress the rebels but had always failed. Finally the governor ordered Li Hung-chang to lead his local corps to suppress these Nien rebels, and in this Li was successful.[21] In subsequent months Li in-

---

[16] *Ibid.* The *chien-sheng* designation was applied to persons who had been accepted nominally as students at the Imperial Academy. It was usually obtained through purchase or recommendation and was often the first step upward in the bureaucracy and gentry through the so-called "irregular route." See, for instance, H. S. Brunnert and V. V. Hagelstrom, *Present Day Political Organization of China,* translated by A. Beltchenko and E. E. Moran (Shanghai, 1912), pp. 505-7; Chang Chung-li, *op. cit.,* discusses the *chien-sheng* in detail.

[17] *Lu-chou chih,* 36:4a.

[18] *Ibid.,* 36:21a.

[19] *Ibid.,* 36:76a.

[20] *Ibid.,* 36:73b.

[21] *Ibid.,* 22:3a.

creased his forces to over a thousand men and performed garrison duty at Yin-ts'ao, where he was credited with having prevented a fleet of Taiping boats from entering the adjoining lake.[22]

From 1853 to 1856, Li remained in the area of Lu-chou and Chao-hsien, and although he received several promotions for his accomplishments, he was still a minor official with only a local reputation.[23] When Lü Hsien-chi, who had originally asked Li to return to Anhwei, was killed in action, Li was transferred to the staff of the governor of Anhwei, Fu-chi. According to popular accounts, Li did not fare well under his new commander. The two men disagreed on questions of military tactics, with Li demanding bolder strategy than the more cautious Fu-chi was willing to permit. Moreover, Li believed that Fu-chi was blocking his chances for advancement. Li finally broke with Fu-chi in 1858 under circumstances which still remain obscure. The explanation usually advanced is that he was dismissed from Fu-chi's staff when he refused to help withstand a Taiping attack and instead escorted his mother and sister to refuge in the city of Chinkiang, Kiangsu.[24]

During these six years of military leadership in his local gentry capacity, Li Hung-chang established two important connections which were to tie him directly to the military leaders of the twentieth century. In 1853, Yüan Chia-san, an official from Honan, famous for his military critiques, was ordered to co-operate in an official capacity with Lü Hsien-chi and Li Wen-an in directing military defenses in Anhwei.[25] Yüan worked closely with the Li family, giving them, and receiving from them, cordial support. According to Chinese custom, the relationship of sons and close relatives of friends, known as *shih-chiao,* is a very strong tie than can operate powerfully in social and political situations. In later years, Li Hung-chang extended constant patronage and support to the sons and nephews of his father's friend, Yüan Chia-san. Yüan Pao-heng, elder son, and Yüan Pao-ling, younger son of Yüan Chia-san, were favored protégés of Li, but most important was Yüan Shih-k'ai, adopted son of Yüan Chia-san's nephew, Yüan Pao-ching. Yüan Shih-k'ai, owing to Li Hung-chang's favor, rose in

---

[22] *Ibid.*

[23] *Ibid.,* 22:7b, 9b, 11b; 96:1a ff.

[24] Hsüeh Fu-ch'eng, "Li Ch'uan-hsiang ju Tseng Wen-cheng kung mu-fu," in *Chung-kuo chin-pai-nien shih tzu-liao, ch'u pien,* Tso Shun-sheng, ed. (Shanghai, 1930), I, 160-61, hereafter cited Tso, *Shih tzu-liao.* A similar account is found in *Ch'ing-ch'ao yeh-shih ta-kuan* (Shanghai, 1916), VII, 147.

[25] Hummel, *Eminent Chinese,* pp. 949-50. See also *Lu-chou chih,* 22:7a.

the ranks of Li's later military organization to a position of strategic power, and ultimately established himself as military strong man of North China, and as President of the Republic of China.[26]

Li Hung-chang's patronage of Tuan Ch'i-jui, another military leader of the early Republic, and one-time Provisional President of China, also originated during these early days of local-corps development at Lu-chou. Tuan's rise under the aegis of Yüan Shih-k'ai is well-known. Less well-known, however, is the fact that his grandfather had served under Li Wen-an and later under Li Hung-chang in militia defense movements. Like Li Hung-chang, Tuan was a native of Ho-fei, and both he and his father spent almost all their lives in Li's military encampments. Tuan's grandfather was given an official title, and thus entered the ranks of the gentry by virtue of the service he had rendered under the Lis at Lu-chou. The grandson was favored in a different but equally privileged manner by being one of the first students admitted to the Tientsin Military Academy founded by Li Hung-chang, and the first of the cadets whom Li sent to Germany for advanced artillery training in later years.[27]

The service of Li Wen-an in helping to initiate gentry defense organization in Lu-chou added tremendously to the status of the family in Anhwei. And Li Hung-chang's own contribution, if not distinguished, could not be overlooked. He had proved himself capable of carrying out with more than moderate success the new military role which rebellion had made available to the gentry. But although this experience was useful in Li's own career as gentry military leader, the loosely organized forces of the Lu-chou gentry provided no strong army for general military defense—or offense. Rather it was in the Hunan area, where Li's patron and teacher, Tseng Kuo-fan, labored painstakingly to perfect a system and an organization, that the first of the great nineteenth-century militia armies, the Hsiang-chün, or Hunan Army, was created.

Tseng Kuo-fan, Li Hung-chang, and the Hsiang-chün

The Chinese historian Liang Ch'i-ch'ao once wrote: "Only because there was Tseng Kuo-fan could there be a Li Hung-chang," and in no aspect of Li's many-phased career does this hold more true than in the

---

[26] Hummel, *Eminent Chinese*, pp. 950 ff; Li Hung-chang, *Li Wen-chung kung tsou-kao*, hereafter cited *LWCK Memorials*, in *Li Wen-chung kung ch'üan-chi*, compiled by Wu Ju-lun (1908), 55:7a; 74:46a; 76:30a, hereafter cited *LWCK Collected Works*. See also Chapter 10.

[27] See Chapter 10.

development of his military organization.[28] Tseng Kuo-fan furnished
the theory, the philosophy, and the pattern that became the model for
Li's own military forces later. Tseng's Hsiang-chün was the trunk
from which Li Hung-chang's own Huai Army appeared as a branch.
The growth and overwhelming importance of the Hsiang Army during
Tseng's lifetime is attributable, in the first instance, to the purpose
and manner of its formation and sustenance.

The Taiping Rebellion, as we have noted, posed a direct threat to the
gentry. One of the means by which the gentry preserved their integrity as a class and guaranteed their privileged status was through
the inculcation of Confucian doctrine upon the people. Through the
imperial examination system, the gentry, or literati, themselves were
subjected to a subtle system of thought channelization which was intended to keep the minds of the scholars occupied and fortify their
loyalty to the throne. And in turn the gentry expounded the ancient
virtues through various means, including "exhortation meetings" in the
villages, publication of local histories, and the control of local education. The gentry's life was one of continual teaching through precept,
and the villagers looked to the gentry as teachers, arbiters, and examples.[29] The success of this system at the local level was largely responsible for the relative stability of the society even in times of great
national and international crisis. The Taipings undermined the security
of the gentry by attacking the whole moral and ethical system upon
which the gentry's position was based, and by preaching, and perhaps
practicing, land redistribution.[30] Although they openly and bitterly
attacked the gentry as "running-dogs," their heterodox doctrine alone
would have been sufficient to ensure the determined opposition of the
gentry.[31]

The gentry's first attempts at self-defense took the form of local
corps. Whatever further purposes the corps served, they were pri-

[28] Liang Ch'i-ch'ao, Chung-kuo ssu-shih nien-lai ta-shih-chi, I ming Li Hung-
chang, in Ying-ping shih ho-chi (Shanghai, 1936), chuan-chi, No. 3, p. 32.
[29] The privileges and prestige of the gentry, and their attempts to defend their
status, have been described minutely by Dr. Chang in The Chinese Gentry, cited above.
[30] The program of land redistribution advocated by the Taipings was described as
"The Land Regulations and Political Economy of the Celestial Dynasty" in a document translated in the North China Herald and Supreme Court and Consular
Gazette, Vol. V, No. 216, Sept. 16, 1854, pp. 26-27, hereafter cited NCH.
[31] Hellmut Wilhelm, "The Background of Tseng Kuo-fan's Ideology," Asiatische
Studien, III (1949), 91-100, describes how Tseng Kuo-fan won over the gentry
through positive action. Dr. Vincent Shih, a member of the Modern Chinese History
Project, University of Washington, has described and analyzed the ideological aspect
of the Taiping program in "The Ideology of the T'aip'ing T'ien Kuo," Sinologica, III
(1951), 1-5. A more extensive study by Professor Shih is forthcoming.

marily used to protect the possessions and authority of their leaders. Until the government realized that these corps were necessary, it frequently treated them as bandits, if not as outright rebels. When the government was finally forced to use the local corps for its own defense, it tried to prevent them from coalescing to form larger territorial units. But the success and loyalty of Hunan leaders like Lo Tse-nan, Chiang Chung-yüan, and Tseng Kuo-fan finally led the government to encourage the creation of militia.[32]

The term *Hsiang-chün* means "the army of Hsiang." Hsiang is the traditional name of Tseng Kuo-fan's native district in Hunan province, and from this region his army took its name. Tseng organized the Hsiang-chün by uniting volunteer forces already in existence in Hunan: The Hsiang-yung, or "volunteers of Hsiang," led by Lo Tse-nan, and the Ch'u-yung, or "volunteers of Ch'u"—an archaic name for the Hunan region—led by Chiang Chung-yüan.[33] While Tseng was building his army by incorporating new local forces, he consistently followed the practice of taking over these corps intact with their commanders and indoctrinating these leaders to ensure their allegiance to himself and his own army. In effect, he was using the clannish spirit of Chinese villagers and their devotion to their native districts as the foundation for the *esprit de corps* of his army. Tseng Kuo-fan's ability to rouse the spirit of his troops and hold the loyalty of his commanders was founded, however, on more than an appeal to provincial or village ties. He was an articulate scholar who effectively applied and built upon Confucian thought to bring out in his followers those qualities of character and conduct necessary for effective campaigning and loyal service.[34]

---

[32] For Lo Tse-nan, see *CSK*, 407:5b-8a, and Hummel, *Eminent Chinese*, pp. 540-41. Lo was a native of Hsiang-hsiang, Hunan, who obtained the *hsiu-ts'ai* degree in 1839 and became a senior licentiate in 1847. He was killed in action in 1856. For Chiang Chung-yüan, see *CSK*, 407:1a-5b, and Hummel, *Eminent Chinese*, pp. 136-37. Chiang was a native of Hsin-ning, Hunan, who attained the highest, or *chin-shih*, academic degree. After failing to repel an attack by the Taipings on Lu-chou, Li Hung-chang's native prefecture, Chiang committed suicide by drowning in 1854. The *Ch'ing-shih kao* biography of Tseng Kuo-fan (405:1a-7b) is by no means a satisfactory account. There is a concise, though still inadequate, English biography in Hummel, *Eminent Chinese*, pp. 751-56, together with a useful multilingual bibliography.

[33] Hummel, *Eminent Chinese*, pp. 751-52.

[34] Hellmut Wilhelm, "The Background of Tseng Kuo-fan's Ideology," *Asiatische Studien*, III (1949); see also Tseng Kuo-fan, *Tseng Wen-cheng kung ch'üan-chi*, compiled by Li Han-chang and others (1876), containing memorials, or *tsou-kao* (hereafter cited *TWCK Memorials*), letters, essays, verses, and his *nien-p'u*, or chronology (hereafter cited *TWCK nien-p'u*). Further materials by Tseng are his extremely revealing forty-volume diary, *Shou-shu jih-chi;* his family letters, or *chia-shu;* his various essays, *chi-wai-wen;* his admonitions, *chia-hsün;* his famous sayings,

In obtaining funds to support his army, Tseng was beset by competition from local and government forces as well as from the enemy. The principal source of revenue in China during this period was the land tax, and struggles arose between local corps and government forces over the question of who was to collect the land tax in the embattled areas. Holding no office when he began to organize his militia, Tseng had no authority to appropriate the revenues of Hunan. Each province within the empire had its governor-general, governor, financial commissioner, and director of grain transport, who were charged with responsibility for raising and remitting various excises and taxes to the capital. Consequently, a running contest was waged between the central officials and Tseng for control of local revenues. On the lower level, leaders of smaller local corps, both gentry and officials, often resisted incorporation of their men into the new army of Tseng Kuo-fan and questioned his right to divert their military and personal revenues to his own forces. Such resistance was often a problem in areas where the authority of the central government was weak or had entirely disappeared. Tseng Kuo-fan insisted that his forces be paid well and regularly. In order to provide them with higher pay and superior equipment, he was especially anxious to attain real financial independence for his Hsiang-chün components. He sought and gained the revenues of his areas of military operation by securing virtually direct control over the revenue-collection agencies. This he achieved, however, only after his successes in battle finally won for him a regular position as a provincial official. Acknowledging his obligation to account for all revenues to the central government, in accordance with official regulations, he nevertheless concealed his actual financial operations, using various pretexts connected with the war situation.[35] Since the central government knew little of Tseng's

---

chia-yen-ch'ao; and his maxims on character development and study, hsüeh-an. Illustrative of his emphasis on Confucianism as a means of character building are the following excerpts from Tseng Wen-cheng kung shu-cha (Nanking, 1945), hereafter cited TWCK Letters. (Unless otherwise noted all citations from Tseng's letters refer to this edition rather than to the shu-cha section of Tseng Wen-cheng kung ch'üan-chi, previously cited.) The excerpts below are from letters which Tseng addressed to Li Hung-chang: "Even barbarian matters, though hard to deal with, need the application of the instructions of Confucius." TWCK Letters, 18:15b; "If we can discipline ourselves no one will dare to humiliate us without reason." Ibid., 19:14b; "To love the people is the first principle in troop movements. You should daily instruct your soldiers to regard this principle as a fundamental matter of life and not just as elaborate phrases." Ibid., 18:18a; "If you win a battle, shift the praise to others. If they lose a battle, go to their aid." Ibid., 18:41a-b.

[35] James T. K. Wu, "Impact of the Taiping Rebellion upon the Manchu Fiscal

financial manipulations, it was unable to oppose his growing financial independence.

The Hsiang-chün did not draw its funds exclusively from land tax revenues diverted from the central government. Tseng Kuo-fan promoted the likin system on a large scale in order to secure funds from new sources. The likin was an ad valorem tax on the sale and transportation of goods. In other words, it was either a transit tax or a sales tax, but in any case it fell directly upon the merchant. The likin was probably first employed in 1853 on an experimental basis. At the suggestion of Kuo Sung-tao, a colleague and relative of Tseng Kuo-fan, it was adopted as a means of tapping new revenue sources for the Hsiang-chün.[36] The likin possessed several distinct advantages for the initiators of the new regional army. The likin collectors for the Hsiang-chün were from the first independent of central government control or regulation, and free of complicating precedents. The likin tax could be levied upon any and all commodities and could be adapted to the special features of the regions in which it was enforced. This made it possible for Tseng Kuo-fan and his followers to move their forces into new areas and still find means of support. At the same time, relief from land taxes—an important measure for winning widespread agrarian support—could be granted in newly recovered areas with small loss to Tseng.[37] As one Chinese historian has put it, "the likin gave wings to the tiger."[38]

Other features of the Hsiang-chün financial system that Tseng promoted with energy were the selling of official titles, a practice that became increasingly common in the course of time, and the establishment of offices in various mercantile centers and ports for the collection of cash contributions.[39] Other military and provincial leaders followed

System," *Pacific Historical Review,* XIX, No. 3 (August, 1950), briefly explains the possibilities open to civil and military officials for financial evasions. See also Franz Michael, "State and Society in Nineteenth-Century China," *World Politics,* VII (1955), 419-33; and "Military Organization and Power Structure of China During the Taiping Rebellion," *Pacific Historical Review,* XVIII (1949), 469-83. I have also had the privilege of consulting Professor Michael's excellent and exhaustive manuscript on this subject, still unpublished.

[36] Kuo Sung-tao's career and contributions are mentioned in Hummel, *Eminent Chinese,* pp. 438, 439. Further details are found in the comprehensive, modern study by Lo Yü-tung, entitled *Chung-kuo li-chin shih* (Shanghai: Commercial Press, 1936), I, 9-33.

[37] James T. K. Wu, *op. cit.,* p. 274.

[38] Hsiao I-shan, *Tseng Kuo-fan* (Shanghai and Nanking, 1946), p. 190.

[39] See, for instance, Tseng's various memorials on the sale of official titles in *TWCK Memorials,* 3:16a, HF 4/7/16; 5:31a, HF 5/2/27; 7:25a, HF 6/2/21; 8:69a, HF 6/10/11; 8:71a, HF 6/10/11; 13:4a, HF 10/12/28.

Tseng's lead in tapping these new sources of revenue, but Tseng alone was able to build a regional army upon them.

While laying the groundwork for the Hsiang-chün in Hunan in 1853, Tseng was already planning a wider strategy against the Taipings. At this time he wrote to Li Hung-chang outlining the plans he had worked out for revitalizing the government forces. The militia was to be re-organized on a "volunteer," or *yung,* basis, and "not even a single regular soldier" would be used. The officers were to be from the same provinces as the men. Tseng disclosed that he planned to send an army of six thousand men eastward. Referring to reports of Li's success in mustering the Anhwei corps, he proposed: ". . . if you will train these troops according to the method of Ch'i Chi-kuang, then next year when the Ch'u [Hunan or Hsiang] army passes through Anhwei, our two armies can be joined. The ten thousand will be united as one."[40]

Tseng's plan for the unification of his and Li's militia did not ma-terialize for many years. Yet from the first Tseng regarded Li as an important aide and a future leader in military affairs. In a letter ad-dressed to Chiang Chung-yüan, governor of Anhwei in 1853, who had formerly distinguished himself as organizer of the successful Ch'u-yung, Tseng recommended Li as "a useful man of talent" and re-quested Chiang to employ the young official in administration and in the conduct of military campaigns.[41] Informing Li's older brother, Li Han-chang, of his recommendation, Tseng revealed that he considered Li Hung-chang "one of the four talented men of the *ting-wei* year" (i.e., of those who took their *chin-shih* degrees in 1847), and of those four the only one who had had an opportunity to demonstrate his ability.[42]

During his years of separation from Tseng, Li kept up a corre-spondence with his former teacher and continued to regard himself as Tseng's disciple. In 1856, while still a member of Fu-chi's staff in Anhwei, Li had already planned to transfer to Tseng's staff. This in-tention was expressed quite clearly in a poem written at the time, which he titled, "On the Occasion of Leaving to Join Tseng Kuo-fan on his Western Campaign," but this opportunity did not come until two years later.[43]

---

[40] *TWCK Letters,* 4:20a-b. Ch'i Chi-kuang was a militia organizer and authority during the Ming dynasty. He was used as a model by Tseng Kuo-fan.

[41] *Ibid.,* 3:35a-b. Since Tseng's letters are undated, we can only estimate (from internal evidence) that this letter was written sometime during the year 1853.

[42] *Ibid.,* Tseng Kuo-fan to Li Han-chang, 3:35a-36a.

[43] *Li Wen-chung kung i-chi,* in *Ho-fei Li-shih san-shih i-chi,* 6:4a. This poem is

The Li Brothers Serve Tseng Kuo-fan

While Li was in Anhwei helping to develop local military forces, a direct connection with Tseng Kuo-fan was maintained through his elder brother, Li Han-chang, who did much to promote Li Hung-chang's career.[44] Li Han-chang was the first of the Li brothers to serve directly under Tseng Kuo-fan. In 1851, Han-chang, who was then a *pa-kung,* or senior licentiate (by special examination), was appointed a district magistrate in Hunan province. In this capacity he led local corps which were being organized in the province under the direction of Lo Ping-chang, one of the most distinguished of Tseng Kuo-fan's colleagues. Li Han-chang's services won for him a sixth-degree rank in 1852, and in the following year he was invited by Tseng Kuo-fan to help form the new Hunan militia, which was later to bear the name of Hsiang-chün. Under Tseng, Han-chang organized local corps and assisted in the establishment of the important military commissariat which provided the forces with equipment and funds. Tseng expressed his appreciation of Han-chang's efficient conduct of military and fiscal affairs by assuring his steady and frequent promotion.[45] His letter to Li Han-chang in 1853, praising the accomplishments of Li Hung-chang in Anhwei, indicates that Tseng was anxious to please Han-chang and to retain him on his staff. When Li Wen-an died, in 1855, Li Han-chang gave up his office, in conformity with regulation, and returned to Lu-chou to observe a period of mourning for his father. At this time Li Hung-chang also gave up office, but since he was serving near his native Lu-chou, he merely remained on the job and designated his activities as "unofficial."[46]

Li Han-chang remained in Anhwei until 1858, serving part of the time as a local-corps organizer and financial manager for the governor, Fu-chi. In 1858, however, he was once more summoned to the camp of Tseng Kuo-fan, then located at Nan-ch'ang in Kiangsi province. Here he was assigned to investigate the financial accounts of Tseng's armies

dated according to the Chinese cyclical system as *ping-ch'en,* which corresponds to 1856.

[44] Wang Wen-shao, "Li Han-chang lieh-chuan" in Li Han-chang, *Ho-fei Li Ch'in-lao-kung cheng-shu,* compiled by Li Ching-yü, Vol. I, pages unnumbered.

[45] *Ibid.* In 1862 Li Han-chang was appointed governor-general of Hu-Kuang.

[46] Although, except under exceptional circumstances, it was necessary for an official to retire and enter a formal period of mourning upon the death of a parent, he was frequently permitted to carry on his duties unofficially, or as a member of the gentry. This was particularly true for local activity, such as the management of defense corps. Not only the Lis, but Tseng Kuo-fan as well, had served with distinction in local military efforts during mourning periods.

and to prepare reports. Later he was recommended for promotion by Tseng, and within a few years became one of the ranking governors-general in the empire, serving notably in Liang-Kuang (Kwangtung and Kwangsi) and Hu-Kuang (Hupeh and Hunan).[47]

Shortly after Li Han-chang resumed his position on Tseng's staff, his younger brother, Hung-chang, appeared at Tseng's headquarters. Two other brothers, Li Ho-chang and Li Chao-ch'ing, also came to serve under Tseng about this time.[48] Tseng's acceptance of the four Li brothers as members of his staff enabled him to win over to himself the leaders of local military forces in Anhwei and made possible the future expansion of the Hsiang-chün by the addition of Anhwei troops.

Li Hung-chang's first experiences at his patron's headquarters have become almost legendary. Apparently Tseng felt that Li was too arrogant and needed disciplining before he could be fully depended upon. Hsüeh Fu-ch'eng, who served at various times as secretary to both Li and Tseng, described Tseng's tactics in an essay entitled "How Li Hung-chang Entered the Secretariat of Tseng Kuo-fan."[49] According to Hsüeh, when Li Hung-chang reported to Tseng's headquarters, he spent one full month attempting to gain an audience with his former teacher, only to be rebuffed on each occasion. His patience exhausted, Li finally prevailed on one of Tseng's assistants, Ch'en Nai, who was his former fellow student and *t'ung-nien,* to ascertain Tseng's opinion of him. Ch'en complied with Li's request and spoke to Tseng on his behalf. He reported that Tseng considered him a good *han-lin* scholar and a man of high ambition but feared that his headquarters were "too shallow a beach in which to harbor so large a ship as Li."[50] Nevertheless, Tseng agreed to employ Li. During the next months Tseng strove to break Li's conceit and cure him of his tendency toward insubordination. For instance, it was Tseng's custom to breakfast with his assistants at an early hour. Li was unwilling to rise at dawn and unhappy at having to attend. One morning Li failed to show up at all, pleading a headache. Tseng first sent ordinary attendants, and finally his personal guard, to fetch Li and to explain that Tseng never ate until all his aides were present. Li hurried to breakfast. Upon his arrival, without saying a word, all began to eat. When the meal was over, Tseng turned to Li and said, "Shao-ch'üan, now that you have entered

[47] Hummel, *Eminent Chinese,* p. 471.

[48] *CSK,* 433:4b-5a; *Lu-chou chih,* 48 *(wu-kung)*:3b-5b.

[49] Hsüeh Fu-ch'eng, "Li Ch'uan-hsiang ju Tseng Wen-cheng kung mu-fu," in *Tso, Shih tzu-liao,* I, 160-61; also, *Ch'ing-ch'ao yeh-shih ta-kuan,* VII, 147.

[50] *Ch'ing-ch'ao yeh-shih ta-kuan,* VII, 148.

my *mu-fu* [secretariat], I have some words to say to you! Around this place, what we most honor is the word 'sincerity,' and that is all."[51] Such an incident, which Chinese raconteurs like to relate, fits into the larger pattern of calculated indoctrination employed by Tseng. He emphasized sincerity and loyalty as the cardinal virtues and tried to soften some of the rough edges of Li's personality. In this he seems to have been partly successful.

For over a year, Tseng retained Li as a *mu-yu,* or personal assistant, employing him first as a clerk, then as a compiler, and finally as a memorial writer, in which capacity Li wrote the drafts of Tseng's memorials to the throne. Recognition came to Li when one day Tseng remarked on the excellence of his documents and predicted for him an outstanding future. Li responded that his former superiors had not directed him upon the road which he wished to follow, and expressed gratification at Tseng's attention.[52]

As a *mu-yu,* or member of Tseng's *mu-fu,* Li was a personal employee of Tseng rather than the holder of an official position. This arrangement was of advantage to the employing official since it permitted him to choose his personal assistants without regard to the regulations of the Board of Civil Offices.[53] Tseng's *mu-fu* constituted a veritable "brain trust" of some of the ablest men of the time. Included within its ranks were distinguished classical scholars; administrators; pioneer modernizers interested in Western physics, mathematics, and engineering; financial experts; foreign affairs specialists; and military commanders. Some of them also held civil or military offices, but most remained with Tseng because he offered them ample opportunity to put their talents to practical use and because of the prestige which the connection afforded. Some of the more important men associated with Tseng's *mu-yu* were Wu Ju-lun, Li Yüan-Tu, Ting Jih-ch'ang, Shen Pao-chen, Li Shan-lan, Jung Hung, and Kuo Sung-tao.[54] Li Hung-chang's association with these men, beginning in most instances with

[51] *Ibid.*

[52] Hsüeh Fu-ch'eng, "Li Ch'uan-hsiang ju Tseng Wen-cheng kung mu-fu," in Tso, *Shih tzu-liao,* I, 162.

[53] Research on *mu-yu,* and other "sub," "under," or "semi" officials during the Ch'ing period has been carried out by Mr. Fang Chia-ying and Mrs. Fang Tu Lien-che, of the Chinese History Project, Columbia University, New York. Manuscript copies of their as yet unpublished materials are available at the Modern Chinese History Project, University of Washington, and have been drawn upon in the present study.

[54] A list of the members of Tseng's *mu-yu* is found in Hsüeh Fu-ch'eng, "Hsü Tseng Wen-Cheng kung mu-fu pin-liao," in Tso, *Shih tzu-liao,* I, 132 ff. Wu Ju-lun was one of the most accomplished literary figures of the time, who distinguished himself in educational affairs and as a prose writer. Hummel, *Eminent Chinese,* p.

his entrance into Tseng's group, provided him with a wide circle of influential friends, many of whom joined him later when he set up his own staff. The continuity of leadership from Tseng to Li in later years was in large measure based upon Li's success in holding the services of a large number of Tseng's *mu-yu,* an accomplishment due in no small part to Tseng's own generosity and foresight.

Tseng's organization came to include most of the distinguished Chinese military leaders who became prominent in the late nineteenth century. Among them were Tso Tsung-t'ang, who rose to fame during the Taiping Rebellion and later distinguished himself by pacifying the northwest and defending it against the Russians; Tseng Kuo-ch'üan, younger brother of Tseng, who was responsible for the capture of the Taiping capital at Nanking; Li Han-chang and Li Ho-chang, brothers of Li Hung-chang; Liu K'un-i, who held power in central China until the turn of the century; P'eng Yü-lin; Ch'eng Hsüeh-ch'i, who deserted from the Taipings in 1861; Kuo Sung-lin; and many others.[55]

Many of these military leaders later joined Li as part of a loose association of provincial leaders, bound together by common experience and loyalty to Tseng. Others became direct subordinates of Li himself. Although rivalries among some of Tseng's followers arose later, a modicum of co-operation was usually maintained. Without the respect and assistance of this group, Li Hung-chang could never have earned the distinction in military and civil affairs which was to make him indispensable to the reigning dynasty for almost half a century.

Table 1, which is based on Lo Erh-kang's data, shows in summary form the native places, backgrounds, and later careers of the Hsiang-chün officers. By far the larger number of the important officers and army managers were from Tseng's own province of Hunan, and most of the key positions in the organization were in their hands. However,

---

870. Wu later compiled the *Li Wen-chung kung ch'üan-chi.* Li Yüan-tu submitted a brilliant letter on military defense tactics to Tseng and was invited to join his personal staff. Tseng was ultimately forced to impeach Li Yüan-tu, but he did so with regret, recognizing that Li's dereliction in duty was a result of his interest in scholarly affairs at the expense of his military duties. Hummel, *Eminent Chinese,* p. 498; see also Hsüeh Fu-ch'eng, "Li Ch'uan-hsiang ju Tseng Wen-cheng kung mu-fu," in Tso, *Shih tzu-liao.* Biographies of Shen Pao-chen, Li Shan-lan, the famous mathematician, and Jung Hung are found in Hummel, *Eminent Chinese.* Jung Hung, also known as Yung Kung, relates his experiences with Tseng in his autobiography under the name (Cantonese) and title, Yung Wing, *My Life in China and America* (New York, 1909). For detailed references to Chinese inventors and engineers on Tseng's staff, see Ch'en Ch'i-t'ien (Gideon Chen), Tseng Kuo-fan, *Pioneer Promoter of the Steamship in China* (Peking, 1935), *passim.*

55 Lo Erh-kang, *Hsiang-chün hsin-chih.* The biographies of Tso Tsung-t'ang, Tseng Kuo-ch'üan, Liu K'un-i, P'eng Yü-lin, and Ch'eng Hsüeh-ch'i appear in Hummel, *Eminent Chinese.*

TABLE 1

HSIANG-CHÜN OFFICERS BY ORIGIN AND CAREER*

	Total	Native Place			Background			Highest Office Attained			
		Hunan	Other	Un-specified	Lit-erary	Mil-itary	Un-specified	Governor-general	Gov-ernor	Other	Un-specified
T'ung-shuai (general)	3	3	0	0	3	0	0	1	2	0	0
Important members of mu-fu	15	10	5	0	15	0	0	7	3	5	0
T'ung-ling (commander)	13	10	3	0	8	5	0	4	2	7	0
Fen-ling (lower commander)	43	28	5	10	26	17	0	2	6	29	6
Ying-kuan (battalion commander)	98	69	8	21	39	52	7	0	0	80	18
Pang-pan (assistant manager)	10	5	4	1	9	1	0	0	0	10	0
Total	182	125	25	32	100	75	7	14	13	131	24

* Translation of a chart in Lo Erh-kang's *Hsiang-chün hsin-chih*, handwritten copy, no pagination.

it should be noted that while the very top military positions seem to have been held almost exclusively by Hunan men, fully one-third of the members of Tseng's *mu-fu* were from other provinces. Among these were men who, like the Lis, commanded local support in their own areas. Through them Tseng considerably extended the influence of his Hsiang organization. As the table shows, fourteen of Tseng's officers went on to become governors-general in later years, and of these seven were from his *mu-fu*. This strongly supports the statement that Tseng was in a position to influence regions outside his own proper sphere of authority, particularly since the *mu-yu* during their period of service were in closer relation to Tseng than any other group. It is also evident from the table that for the highest posts in his organization Tseng preferred to have men who, like Li Hung-chang and his brothers, had been trained in the traditional literary fashion.

In a memorial to the throne written in mid-1859, Tseng Kuo-fan summarized Li's background and requested permission to avail himself of his services as an official and military commander. Tseng wrote:

> The already recommended judicial commissioner bearing the title of circuit intendant, the compiler of the Hanlin Academy, Li Hung-chang, was ordered in the third year of Hsien-feng to follow the vice-president of the Board of Works, Lü Hsien-chi, to manage local defense affairs in Anhwei. Subsequently it was memorialized that the provincial commander-in-chief, Ho-ch'un, and the Anhwei governor, Fu-chi, retain him in their service to assist in general management. A former edict is already on record stating that the said circuit intendant's management of his Anhwei battalion's affairs has been completed.
>
> In the winter of last year he went to Kiangsu to see his mother, after which he desired to return to the capital. However, because the said circuit intendant has long been active in civil and military affairs, I retained him to assist me in my military business. Yesterday I sent Li Hung-chang together with my brother to attack Ching-te-chen. . . .[56]

The attack by Tseng's brother, Kuo-ch'üan, and Li Hung-chang upon the Taiping forces at Chiang-te-chen was successful, and shortly afterward Li was promoted to the post of circuit intendant in Fukien, an office he held only nominally. Li Han-chang had also participated in the battle at Ching-te-chen, and for his efforts received imperial recognition in the form of a circuit intendancy in Hunan. Shortly thereafter, Tseng Kuo-fan appointed Li Han-chang to manage the likin affairs for his army in Kiangsi.[57] At about the same time he put Li Hung-chang

[56] *TWCK Memorials,* 11:4a, HF 9/5/26.

[57] Wang Wen-shao, "Li Han-chang lieh-chuan," in Li Han-chang, *Ho-fei Li Ch'in-lao-kung cheng-shu,* Vol. I.

in command of a battalion of water troops.[58] Among Li's duties was responsibility for inspecting and reporting on the commanders of the various battalions of the Hunan troops. Even as he assigned Li to this task, Tseng took the opportunity to warn him to temper his manner and approach:

Your ability is great and your aspirations reach far. But though I believe you can save our civilization, you must yet pay attention to time and place. Furthermore, there are sometimes mystical forces behind things which cannot be controlled. Of this I warn you as a friend. . .[59]

Li, however, continued to appear headstrong and finally came into conflict with Tseng himself. After continual bickering on questions of strategy, Li finally exhausted Tseng's patience by refusing to draft for him a memorial to which he took exception. Rather than write it, he threatened to leave, whereupon Tseng relieved him of his post.[60]

Li remained away for one year, residing in Kiangsu, but continued to correspond with Tseng. Unfortunately, none of Li's correspondence written before 1861 has come to light. Tseng's letters to Li, however, indicate that the older man regretted the breach in their relations and was willing to let bygones be bygones. The occasion for reconciliation was a letter from Li to Tseng congratulating the latter on the capture of Anking, Anhwei, late in 1861.[61] But Tseng's correspondence reveals that on at least three previous occasions in the course of the year 1860-61, Tseng had attempted to persuade Li to return to his service. On the first occasion, Tseng warned that the province of Kiangsi was in imminent peril, and that if Kiangsi fell, Hunan would soon fall as well. He requested Li "to persuade Fu T'ang to support me."[62] He then asked Li to return to manage the garrison at the capital of Kiangsi, re-

---

[58] "Kuo-shih pen-chuan," in *LWCK Collected Works*, Introductory *chüan*, pp. 12a-34a.

[59] *TWCK Letters*, 8:22a.

[60] Hsüeh Fu-ch'eng, "Li Ch'uan-hsiang ju Tseng Wen-cheng kung mu-fu," in Tso, *Shih tzu-liao*, I, 161-62.

[61] See, for instance, Hummel, *Eminent Chinese*, p. 464. On the other hand the *CSK* biography completely omits reference to the alleged break and reconciliation, as does the "Kuo-shih pen-chuan," in *LWCK Collected Works*, p. 13a.

[62] Fu T'ang was the *hao*, or style-name, of Li Huan, third son of the famous military leader, Li Hsing-Yüan, also a native of Hsiang-hsiang, Hunan. Li Huan served Tseng Kuo-fan in Kiangsi, but had been offended by Tseng Kuo-fan's reporting of a minor error in his accounting and snubbed Tseng Kuo-fan for several years thereafter. In his letter Tseng apparently hoped to persuade both Li Hung-chang and Li Huan to return to him. At this time Li Huan was serving in Kiangsu and apparently had some connection with the revenue administration in that province. It is possible that Tseng was for this reason anxious to regain Li Huan's friendship through the good offices of Li Hung-chang. See Hummel, *Eminent Chinese*, p. 458.

minding him that the life of his own brother, Han-chang, who was then serving in the area, might thus be saved. If Li consented, Tseng was willing to give him a regular appointment and attach a special note to the memorial formally recommending him.[63]

Shortly afterward, Tseng again wrote to Li complaining that since he had left his camp in the previous year he had waited in vain for him:

My whole army is now at Ching-te-chen. For a long time you have not come to my headquarters, and I do not understand why. In so far as public duty is concerned you have responsibilities toward your water troops and cannot just abandon them. As far as personal affection is concerned, when you left you did not say you would not return. Only this spring Ch'i-men was in danger, and still you did not come. In the summer Tung-liu was hardly safe. Now I suffer a rash because of the heat. I am sick within and without. For fifteen days I have not written a memorial. If you bear me no ill feeling, I hope that you will come back to me.[64]

Finally, after the capture of Anking, in September, 1861, Tseng again wrote that if Li had finished his family affairs, he hoped Li would come to his camp in order to clear up Tseng's accumulated affairs.[65] Only then did Li rejoin his old patron.

When Li left Tseng Kuo-fan in 1860, he had been the commander of a single unit popularly known as the Huai-yung shui-shih, or Huai volunteer water troops. After he returned in 1861, he was ordered to raise and command an entire army—the Huai-chün.

---

[63] *TWCK Letters,* 14:17a-b.
[64] *Ibid.,* 15:39a ff.
[65] *Ibid.,* 16:30a.

II. The Rise of the Huai-chün

THE capture of the city of Anking by the troops of Tseng Kuo-ch'üan, acting under the orders of Tseng Kuo-fan, was the only bright spot in the government campaigns of 1861. Six months before, the Taipings, in a resurgence of strength, had won spectacular victories in Kiangsu province. The capital city, Soochow, had fallen in June, 1860, and Ch'ang-chou and other important points along the Grand Canal were occupied by the Taipings. The victory at Anking, however, gave Tseng Kuo-fan a strong foothold in the Yangtze valley from which troops could be sent by land and sea to attack the Taipings at their capital, Nanking.

The Taiping armies had been centered around Nanking since 1853. They had maintained intermittent control over the important trade routes of southern Liang-Chiang, disrupted the economy of the entire region, and threatened to cut the central government off from its two most important sources of revenue, the grain tribute and the salt tax. Nanking was the heart of the Taiping movement. There the Taiping T'ien Wang, the Heavenly King, held court and concentrated a wealth of fighting men and resources. The Taipings themselves described Nanking as "an extraordinary place," strategically located, well fortified, and abundant in grains and riches.[1] So far as the Manchu government was concerned, only the fall of Nanking could remove the would-be usurper and destroy the primary base of the rebels.

---

[1] Among the more important documents revealing the Taiping attitudes toward Nanking are a series of forty-four treatises supposedly written by candidates for office among the Taipings which deal with the subject "On the Establishment of Nanking as the Heavenly Capital." See "Chien T'ien-ching yü Chin-ling lun," in Ch'eng Yen-sheng, *T'ai-p'ing t'ien-kuo shih-liao, ti-i-chi* (Peking, 1926), III, 2a-23a.

The Problem of Defending Kiangsu

The only two important cities in Kiangnan still holding out against the Taipings were Chinkiang and Shanghai. Chinkiang lay forty miles to the east of Nanking, commanding the confluence of the Yangtze River and the Grand Canal, and it was an obvious base for a possible westward thrust by government forces against Nanking. It controlled the inland transportation route upon which the central government depended for shipment of tribute. Eighteen years earlier, during the Opium War, the British had thrown the Manchu government into a

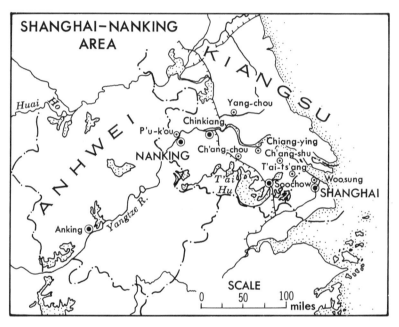

panic by capturing Chinkiang, thus gaining control of the Grand Canal. This was such a serious blow that the Manchu government had been forced to capitulate to the stiff British terms that ended the war.[2] To prevent the Taipings from gaining such an advantage, the government had arranged for the transportation of tribute by sea. Nevertheless, the Grand Canal and the Yangtze River remained the main artery of China, and the government could not afford to lose Chinkiang.[3]

Shanghai, farther to the east, was the most important of the Chinese

---

[2] Lo Erh-kang, *Hsiang-chün hsin-chih, chüan* 12.

[3] Harold C. Hinton, "Grain Transport Via the Grand Canal, 1845-1901," *Papers on China,* from the East Asia Regional Studies Seminars (mimeographed for private distribution by the East Asia Program, Committee on Regional Studies, Harvard University), IV (1950), 36.

ports opened to trade under the terms of the treaty of Nanking in 1842. By 1861 its population had grown to more than a million. It had rapidly surpassed Amoy, Foochow, and Ningpo, the other ports originally selected by the Western merchants and governments as promising trade centers.[4] Within two decades after its opening, Shanghai had supplanted Canton as the chief center of foreign trade. A report by a China Maritime Customs officer emphasized the effect of the Taiping Rebellion upon this development:

A very striking change in this period [1843-1858] was the gradual supplanting of Canton by Shanghai as the chief centre of foreign trade. Canton lost her supremacy partly owing to the development of Hongkong as the first port of call in Chinese waters ... and partly owing to the devastation caused by the Taiping Rebellion and the consequent disorganisation of those trade routes in the interior by which Canton had been supplied from time immemorial. Shanghai was nearer both the tea and the silk districts, particularly the latter.... The total effect of the Taiping Rebellion on the foreign trade of China is, of course, incalculable; the development that might have taken place if the sources of supply had not been devastated, and if widespread ruin and impoverishment had not cut down demand, can only remain a matter of speculation. It is remarkable that, even in spite of the fact that at the close of our present period [1843-1858] this terrible and ruinous civil war was at its height, so much progress in foreign trade has actually to be recorded.[5]

An American consular official who witnessed the development of Shanghai described its growth as follows:

By 1846 Shanghai was contributing one-seventh of the total exports from China; by 1851, this share in the export trade had grown to one-half, and after 1851, it was never much less than a half.[6]

From its very opening, therefore, Shanghai proved to be a flourishing port. Not only did it draw coastwise trade, but it was also the gateway to the interior via the city of Soochow and the Grand Canal. It was estimated in 1861 that there were 14,000 to 20,000 Shanghai junks engaged in the traffic to the north alone.[7] In the silk trade, the export mounted from 6,433 bales in 1845 to 84,970 bales in 1858.[8] The shipments of tea from Shanghai grew from approximately one million

---

[4] "A History of External Trade, 1834-1881," in China: The Maritime Customs, Decennial Reports, 1922-31, Statistical Series No. 6 (Shanghai: Inspectorate General of Customs, 1933), I, 23-25.

[5] Ibid., pp. 22-23.

[6] Ibid., p. 23, quoting from Commercial Reports from British Consuls in China, 1872, p. 149.

[7] "A History of External Trade, 1834-1881," p. 25.

[8] Ibid.

pounds (weight) in 1844 to over eighty million pounds eleven years later.[9] Because of its favorable climate, its easy access to the principal silk and tea producing area, and its proximity to the main interior trade routes, Shanghai attracted more foreign attention than any other port in China. Both Shanghai and Chinkiang were in constant danger of being attacked and occupied by the Taipings. Shanghai was guaranteed protection by the Western powers who maintained small forces in the area, but it was the wealthiest center in Kiangsu still free, and foreign protection alone could never be considered sufficient for its permanent security.

Tseng Kuo-fan, as governor-general of Liang-Chiang and Imperial Commissioner for Bandit Suppression, was responsible for laying down the over-all strategy for clearing his provinces of the rebels. He was torn between the desire to crush Nanking at the earliest possible moment by throwing his full force against that city and his realization of the need to provide strong forces for the relief of Chinkiang and Shanghai. Realizing that Nanking could be taken only by a strategy of encirclement, Tseng became more and more convinced that Chinkiang offered the key to victory. This course had been pressed upon him even before his victory at Anking by Feng Kuei-fen, a prominent member of the Soochow gentry, then taking refuge in Shanghai.[10]

Feng's opinion at that time had been that despite two years of depredation by the Taipings, the situation in Kiangsu still was not hopeless. He warned, however, that although Shanghai was still undisturbed the city was in constant danger. Reminding Tseng that desertions from the Taiping ranks had been observed, he argued that the presence of Tseng's army might immediately increase this tendency. He also informed the governor-general that the small government garrison still stationed at Chinkiang was without revenue and could not sustain itself much longer. Similarly, the garrisons at Hanghow and Hu-chou lacked funds and equipment and were under continual enemy pressure. The situation there would remain extremely difficult unless Tseng's army came to offer protection. On the other hand, he noted:

Shanghai has revenue but no garrison. Here trade and commerce are concentrated. Nominally there are ten thousand soldiers, but in fact only a few thousand are suitable for defense purposes. If your army comes, Shanghai can provide revenue for both your land and water forces. But this place is cut off and isolated. The bandits surround it heavily. The disbanded vol-

---

9 *Ibid.*, p. 26.
10 Feng Kuei-fen's biography is concisely related in Hummel, *Eminent Chinese*, pp. 241-43.

unteers and rascals here cannot be driven to fight them; therefore the situation cannot long remain as it is.[11]

Feng proposed that Tseng use a "surprise" army of ten thousand men led by a vigorous commander and send them to Shanghai by a short-cut. If attacks were launched at the same time at various points within Kiangsu and the Taipings were encircled as they moved, "the various bandit leaders would be thrown into chaos, and your [Tseng's] army at Wuhu could proceed directly to Nanking."[12]

These were the problems Tseng was facing when Li Hung-chang rejoined him in late 1861. He had not yet decided that Shanghai was essential to victory, and he excused his indecision in these words: "I am at a great distance from Kiangsu and Chekiang, and my communication with this area is frequently interrupted. I cannot investigate minutely and study and evaluate the situation."[13]

Tseng also felt a repugnance for the city because it was heavily under the influence of foreigners, whom he considered to be corrupt and unscrupulous. He described the city in the following terms:

The Shanghai "corner" is a place where all the Westerners come together. The people are like the seas and the goods are [piled up] like the mountains. The Chinese and foreign merchants and officials, both civil and military, rub shoulders there, and their carriage wheels tangle with each other's. Day and night noises fill the air. The place is small but the men there are numerous. We have more personnel available there by far than we can use.[14]

Unless this city, whose tremendous wealth Tseng had described, was in dire trouble, it could be left alone for the moment. Pressed by other worries and lacking sufficient control of the area, he did not take the initiative in securing the city.

The Role of the Gentry at Shanghai

During the years of rebellion, Shanghai became host to a new group of gentry, merchants, and officials. The powerful gentry of Soochow, Ch'ang-chou, and T'ai-ts'ang thronged into the city to escape the Taipings who had overrun their lands. The gentry and merchants of Chekiang, who originally had come to Shanghai to participate in the growing trade, now ensconced themselves in business and in government offices and made Shanghai their second home. The fall of Soochow, the provincial capital, had brought a host of officials, high and low, the gov-

---

[11] Feng Kuei-fen, Hsien-chih-t'ang kao (1877), 5:3a-6b.
[12] Ibid.
[13] TWCK Memorials, 14:66b.
[14] Ibid., p. 67a.

ernor as well as petty officeholders, to Shanghai, which became a temporary capital. Although there were conflicts of interest among these groups, and men of one province competed with those of another for wealth and power, all were agreed that the Taipings were their principal enemy, and they worked together for their common security.[15]

A defense organization was established by the gentry and merchants to finance and direct a European-style defense corps. This force was placed under the command of an American adventurer, Frederick Townsend Ward, son-in-law of one of the leading Chinese gentry merchants, Yang Fang. Yang Fang was known among foreigners as "Takee," and for many years he managed the finances of the army. The success of this small, hard-hitting force in clearing the seaboard area around Shanghai gave it the name of the Ever Victorious Army. In later years it was to achieve world renown under the command of Colonel—later General—Charles ("Chinese") Gordon.[16] The Ever Victorious Army served as an adjunct to the poorly organized, poorly trained, and poorly disciplined provincial forces of the governor, Hsüeh Huan. Although its officers were Europeans and Americans and many of the soldiers were Filipino seamen, the Ever Victorious Army was a Chinese army, subject to the command of Chinese officials and gentry. Unlike the regular British and French forces, which confined their operations to a well specified area around Shanghai (a thirty-mile perimeter), the Ever Victorious Army was free to move in offensive action against the Taipings.

Although gentry, merchants, and officials worked together to support the campaigns of the Ever Victorious Army, they differed in their ultimate aims. The Chekiang merchants and gentry, who were well established in Shanghai and had infiltrated the local bureaucracy, were most concerned with protecting the city and the trade routes leading to it. But the Kiangsu gentry, relative newcomers to the port, even though they too were beginning to build for themselves a place in the Shanghai mercantile world, were still primarily interested in freeing their home districts. Tseng Kuo-fan's campaign strategy directly affected their own plans. They realized that the Hsiang-chün was the only army capable of driving out the Taipings. If Tseng chose to attack Nanking from upriver, neither Shanghai nor the rest of eastern Kiangsu would be any more secure for a long time to come. Even if

---

[15] Hsüeh Fu-ch'eng, "Shu Ho-fei Po-hsiang Li-kung yung Hu p'ing Wu," in Tso, *Shih tzu-liao,* I, 163-67.

[16] Feng Kuei-fen, in *Hsien-chih-t'ang kao,* 4:14a-b.

Tseng's forces by-passed Nanking, reinforced Chinkiang, and wheeled back upon Nanking, the situation would still be no better in eastern Kiangsu. Only the dispatch of a strong force overland from Shanghai to Nanking would make Shanghai secure and clear the area between the two cities.

Gentry Pressure for the Protection of Shanghai

While Tseng vacillated, the gentry found their situation becoming ever more precarious. One gentry resident of Shanghai wrote at the time that the 55,000 volunteers upon whom the governor depended were "only ruffians and rascals of the street whose fighting ability was negligible."[17] The Ever Victorious Army was far too expensive, costing ten times as much as ordinary troops. Moreover, it was a small force with unruly commanders who were principally interested in keeping free the important trade areas of Sung-chiang.

In this atmosphere of insecurity, the gentry leaders in Shanghai met late in 1861 to decide what should be done. Dominating the meeting were the gentry from the neighborhood of Soochow: P'ang Chung-lu, the commissioner of local militia and a man of great influence, was a native of Ch'ang-shu.[18] Other men from the Soochow region were the former senior secretary of the Board of Punishments, P'an Tseng-wei; the Hupeh salt intendant, Ku Wen-pin; and Feng Kuei-fen. All of these men were actively interested in the recapture of Soochow, the principal city of their home area.[19] A younger member of the group was Ch'ien Ting-ming, who had risen to prominence as a local-corps leader in this region. Ch'ien came from T'ai-ts'ang, a short distance north of Soochow.[20]

---

[17] *Ibid.*

[18] P'ang Chung-lu is mentioned in the biographical dictionary, compiled by Tsang Li-ho, *Chung-kuo jen-ming ta-tz'u-tien* (Shanghai, 1934), p. 1764, as having obtained his *chin-shih* degree during the Tao-kuang reign. He rose from the office of *pien-hsiu* [compiler] to that of subchancellor to the Grand Secretariat, but subsequently had to retire to his native place for mourning. When the Taiping Rebellion arose he became an official in the local corps organization. After the fall of his native Ch'ang-shu he went to Shanghai. He presented the case for the protection of Shanghai to Tseng Kuo-fan, after which he returned to Shanghai and participated in the recapture of Soochow and Chang-chou. During the Kuang-hsü period he rose to the rank of president of the Board of Punishments. See Feng Kuei-fen, *Hsien-chih-t'ang kao,* 4:19a-21a, "The Organization of the Mutual Defense Force in Shanghai," for a good description of the activities of P'ang Chung-lu, P'an Tseng-wei, and Ku Wen-pin. See also *Li Wen-chung kung p'eng-liao han-kao,* 1:15a, TC 1/3/25 (hereafter cited *LWCK Letters),* in *LWCK Collected Works.*

[19] *LWCK Memorials,* 24:29a-b, TC 13/11/12.

[20] *CSK,* 425:7a.

The details of this meeting have been handed down by Feng Kuei-fen, who was one of the finest historians and scholars of his period and a prolific writer on many subjects. The purpose of the meeting was to decide upon ways and means of inducing Tseng Kuo-fan to occupy Shanghai. Ku Wen-pin, who earlier in the year had passed through Anking, had been favorably impressed by the Hsiang-chün troops. Upon his return to Shanghai, he had called upon Feng Kuei-fen, and they had discussed the uselessness of the Shanghai troops, comparing them with the Hsiang-chün. So far as they could see, the Hsiang-chün was available. They then had called in P'an Tseng-wei, and he had agreed to join them in inviting Tseng Kuo-fan to Shanghai.

In the course of their conference, the gentry leaders discussed the possible difficulties. They anticipated that the governor, Hsüeh Huan, might not consent. Opposition was also expected from the Western merchants and officers, who were maintaining a policy of neutrality and might not want to see their trade center turned into a military base. The biggest problem of all was Tseng Kuo-fan himself, for the gentry considered him to be a cautious man who might not be willing to let his troops pass through dangerous enemy territory.

Having reviewed the obstacles, the gentry set about overcoming them. When they approached the governor, Hsüeh Huan, their first fears were realized. Hsüeh opposed their plan, but lacking any suitable excuse for his opposition, adopted a tactic of hesitating and delaying, apparently hoping to wear down the advocates of the scheme. He did not welcome the lessening of his authority and the close critical scrutiny to which he would be subjected if Tseng or his deputy came to Shanghai. Hsüeh had been roundly criticized for maladministration, and he may even have been aware that his muddled efforts at defense were being brought to the attention of Tseng and the court. Governor Hsüeh, however, was in no position to block the gentry directly. He was dependent upon the acting judicial commissioner, Circuit Intendant Wu Hsü, an official from Chekiang, powerful in the mercantile world and firmly entrenched in the Shanghai bureaucracy. Exercising strong control over the revenues, Wu could make his influence felt. Although Hsüeh Huan was the ranking official in Shanghai, as one observer noted, "He could only 'yes' Wu Hsü."[21] When Wu Hsü, desiring the presence of a strong government army, fell in with the plans of the gentry, he put an end to Hsüeh Huan's dilatory tactics.

---

[21] Hsüeh Fu-ch'eng, "Shu Ho-fei Po-hsiang Li-kung yung Hu p'ing Wu," in Tso, *Shih tzu-liao,* I, 163-64.

The task of convincing the British and French of the importance of the proposed relief expedition and of securing their help was entrusted to the prefectural magistrate, Ying Pao-shih, who was associated with the gentry in directing the United Defense Bureau (established in 1860) in Shanghai. While the British consul, Medhurst, refused to co-operate, Admiral Sir James Hope, who was in charge of British forces in the area, consented quite readily. Ying Pao-shih next approached the foreign merchants and, by offering a good price, secured their willingness to rent their steam vessels for the transportation of an army from Anking. The gentry believed that swift steamers were the answer to Tseng's reluctance to send his troops on a hazardous land march or to commit them to the dangers of running the Taiping blockade on the Yangtze River.

The Shanghai Gentry Approach Tseng

It remained for the gentry to convince Tseng Kuo-fan of the feasibility of their plan. Tseng was finally approached by Ch'ien Ting-ming, who made the trip to Anking by steamer, carrying with him a letter written by Feng Kuei-fen with the assistance of other gentry leaders. Ch'ien's role in urging Tseng to save Shanghai has been described in several contemporary accounts. All accounts agree that the selection of Ch'ien Ting-ming to plead the case of the gentry group in Shanghai was a happy decision. Instead of an ordinary letter, Tseng received a message delivered personally by an eloquent spokesman. Feng Kuei-fen himself described the mission as follows: "In the middle of the tenth month, Ch'ien Ting-ming went to Tseng Kuo-fan to report that Shanghai was in peril. Ch'ien shed tears. Tseng Kuo-fan responded with sympathy and said: "Cease your crying. Although I am not able to send my main army, I shall send a 'surprise' force."[22]

Despite his encouraging words to Ch'ien, Tseng still did not act. He was still convinced that Chinkiang was the most important strategic point in the area,[23] and he planned to station Li Hung-chang there. It was his hope that from Chinkiang, Li and the forces at Hangchow could immediately launch an attack upon Nanking. Later the combined army could proceed to recover Soochow and Ch'ang-chou, thus relieving the pressure on Shanghai.

---

[22] Feng Kuei-fen, *Hsien-chih-t'ang kao,* 4:14a-b.
[23] Hsüeh Fu-ch'eng, "Shu Ho-fei Po-hsiang Li-kung yung Hu p'ing Wu," in Tso, *Shih tzu-liao,* I, 164.

Tseng Decides to Reinforce Shanghai

Governor-general Tseng's final decision, when it came, was largely due to the influence of Li Hung-chang. Feng Kuei-fen reports that Tseng Kuo-fan, upon hearing Ch'ien Ting-ming's description of conditions around Shanghai, remarked that in view of the emergency situation he would consult Li Hung-chang of Ho-fei. Li then expressed his agreement with Ch'ien's plan and requested permission to go to Shanghai.

Another account, by Hsüeh Fu-ch'eng, relates that Ch'ien first called upon Tseng and told him of the great suffering of the people in the southeast. He then went to see Li Hung-chang, who was in Tseng's *mu-fu* at that time, and recounted the advantages of Shanghai, its thriving trade, its income from foreign customs and likin, all excellent sources of military revenues. It can be assumed that Li already had a fairly good idea of what Shanghai offered. He was no stranger to Kiangsu province, where his family had lived in exile since 1858. His mother had taken up residence in Chinkiang, and Li had visited her there in 1860. On that occasion it is quite likely that he had also visited Shanghai, since Tseng Kuo-fan had asked him to induce the financial officials of Kiangsu to send funds to Tseng's headquarters, and these officials presumably were living then in Shanghai. Whether it was owing to Li's experience or his own eloquence, Ch'ien had no difficulty in impressing upon Li how regrettable it would be if the rich revenues of Shanghai fell to the enemy rather than to Li's forces. As a result of this conversation, Hsüeh Fu-ch'eng records, Li Hung-chang determined that Shanghai should be the immediate objective of his army. Accordingly he approached Tseng, described the situation to him once more, and settled upon the plan for relieving Shanghai from the rebel threat.[24]

Still another source emphasizes Li's role as follows:

In the eleventh year of Hsien-feng, the Taipings endangered the Soochow and Shanghai sector. At that time Tseng Kuo-fan had just taken Anking. The local-corps high commissioner P'ang Chung-lu and others begged for aid from Tseng Kuo-fan. But Tseng Kuo-fan considered Shanghai as militarily hopeless and was indecisive about the matter. Li Hung-chang then expressed to Tseng his determination to go.[25]

---

24 *Ibid.*

25 This description is found in a memorial written by Sheng Hsüan-huai on behalf of the gentry of Shanghai who had requested the erection of a shrine in that city commemorating the exploits of Li Hung-chang. *LWCK Collected Works,* Introductory

Li Hung-chang's conversations with the representatives of the Soo-chow gentry marked the beginning of a period of co-operation which lasted for several years. On the basis of their understanding it became possible for Li to plan the future development of an army and decide on the part it should play in liberating Kiangsu from the Taipings.

---

chüan, pp. 49a-b. Confirming evidence is found in the official biography of Ch'ien Ting-ming, reproduced in *Ch'ien Min-su kung tsou-shu* (1878), which states:

"Ch'ien Ting-ming was born in T'ai-ts'ang [Kiangsu]. His father . . . had been governor of Hupeh province. He [Ch'ien Ting-ming] received his *chü-jen* degree in the twenty-sixth year of Tao-kuang. In the thirtieth year he passed the examination as tutor in the Ching-shan Academy. At the special examination of Hsien-feng third year he entered the second rank as a local commissioner of education. At this time the Taipings had occupied various prefectures [in Kiangsu] and the court thereupon ordered his father to organize local corps at his native place. Ch'ien Ting-ming assisted his father in this work. Later the bandits caused trouble in Shanghai and occupied Ch'ing-p'u and Chia-ting. In collaboration with a *chü-jen* from Chia-ting, Ch'ien Ting-ming summoned volunteers to recapture Chia-ting and apprehended the bandit leader. This has been officially recorded.

". . . During the latter part of the Hsien-feng reign his father died and he retired from office [at the capital] in order to observe a period of mourning. In the tenth year of Hsien-feng the Taipings caused trouble in Soochow, T'ai-ts'ang, and other places. At this time the governor of Kiangsu, Hsüeh Huan, hurried to Shanghai to protect that city. The governor-general, Tseng Kuo-fan, had stationed his army at Anking, one thousand li from Shanghai and therefore could not protect that city owing to its great distance from Anking. Therefore, Ch'ien Ting-ming suggested to Hsüeh Huan that the armies from the upper river [i.e., stationed in Anhwei] should take a commanding position from higher land. At this time the various local-corps commissioners had a conference in order to request help from the Hsiang-chün, but no one wished to risk the journey. Ch'ien Ting-ming thereupon volunteered to go. He then embarked on a boat and passed through the Taiping blockade, risking the shells of the rebels which struck his boat. He finally arrived at Tseng Kuo-fan's headquarters and made clear to Tseng the critical situation prevailing in Kiangsu and Chekiang. He told Tseng that Shanghai was a trading port where both foreign and native merchandise were handled. The revenues there were so tremendous that it was unthinkable to abandon them to the rebels. He presented thousands of such words to Tseng Kuo-fan and wept greatly. Tseng Kuo-fan also wept. Tseng was so moved that he permitted the dispatching of a rescuing army to Shanghai.

"Previously Hsüeh [Huan] had called for twelve thousand volunteers from Huan, and these volunteers were already en route to Shanghai. But Tseng Kuo-fan told Ch'ien Ting-ming that the volunteers whom Hsüeh had so engaged were the same ones Tseng had previously disbanded, and were not fit to be used. Ch'ien thereupon offered to meet the volunteers half-way and disband them. He then met them at Hankow. Selecting only nine hundred of the original twelve thousand, he demobilized the rest. While ordinarily disbanded volunteers were prone to mutiny, in this case they remained passive. Ch'ien Ting-ming then went alone to Shanghai where he conferred with the local-corps commissioners and arranged for the transportation of the relief army. They then decided to employ foreign steamships for that purpose, and raised 180,000 taels, with which they hired five steamers. Ch'ien Ting-ming himself led the five steamers to Anhwei. At that moment Tseng Kuo-fan ordered the *an-ch'a-shih* Li Hung-chang to lead five thousand Huai-chün troops to rescue Shanghai. Thus in the third month of the first year of T'ung-chih, Ch'ien met Li's armies and welcomed them aboard the steamships."

Another account, written by members of the gentry requesting the erection of a shrine in honor of Ch'ien, states: "Li Hung-chang was in the headquarters of

Once Li had succeeded in convincing Tseng of the importance of strongly reinforcing Shanghai, the governor-general acted quickly. He ordered Li to return to Ho-fei and raise an expeditionary force. Meanwhile, Tseng paved the way in Kiangsu for the appointment of a new governor belonging to his own military organization as a substitute for the ineffectual Hsüeh Huan. The opportunity to replace Hsüeh was provided by an imperial edict questioning Hsüeh's official conduct. This edict was dated Hsien-feng eleventh year, tenth month, seventeenth day, and received by Tseng on the thirteenth day of the following month. The imperial edict was sent one day after Ch'ien Ting-ming's arrival at Tseng's headquarters. Evidently at the court as well as at Anking the Soochow gentry were stirring up interest in Shanghai.[26]

Twelve days after receiving the edict, Tseng Kuo-fan answered the imperial inquiry. He charged that Hsüeh had refused to give up his life of pleasure in Shanghai in order to inspect the few areas in Kiangsu where government authority still prevailed. Nor had he made any serious effort to supply adequate funds to these beleaguered outposts. Tseng also stated that Hsüeh had shown poor judgment in recruiting provincial troops from among Taiping deserters and vagabonds of Kwangtung province, poorly disciplined soldiers who harassed the merchants, looted foreign ships, and killed local-corps leaders and their followers.[27] Tseng went on to compare Hsüeh Huan with the proverbial Chinese peasant who saw a rabbit kill itself by running into a tree and thereafter spent his days by the tree convinced that he had discovered an effortless way to bag game. Instead of attending to military affairs, the governor indulged in the pleasures of curio-collecting and wine. Meanwhile his subordinates embezzled funds and taxed the people so oppressively that widespread complaints had arisen. Tseng declared that Kiangsu, with its rich revenues, was too important to be entrusted to a man like Hsüeh, who was "incapable of shouldering his heavy responsibilities."[28]

Tseng's denunciation of the governor was evidently based on information supplied by the Kiangsu gentry. He sympathized particularly with their complaints about the conflict between the governor's troops and their own defense corps. Although Hsüeh Huan's troops were

Tseng Kuo-fan and was just at the point of using his Huai-chün to rescue Chinkiang, but on the basis of Ch'ien Ting-ming's request he was ordered instead to save Shanghai." *Ibid.*, pp. 12a-15a. Further accounts of Ch'ien's exploits are found in *CSK*, 425: 7a-b; and *LWCK Memorials*, 61:62a ff., KH 13/12/14.

   26 *Ch'ing-shih-lu*, HF 11/10/17. *TWCK Nien-p'u*, 7:15a-16a.
   27 *TWCK Memorials*, 14:65a.   28 *Ibid.*, 14:64a, 68a-b.

probably no worse than most others,[29] the reports Tseng received about them caused him great concern. How often in his own rise to power as a gentry military leader had he come into conflict with rival power groups. How often had he despaired of the waste and obstruction that lethargic government forces had caused. They were a military and political liability. This was especially true of Hsüeh Huan's troops— former prisoners, deserters, and displaced peasants who had no special devotion to Shanghai, Governor Hsüeh, or the central government under whose banner they served. The gentry leaders in Shanghai had unmistakably indicated that they were willing to support Tseng and make available to him the resources of the city. They stood apart from the provincial administration of Hsüeh and now waited for Tseng to supply an administration they could support. In responding to their invitation and denouncing Hsüeh, Tseng paved the way for Li Hung-chang to take over Shanghai for him.

Tseng's General Strategy

Tseng Kuo-fan's confirmation of Li's decision to secure Shanghai was not yet his final action in the matter. He had good cause to weigh every move carefully and to reconsider previous decisions. Large areas of Anhwei were in Taiping and Nien hands. Kiangsi province was held at only a few points. Kiangnan, as we have seen, had fallen completely, except for Chinkiang, Shanghai, and a few other districts. The situation was even worse in Chekiang, to the south. A false move, another Taiping victory, could not be afforded. The tide of battle shifted daily, and Tseng had to use his troops and position accordingly. Nevertheless, he laid down a clear over-all strategy, to which he consistently adhered. He divided the Yangtze region into three military areas. The southern sector was entrusted to Tso Tsung-t'ang, a former member of his *mu-fu* from Hunan. Tso fought his way down to Kiangsi province and then, proceeding eastward, entered Chekiang. His task was to clear Chekiang of the Taipings and at the same time to prevent the Taiping armies in Kiangsu and Anhwei from filtering southward. The central sector remained under Tseng's direct command. Here the main effort was to be carried on by his brother Tseng Kuo-ch'üan, who was given the difficult assignment of clearing the environs of Nanking and assaulting the city itself. The third sector was eastern Kiangsu, which had to be cleared in order to protect Tseng

---

[29] Even Li Hung-chang retained Taiping prisoners and deserters to garrison Shanghai for several months after his arrival, but he gradually demobilized them.

Kuo-ch'üan's flank and to keep the wealthiest part of the province in government hands.[30] It was this sector that was finally given to Li Hung-chang.

Appointment of a New Kiangsu Governor

When Li went back to Anhwei late in 1861 to raise troops, Tseng had not yet fully decided whom to appoint as governor of Kiangsu. He had been informed by the court that if he found Hsüeh Huan unsuitable for that post, he was free to select another man. The court at the same time informed Tseng that it was sending to his headquarters Shen Pao-chen, in whose career Tseng had shown favorable interest. Shen was an official nominally assigned to Kiangsi province, who had attracted notice as a local-corps leader in his native province of Fukien.[31] The court implied that it considered Shen worthy of appointment as governor of Kiangsu. Tseng, too, apparently had a high opinion of Shen and did not lightly dismiss this recommendation. However, after some thought, Tseng decided on another post for Shen and recommended Li Hung-chang as governor of Kiangsu. Li had more military experience than Shen, and this weighed heavily in Tseng's judgment.[32]

Moreover, Li was far more important to Tseng personally. Tseng Kuo-fan had never given up his early idea of integrating Anhwei forces into his own Hsiang-chün. Indeed, steps in that direction had been made over the past ten years. Li's own services as a commander under Tseng had been as the head of Anhwei units, and these forces had given a good account of themselves in battle. The spirit of the Anhwei troops, the kind of arrogance they displayed, which Tseng liked but tried to modify in Li himself, commended them highly to his regard. Further, because they were of much the same stock as Kiangsu people, closely related through historic, cultural, and economic ties, they were most suitable, in his opinion, for extended campaigning in Kiangsu province. Mustering Anhwei soldiers into his own ranks made it possible for Tseng to make loyal soldiers out of potential bandits and at the same time to strengthen his army. One part of Tseng's technique had always been to outbid other military leaders, whether loyal or rebel, and to buy out opposition before it ever started. Among other

---

[30] See the concise description by Sheng Hsüan-huai, an intimate of Li, in *LWCK Collected Works*, Introductory *chüan*, pp. 49b-50a.

[31] Hummel, *Eminent Chinese*, p. 643.

[32] Hsüeh Fu-ch'eng, "Shu Ho-fei Po-hsiang Li-kung yung Hu p'ing Wu," in Tso, *Shih tzu-liao*, I, 163.

things, he wanted to buy Anhwei men, lest they turn rebels and increase his problems.

Tseng's Need for New Forces

The need for the Anhwei reinforcements was particularly urgent at this time because of the condition of the Hsiang-chün itself. After almost ten years of bitter warfare and strenuous campaigning, Tseng's army was showing unmistakable signs of weakness. With the morale of his troops beginning to ebb, he realized that demobilization of at least some units could not long be delayed. His battle-weary troops were becoming increasingly difficult to control, and he feared that once a decisive victory was gained they would get completely out of hand.[33] He favored partial demobilization of the Hsiang-chün not only for military reasons but for financial and political reasons as well. Tseng had always adhered to a policy of paying his soldiers in full and not accumulating indebtedness to them. Abrupt demobilization of a large part of his forces after victory would be financially impossible. He was anxious therefore to whittle his army down by degrees, paying off the released soldiers in full. To have released them with less than full pay would have brought into being a new and dangerous host of restless malcontents.[34] In 1861-62, it was still too early to demobilize, for the greatest battles still loomed ahead. But by bringing in a new, independently financed army, Tseng was shrewdly preparing for the future.

Tseng's political reasons for having someone else create for him an army of Anhwei troops were equally farsighted. Jealousy of his great power was already evident in various quarters. Anticipating that the dependence of the government upon him would decrease after the rebellion was crushed, he foresaw that the court might then readily set him aside. A careful student of history, Tseng was aware that successful generals in the past had frequently been disposed of, even put to death, on one pretext or another once their services were no longer required. He wished to hold on to his power while lessening the jealousy and fear that such great power invariably inspired at court.[35] This he hoped to do by controlling a second army, the command of

---

[33] Later events were to prove the correctness of Tseng's apprehensions. See, for instance, his remarks on the demoralization of the Hsiang-chün in *TWCK Letters*, 24:31b. See also *LWCK Memorials*, 8:27a ff., TC 4/4/14.

[34] *TWCK Letters*, 24:29b, describes mutinies among the troops of Pao Ch'ao, one of Tseng's commanders from Szechwan province, arising from the nonpayment of rations at the time of demobilization.

[35] Lo Erh-kang, *Hsiang-chün hsin-chih, chüan* 12, cites the diary and the letters of Tseng Kuo-fan to establish that this was indeed Tseng's position.

which would be directly exercised by another. Li Hung-chang served
this purpose admirably. He was attached to Tseng through family ties,
and his brothers were all in Tseng's service. As a *mu-yu*, he possessed
a firsthand knowledge of Tseng's organization and enjoyed intimate
relations with Tseng's staff. He had personally led local forces in
Anhwei for years, adding good military reputation to the solid standing
he already possessed as a member of one of Anhwei's most respected
gentry families. His examination record was excellent, and his training as a secretary and memorial writer for Tseng qualified him well for
a high bureaucratic post. It is not difficult to see why, without too
much hesitation, Tseng caused Li to be appointed governor of Kiangsu.

Anhwei Local Corps Become the Huai-chün

While Tseng took these steps to assure Li's future authority in
Kiangsu, his protégé was gathering forces in Anhwei. This was not a
difficult task. Li had only to contact the important local-corps leaders
in the province, bring them with their troops under his command, and
lead them to Anking for reorganization and further training. The
forces already existed, and he needed only to pull them together. Li
himself attributed his rapid success in forming the new army to the
groundwork laid by his father almost ten years earlier. The early history of the Huai-chün, as Li's army came to be called, was noted by Li
in a tomb inscription at Ho-fei, Anhwei. He wrote:

In the third year of Hsien-feng, the rebels attacked and seized Lu-chou
and quickly moved north. The emperor, Wen-tsung, heeded the recommendations of his high officials and ordered my father to lead and manage
the local defense efforts in Anhwei. My father started out alone on his
journey. He went for a while to Lin-huai, where he recruited and trained
local corps, and then went to to Lu-chou to support government troops by
harassing the rebels. He won frequent victories. Furthermore, he crossed
the Chao lake and defeated the enemy Ch'en Yü-cheng's great horde, which
was then located below Po-shih-shan. He thereupon attacked Chao-hsien
but could not recover it. The onset of illness caused him to withdraw.

But in a letter written by his own hand, he instructed me, saying: "The
power of the rebels is that of a mad herd, and the people have no means of
sustaining their lives. We, both father and sons, have been graced by the
imperial favor. If these rebels are not exterminated, then what purpose can
our family serve? You, my sons, must exert your utmost strength in order
to fulfill my will." As he lay at the threshold of death these were his only
words. Alas! How tragic!

After the death of my father, the situation in Anhwei deteriorated by the
day, and the prefectures and districts of the southern Huai region all fell
to the rebels. But the leaders of my father's old local corps remained, and at

their respective villages they raised mud walls, killed rebels, and protected themselves. Finally, they were formed into a strong army which followed me and my brothers to subdue and pacify Kiangsu and Chekiang, and bring peace to the central plain. [This army] is known today by the name of the Huai-chün. Thus is the ambition of my father to a small extent satisfied.[36]

Principal Huai-chün Units

The leaders of the "old local corps" to whom Li referred were still active in Anhwei when he returned to that province to assemble his new army. The four principal units, which were to be the nucleus of the Huai-chün, were the Shu, Ting, Ch'ing, and Ming battalions. The Shu battalion, or Shu-tzu-ying, was a corps organized by Chang Shu-sheng and Chang Shu-shan, two brothers from Ho-fei, Li's native village. Chang Shu-sheng, who commanded the battalion, had led local corps against the Taipings since 1853,[37] and Chang Shu-shan was also credited with forming a small force for local defense in that year.[38]

The Ting battalion, or Ting-tzu-ying, was commanded by P'an Ting-hsin, of Lu-chiang, Lu-chou prefecture, directly across Lake Chao from Ho-fei. P'an's father had been a local-corps leader who was killed in action against the rebels. Vowing revenge, P'an Ting-hsin joined the local corps in Anhwei in 1857 and soon rose to comand his own unit.[39]

The Ch'ing battalion, or Ch'ing-tzu-ying, had distinguished itself in Anhwei under the command of Wu Ch'ang-ch'ing, who was also a native of Lu-chiang. In 1854 Wu's father had organized a local corps and for his distinguished service in the following years was rewarded with a hereditary title. In 1855 the governor of Anhwei, Fu-chi, placed Wu Ch'ang-ch'ing in command of all local corps at Su-ch'eng and Lu-chiang, Anhwei.[40]

Probably the most famous of all the early Huai-chün components was the Ming battalion, or Ming-tzu-ying, of Liu Ming-ch'uan. Liu was the leader of a band of salt smugglers from Ho-fei. It was said that at the age of eighteen he murdered a local man and soon entered a career as a bandit. But when the Taipings advanced into Anhwei, he converted his band of freebooters into a local corps and distinguished

---

[36] *Li Wen-chung kung i-chi*, in *Ho-fei Li-shih san-shih i-chi*, 4:3a. *LWCK Memorials*, 74:3a-4b, KH 18/2/9, gives a broader though less detailed survey.

[37] Chang Shu-sheng's basic data is in *Ch'ing-shih lieh-chuan*, 54:13a. See also *LWCK Memorials*, 13:6a ff., TC 7/1/12.

[38] Chang Shu-shan's biography is recorded in *Ch'ing-shih lieh-chuan*, 51:25b.

[39] P'an Ting-hsin's biography is recorded in *ibid.*, 55:2a-b.

[40] *Ibid.*, 56:19a.

himself in defending his district against the rebels. He served directly under Li Hung-chang's father in the campaign against the Taiping prince Ch'en Yü-ch'eng. He continued to serve in Anhwei until 1861, when he agreed to join Li Hung-chang.[41]

In addition to these four units, a fifth battalion was formed under Li's direction at the same time. In early 1862, he persuaded two Ho-fei local-corps leaders, the brothers Chou Sheng-po and Chou Sheng-ch'uan, who had been engaged in local-corps activity since 1853, to come formally under his new command. They called their reorganized army the Sheng battalion, or Sheng-tzu-ying.[42]

All of these local corps were personal armies of their leaders. Even their names came from the names of their leaders: Shu from Chang Shu-sheng, Ting from P'an Ting-hsin, Ch'ing from Wu Ch'ang-ch'ing, Ming from Liu Ming-ch'uan, and Sheng from Chou Sheng-po and Chou Sheng-ch'uan. But when formed into an army by Li Hung-chang, they all shared the regional designation Huai-chün, or Army of the Huai.

Structure of the Huai-chün

In the first month of 1862, all of these units made their way to An-king, where Li and Tseng set about making them an effective branch of the Hsiang organization. The structure of these irregular battalions was now standardized to correspond to the structure of Tseng's Hsiang-chün.[43] The basic organizational unit was the *ying*, or battalion, commanded by a *ying-kuan*, or battalion commander. These battalions, 504 men at full strength, were divided into four companies; front, rear, left, and right, each under a company commander, or *shao-kuan*.

Companies were subdivided into eight platoons, or *tui*, designated according to the weapons they used and consisting of either ten or twelve regular soldiers ("privates") in addition to one sergeant and one cook. The eight platoons of soldiers had a total of 100 men. In addition, attached directly to the company comander were an assistant company commander, or *shao-chang*, five company guards, or *hu-yung*, and a cook, *huo-yung*. A company at full strength, including the company commander, amounted to 108 men. (See Table 2.)

A special corps in each battalion was the *ch'in-ping*, or personal

---

[41] Hummel, *Eminent Chinese*, p. 526.

[42] See the biography of Chou Sheng-po in *Ch'ing-shih lieh-chuan*, 56:22a; and for the biography of Chou Sheng-ch'uan see *ibid.*, 56:23b.

[43] Chou Shih-ch'eng, *Huai-chün p'ing-nien chi* (Shanghai, 1877), 11:1a, states: "The origin of the Huai-chün was in the first year of the T'ung-chih reign. Its military organization was patterned exactly after the Ch'u-chün [Hunan Army, or Hsiang-chün]."

TABLE 2

Huai-chün Company and Personal Guard Organizations

HUAI-CHÜN COMPANY, OR *SHAO* ORGANIZATION

Company Commander
Assistant Company Commander
5 Guards
1 Cook

1st Platoon Rifle	2nd Platoon Sword and Spear	3rd Platoon Small Arms	4th Platoon Sword and Spear	5th Platoon Rifle	6th Platoon Sword and Spear	7th Platoon Small Arms	8th Platoon Sword and Spear
14 men: 1 sergeant 1 cook 12 soldiers	*12 men:* 1 sergeant 1 cook 10 soldiers	*12 men:* Same as 2nd	*12 men:* Same as 2nd	*14 men:* Same as 1st	*12 men:* Same as 2nd	*12 men:* Same as 2nd	*12 men:* Same as 2nd

Total: 108 officers and men

HUAI-CHÜN PERSONAL GUARD, OR *CH'IN-PING* ORGANIZATION

Battalion Commander

1st Platoon Cannon	2nd Platoon Sword and Spear	3rd Platoon Cannon	4th Platoon Sword and Spear	5th Platoon Small Arms	6th Platoon Sword and Spear
12 men: 1 sergeant 1 cook 10 guards	*12 men:* Same	*12 men:* Same	*12 men:* Same	*12 men:* Same	*12 men:* Same

Total: 72 men

guard of the battalion commander. This guard was organized as a
company consisting of seventy-two men, divided into six platoons of
ten regular soldiers, a sergeant, and a cook. Like the regular battalion
platoons, the *ch'in ping* units were named for the weapons they used.
(See Table 2.)

Four companies of 108 men each, plus one company of battalion
commander guards, or seventy-two men, formed the force of 504 men.
Within this force were two *p'i-shan-p'ao* ("mountain-breaking cannon") platoons, eight *t'ai-ch'iang* ("carrying firearms") platoons, nine
hsiao-ch'iang ("small arms") platoons, and nineteen *tao-mao* ("sword
and spear") platoons, making a total of thirty-eight platoons, thus
armed and designated.[44]

For each battalion there were 180 laborers, or *chang-fu,* assigned in
varying numbers to the companies and platoons. When heavy work,
such as the transportation of cannon and other field pieces, was required, the *chang-fu* were summoned from the companies and platoons
to which they were assigned to perform this special labor. The *chang-fu*
swelled the size of the battalion to 684 men in all, and were an important part of the total force. For every one hundred fighting men it was
necessary to have thirty-six laborers.

Above the battalion level, the organization of the Huai-chün was
looser. The detachment commander, or *t'ung-ling,* might have a few, or
ten, or even several tens of battalions under his command. For this
there were no fixed regulations.[45]

Only in one minor detail does there seem to have been any variation
between the organization of the Huai-chün of Li Hung-chang and
Tseng's Hsiang-chün. No indication of the presence of a special company commander, assistant company commander, guards, sergeant, or
cook has been given in the principal sources on the Hsiang-chün. Thus
the Hsiang-chün battalion would appear to have had thirty-two men
less than its Huai-chün counterpart.

The organizational structure of the Huai-chün gives only a general
idea of actual manpower. Undoubtedly there were fragments of battalions on special assignment and small corps not yet integrated within
the general structure, neither of which were likely to have been on
regular battalion lists. Furthermore, the numbers were only theoretical, and the muster rolls probably were padded, for officers received
funds according to the number of names they carried on their rolls.

---

44 *Ibid.,* 11:1a-b.
45 *Ibid.,* 11:2a.

It is well to bear in mind that all statements on the number of troops employed at various times are, at best, only estimates and are probably sometimes far from accurate.

The battalions that Li Hung-chang brought to Anking and organized into a smaller replica of the Hsiang-chün were trained for several months. Tseng Kuo-fan himself took an active interest in their progress and advised Li on how best to discipline and indoctrinate them. Early in 1862, Tseng and Li believed that the new forces were ready for action. But once again the question arose of exactly where they were to go.

New Pressure for the Occupation of Shanghai

Ever since the gentry at Shanghai had decided to seek Tseng's aid, they had exerted unremitting pressure on him, both directly and through the court. Several of them, including Ch'ien Ting-ming and Ku Wen-pin, had served for considerable periods at the capital, and their acknowledged local leader, P'ang Chung-lu, was a former member of the Grand Secretariat, one of the highest government councils. Through friends and letters they could make their case well known to the court. How well they succeeded is clearly revealed in the *Ch'ing-shih-lu*, or "Veritable Records," of the court.

After the first imperial inquiry on the conduct of Hsüeh Huan, a series of edicts was handed down with reference to the situation in eastern Kiangsu.[46] The first of these edicts noted that certain persons had reported that efforts should be made to recover Soochow and Ch'ang-chou in view of the importance of those places to the national economy. The court therefore ordered Tseng Kuo-fan to determine whether an offensive could be launched against the rebels in that area from three directions by the armies of Tseng, Tso Tsung-t'ang, and Hsüeh Huan.[47] Two weeks later the court ordered Tseng to take over formal command of all military operations in Kiangsu, Kiangsi, Anhwei, and Chekiang. This was no new authorization but merely a confirmation of previous orders which Tseng, according to traditional practice, had declined to accept.

These edicts were only a prelude to the flurry of orders that now

---

[46] *Ch'ing-shih-lu,* 8:33a ff., HF 11/10/24. This was actually the second edict on Hsüeh, suggesting that if Hsüeh were found incompetent as charged, Tseng could recommend a candidate familiar with military, local, and foreign affairs in Shanghai as a replacement. The court notified Tseng that it had ordered Shen Pao-chen to report to him, and that if Tseng wished to recommend him for a post he could do so.

[47] *Ibid.,* 12:1a-b, HF 11/12/1.

issued from Peking. Impressed, finally, by the importance of eastern Kiangsu, the court itself attempted to direct the campaign. But the court was ill informed, and its edicts were outdated before they were even sent off. One month after Tseng had agreed with Ch'ien and Li that the latter would muster the Huai-chün and take it to Shanghai, the court ordered Tseng to dispatch Li to Chinkiang immediately.[48] This order was to be repeated constantly in the ensuing months until Tseng himself wavered and prepared to carry out the new instructions, which were based on his own earlier recommendations.[49] There was poor co-ordination between the court and Tseng, and poor co-ordination as well between the representatives of the Kiangsu gentry in the capital and the gentry in Shanghai itself. It had been arranged that Li was to reinforce Shanghai and Tseng Kuo-ch'üan to attack Nanking, and that the interlying region was to be cleared by a westward thrust by Li's troops. But now the court ordered Tseng Kuo-ch'üan to hasten to Shanghai and establish defenses for that city. As soon as this was accomplished, he was to march on Ch'ing-p'u and then recover Soo-chow and Ch'ang-chou.[50] Tseng Kuo-fan failed to follow the imperial instructions, giving his reasons as follows:

In the first year of T'ung-chih, after the fall of the port of Hangchow, the court was greatly concerned about the critical situation in the Sung-chiang–Shanghai area and ordered Tseng Kuo-ch'üan to lead troops to Shanghai to recover Soochow and Ch'ang-chou. Several edicts were handed down urging this action. Tseng Kuo-fan wrote to Kuo-ch'üan and consulted him on the matter. Tseng Kuo-ch'üan answered that "the wealth of Sung-chiang and Shanghai is the foremost in the country, and it is therefore an easy matter to obtain revenues for the armies there. The nest of the rebels, however, is in Nanking. If the nest were attacked, the other rebel armies would wholeheartedly go to its aid, and Soochow and Hangchow would thereupon be relieved. I [Kuo-ch'üan] was willing to undertake this difficult task." Tseng Kuo-fan agreed and therefore made Kuo-ch'üan responsible for the recovery of Nanking.[51]

If the imperial edicts were more concerned with eastern Kiangsu than with Nanking, it was because they were inspired by Weng Hsin-ts'un, an official at the court, tutor of the young emperor, and a Grand Secretary. He was a member of the Ch'ang-shu gentry and therefore a resident of the same area that the court suddenly wanted Tseng to

---

[48] *Ibid.*, 13:13a, HF 11/12/14.
[49] *Ibid.*, 15:11a; *also ibid.*, 15:28a, TC 1/1/7.
[50] *Ibid.*, 14:26b-27b, HF 11/12/25.
[51] Tseng Kuo-ch'üan, *Tseng Chung-hsiang kung ch'üan-chi* (1903), *nien-p'u*, 1:16a-b.

recover. A later edict, which again ordered Li to hasten to Chinkiang and reiterated instructions that Tseng Kuo-ch'üan move to Shanghai, referred directly to a report by P'ang Chung-lu. It will be remembered that it was P'ang who first proposed to the gentry leaders at Shanghai that Tseng should be approached.[52]

During the first three months of the first year of T'ung-chih (February, March, April, 1862), the court repeatedly ordered Tseng to dispatch Li to Chinkiang and send Tseng Kuo-ch'üan to Shanghai.[53] But neither of the Tsengs was anxious to move the Hsiang-chün to that city. Then the court changed its plan and ordered Tseng to send the judicial commissioner of Kiangsu, Ch'en Shih-chieh, to Shanghai, but again commanded that Li go to Chinkiang.[54] With orders and counterorders, and with pressure mounting on all sides, the question of where Li was to go again came to the fore. Tseng placated the court by giving assurance that Li would be sent to Chinkiang as soon as the Huai-chün's training had been completed, but he prepared to wait for further developments before taking any such action.

Preparations for the Huai-chün Expedition

Tseng did not have long to wait, for while he pondered the contradictory edicts that the gentry leaders of Kiangsu had advocated at court, the gentry at Shanghai took matters into their own hands. Upon returning to Shanghai from Tseng's headquarters, Ch'ien Ting-ming, in accordance with his understanding with Li and Tseng, met his fellow gentry leaders and made known the agreement that had been reached. They now instructed Ying Pao-shih, the local official who had made the preliminary inquiries about hiring steamers, to proceed with the arrangements. When the time came to rent the vessels, it was found that the Western merchants demanded a sum of 205,000 taels for arranging to carry stoves, donkeys, and weapons and for transporting troops. Hsüeh Huan, who was still in office, used the high price demanded as another reason for abandoning the expedition. He hinted that Wu Hsü should tell Tseng Kuo-fan that the price for transportation was too high and that the troops should go by land. Feng Kuei-fen recounts:

[52] *Ch'ing-shih-lu*, 17:35a; biographical material on P'ang has been given in note 18 above.

[53] *Ch'ing-shih-lu*, 15:28a, TC 1/1/7; 16:45a, TC 1/1/18; 17:13a, TC 1/1/23; 17:35a ff., TC 1/1/26.

[54] *Ibid.*, 18:15b, TC 1/2/4; see also 21:20a, TC 1/3/5.

At this time P'ang Chung-lu also went to the north, and only Ku Wen-pin stayed behind. He discussed the matter with Wu Hsü, stating that the plan could not be abandoned. He said: "Tseng Kuo-fan is the governor-general, while Hsüeh Huan is only the governor. We should obey the orders of the governor-general. Let us send the ships first, and if the governor wishes to impeach us, the ships will at least already be on their way." In spite of all this, the governor still remained adamant, and inquired about the source of the funds for the expedition. Ku Wen-pin told him that he could give the money, whereupon Hsüeh Huan asked him where he would get it. Then Wu Hsü said: "We have already obtained the money from the foreign merchants." At this the governor fell silent.[55]

The quibbling in Shanghai and the resultant delay in sending steamships to pick up Li's troops at Anking caused Tseng Kuo-fan to change his mind once more. He reverted to his original plan of sending Li to Chinkiang by land. Only the sudden arrival of Ch'ien Ting-ming and his steamship flotilla at Anking in April, 1862, forestalled the now twice-planned land expedition of the Huai-chün to Chinkiang. The circumstances were related by Tseng Kuo-fan in his important memorial that month:

This memorial is to report the date on which Li Hung-chang's army started on its journey to Shanghai via the water route as a result of a change in routing, and respectfully beseeches imperial guidance in this matter. The recruiting and training of the Hsiang and Huai volunteers under the command of your subject, Circuit Intendant Li Hung-chang, has been completed. It was originally determined that on the second day of the third month, the troops would be mustered and commence their journey to the area of Ch'ao-hsien, Han-shan, and Ho-chou, leading to Chinkiang. On the twenty-second day of the second month, I, your humble servant, memorialized respectfully on the subject and thereupon formally ordered the said intendant [Li Hung-chang] to make the necessary arrangements for the journey. Subsequently, on the twenty-eighth day, I received a communication from the Kiangsu gentry P'an Fu, Ch'ien Ting-ming, and others, who came to Anhwei from Shanghai to present a petition to the following effect:

Although the Shanghai sector has obtained troops dispatched by the English, French, and other nations for the purpose of assisting in defense, and although they have scored victories at Kao-chiao and Hsiao-t'ang, the rebels still press from all sides and merchants cannot come through [to Shanghai]. The situation is extremely perilous. The Shanghai bureau has already taken measures to raise 180,000 taels for the purpose of engaging steamboats to enter the Yangtze River and come here to take my troops on board in the hope that they can strongly defend important places, and for other such reasons.

It is the opinion of your humble servant that Chinkiang is a place stra-

---

[55] Feng Kuei-fen, *Hsien-chih-t'ang kao,* 4:17a-b.

tegically advantageous for the advancing of troops. Shanghai is an extremely fertile place for the raising of revenues. Both are of equal importance, and neither can be in the least neglected and permitted to be lost. Formerly, because foreign boats were not permitted to be hired out for the transport of troops, Li Hung-chang's forces were to advance by land to Chinkiang in successive stages. This was truly a plan born of extreme desperation!

I, your humble servant, consider the land route full of obstacles and too long. Along every point of the way there are rebels. Consequently, I have been anxious over the difficulty of moving the baggage trains which must accompany the army, and I have been apprehensive of the great delay that this journey will entail.

I have respectfully received, moreover, the two proclamations of the fourteenth and twenty-fourth days of the second month, which are also profoundly concerned over the delay and laxity in the journey of Li Hung-chang.

Now I have the news that the previously mentioned gentry and the foreign merchants have engaged steamboats to come to Anhwei and have already paid for them. Consequently, I have seized upon the following over-all plan:

It is best to approach Shanghai first in order to satisfy public feelings, and I have already dispatched several battalions on the seventh day of the third month on board ships. Li Hung-chang himself embarked on the eighth day. They will arrive in not more than four days time, we will then await the return of the ships and load them up again in succession. They will make the round trip three times, one following immediately upon the other. The transportation of the entire army to its defense station down the river will not require [even] a month's time.

After the disposition of the troops at Shanghai has been settled, Li Hung-chang will go personally to Chinkiang to examine the circumstances prevailing and decide how to divide his forces in order to protect that area. At that time he will memorialize on how the situation may be handled.

As for the water troops of Li Hung-chang and Huang I-sheng, they will, as already decided, go from Liang-shan and break through the rebels' concentration at Nanking and then be in a position to penetrate to Chinkiang. I will await the fixing of a date for this expedition and then prepare a supplementary memorial.[56]

Prompt action on the part of Ch'ien Ting-ming and the energetic gentry group in Shanghai had at last brought about the long awaited expedition. The Huai-chün, safely embarked upon swift river steamers, quickly ran the Taiping blockade on the Yangtze River and arrived in Shanghai without incident. Once Li had occupied Shanghai, the court did not delay in following Tseng's recommendation, and appointed Li acting governor of Kiangsu.[57] At the same time, he was

[56] *TWCK Memorials,* 15:59a-60a, TC 1/3/8.
[57] *Ch'ing-shih-lu,* 23:29a-32a; 25:30a ff., TC 1/4/16; Hsüeh Fu-ch'eng, "Shu Ho-fei Po-hsiang Li-kung yung Hu p'ing Wu," in Tso, *Shih tzu-liao,* I, 164.

ordered to strengthen the defenses of the city carefully and to maintain good relations with the foreigners there.

Li Hung-chang was only thirty-eight years of age when he arrived in Shanghai at the head of his army. As the junior partner in the expansion of Tseng Kuo-fan's military organization, and as the appointed protector of the influential gentry in Shanghai, he had risen almost overnight to the governorship of the richest province in China. With the newly-formed Huai-chün at his back, a rich economic potential before him, and a shrewd understanding of power politics, he made his temporary position the solid foundation for the development of an outstanding political career.

III. Li Hung-chang
Takes over Kiangsu

THE warm reception given Li Hung-chang by the gentry in Shanghai did not lead him to overlook the hostility his arrival aroused among the provincial and local officials. They regarded him as an upstart who, with his army of twenty-five hundred men and the seal of the governor of Kiangsu, had sufficient force and authority to displace men in entrenched positions and rob them of their offices and means of easy wealth. Li was well aware that a struggle would be necessary before he could establish his own control. His predecessor, Hsüeh Huan, had been a tool in the hands of Wu Hsü, the customs circuit intendant, and other officials who controlled the financial offices of the province. Li knew the corruption of the Shanghai bureaucracy, and he particularly distrusted the natives of Chekiang, who dominated the government offices and mercantile establishments. "When I entered Shanghai," he wrote later, "it was like entering a camp of Hsiung-nu [the Huns, or northern barbarians of the past]."[1] In a letter written to Tseng Kuo-fan at this time, Li complained that of every ten underofficials in Shanghai, seven or eight were natives of Chekiang.[2] Heading this group were Wu Hsü and Yang Fang, whose wealth Li needed and whose power he coveted.

Displacement of the Old Bureaucracy

Although Li despised these men, he knew that for the time being they alone were experienced enough to deal with the Westerners and control the vast complex of officeholders, clerks, and yamen runners who supervised the customs, collected the likin, and carried on the

[1] *LWCK Letters,* 1:43a, TC 1/7/8.
[2] *Ibid.,* 1:9a-12b, TC 1/3/15.

day-to-day business of government. They also controlled the United
Defense Office of Shanghai and the Ever Victorious Army, which was
financed by this office.[3]

The Kiangsu gentry, who were also concerned with these matters,
had little control of financial offices, since they were barred by regulation from holding important offices in Shanghai. Most of the financial
offices embraced areas as large as a circuit or province, and therefore
a native of Kiangsu holding such a post would have been serving in his
native locality and violating the rules of the Board of Civil Office. But
the Kiangsu gentry were not content to leave matters in the hands of
the incumbent officials. Their earlier attacks on the former governor,
Hsüeh Huan, had been motivated by a desire to bring in a new official
group more amenable to their interests. They had taken every opportunity to inform Tseng Kuo-fan and Li Hung-chang of the mal-
feasance of the officials they were anxious to remove. Acting on this
information, Tseng had warned Li, "Unless Wu Hsü is eliminated, our
power in Shanghai can never be complete."[4]

Wu Hsü had served in the Shanghai area since 1854.[5] In 1859 he
had been appointed to serve as circuit intendant in Shanghai, where he
was responsible for customs collection. This office was so lucrative that
candidates for the post had to pay enormous sums to obtain the appointment. Yang Fang, who had obtained the title of circuit intendant
through purchase, was considered to be one of the wealthiest compra-
dors, merchants, and moneylenders in Shanghai. One of his most
important activities was managing the finances of the Ever Victorious
Army, which his son-in-law, Frederick Townsend Ward, had organized.[6] Neither Wu Hsü or Yang Fang could be displaced immediately.
The most Li could do was to familiarize himself with their work and
wait for an opportunity to act. Even Hsüeh Huan, the former governor,
was retained in Shanghai. As circuit intendant and later as governor,
he had been responsible for the over-all conduct of foreign affairs since
1857.[7] Upon being relieved of office by Li Hung-chang, he was appointed Commissioner of Foreign Trade.[8] Although Li felt that Hsüeh

---

[3] *Shanghai hsien-chih* (1872), 12:24a; Feng Kuei-fen, *Hsien-chih-t'ang kao,* 4:23b-
24a.

[4] Hsüeh Fu-ch'eng, "Shu Ho-fei Po-hsiang Li-kung yung Hu p'ing Wu," Tso, *Shih
tzu-liao,* I, 165.

[5] *Shanghai hsien-chih,* 12:24b-25a.

[6] An interesting fictional account, based on good historical evidence, describing Yang
Fang's position and career, is contained in H. B. Morse, *In the Days of the Taipings*
(Salem, Mass., 1927).

[7] *Shanghai hsien-chih,* 12:24a.

[8] *TWCK Memorials,* 16:73a-74b. Hsüeh Huan was subsequently appointed to mem-

Huan was a bad official, he was forced to acknowledge that for the time being he was unable to replace him in the management of foreign affairs.[9]

Li was conscious of the weakness of his position. He lacked the support of the local bureaucracy. He was totally inexperienced in dealing with foreigners and with the complicated problems that arose from their presence in Shanghai. He had no real control over the finances of either the Ever Victorious Army or the fifty to seventy thousand troops which had been raised by Hsüeh Huan. Although several thousand Huai and Hsiang soldiers had moved into Shanghai, these troops were at first considered a laughing matter.

When the foreigners saw the men of the Huai-chün dressed in simple garb, they gave vent to their mirth. Whereupon Li Hung-chang said: "Is it more important that the troops be smartly dressed than that they be able to fight? You would do better to wait until we have been tried in battle; then it will still not be too late for you to laugh."[10]

However, the derision of the Westerners, who were acknowledged to be experts in modern military affairs, was a blow to the prestige of the new governor.

Li's original orders had directed him to reorganize the military forces in Shanghai, encourage the interest of Westerners in protecting the city, and then proceed swiftly to Chinkiang, leaving Shanghai under the command of the judicial commissioner, Liu Hsün-kao, or some other capable official.[11] Once in Shanghai, however, Li showed no inclination to move on to Chinkiang as directed. In the first memorial Li ever addressed to the throne, dated May 16, 1862, he laid the groundwork for a long stay at Shanghai. He claimed that for military reasons and "because I cannot leave all the unfinished business," he would not be able to move on to Chinkiang for some time.[12] One month later, Li again addressed the throne on the same subject. Acknowledging that Chinkiang was important and that Tseng Kuo-ch'üan needed Li's help there for the taking of Nanking, he argued that his army at the time consisted only of several thousand men, and "if my army is divided between Shanghai and Chinkiang, there will be two

---

bership in the new Ministry of Foreign Affairs, or the *Tsung-li ke-kuo shih-wu ya-men pan-li*. See Wen Ch'ing, Chia Chen, and others, *Ch'ou-pan i-wu shih-mo* (Peiping, 1929-30), 25:36a.

[9] *LWCK Letters*, 1:29a, TC 1/5/7.

[10] *CSK*, 411:1b.

[11] *LWCK Memorials*, 1:1a-b, TC 1/4/18.

[12] *Ibid.*, 1:1a-4b *passim*.

weak points."[13] He also stressed Shanghai's importance as a vital source of revenue:

I am acting governor of Kiangsu, and both Shanghai and Chinkiang are under my jurisdiction. I can neither give up Shanghai, where we have 200,000 taels of revenue each month, nor can I give up Chinkiang, which controls both the north and the south. I do not know how to choose in this dilemma. This new army at Shanghai cannot be commanded without me. There are some faithful and brave commanders, but none are popular enough to take the leadership.

The people and the army both put great hope in my remaining at Shanghai. I cannot abandon them, and for the time being Tseng Kuo-fan does not have suitable personnel to send to Shanghai [in my place]. Until I have put things in order in Shanghai, I cannot go to Chinkiang.[14]

To Tseng Kuo-fan, Li confided a special reason for remaining in Shanghai. The occupation of Chinkiang by a large Huai-chün force might precipitate a struggle for revenue in that area. The garrison of Feng Tzu-ts'ai, already at Chinkiang, sorely lacked revenues. To bring in heavy reinforcements would only intensify this problem, making it necessary to look north of the river for additional revenues. But the wealth of the districts on the north bank was already monopolized by the Manchu commander Tu-hsing-a, who, according to Li, was seizing revenues without scruple. Unwilling to be placed in a position of outright competition with the Manchu commander, Li preferred to stay away from this potential trouble spot.[15] Li decided that it would be cheaper and less hazardous to send a subsidy of 30,000 liang to Chinkiang than to move there himself.[16] Li's instructions from Tseng covered this eventuality. Tseng had written: "The revenue from Shanghai should first support the Shanghai army. If any is left it should then support the Chinkiang army. If there is still a remainder, send it to me."[17] At the same time Tseng approved Li's policy of caution in building himself up firmly at Shanghai before venturing afield. He suggested:

The corrupt camps filled with corrupt volunteers should be broken up because they not only violate the sensibilities of the people but also give cause for the barbarians to create scandals. Consider all this. If the disbanded volunteers cause trouble in local areas, can you cope with them? . . . Do not go into battle too hastily before training is sufficient. If the court

---

[13] *Ibid.*, 1:29a-30b, TC 1/5/27.
[14] *Ibid.*
[15] *LWCK Letters*, 1:32a-34a, TC 1/6/3.
[16] *LWCK Memorials*, 1:53a, TC 1/7/13.
[17] *TWCK Letters*, 18:15b ff.

complains, you can shift the responsibility to me. Then when your troops are trained, we can launch a drastic campaign.[18]

As Tseng's needs for revenues increased, he gave strong support to Li's efforts to entrench himself in Shanghai. He particularly wanted Li to gain firm control over the revenue offices. In requesting funds from Li, he wrote:

> You cannot, at least for the moment, go to Chinkiang, and I have addressed the throne on this matter. I think you should take your time now in reorganizing the income and expenditures of Shanghai, because once you go to Chinkiang, no one will do that work any more. Even though Huang I-sheng can succeed you in military affairs, no one can manage the military ration affairs.
>
> The Anhwei headquarters treasury has been getting rigid of late. The Canton likin has sent no news. I do not know how to answer the urgent needs of the starved soldiers at Nanking and Ning-kuo. I wonder if you can spare me 30,000 or 50,000 liang at once.[19]

Li lost no time in beginning his activities to undermine the Shanghai officials. He was particularly careful in dealing with Wu Hsü. Since Wu had provided Li with an initial official loan of 100,000 taels to support the Huai-chün even before it reached Shanghai,[20] Li was in no position to launch an attack upon him. Li admitted to Tseng that he saw no way of getting rid of Wu, but asked Tseng to look for suitable candidates whom he could install in office at some future time.[21] Tseng Kuo-fan, always cautious and often noncommittal, warned Li that Wu Hsü could never be replaced as customs intendant of Shanghai,[22] apparently reversing his position of a few months earlier. In the ensuing weeks and months, Li's denunciations of Wu Hsü grew increasingly bitter, as he informed Tseng that to gain favor with the foreigners Wu Hsü was "snatching" all the customs revenues to support the foreign troops.[23] More serious was Li's charge that Wu Hsü was involved in an attempt to have Shanghai turned over completely to foreign control.[24]

Li secretly impeached Wu Hsü for irregularities in raising military funds. Later, as he came to realize Wu Hsü's great influence and power, Li resorted to a more subtle and effective technique. Masking

---

[18] *Ibid.*

[19] *Ibid.*, 19 :8b.

[20] *LWCK Letters,* 1 :4b, TC 1/2/8. Also see a letter from Li Hung-chang to Wu Hsü, *ibid.,* 1 :7a, TC 1/2/14.

[21] *Ibid.,* 1 :20b-21a, TC 1/4/2.

[22] *TWCK Letters,* 18 :15b.

[23] *LWCK Letters,* 1 :43a, TC 1/7/8.

[24] *Ibid.,* 1 :46b, TC 1/7/19.

his hostility to Wu, he gradually began establishing new bureaus which gradually took over the functions that Wu and his followers had monopolized.[25] At the same time, Li systematically impeached members of Wu's staff. In concentrating his main overt attack upon the lower officials at Shanghai, Li was striking at the roots of the entire Shanghai bureaucratic structure and preparing the ground to establish his own group in power.

Tseng Kuo-fan tried to persuade Li to adopt a more cautious and conciliatory policy. In response to a letter from Li complaining that Wu was interfering with the proper collection of customs revenue, Tseng cautioned Li not to shift the blame to Wu but to bear the responsibility himself.[26] When in July, 1862, Li formally impeached several of Wu Hsü's subordinates and requested imperial approval of replacements selected by Li himself, Tseng responded:

> Your memorial on the impeachment and selection of six officials has pleased public opinion, but bear in mind that if you touch the branch of a tree the heart of the tree will be hurt. Now you are impeaching Wu Hsü's men and his heart will therefore be uneasy.[27]

Tseng warned Li that he might be held responsible for any malpractices committed by Wu and his other subordinates. He reported that Chang Chung-yuan had already complained about the conduct of Wu Hsü and had implicated Li, and even Tseng. "But," said Tseng, "actually we have never protected such men [as Wu]."[28] He then asked Li to co-operate with Chang Chung-yuan, who had been authorized to carry out a thorough investigation of corruption in the Shanghai customs administration.

The investigation by Chang Chung-yuan provided fresh ammunition for Li, who sent Tseng the following information about Wu Hsü and his activities:

> The said customs intendant [Wu Hsü] has had his origin as the cunning member of a local money-raising bureau. He is expert in accounting and skillful in hiding deficiencies. Wu Hsü always claims that he devotes his heart and blood to public business, yet never attempts to economize or save money if it is in the public interest. But actually under the pretext of borrowing funds [for official purposes] his hand is deft at adjusting transac-

---

[25] Hsüeh Fu-ch'eng, "Shu Ho-fei Po-hsiang Li-kung yung Hu p'ing Wu," in Tso, Shih tzu-liao, I, 165.

[26] TWCK Letters, 19:5b.

[27] Ibid., 19:17a; Li Hung-chang's memorial impeaching the subordinates of Wu Hsü is found in LWCK Memorials, 1:23a ff., TC 1/5/9.

[28] TWCK Letters, 19:17a.

tions to his own convenience. He always succeeds in confusing outsiders.

Now I shall temporarily draw a line with him. The Chinese army military revenues will be drawn from the likin and contributions; [the funds for] the foreign army and the funds for Chinkiang will be supplied from the foreign customs. From now on if there is any borrowing, or if he has used empty figures and claims he has borrowed, under either circumstance he will not be able to use our military revenues as an excuse.

Watching an official is like watching a bandit. It is very difficult to be Wu's superior. Wu has started a company for foreign trade, has constructed houses in the foreign bund, and has bought steamers and *sha-ch'uan* [a type of sea-going junk] with which to navigate the Yangtze River and the sea. All these enterprises are shared with Yang Fang and are concealed under foreign names. The public all know this as well as I, but they [Wu and Yang] are exceedingly skillful at hiding their malpractices. No one can put his finger on them. When one investigates, one can prove nothing. . . .

Wu Hsü buys up the contribution tickets issued in Shanghai at one-tenth of their face value and then sells them.[29] This is the natural practice of a city slicker.

If a man wishes to buy a position as an underofficial, which requires a ticket valued at 100 liang, he can get it for 30 liang. Wu Hsü then makes a profit also of 20 to 30 liang per ticket. If a buyer has a receipt for a ticket today, he can use it tomorrow and have an appointment. In a wink the buyer can make a manifold profit. He can use his new position to feed his family and to be secure from disorder.

These buyers are almost all men from Chekiang, and the system has been created by a Chekiang man. I wonder when we can clean out this administrative machine. Lacking even a single assistant, I cannot carry out any reform.[30]

The personal letters exchanged by Li and Tseng reveal more clearly than official correspondence or memorials the actual conditions that prevailed. Officials more often than not tried to hide evidence of malpractices carried on in their areas of jurisdiction lest they become involved and be held responsible. For instance, Wu Hsü was not permitted to engage in private mercantile activity, yet it was an open secret that he did so. Li's description of Wu's financial manipulations helps to show how practices initiated to meet the emergency situation became a source of private wealth for officials. The sale of "contribution tickets," or licenses, was a means of raising military funds. In return for a donation the contributor received an official title, or even, on occasion, actual office, according to a fixed schedule. However,

---

[29] The sale of "contribution tickets" or licenses was a fairly common means of raising revenue during and after the Taiping Rebellion. These licenses or tickets entitled the holder to an official title, and on occasion office was even bestowed upon the bearer.

[30] *LWCK Letters,* 1:47a-49a, TC 1/7/26.

clever officials benefited far more than the military budget from this practice. "Contributions" were often raised through coercion. When officials and merchants who participated in Shanghai's booming foreign trade ran afoul of regulations, the payment of a sufficient "contribution" protected them from action by their superiors.

Li was well aware of what was going on under the surface of bureaucratic routine and used this knowledge for his own purposes. In his campaign to build up his own loyal following among the lower officials, he went out of his way to protect men who, though corrupt, could be fitted into his own organization. An interesting case is that of the candidate for magistrate, Chin Hung-pao. Charges had been leveled against Chin at court, and Li Hung-chang was ordered to investigate locally and render his verdict in a memorial. Accordingly, Li submitted the following information and opinions on the matter:

Magisterial candidate Chin Hung-pao was originally a private employee of Wu Hsü. Formerly the administration in Kiangsu province was usually corrupt; the higher officials started the corruption and the lower officials continued it. In my opinion the corruption cannot be attributed entirely to the lower officials.

In the fifth month it was memorialized that on the gate of the circuit intendant's yamen someone had drawn a large turtle, and that this was the result of a conspiracy by Chin Hung-pao and Yü Ping. Yü Ping was alleged to have started the conspiracy, Chin Hung-pao was behind the curtain, and Min Tsao was the author of the plot. All of these men are able but corrupt.

Yü Ping managed the tribute in Shanghai with great corruption. Min Tsao has connections with the staff of the Customs Office. I believe that there is indeed a plot there.

I have observed, however, that Chin Hung-pao's ability is above that of Yü Ping and Min Tsao. He is familiar with the inner workings of the tribute office in Shanghai and that is why I have been compelled to use him. . . . The tribute office relies upon Chin Hung-pao and his plans. Chin himself managed the commodity tribute which is the principal part of the likin income. Chin's monthly income is between 80,000 and 100,000 liang. It is because Chin is so rigid and strict that jealousy and complaints arose. I have already secretly investigated him and have found that in the past he perhaps did involve himself in a little graft. But today, under the influence of my efforts to clean up the situation, he has become an upright man. During this period of military and financial desperation, it is difficult to obtain men of talent. If a man had but a single ability, I should not dismiss him. However, I shall continue my investigations, and if this man is found to be really corrupt, I shall never defend him.[31]

---

[31] *LWCK Memorials,* 2:41a, TC 1/10/25.

The longer Li Hung-chang remained in Kiangsu, the less frequent became his impeachments and complaints. This does not necessarily indicate that corruption had been wiped out, but rather that the elements which had jeopardized Li's organization had either been eliminated or brought under his own control.

Li made his final moves against Wu Hsü toward the end of 1862. At that time he appointed Wu Hsü to a position of command in the Ever Victorious Army and sent him out to fight the Taipings. Since Wu was one of the founders of that army, he was in no position to decline command. Meanwhile, Li adopted a more conciliatory attitude toward Ward and the foreigners.[32] As long as Wu Hsü, Yang Fang, and Hsüeh Huan had been on hand, Li could afford to remain aloof and even to show hostility toward the foreigners. But now Li realized that foreign support was indispensable for his own military development, and he wanted to be rid of all dependence on Wu, Yang, and Hsüeh.

While Li stayed in Shanghai, fortifying his position, Wu Hsü found himself embroiled in difficulties with the Ever Victorious Army, which refused to move out under his command unless they received the back pay owing to them.[33] Unfortunately for Wu, his old friend and foreign associate, Ward, had been killed in battle and had been replaced by the self-seeking, hot-tempered American freebooter, Henry A. Burgevine. Wu's inability to make the Ever Victorious Army move forward as ordered placed him in the position of failing to carry out military orders. As Wu's position became weaker, Li Hung-chang denounced him more and more openly.[34]

Wu's private partner and erstwhile official colleague, Yang Fang, was also being discredited. By clearly dividing the Shanghai revenues and making Wu and Yang solely responsible for all foreign payments, Li had placed on their shoulders a larger share of financial obligations than they had hitherto assumed. Faced with the prospect of digging into his own pocket in order to pay Burgevine and his troops, Yang balked and delayed. As a result, Burgevine raided his office, carried off the funds he claimed, and as a parting gesture slapped Yang's face. The affair became a *cause célèbre* in Shanghai, China, and even abroad. Under the circumstances, Li dismissed Burgevine, whom he, as well as the British, had never cared for, and also dismissed Yang Fang from

[32] *LWCK Letters*, 1:54a, TC 1/8/15.

[33] *Ibid.*, 2:2a, TC 1/8 int./7; 23a, TC 1/9/27.

[34] *Ibid.*, 2:37b, TC 1, 1st day of winter; 44a, TC 1/12/4; Hsüeh Fu-ch'eng, "Shu Ho-fei Po-hsiang Li-kung yung Hu p'ing Wu," in Tso, *Shih tzu-liao*, I, 165-66; Hummel, *Eminent Chinese*, p. 465.

office.[35] On this occasion Tseng Kuo-fan commented: "Burgevine beat Circuit Intendant Yang, and it pleases me because this will be a lesson to those who rely on foreigners and use foreigners as the basis of strength with which to threaten their own countrymen. From now on, such men will be humbled."[36]

Li attempted to use the same tactic with Hsüeh Huan, who was now Commissioner of Foreign Trade, but was warned by Tseng that such behavior was unbecoming and ill designed to make Li popular.[37] Hsüeh's experience in foreign affairs, Li soon learned, made him a valuable addition to his staff. Hsüeh was later appointed to the newly-formed Tsungli Yamen (Office of Foreign Affairs) at the capital.

Li Hung-chang Installs His Political Machine in Shanghai

As Li Hung-chang created vacancies in the various offices at Shanghai, he brought in new men of his own choosing. It was only natural that he made his first appeals for personnel to Tseng Kuo-fan. Within two weeks of his arrival in Shanghai, Li asked Tseng to permit him to appoint Huang Fang, a *chü-jen* from Ch'ang-sha, Hunan, as customs intendant in Shanghai, to help in reorganizing the Shanghai customs bureau.[38] Huang had previously served in Shanghai, in 1855, and therefore possessed the necessary experience.[39] Voicing regret that Huang was an opium smoker, Li nevertheless assured Tseng that he considered Huang a good man of loyal qualities. The selection of a Hunanese for so important a post was an assurance to Tseng that Li intended to keep vital appointments within the "family." As Li had anticipated, Tseng dispatched Huang to Shanghai without delay.[40]

Next Li asked Tseng for help in the appointment of another Hunanese, Kuo Sung-tao, who had formerly been associated with Tseng.[41] Kuo is perhaps remembered best for his part in the introduction of the likin tax system in Hunan in the early days of the Taiping Rebellion,

---

[35] *LWCK Letters,* 2:44b, TC 1/12/4; Hsüeh Fu-ch'eng, "Shu Ho-fei Po-hsiang Li-kung yung Hu p'ing Wu," in Tso, *Shih tso-liao,* pp. 165, 166; Hummel, *Eminent Chinese,* p. 465.

[36] *TWCK Letters,* 20:29b; *LWCK Letters,* 1:44b, TC 1/7/9.

[37] *TWCK Letters,* 18:18a, 41a-b. Tseng had already impeached both Wu Hsü and Hsüeh Huan, recommending, however, that Hsüeh Huan be retained for service in foreign affairs for the time being. *TWCK Memorials,* 16:73a-74b, TC 1/8/29.

[38] *LWCK Letters,* 1:14b-17b, TC 1/3/25.

[39] *Shanghai hsien-chih,* 13:17a-18a; 12:24b-25a. In the fifth year of Hsien-feng, Huang had served as magistrate of Shanghai *hsien* (district), and in the eighth year of Hsien-feng he was listed as subprefect of coastal defense in Sung-chiang prefecture.

[40] *TWCK Letters,* 18:45b; 19:36a.

[41] *LWCK Letters,* 1:14b-17b, TC 1/3/25.

which made possible the development of the Hsiang-chün.[42] Later Kuo became China's first minister to England and France. Li was anxious to bring Kuo into a post of major responsibility, and discussed with Tseng the possibility of appointing Kuo as grain intendant for the Su-Sung (Soochow, Sung-chiang) circuit. This pleased Tseng, and he assured Li that he would make every effort to speed Kuo to Shanghai.[43]

The appointment of Kuo Sung-tao to a high post in Kiangsu province was clearly in violation of central government regulations. Kuo and Tseng Kuo-fan were related, Kuo's son having married Tseng's daughter. Since Tseng Kuo-fan was governor-general of a region that included Kiangsu, Kuo was automatically prohibited from holding office there. This kind of prohibition was essential to the civil service system of the empire, which was designed to prevent local and provincial officials from building up their own power centers. Tseng and Li exchanged letters on the matter. Since Kuo was to be proposed for a regular post, imperial approval would be necessary. The more experienced Tseng counseled Li on how to go about the delicate task of convincing the court:

> If you must use him, memorialize the court yourself. Make it clear that Shanghai needs able men and is faced with an emergency; consequently you cannot avoid having him. Point out that his character is sincere and he is extremely loyal. We should not fear that he lacks ability, but only that he will be too impatient to perform his duties. If you are really well disposed toward him, put him in an independent post as grain intendant, without other offices and without responsibility for managing military and revenue affairs. Thus his power will be light and will not tend to increase the jealousy of others.[44]

In May, 1862, Li memorialized the throne, requesting the appointment of Kuo. He stressed the need for able and incorruptible men in Kiangsu, and stated that the *han-lin* compiler Kuo Sung-tao was then in retirement at his native place. In reviewing Kuo's service since 1853, Li mentioned that since 1860 Kuo had adamantly declined the various summons of the governor of Hupeh, Hu Lin-i, and the governor of Anhwei, Li Hsü-i. Li explained Kuo's unwillingness to serve the provincial officials as follows:

> He considers himself a close servant of the central government, who should take into rigid consideration his entry into or retirement from serv-

---

[42] Hummel, *Eminent Chinese,* p. 438.
[43] *TWCK Letters,* 18:45b.
[44] *Ibid.,* 19:36a.

ice. If he should be granted an inch or foot of power so that he can use his ability, I do not think he will be content with inactivity.[45]

Li thus attempted to convince the court that Kuo's record proved he was not likely to put service to Tseng or himself before loyalty to the central government. Disregarding Tseng's injunctions to invest Kuo with light duties, Li recommended that Kuo be appointed grain intendant of Kiangsu because he could manage military provisions and revenues, supervise officials, and deal with various matters relating to the "barbarians." He knew the Hunan military officials and could therefore effectively co-operate with the Hunan Army stationed on the upper and lower reaches of the Yangtze River.

Kuo Sung-tao proved to be popular in Shanghai. Li Hung-chang found him a man of rare ability and vision.[46] Although Kuo was one of the key men at Li's headquarters, he still refused to accept any official appointment. Li was anxious to have Kuo officially confirmed in office, and six months after his first recommendation again memorialized on behalf of Kuo, saying that Kuo was still unwilling to accept any post and asking the court to order him to do so. As before, he noted Kuo's unusual merits and again suggested that he be appointed grain intendant of Su-Sung. Li argued that although Kuo was doing a splendid job in Shanghai, he would be more valuable in the campaign against corruption and demoralization in Kiangsu if he held office.[47] A few days later, in a private letter to Tseng, Li discussed Kuo's position:

> The seal either of Commissioner of Salt Transportation or of Financial Commissioner could well be entrusted to him. But he is your close relative and should avoid such posts. I have informed the throne that he is only an assistant in my headquarters. This will seem to be in proper taste. I intend as before, however, to direct him to manage the contributions and likin offices simultaneously and assist in training.[48]

The court was in no position to uphold its own regulations. Under the subtle pressure of Li and Tseng, it consented to the formal appointment of Kuo as grain intendant of Kiangsu and later approved his appointment as salt commissioner of Liang-Huai, in the same general area.[49]

With the appointment of the two officials from Hunan, Huang Fang and Kuo Sung-tao, Li had brought the two most important revenue

---

[45] *LWCK Memorials*, 1:7a-b, TC 1/4/18.
[46] *LWCK Letters*, 2:23a, TC 1/9/27.
[47] *LWCK Memorials*, 2:28a-b, TC 1/9/19.
[48] *LWCK Letters*, 2:23a ff., TC 1/9/27.
[49] Miao Ch'üan-sun, *Hsü pei-chuan chi* (1910), 15:5b.

collection offices in Kiangsu under his direct control. In doing so, he had violated in one case a central government regulation forbidding employment of relatives but had conformed at least to the requirement that officials should not serve in their home areas. Tseng, for his part, tried to avoid initiating appointments of his fellow Hunanese to posts under his own jurisdiction as governor-general of Liang-Chiang. He preferred to let Li make the proposals, which he then merely confirmed. For Li it was extremely fortunate to have men serving under him from whom he could expect personal loyalty because of their connection with his senior partner, Tseng.

The important task of administering the growing likin and customs revenues required a good deal of local help. The likin tax system, which had been developed because of the emergency situation, had been left in many cases to the supervision of the local gentry. They knew the local economic situation and which forms of enterprise could be most profitably taxed. The Kiangsu gentry at Shanghai understood these problems particularly well. Men like Feng Kuei-fen had spent years studying local conditions and advising regional leaders accordingly. Li could not dispense with their services if he was to increase his revenues and finance his own and Tseng's armies. He called upon the Kiangsu gentry to assist him and appointed them to special supervisory jobs connected with revenue collection. In doing so, he contravened in spirit the regulations that prohibited the gentry from holding office in their own provinces. He did not ask to have them appointed to specific provincial offices but rather attached them to his provincial staff in a somewhat vague manner. His first such appointment was Feng Kuei-fen, who had been an official of the fifth rank and held the title of Expectant Secretary of the Supervisorate of Imperial Instruction. An outstanding member of the Kiangsu gentry, Feng had been active in his native province since 1855 and had rendered impressive service in militia and revenue affairs. His part in bringing Li and the Huai-chün to Shanghai has already been described.[50]

Another member of the local Kiangsu gentry whom Li added to his staff during the first months of his stay in Shanghai, was Ch'ien Ting-ming. Besides persuading Tseng and Li to send an expedition to Shanghai, Ch'ien had personally gone to Anking with the steam flotilla that brought the Huai-chün eastward down the river.[51] The third member of the Kiangsu gentry whom Li called upon to manage the Shanghai

---

[50] See Chapter 2.
[51] See Chapter 2.

revenues was the second-rank *han-lin* compiler Wang K'ai-t'ai.[52] All three of these men were well-known members of the local gentry, and they were of great help to Li in securing control of revenues.

In his efforts to concentrate around him men whose ability and loyalty to himself could be counted upon, Li did not overlook officials who had worked well with him in his native province. In the middle of 1862 Li asked the court to summon the expectant circuit intendant Wang Ta-ching and the expectant department magistrate Yen Wei from service in Anhwei.[53] Wang had held office in Anhwei since 1853, and had been found co-operative in military affairs. Yen Wei, according to Li, had particularly distinguished himself in handling likin. Their co-operation with the Anhwei gentry now paid off, as Li gave them his patronage.[54]

Li also proposed to add to his staff Hsüeh Shih-yü, an expectant district magistrate for Chekiang province, then holding the title of subprefect.[55] Hsüeh was a native of Anhwei.[56]

Ying Pao-shih, a local underofficial from Chekiang, was singled out for the important job of deputy to the new customs intendant, Huang Fang. On more than one occasion, Li had expressed deep aversion to Chekiang officials, but this aversion did not extend to Ying. Ying had served Li well in arranging for the Huai-chün expedition to Shanghai and had a good reputation as a local official.[57] In later years, Li recorded Ying's contributions as follows:

> The late *an-ch'a-shih* Ying Pao-shih in the tenth year of Hsien-feng, when the Taipings captured Soochow and Sung-chiang, participated in the establishment of local corps, with which he retook Sung-chiang. In the eleventh year of Hsien-feng, the capital of Chekiang fell to the rebels, and with the exception of Shanghai, which was the key to the entire situation, all of the southeast also fell. Ying Pao-shih consulted with the officials and gentry and built up a united defense bureau. He raised revenues, summoned volunteers, and maintained connections with the outside world. Shanghai had become an isolated city, and in view of the more than one million refugees in the city and the importance of its foreign trade and revenues, Ying did his best to hold the city. He consulted the officials, gentry, and people, and persuaded them to receive the Huai-chün, contribute funds, and hire steamers. So great were Ying Pao-shih's efforts that the eastward journey of my armies was actually the culmination of his efforts. And the eastward journey of

[52] *LWCK Memorials*, 1:23a-b, TC 1/5/9. See also Miao Ch'üan-sun, *Hsü pei-chuan chi*, 27:11a ff.

[53] *LWCK Memorials*, 1:23a-b, TC 1/5/9.

[54] *Ibid.*, 9:74a, TC 4/12/19; 1:23a-b, TC 1/5/9.

[55] *Ibid.*

[56] Miao Ch'üan-sun, *Hsü pei-chuan chi*, 80:15a ff.

[57] *Shanghai-hsien hsü-chih* (1918), 15:1b.

my armies was the turning point of the situation.... When he took the steamers up the river to welcome me, jealous people hampered him, and the English consul, Meadows, tried to dissuade him. But Ying was fairly well acquainted with the foreign leaders and explained to them why he should go. He succeeded in persuading Admiral Hope, and went further, paying money to the foreign merchants. As a result, the foreigners became willing to furnish him with steamers, and he even arranged to provide stoves for cooking aboard the steamers and to transport munitions and horses on the same boats. At Anhwei, he did everything to my satisfaction. This use of steamers may be credited solely to Ying Pao-shih, and the story itself has been carefully recorded by Feng Kuei-fen.... Feng was present at these arrangements and witnessed the events himself. Thus, even today [1891] the people of Kiangsu still recall this expedition.[58]

Ying was a valuable addition to Li's organization, because he had demonstrated ability to get money when it was needed and to convince Westerners that their interests and local interests were identical. Li now had the advantage of the service of an experienced Chekiang customs assistant, directly controlled by a loyal Hunanese, Huang Fang.

All of these men, according to Li, had been selected to spearhead his drive to eliminate corruption in Shanghai. Whether or not they actually did this, their appointment eliminated opposition to Li within the Shanghai bureaucracy. In only one instance did the central government oppose Li's selection. In 1862 Li had also requested for service in Shanghai a district magistrate of Kiangsi, Wang Hsüeh-mo.[59] The court had quickly approved the appointment, but the following month the Board of Civil Offices, upon checking, reported that the assignment of Wang would be contrary to regulations. On the board's advice, the court ordered Wang to Peking for an interview and thence to his regular post in Kiangsu.[60]

During this period Li developed his own *mu-fu*, or staff of personal advisers and secretaries. Since these men were not officially appointed, there was no need for Li to report their names or activities to the central government until such time as he might wish to appoint them to regular offices.[61] Almost all these staff members, both civil and military, were from Li's native prefecture, Lu-chou. In later years many of Li's top official assistants came from his *mu-fu*, just as Li himself had risen from Tseng's.

---

[58] *LWCK Memorials*, 71:50a ff., KH 17/4/15.
[59] *Ibid.*, 1:23a-b, TC 1/5/9.
[60] *Ibid.*
[61] *LWCK Letters*, 2:35a, TC 1/10/22.

What Li had done within a year's time was to create a new power organization within the bureaucracy. It was a bureaucratic machine, which carried on the functions of government with as little reference to the central government as possible. At the head of this machine was Li Hung-chang. He had developed a personal army with a group of commanders loyal only to him, and, in fact, controllable only by him. To sustain this army, Li had to have direct control of local revenue sources. His military power gave him a decisive advantage in extending the sphere of his authority; and each extension of authority in turn guaranteed him closer control of revenue and personnel.

Under ordinary conditions the central government was quick to note and frustrate any tendencies toward local concentrations of power. The entire civil service system was aimed at protecting the security and decisive authority of the court and its boards. The Board of Civil Office had the power of assigning all officials to their posts. Their records were periodically reviewed, and no appointment could be made without the board's assent. All officials, according to regulations, were required to pay audience to the emperor before taking up their new posts, and were thus individually screened. Once on the job, they were subject to fitness reports by their superiors and were in turn required to report from time to time on their subordinates and other colleagues as demanded. They were not permitted to remain at one post too long. The customary practice was to transfer an official every two or three years, before he could build up a personal following. Regulations that prevented officials from serving in their native areas or from employing relatives were designed for the same purpose. None of this made for efficiency, but all contributed to the security of the court.

In order to lessen the danger of corruption among local officials, the government prohibited them from buying land in the area under their jurisdiction as well as from engaging in commerce. It was hoped that as a result of these safeguards, the officials would serve only one interest, that of the court, and would stand as impartial arbiters in the districts to which they were assigned. Intercourse between officials and gentry was essential for good local government, but by encouraging separation of functions and interests between the officials and gentry, a balance of power was sought in which the central government would retain control.

In practice, such a system could never work as planned. It was impossible to compel responsible officials to adhere completely to regulations that tended to cut them off from the communities they served and prevented them from building the following they needed to carry out their minimum functions. In the interests of efficiency alone, it was advantageous for officials to have their friends and fellow townsmen, as well as local gentry, at hand. In many instances the special problems of certain areas required men with special training and experience, and it was hardly practicable to shift them to new posts periodically, or dispense with their services because a regulation was being violated. This was especially true in periods of civil war and emergency, when special talent, local power coalitions, experience, and greater sources of wealth were necessary for keeping localities prosperous and loyal to the central government. It was for the court to decide, however, whether violations of its ordinances were justified and whether offending officials should be punished. The extent to which the government could or did punish violations was one measure of its power and security.

Li Hung-chang's development of his own bureaucratic machine in Shanghai was possible only because he was able to violate regulations and run counter to the restrictive spirit of the Chinese civil service system. Such breaking of tradition and rule was in turn possible only because Tseng's army and Li's own newer army were needed by the government for its survival. The Taiping Rebellion, and the Shanghai emergency in particular, created conditions in which the development of strong personal power among regional officials like Li Hung-chang and Tseng Kuo-fan was as important to the central government as to the officials themselves.

The Bureaucratic Machine and Kiangnan Revenues

The primary task of Li Hung-chang's bureaucratic machine was to collect and hold for him the revenues of the region in which it was ensconced. The key to military power was military revenue. It was for this that Li had come to Shanghai, and upon this depended the future of the Huai-chün.

Li's first general report on his administration of finances in Kiangsu, which for the most part meant Shanghai, was summed up in four sets of figures which he presented to the central government in 1865 under the title "First Report, T'ung-chih 1/4 to 2/6 [May, 1862, to July, 1863]."[62]

---

[62] *LWCK Memorials*, 8:12a-13a, TC 4/2/17. The balance of some 10,000 taels was, according to Li, already committed, since he owed considerable sums to foreign merchants at Shanghai, owed money for ammunition bought on credit, and had given his troops official certificates and honors in lieu of pay. See also *ibid.*, 9:12a-13a, TC

Received

        4,433,598.13723   silver taels
           59,197.426   strings of copper coins

Paid Out

        4,423,666.653142 silver taels
           34,271.00   strings of copper coins

Behind this statement was a record of more than a year of intense struggle over the possession and use of regional wealth.

Shanghai's mercantile wealth had continued to increase under Li Hung-chang's administration. This was noted and described in the following terms by George Seward, United States consul at Shanghai, in 1862:

> In the general movement of the enterprise of the Western nations towards the shores of the Pacific this point is the centre.... A fleet of Steamers increasing in numbers almost daily is carrying new ideas of the utility of things up the course of the great river at whose mouth we are located to the very heart of the continent.[63]

It was natural that a foreign consul would emphasize the importance of trade in Kiangsu's leading port, but the province was wealthy too as an agricultural and salt-producing region. Its wealth was drawn upon through several forms of taxation. The first was the land tax and grain (principally rice) tribute, intended for the imperial government primarily, and collected according to regulations by various tax-collecting and other official agencies, which transmitted it to Peking. The second tax system was the foreign customs, administered in part by the Imperial Chinese Maritime Customs Administration, a joint Chinese-Western organization. Because the Taipings occupied most of Kiangsu, Shanghai had become the province's only center for the collection of foreign customs.

Domestic commerce was taxed through the likin, collected at various tollhouses along the trade routes and through licenses issued to mer-

---

4/6/1; 8:12a-13a, TC 4/2/17; 8:11a ff., TC 4/2/17; and *TWCK Letters*, 20:16b. In Chou Shih-ch'eng, *Huai-chün p'ing-nien chi*, 11:15, it is claimed that Li Hung-chang also paid out 30,000 liang to Governor-general Yang Yüeh-pin, who was in command of the campaign against the Moslem rebels in Kansu during the third year of T'ung-chih. Although Li was ordered by the throne to make this payment, he pleaded that he was unable to afford the funds and announced that the requested payment would not be made. See *LWCK Memorials*, 7:42a ff., TC 3/10/7.

[63] Consul Seward to Secretary of State, U.S. State Department, *Despatches from United States Consuls in Shanghai*, July, 1862, hereafter cited *Shanghai Consular Despatches*.

chants and shippers by local authorities. Salt provided revenues through at least two systems of taxation. The regular salt tax was collected for the imperial government from the licensed salt merchants, for technically the production and distribution of salt was a government monopoly. In addition the provincial authorities levied a likin tax upon salt. Transport taxes were also collected from merchants in various areas and generally passed into the hands of the local controlling authorities. In addition to the taxes, likin, and license fees, an important new type of income was derived from the contributions of wealthy merchants and gentry. These contributions were a form of emergency tax, since they were not always voluntary. Although an incentive was sometimes provided by the bestowal of an official title upon the contributor, official coercion was often used.

The earliest fairly detailed statement of Li Hung-chang's financial position in Shanghai was made necessary in mid-1862 by an imperial edict inquiring into Li's action in appropriating, at Shanghai, customs revenues collected on behalf of the customhouses at the river ports of Kiukiang and Hankow. He was ordered to remit the funds in question to an agent who had been sent to Shanghai to receive them. Li refused to give up these funds or similar funds collected in the future, pointing out that the practice of collecting this revenue at Shanghai had been established several years before he took office. He could not, he claimed, determine which taxes were due to Kiukiang, which to Hankow, and which to Shanghai. Customs officials at Shanghai entered all receipts in one book, because it was impossible to control the destination of a ship after it had passed Shanghai and proceeded upriver.

Li went on to state his case in the more convincing terms of practical necessity. He pointed out that Shanghai had been isolated since Soochow and Ch'ang-chou had fallen to the Taipings in 1860 and that Hsüeh Huan, then governor, had been forced to use the customs revenues collected at Shanghai, as well as likin and tribute, to maintain the garrison there. In the past winter and spring, the Shanghai garrison alone had numbered 50,000 men, and the existing income was insufficient to maintain it. Li estimated that the income from the Shanghai customs in 1862 was over 2,000,000 liang per year, or over 200,000 per month. Twenty per cent of this revenue went to England and 20 per cent to France, leaving a remainder, including the disputed Kiukiang and Hankow revenues, of only a little more than 100,000. With the additional income from likin and contributions, this total income amounted to over 200,000 liang per month.

But Li's expenses were high. Army rations and munitions alone required over 300,000 liang each month. In addition, Shanghai sent a subsidy to the garrison at Chinkiang and had to pay for official salaries in the province and other military and civil expenses. When Li was in Anking he had been informed that he could expect an income of 400,000 or 500,000 per month, but this was far from true. Because the foreign customs were managed for foreigners and therefore were not corrupt as were the native customs, he did not believe that reform would increase this income. The report of the foreign customs bureau that the customs income was only 200,000 monthly could be relied upon as true.

Li claimed that the funds he had collected on behalf of the two Hupeh customhouses since his arrival were negligible. He had used the money to send tribute to the capital, and the amount he had sent, 70,000 liang, was exactly what Hupeh province had been responsible for remitting.

Returning to the problem of military necessity, Li emphasized that Shanghai was a revenue source and therefore the principal object of attack by the Taipings in Kiangsu. A new, separate army must be trained to defend Shanghai. Although Li had reduced the old garrison at Shanghai by 15,000, he still had his own Huai Army, numbering over 10,000 water and land troops. Together with British and French artillery volunteers and surrendered Taipings, his total force in mid-1862 came to 40,000. For these troops he needed at least 300,000 liang per month. There were still other expenses: 113,000 liang to meet the rice requirements of the capital; 250,000 for the steamers and munitions that Robert Hart was procuring; and a subsidy of 20,000 liang per month for Yüan Chia-san's army fighting in Anhwei. In conclusion Li reiterated:

Last month we took in a little more than 100,000 in likin and tribute, and a little more than 100,000 in customs taxes. With this sum we cannot sustain our own army. I therefore respectfully request that Your Majesty allow us to use the Hankow and Kiukiang taxes to fill our own gaps.[64]

One week after addressing this memorial to the throne, Li Hung-chang described the situation somewhat differently to Tseng Kuo-fan. He stated that his total revenues in Shanghai came to 300,000 per month and that his total military expenses for both foreign and Chinese troops amounted to 200,000. Additional expenses arose from the neces-

---

[64] *LWCK Memorials*, 1:32a-35b, TC 1/5/27.

sity of paying back debts and meeting indemnity payments. He estimated that two-thirds of his local income was spent on the foreign and
local troops under his command. He admitted that the accounts were
not clear and that both he and the foreigners would be pleased to see
them clarified.[65]

In subsequent months, besides withholding funds from Hupeh
province, Li also appropriated revenues collected on behalf of the
customhouses at Tientsin, Newchwang, Teng-chou, Canton, Shan-t'ou,
Foochow, and Sha-men. He again vigorously defended his actions as
being a result of the emergency. Later, he went further and attacked
the accusation of the governor of Hupeh that he was illegally holding
funds. He was aware that his position, for the moment, was strong.[66]
Once the rebellion was over and other provinces were able to reopen
their customhouses, it would be impossible to prevent them from collecting their own revenues. Meanwhile, Li took advantage of Shanghai's momentary quasi monopoly on foreign customs to increase the
resources of his Huai Army and establish it firmly for the future.

The court was greatly concerned over Li Hung-chang's usurpation
of funds rightfully due his colleagues in other regions. One of the
important functions of the central government was to maintain a certain balance in the distribution of wealth among the provinces. The
court and its Board of Revenue were expected to enforce the payments
due from one province to another, but because of unsettled conditions
and the growing importance of Li's new army, the court was helpless
to intervene effectively. It was quite another matter when Li began to
seize and hold funds that the central government claimed for itself. If
the central government allowed such a move to go unchallenged, not
only would it be abandoning its jurisdictional role but it would be
losing its hold on its main source of support. Since the court was almost
entirely dependent on the revenues from the provinces, any governor
or governor-general who withheld funds was threatening its very
existence.

At the close of 1862 the court ordered Li Hung-chang to account for
his management of the Shanghai customs and also make restitution for
funds that had been misappropriated before he took office. The edict
stated that between Hsien-feng 10/7/26 (1860) and Hsien-feng
11/7/25 (1861) the foreign customhouse at Shanghai had collected
revenues on shipping, opium, transit dues, export tax, and other items.

---

[65] *LWCK Letters*, 1:32a-34a, TC 1/6/3.
[66] *LWCK Memorials*, 1:55a ff., TC 1/7/13; 57a ff., TC 1/7/13.

With 40 per cent of the income turned over to the British and French for indemnities, the balance of the revenues amounted to 1,318,077 liang. According to an earlier memorial by Li Hung-chang this money had been used to provide urgently needed military funds. The rule, however, was that these taxes were to be delivered to the capital. If there was any balance, it should be broken down into the proper categories and delivered to the Board of Revenue. Even if military necessity had compelled Li to borrow from these funds, he should first have memorialized and transferred the funds only after permission was granted. Transfers could not be made without authorization.

The court reminded Li that, according to proper procedure, when the Shanghai customs collected the silk tax on behalf of other customhouses further inland, the receipts should have been sent on to the other customhouses. Instead Li had transferred those funds as well as the foreign customs revenues to his own military treasury. All this was definitely contrary to the regulations. Especially wrong was Li's appropriation of the transit dues and the taxes on native goods, which were new imposts and not usually handled by the Shanghai customs. Li was directed to order the customs intendant to return to the treasury the revenues from foreign customs and to report on the revenues from transit dues and native goods and turn them in as well. Should the former intendant at Li's customs office, Wu Hsü, delay in reporting, he would be liable for punishment. Moreover, all foreign customs revenues, transit dues, native goods taxes, and silk taxes collected after Hsien-feng 11/7/25 (1861) were to be delivered in full to the Board of Revenue.[67]

The edict ordered Li Hung-chang to respond. Li made no reply. Six months later, when he received another edict calling him to account, he at last answered the charges.[68] In his reply, Li first made it clear that the collection of taxes before 1861 was not his concern. Wu Hsü would have to be held responsible, for although Wu had been dismissed from office on other charges, he had been in actual management for many years and was particularly concerned with customs affairs.[69] Li

---

[67] *Ibid.,* 3:71a-73a, TC 2/5/30.   [68] *Ibid.*

[69] *Ibid.* See also *TWCK Memorials,* 16:33a-34b, TC 1/8/29. This memorial provides the detailed charges submitted to Tseng against Wu Hsü and Hsüeh Huan. Tseng confirmed the truth of the charges, thus causing Wu's dismissal. It should be noted that Li Hung-chang had also impeached Wu. The practice of retaining dismissed officials in office was common under the Ch'ing bureaucratic system. Such officials frequently continued at their posts for many years after their official "dismissal," and there are numerous cases where they were ultimately officially reinstated and even promoted.

had nevertheless ordered the incumbent customs intendant, Huang Fang, together with Wu Hsü, to draw up a report on the period in question. On the basis of their report, Li was able to state that for 1857, 1858, and 1859 all foreign customs revenues collected at Shanghai had been duly remitted to the Board of Revenue. Such funds were not appropriated for military purposes until the loss of Soochow and Ch'ang-chou in 1860. Owing to that disaster the customs intendant had found no way to forward the funds to the capital. Soon afterwards T'ai-ts'ang, Chia-t'ing, and Ch'ing-p'u had fallen, and Shanghai was isolated and in peril. The former governor, Hsüeh Huan, had raised troops and gathered funds to pay them and to assist Chinkiang. This required huge outlays. In the twelfth month of Hsien-feng 10 (1861), Hsüeh Huan requested authority to use the customs revenues, transit dues, native taxes, and opium tax as military reserves. Since this had been memorialized and authorized, Li argued that it could not be regarded as an arbitrary measure.

Li then went on to discuss the question of turning over to the Board of Revenue the more recently collected taxes. Although his forces had already recovered various cities in Kiangsu, both Soochow and Ch'ang-chou were still occupied by the rebels, and Li was still increasing his army. The need for revenue was still growing. Since 1861 he had paid subsidies to Chinkiang and supplied funds for the barracks and transportation of the British and French troops stationed in Shanghai. In addition, the Board of Foreign Affairs had asked Li to have 6,800 of his troops trained by the British and French in the use of Western weapons, an expense of 40,000 to 50,000 liang each month. Then the Ever Victorious Army "with its more than 4,000 men" required twice as much as any other army. High expenditures were necessitated by the use of foreign munitions and steamships. Not only did Li have to supply his own and the Ever Victorious Army, but he had to send munitions to other armies. Further expenses were incurred in the payment of salaries to civil officials. Even the officials paid by the Office of the Financial Commissioner cost Li money, since that office was borrowing the funds from him. In fact, said Li, his total expenses were between 400,000 and 500,000 liang each month.

Li pressed his case further by showing that the opening of the Kiukiang and Hankow customs offices, early in 1863, had greatly diminished the Shanghai revenues, since those ports now carried trade on the Yangtze River. Changes in the system of customs exemptions resulted in further reductions of income. As a result, even with the appropriation of the foreign customs revenues, the transit dues, the native goods tax, and the opium tax, Li could not raise even 100,000 per month. This sum could meet only a part of his military needs. He was therefore making up the deficiency through other means, using likin and contributions. Li then warned: "If we carry out the orders of this edict and return these revenues to the Board of Revenue, the lack of rations among my troops will lead to mutiny. I therefore respectfully request permission to hold these revenues in Shanghai."[70]

Li's seizure of customs revenues was one more step in the weakening of the central government. Although this was a temporary measure for an emergency situation, the central government's authority had been challenged at its core. The foreign customs, during and after the Taiping Rebellion, were administered by a foreign inspectorate, which justified its usefulness to China by guaranteeing revenues to the central government. Nevertheless, customs receipts were held back and spent by regional authorities without permission. It is true that Li promised to restore the funds when the rebels were defeated;[71] but throughout the latter half of the nineteenth century, China was subject to a succession of emergencies that provided ample excuse for constant delay in repayment.

During Li's years in Kiangnan the court also requested that he raise and send to the capital huge contributions of rice. Because of market conditions, Li felt it would be cheaper to send cash and memorialized the throne to that effect, indicating also that Kiangsu was not an unfailing source of revenue for the capital and that the merchants of Kiangsu had a prior obligation to their own region. While not openly refusing to send the increased contributions, Li indicated his reluctance by writing, "Since we started fighting in Kiangsu, our army has relied for everything upon the merchants. Now the merchants are exhausted; nevertheless, because of their loyalty, they will do their best."[72]

Li's contest with the central government for the control and disposition of the wealth in his region never took the form of open defiance. It was a series of delays and evasions, always excused on grounds of emergency, sometimes justified by the danger of mutiny. Whatever the reasons Li gave, he achieved his ends. Regional interests were winning out over the interests of the central government. Li's actions were taken ostensibly for the sake of the general security of the court, but in fact they undermined its authority and economic basis.

[70] *LWCK Memorials,* 3:73a-75b, TC 2/5/30.
[71] *Ibid.,* 3:75a-b, TC 2/5/30.
[72] *Ibid.,* 3:28a-29b, TC 2/4/7.

The Struggle to Meet Military Expenses

Li's administration of revenues was determined by the very real problem of sustaining and expanding military forces in a region ravaged by warfare. He relied almost entirely on customs, likin, and salt revenues, and although they yielded high returns, they were not sufficient for his needs. As the Huai armies of Li and the Hsiang armies of Tseng Kuo-fan, Tseng Kuo-ch'üan, and Tso Tsung-t'ang recaptured from the Taipings areas in which customhouses were located, Shanghai lost its monopoly on the regional customs. Li described the seriousness of the situation to Tseng Kuo-ch'üan in a private letter written in the middle of 1863. During the previous months the Shanghai customs revenues had dropped from 100,000 to 60,000 or 70,000 liang a month.[73] At the very time Li had finally succeeded in ousting the Chekiang clique from control of the customs, the decline was under way. He had planned to divide his customs money in the following manner: 50,000 liang for Western troops and officers, 30,000 for the Chinkiang garrison, and 20,000 for munitions. Even when he expected to have 100,000 liang a month to draw upon, there would be no surplus. As Li put it, "Although many people suspect that I am rich, I am actually not so at all."[74]

He had attempted to cut corners by partially demobilizing the Ever Victorious Army in 1862, but the British apparently were unwilling to permit much reduction. Li had set aside most of the customs revenues for expenses on "foreign" items, by which he meant the Western army and munitions as well as personnel. In a later accounting to the central government, Li reported these expenditures separately, since the traditional form of report made no allowance for foreign items. The general theory behind Li's division of expenditures was that foreign expenses should be met with foreign income.[75] As the Ever Victorious Army proved again and again that it was a valuable adjunct to the Huai-chün, Li later gave up any idea of dispensing with it and was quite willing to bear the high cost of maintaining it. In the face of diminishing customs returns, Li had to rely more and more on other sources of income.

One of these was the likin, with which Li had been concerned from the very beginning. In his very first memorial to the throne after his arrival at Shanghai, Li had mentioned his concern that the various

---

[73] *LWCK Letters*, 3:30b, TC 2/4/28.

[74] *Ibid.*, 3:2a, TC 2/1/6.

[75] A case in point is provided in *LWCK Memorials*, 2:4a-b, TC 1/8/2. Wu Hsü collected 18,300 taels for the construction of fortifications around Shanghai by engineers from the foreign military establishments.

water forces of the government army operating north and south of the Yangtze River had established for themselves spheres of influence within which they independently imposed and collected likin taxes,[76] a problem for which Li had no immediate solution. Although the likin income in the summer of 1862 had exceeded customs income by only 20,000 to 30,000 liang, it was by far the more flexible of the two. The customs were saddled with a deductible indemnity, drawn in installments by the foreign inspectors of customs, protected by treaty and impossible to evade. Moreover, Li had temporarily left the customs administration in the hands of Wu Hsü, upon whose shoulders fell the blame for any deficits arising from the high costs of Western munitions and the employment of European officers.[77] Finally, customs income depended upon the volume of foreign trade, which could not be controlled or relied upon with confidence. The likin, on the other hand, was imposed and collected locally, and once Li's machine was entrenched, it was under the governor's direct control. It was for Li to decide when, where, and to what extent likin could be levied.

Li's initial efforts to reform the various likin bureaus in Shanghai by putting them under the control of his colleagues from Hunan and the Kiangsu gentry brought quick returns. By August, 1862, the likin income at Shanghai had risen to over 200,000 liang per month.[78] This income held steady until 1863.[79] But as the Huai-chün grew to a major command of some 60,000 troops, Li was driven to seek new sources of likin revenue. At the beginning of 1863, he levied new likin impositions on sugar, soybeans, housing, banking, and other businesses in Shanghai,[80] and established many more likin stations (similar to tollhouses) along the roads in the Shanghai area. He reported to Tseng that the new likin on banking was bringing in about 10,000 liang each month and that the new stations were yielding an additional 40,000 monthly.[81] He described to Tseng some of the lucrative enterprises in Shanghai that he hoped to tap: the silk industry, the opium shipments from Fukien and Kwangtung, lumber and miscellaneous goods from Ningpo.[82] But just as new imposts on these items began to bring profit, new Taiping incursions in Kiangsu cut off important areas, and his total likin in the province declined, according to his report, by some 50 per cent.[83]

[76] LWCK Letters, 1:17a, TC 1/3/25.
[77] Ibid., 1:47a-49b, TC 1/7/26.
[78] Ibid., 1:46b, TC 1/7/19.
[79] Ibid., 4:14b-15a, TC 2/9/19.
[80] Ibid., 3:11b, TC 2/2/16.
[81] Ibid., 4:3b, TC 2/7/17.
[82] Ibid., 3:18b, TC 2/4/4.
[83] TWCK Letters, 20:34b.

Besides meeting the mounting costs of maintaining the Huai-chün, Li was called upon more and more frequently to assist Tseng Kuo-fan in the financial crises of the Hsiang-chün. Tseng had come to look upon Li as his Shanghai financial agent, who could always produce funds when they were needed by his various commanders. After reading Li's frequent letters on the situation in Shanghai, however, Tseng was forced to admit, "In Shanghai the revenue founts grow drier every day."[84] Li attempted to meet the responsibilities he had taken upon himself when he first went to Shanghai. In October, 1862, Li had sent Tseng Kuo-ch'üan weapons and ammunition purchased with funds he had raised from fines. At the same time, he ordered the general bureau of likin and tribute to raise an additional 40,000 liang, which was half the total income expected from fines to be imposed in October and November of that year. All these funds were reserved for the exclusive use of Tseng Kuo-fan.[85] When the promised money failed to reach Tseng's headquarters on schedule, Tseng wrote to Li, urging him to meet his obligation.[86] Li sent the money, and in return received a cordial letter from his old commander, thanking him for his help and commenting on Li's recent victories. Tseng went out of his way to play upon Li's vanity:

I know that on the twenty-third day you gained a sweeping victory and defeated over ten thousand rebels.... This greatly enhances our position. I have been with the army for ten years, but I have never gone into battle or slain a single bandit with my own hand. When I read your letter, I feel ashamed as well as happy.

Tseng went on to express his concern over the financial situation in Shanghai:

You have afforded me 40,000 silver taels and 10,000 in ship tribute. I am grateful, but Shanghai has already been exhausted. After a while there will not be much prospect of getting additional money from Shanghai.[87]

Tseng's concern did not prevent him from soon requesting an additional 50,000 liang from Shanghai, but led him to recommend that Li stay on in the Shanghai area instead of planning an early campaign.[88]

---

[84] *Ibid.*, 19:5b.

[85] *LWCK Letters,* 2:23a, TC 1/9/27.

[86] *TWCK Letters,* 19:23b.

[87] *Ibid.*, 20:13a.

[88] The funds requested here by Tseng were intended to compensate him for expenditures made for the support of the army of Wu Ch'ang-ch'ing, one of Li's original Huai-chün commanders. *Ibid.*, 20:29b.

In defending his appropriation of the Hupeh customs revenues several months earlier, Li had made a great point of his obligation to provide the forces of the Honanese Hsiang-chün commander Yüan Chia-san with a regular military subsidy of 20,000 liang. In the last quarter of 1862, Li reduced this remittance to 10,000 liang on the grounds that he had insufficient funds and could not further jeopardize the support of the Huai-chün.[89]

The same theme of financial stringency prevailed when late in 1862 Li reported that he had finally been forced to reduce the Ever Victorious Army to only 4,500 men, for whom he provided 70,000 taels per month.[90] If the army were kept at this size, its expenses would not exceed the customs income Li had reserved for this purpose.

This report by Li provides one of the few instances in which his information can be checked against independent Western sources. Li's report, based on figures supplied by Wu Hsü, was submitted on the occasion of the death of the commander of the Ever Victorious Army, Ward. It stated that command had been assumed by the American officer Burgevine. At this time Burgevine himself wrote a letter to the American consul, George Seward, relating the details of his new command and enclosing a muster roll of the army as of that date. The records of the United States Archives reveal that in September, 1862, the official muster roll of the Ever Victorious Army showed 3,126 officers and men.[91] In allowing 70,000 liang as the required sum to support 4,500 men, Li was providing an average of 15.5 liang per man. On the basis of this average, a force consisting of only 3,126—as claimed by Burgevine—would have required only 48,453 liang. By falsifying the size of the army, Li, Wu Hsü, or their subordinates were able to divert some 21,500 liang each month. This could have meant a quarter of a million liang per year surreptitiously flowing into the purse of some bureaucrat.

The pressure from Tseng Kuo-fan continued. In order to avert mutinies among troops under his command, he urged Li to draw upon customs revenues and remit the money as soon as possible. He reminded Li that the Shanghai customs owed him a considerable sum and explained why he needed the money at once:

The bandits in Nanking still seem to have provisions. The campaign at

---

[89] *LWCK Memorials*, 2:9a-b, TC 1/8/30.

[90] *Ibid.*, 2:13a-17b, TC 1/8 int./6.

[91] Enclosure in a dispatch from Consul Seward to Secretary of State Seward, *Shanghai Consular Despatches*, September, 1862.

Nanking will therefore continue for some time yet. But our own rations are extremely low. We have never faced such hardship before. I fear a mutiny among the troops under Pao Ch'ao . . . they have only received 50 per cent of their rations this year. My brother's troops, however, receive only 30 per cent. Thus you can see that I do not favor my brother over Pao Ch'ao.

Because of this prevailing situation I have sent a special commissioner . . . to appropriate some of the funds which were supposed to be sent to the Ministry of Foreign Affairs in Peking, amounting to a total of 200,000 liang and coins totaling 16,000 yüan. I hope that you can give him this sum as soon as possible. Ninety thousand liang will be distributed to Pao Ch'ao and the remaining 110,000 liang in addition to the coins will be sent to my brother. Only by doing this can we guarantee that for the fourth and fifth months there will be no mutiny and that we can then finally bring the Nanking campaign to a conclusion.

Further, the Shanghai customs office still owes us 50,000 liang in addition to the funds originally provided for the purchase of steamships but never spent. Altogether, this should amount to 240,000 liang. I hope you can get this all together and send it to me.[92]

In this letter Tseng also remarked how much he missed Li's presence at his own headquarters. "Since you went to Shanghai," he wrote, "the selection of officers, the reorganization of soldiers, the appointment of personnel, and the arrangement of financial affairs here have departed from the practical way. The empty and vain appearance here grows day by day."[93]

In the year and a half following Li's arrival at Shanghai his personal army had grown from some five thousand officers and men to a major command of some sixty thousand troops.[94] In order to sustain this expansion, he continued his fund-raising campaign without abatement. Initiating a program similar to that of Tso Tsung-t'ang in Chekiang, he turned to the wealthy people of Shanghai for assistance, demanding contributions of rice.[95]

The quest for new revenue sources brought Li into conflct with other regional leaders. One of the most famous and bitter rivalries in nineteenth century provincial officialdom was that between the two Hsiang-chün protégés, later independent regional military leaders, Li Hung-chang and Tso Tsung-t'ang. Tso's branch of the Hsiang-chün was his own personal army in the same way that the Huai Army was Li's. Tso had been appointed governor of Chekiang province at about the

[92] *TWCK Letters*, 23:36b.
[93] *Ibid.*
[94] *LWCK Letters*, 4:14b-15a, TC 2/9/19.
[95] *Ibid.*, 4:16a-b, TC 2/9/27.

same time Li was given charge at Shanghai. Responsible for the embattled and ravaged sector to the south and west of Kiangsu, Tso was hard pressed for funds to sustain his armies, and levied high taxes, or "contributions," upon the Chekiang merchants and gentry in his area.

The more enterprising and fortunate gentry and merchants of Chekiang, like their counterparts in Kiangsu, had fled to Shanghai. Indeed, Shanghai from the first had been a mercantile center for Chekiang entrepreneurs, who counted Chekiang as their homeland but lived, and often lived well, in Shanghai. When Li exacted funds from them it was difficult, considering the emergency, to withstand his pressure. It was another matter, however, when Tso Tsung-t'ang sent agents to Shanghai to collect from them the contributions that as Chekiang natives they were expected to pay. The struggle for funds between Tso and Li became the basis of a long-standing enmity between the two governors.

Some interesting details of the revenue issues underlying regional and personal rivalries are provided by Tso Tsung-t'ang himself. He reveals, in addition, the means through which some of the fabulous gentry-mercantile fortunes of the period were accumulated. It has been mentioned that Yang Fang was originally from Chekiang and had taken refuge in Shanghai, where he not only held office but also engaged in extensive commercial and banking activities. In 1863, while Yang, despite his removal from office by Li, was enjoying the comparative security of Shanghai, where he continued in business, Tso Tsung-t'ang was casting about anxiously for sources of revenue. Annoyed by Yang Fang's refusal to assist in his fund drive, Tso addressed a bitter memorial to the throne:

> The circuit intendant of Kiangsu, Yang Fang, and others have their native places in Chekiang province. The wealth of their families amounts to many tens of thousands of liang. Yet they disregard the plight of their country and their clans, who suffer from terrible devastation. They do not render assistance to those in distress.
>
> Formerly, I appended a note to a memorial explaining all this. I then was favored with an imperial edict stating that my intention to order the rich member of the gentry Yang Fang and others to collect energetically a huge sum in order to buy a large amount of grain and thus to alleviate the emergency quickly, was approved. If any were to dare disobey, I was authorized to employ strict measures.

Having demonstrated that he was acting in full accordance with imperial authority and had the right to enforce his orders under central government sanction, Tso went on to denounce Yang Fang:

This rich member of the gentry, Yang Fang, who is an official, was deputed to collect 50,000 tan of rice. The circuit intendant of Ning-Chao-T'ai, by the name of Shih Chih-o, was previously commissioned to press for this remittance [from Yang Fang]. According to the petition of Shih Chih-o, his special deputy, the expectant district magistrate Wang Ch'in-yu went to Shanghai to influence, urge, and order. But the said official [Yang Fang] gave an excuse and declined. He offered opposition and refused to recognize his obligation to contribute. He was warned three times but to no avail. These were the circumstances as they were brought to my attention.

It is my humble opinion that Yang Fang, by being a "middleman," became intimate with the foreign merchants in order to reach for wealth. In a period of ten years, he has come into the possession of over 1,000,000 liang. He purchased the title of customs intendant.

Formerly, when in Chekiang, he dealt in Western affairs in order to grasp a fortune. This is all public knowledge. For example, in the sixth year of Hsien-feng (1856), the former governor of Chekiang borrowed several steamships from the English merchant "P'ili." The boats were kept not even three months, yet the final payment was over 79,000 liang in foreign silver. This he [Yang] called payment to the foreigner, but actually some of it was taken out and put in his own purse. Thus does he becloud virtue in his lust for profit.

At this time, because Chekiang province is cruelly devastated, he has been ordered to contribute 50,000 tan to give succor to the calamity-stricken populace. In the end he dares to oppose contemptuously and fails to comply. It is not proper that the deputy should have to urge him. Having already attained wealth through wickedness, he [Yang] as a wealthy man compounds [his wickedness] by being without benevolence. It is proper that steps be taken to handle the situation.

According to a petition from Yang Fang which I have received from that official, he has acknowledged obligation for and contributed 10,000 liang in silver. He also asks to provide grain for the capital to the value of 10,000 liang and to return an equal sum to Chekiang as his contribution.

It is my opinion that because in recent years the transportation of grain from the south by water has been interrupted, the granary at the capital very urgently needs rice. Your minister, the governor of Kiangsu [Li Hung-chang] has ordered the official in question to contribute 100,000 tan of rice for the capital. Yang naturally should completely carry out the raising of the funds and hand it in. But how can he shift it and make out as if this were a contribution to the Chekiang relief fund?

If we discuss and compare the quota of rice that I have asked him to contribute, that is, 50,000 tan, with Yang's contribution of 10,000 liang in silver, in terms of the prevailing cost of rice, his contribution barely reaches one-thirtieth of his assigned allotment. That he merely wishes to evade the Chekiang collection is obvious. It is a curious way to shirk. His attitude furthermore is deceitful.

I respectfully request that an imperial edict be issued to the governor of

Kiangsu [Li Hung-chang] ordering that the already dismissed circuit intendant Yang Fang be compelled to pay his contribution of rice to the capital and that the rice be duly handed over; and furthermore that he be sent back to Chekiang in custody in order to pay his relief contribution, thus preventing an evasion of the regulations.[96]

Tso's statement of affairs shows what enormous wealth Li Hung-chang had begun to tap in Shanghai. The extent of his victory over Wu Hsü, Yang Fang, and the Chekiang clique comes into perspective only when it is realized that he had been pitted against the holders of some of the largest fortunes of his period. Tso Tsung-t'ang's memorial implied that Li Hung-chang was apparently willing to protect Yang provided the latter assumed some of the financial burdens for which Li, as governor, was responsible.

Li's strategic position in the new financial and trade center of China offered him decisive advantages in contests for revenue. By becoming the protector of local interests, he assumed at the same time the enviable role of exploiter of the newly rising Chinese commercial interests, which were concentrated most strongly in Shanghai.

The Military Build-up in Kiangnan

A former secretary of Tseng Kuo-fan and Li Hung-chang, in describing the growth of Li's organization and his success in raising revenues, entitled his essay "How Li Hung-chang used Shanghai to Pacify Kiangsu."[97] Li's efforts to consolidate his position in Shanghai were aimed at developing and strengthening his army for the struggle to wrest Kiangsu from the Taipings. Shanghai was the base at which revenues were collected and the Huai military organization outfitted and trained for the crucial campaign ahead. While Li slowly disbanded the ragamuffin army previously raised by Hsüeh Huan, the numbers of Huai and Hunan troops moving into Shanghai constantly increased. The armies that had earliest been organized into proper battalions, such as the Ming-chün of Liu Ming-ch'uan and the Sung-tzu-chün of the Hunanese Kuo Sung-lin, were the first sent out to battle. In general, however, Li followed Tseng Kuo-fan's cautious advice and waited a few months before he committed the bulk of his troops to the field.

The battalions of Liu Ming-ch'uan were assigned to co-operate with another important force, the army of Ch'eng Hsüeh-ch'i. Ch'eng, like

[96] *Tso Wen-hsiang kung ch'üan-chi, Memorials*, 6:6a ff., TC 2/6/10.

[97] Hsüeh Fu-ch'eng, "Shu Ho-fei Po-hsiang Li-kung yung Hu p'ing Wu," in Tso, *Shih tzu-liao*, I, 163-72.

most of the principal commanders under Li, was a native of Anhwei.
He had taken part in local defense during the early days of the Taiping Rebellion, but in the course of time had gone over to the Taipings
and had risen in the ranks of the Taiping army. When Tseng Kuo-fan
took Anking, Ch'eng offered himself to Tseng as a commander and in
the following months gained Tseng's confidence as one of his stoutest
fighting commanders. On being assigned to Li Hung-chang's command
in 1862, Ch'eng readily accepted the authority of a fellow Anhweinese
and in the ensuing years proved to be a strong and loyal aide.[98]

Another experienced force numbering over four thousand arrived at
Shanghai some time after the main body of Li's troops. This army was
the Huai-yang "water troops," which Li himself had personally commanded while serving under Tseng in Kiangsi four years earlier.[99]
Now under the command of Huang I-sheng, it scored conspicuous victories in numerous battles along the Yangtze River and on the lakes in
Kiangsu. Converging upon Kiangsu at the same time were other detachments. Most of them were Hsiang-chün battalions which Tseng
assigned directly to Li's command. Only a few battalions were from
provinces other than Anhwei and Hunan. Notable among these were
the Szechwan troops of Yang Ting-hsün. All of these forces became
integral parts of the Huai-chün and remained loyal to Li for many
years to come.

While in Shanghai Li was deeply impressed by the performance of
the Ever Victorious Army, the nominal command of which he had inherited from Hsüeh Huan. He was equally impressed by the British
and French forces that were co-operating in the defense of Shanghai.
On one occasion he wrote to Tseng:

I have been on board the war vessels of the British and French commanders, and I have observed the fine construction of their cannon, the

---

[98] Hummel, *Eminent Chinese*, pp. 115-16 (biography of Ch'eng Hsüeh-ch'i).

[99] In working on Li's campaign in Kiangsu I have had the privilege of consulting
and using an unpublished doctoral dissertation in the Cambridge University Library,
Cambridge, England, by J. C. Cheng, entitled "Some Aspects of the Taiping Rebellion
in China, 1850-1864" (Cambridge, 1950). A copy of this work was made available to
the Modern Chinese History Project, University of Washington, and to the writer,
through the courtesy of the late Professor Gustav Haloun of Cambridge University.
The section entitled "Li Hung-chang's Account of the Suppression of the Rebellion,"
pp. 200-301, consists of translations from the letters and memorials of Li. Mr. Cheng
has not attempted to organize or collate these materials but presents them chrono-
logically as they occur in Li's own collected works. Where I have drawn upon these
translations I shall refer to Mr. Cheng's work in addition to citing the original source.
On p. 272 Dr. Cheng quotes a letter from Li to Tseng which states: "This [Huai-
yang water] corps has followed me longest and most faithfully." See also *LWCK
Letters*, 4:22a ff., TC 2/10/22.

skilled workmanship of their cannon balls, the newness of their mechanical work, and the strength and order of their troops. Truly, those of China cannot measure up to them.[100]

After criticizing several aspects of foreign military life, particularly the methods of encampment, Li went on to admit:

While I dare not believe in their depraved teachings in seeking benefits, I am in general deeply concerned because China's military implements are so far behind those of the people from overseas. Consequently, I daily exhort my officers and soldiers to be of unprejudiced mind and to stand prepared to study some of the methods of the Westerners, so that we may add what they have [to our own accomplishments] and use it in battle.... Ch'eng Hsüeh-ch'i and Kuo Sung-lin are both extremely obstinate and are consequently unwilling even to attempt to learn. Liu Ming-ch'uan is gradually gaining some understanding and is now anxiously awaiting some real howitzers and cannon, which he has not been able to obtain. Should we remain long in Shanghai and not be able to acquire the strong points of the foreigners, it will be regrettable indeed.[101]

Li took advantage of the foreign officers under his command to initiate Western military methods in the Huai-chün. Although the Ever Victorious Army was to play a conspicuous, though perhaps not decisive, role in the final victory over the Taipings, its most lasting contribution was as a model and training group for China's first relatively modern army, the Huai-chün.

Li's Military Campaigns, 1862 and 1863

The over-all campaign carried out by Li falls into three principal phases, corresponding roughly with the years 1862, 1863, and 1864. The first phase was devoted to rendering Shanghai, Chinkiang, and other river and seaports secure from Taiping attacks, and to recapturing some neighboring areas. The second phase was the inland penetration by the Huai-chün, the expulsion of the Taipings from key interior cities, and the establishment of Huai garrisons in vital areas. During this phase the requirements of the gentry leaders in refuge at Shanghai were met; their homes were restored to them and the local trade routes safeguarded. The final phase involved a further westward push, which forced Taiping armies into two major centers, Ch'ang-chou and Nanking, and resulted in conclusive victories and the end of large-scale organized resistance by the Taipings.

---

[100] *LWCK Letters,* 2:46b, TC 1/12/15. See also *Ibid.,* 1:46b, TC 1/7/19; p. 5a, TC 1/8/15; 2:26b, TC 1/10/6.

[101] *Ibid.,* 2:47a, TC 1/11/18.

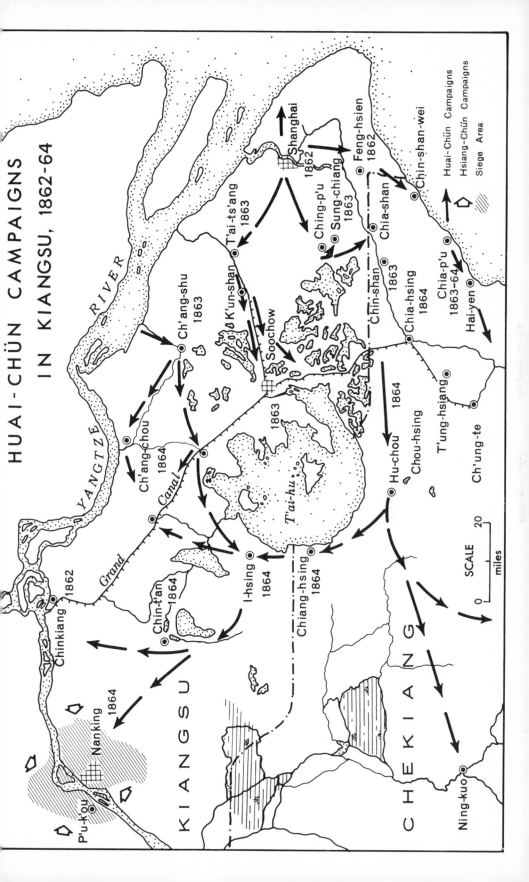

HUAI-CHÜN CAMPAIGNS
IN KIANGSU, 1862-64

Shanghai

Feng-hsien
1862

Chin-shan-wei

Ch'ing-p'u   Sung-chiang
1863

T'ai-ts'ang
1863   Chia-shan

Chia-hsing
1863

Chia-p'u
1863-64

Hai-yen

Huai-Chün Campaigns

Hsiang-Chün Campaigns

Siege Area

Ch'ang-shu
1863

K'un-shan

Soochow

1863

Chin-shan

Hu-chou
1864

Chou-hsing   T'ung-hsiang

Ch'ung-te

YANGTZE   Ch'ang-chou
1864

Grand   Canal

I-hsing
1864

Chiang-hsing
1864

RIVER

SCALE

0   20
miles

Chinkiang
1862

Chin-t'an
1864

K I A N G S U

C H E K I A N G

Nanking
1864

P'u-k'ou

Ning-kuo

During the first phase of the campaign in 1862, the British and French regulars and the Ever Victorious Army cleared the outskirts of Shanghai and occupied strategic neighboring localities. The troops of Liu Ming-ch'uan and Ch'eng Hsüeh-ch'i, with the assistance of the Ever Victorious Army, brought the Huai-chün its first victories by attacking and subduing the cities of Chin-shan, Chin-chan-wei, Feng-hsien, and Sung-chiang. Pao-shan was also occupied in strength. By the end of the year 1862, Shanghai was no longer in danger of attack, and government troops were well entrenched along the coast. The east was secure. Meanwhile, Li Hung-chang had dispatched strong reinforcements, consisting largely of Huai-yang water battalions, to Chinkiang, and by November, 1862, Taiping pressure on that city was eased. Even before this time, Tseng Kuo-ch'üan's Hsiang-chün troops had succeeded in reaching Yu-hua-t'ai, under the very walls of Nanking, and commenced the siege operations which were to be maintained without abatement until the final collapse of that city.

Although several of the cities taken by Ward's Ever Victorious Army had to be relinquished in the face of strong thrusts by Li Hsiu-ch'eng's Taiping forces in the summer of 1862, they were reoccupied by Li Hung-chang in the fall of 1863. At that time Li Hung-chang led Liu Ming-ch'uan and Ch'eng Hsüeh-ch'i in an offensive to retake Chia-t'ing, Ch'ing-p'u, and Sung-chiang. Despite Li's reluctance to permit regular British and French armies to carry on operations in the interior, he used the Ever Victorious Army, by then under the command of Gordon, to assist his forces in their advance north and west to T'ai-ts'ang, Fu-shan, Ch'ang-shu, and Chiang-yin. Striking southward during the last months of 1863 and the beginning of 1864, Huai-chün troops, battling without the assistance of the Ever Victorious Army, seized Cha-p'u, Hai-yen, and Chia-shan in northern Chekiang.

The provincial capital, Soochow, fell to Li in December, 1863, climaxing a year of hard campaigning. The collapse of the city came about partly as a result of treachery and incompetence in the Taiping military command. At the same time the Taiping leaders were faced by one of the mightiest armies ever assembled in Kiangsu and were subjected to the strongest assault they had encountered in the three years they had held Soochow. Several armies, including branches of the Hsiang-chün and the Ever Victorious Army, personally led by Gordon, and a powerful array of artillery were used to surround the city. The fall of Soochow provided the background for one of the most famous incidents in Li's career. It involved Colonel Gordon and therefore has been recorded widely in English writings.[102] At the time of the concerted attack upon Soochow, Gordon had privately arranged for the surrender of the Taiping leaders, guaranteeing in return their personal safety. While Gordon was engaged in restoring order to the city after the capitulation of the Taipings, Li Hung-chang secretly executed the Taiping leaders. Gordon was furious when he heard of this violation of his pledge, and partly because of this resigned his command not long afterwards. Li had to exercise all his newly acquired techniques of diplomacy and persuasion to induce Gordon to return.

The victory at Soochow made it possible for the provincial government to return to its official seat. Within a matter of days Wu-hsi also fell to the Huai-chün, bringing the Grand Canal south of the Yangtze under control and opening the route for an all-out attack on Ch'ang-chou. Now that the capital area was clear, the court ordered Li Hung-chang to establish himself at Soochow, the proper residence of the governor of Kiangsu. Such a move would demonstrate that order had been restored in the province and that the normal way of life and processes of government were being resumed. Li did not agree. He acknowledged the advantages and propriety of having his residence at Soochow but maintained that there were equally strong reasons for his retaining close personal control over Shanghai. He informed the court that as long as his army was chiefly dependent upon the financial resources of Shanghai, he could not afford to neglect that city. He mentioned that since he was developing a good corps of revenue collectors at Shanghai, including such men as Huang Fang, Ying Pao-shih, and Hsüeh Shu-t'ang, he felt the city would soon be in safe hands.[103]

Regional Administration Versus Central Government in Land-Tax Policy

The victories of the Huai-chün opened the way for Li Hung-chang and Tseng Kuo-fan to initiate a program of land tax reform in the newly recovered regions of Kiangsu. The success of this program was largely due to Feng Kuei-fen, who had originally proposed it and

---

[102] In addition to the various biographies which deal with the Kiangsu campaign, certain biographies of General Charles "Chinese" Gordon may profitably be consulted, for example, Samuel Mossman, *General Gordon's Private Diary of his Exploits in China* (London, 1885); and Bernard M. Allen, *Gordon in China* (London, 1933). Particularly important is Andrew Wilson, *The Ever Victorious Army* (London, 1868), which is based on primary materials from Chinese and British sources, and contains useful campaign maps.

[103] *LWCK Memorials,* 5:46a ff., TC 2/11/28.

worked it out in detail for Li Hung-chang. Feng had first proposed the
measure as a means of reducing tax evasions among the people. Stated
simply, Feng's original argument was that the people of Kiangsu were
using every available means to avoid tax payment. The more the
government asked, the less it received; consequently, the best thing for
all concerned would be to reduce the tax and so reduce the incidence
of evasion.[104] Undoubtedy a reduction in the land tax would have been
most beneficial for the landowners, particularly the larger ones. The
leaders of this group were the gentry, and Feng Kuei-fen, who had
served them so well in planning for their restoration in Soochow, was
now their spokesman in pressing for land tax reductions. Tseng Kuo-
fan was concerned lest the reductions should appear to be favorable to
the gentry and large landowners, and he warned Li Hung-chang that in
carrying out the reform he should deal with the various areas impar-
tially. He added: "Do not reduce both the grain tribute and the land
tax. Just proclaim a general reduction by one-third and one-tenth so
that the large families *(ta-hu)* and small families *(hsiao-hu)* will know
that they are receiving impartial reductions."[105] The reduction of the
existing land tax by one-third covered the area of Soochow—Sung-
chiang–T'ai-ts'ang, and the reduction of one-tenth covered the Ch'ang-
chou–Chinkiang area. In advising Li, Tseng informed him that the
Board of Revenue favored the measure but warned that the Soochow,
Sung-chiang, and T'ai-ts'ang gentry would request even further reductions, since "the appetite of Su-Sung-T'ai cannot be easily satisfied."[106]
These tax reductions in important areas of Kiangsu were encouraging
gestures to the leaders of the gentry resistance as well as to the
peasants.

Li Hung-chang's interest in the land tax was by no means comparable with his interest in the likin or the customs. The land tax collection was regulated by central government quotas and was intended
principally for Peking. A good deal of the intake was appropriated by
the local tax collectors and the local and regional officials, but such
appropriations were a form of extortion and not properly assigned to
the collecting officials. The land tax quota was often raised to offset a
decrease in the central government's actual receipts as a result of

---

[104] Feng Kuei-fen, *Hsien-chih-t'ang kao,* 5:7a-9b; see also 10a-13b, 14a-15a, 16a-
19b, for additional details on the procedures employed and on the systems of measure-
ment proposed.

[105] *TWCK Letters,* 23:26a. The term *ta-hu,* meaning literally "big families," generally refers to wealthy, powerful gentry families. The term *hsiao-hu,* meaning literally
"small families," generally refers to the less distinguished, "commoner" households.

[106] *Ibid.*

excessive "squeezing" by local collecting agencies. Correspondingly, a lowering of the land tax quota could be manipulated so as to give avaricious collectors more leeway in taking a larger cut of the taxes collected. Li Hung-chang was aware of this possibility and attempted to avoid it by widely proclaiming the new land tax reductions. In this way he hoped to prevent the land tax collectors from collecting the taxes at the old rate and merely sending on to Peking the lesser amount demanded by the new quota.[107]

Li and Tseng had no reason to object to the demands of the gentry for reduction of the land tax. The officials continued to deduct their regular salaries from the remittances before passing the balance on to the central government, which was, in fact, the only loser. For Li and Tseng, the reduction of the land tax was a helpful measure. The heavy burden of payment which rested on both peasants and gentry was lightened. This in itself assisted the officials in maintaining order and rehabilitating the population of war-devastated areas. It is even possible that by increasing the purchasing power of the agrarian population the land tax reduction stimulated trade and helped increase the likin tax receipts, which were paid by merchants and depended upon the volume of sales and transportation of goods.

The land tax reform program, which was suggested by the local gentry and carried out by Li and Tseng, was part of the conflict between regional officials and the central government. The likin exactions were a form of competition with the central government for revenues. When the likin was first instituted, the revenues were kept by the local and regional officials and rarely even reported upon. Later, as the government tried to regularize the new tax and take it for itself, the regional officials resisted and continued to regard it as primarily local income. So long as Li and Tseng could continue to draw likin revenues independently, they had no personal reasons for guarding the land tax interests of the central government beyond their normal obligation to assure regular delivery of the tax receipts. On the contrary, by advocating reductions in the land tax, they gained the support of the interested local gentry and tightened their control over their areas of jurisdiction.

Li Hung-chang had encountered little opposition to his measures to increase his likin revenues by levying taxes upon new items and estab-

---

[107] In one letter addressed to Li Hung-chang, Tseng Kuo-fan stated: "The yamen runners [local tax-collectors and official servants] cannot make tricks out of this change because the people themselves will be apprised of what has been proclaimed." *TWCK Letters,* 23:26b.

lishing new toll stations so long as Shanghai and the Su-Sung-T'ai area
were in imminent peril from the Taipings. Shanghai was largely popu-
lated by refugees from areas endangered by the Taipings, rich merchants and gentry who had wanted him and his army. They could
scarcely protest measures that supported Li and his troops. But when
Shanghai and their native lands were again secured, their stake in the
continuance of Li's campaign diminished. With fewer immediate gains
to be had and with increasing exactions being demanded, a chorus of
protest began to be heard from Shanghai. The merchants claimed that
their likin burden had become insupportable.

Li Hung-chang used their complaints to try to raise additional likin
revenues. He agreed that an excessive likin would crush the merchants,
and destroy the major source of his income,[108] but within a few months
he suggested an increase of 40 per cent in the likin on the north bank
of the Yangtze. This measure would be equitable, he claimed, because
the likin at Shanghai was by then the highest in all China, and the
proposed increase in the north would level it off.[109] Li knew, of course,
that such an increase would not help the Shanghai merchants. In a
letter to Tseng Kuo-fan he mentioned the protests of the Shanghai
merchants at the excessively heavy excises and his concern that the
British and French consuls were supporting the merchants' complaints.[110]

Although Li himself exploited the merchants as major providers of
revenue, he was quick to defend them against outside impositions.[111]
In early 1863 the Board of Revenue and the Ministry of Foreign Affairs
wished to levy a license tax on opium. The boards recommended that
the provinces of Kiangsu, Chekiang, Hupeh, and Kiangsi follow the
lead of Kwangtung, which collected for them a fifteen-liang tax and
a one-liang surtax on every hundred chin of opium sold or transported,
while retaining the likin and tribute imposts at their previous rate.[112]
Li objected to the proposal as a threat to his own finances. He replied
that he had taken the matter up with his assistants, the manager of
the general office of likin and tribute, Hsüeh Shu-t'ang, and the acting
customs intendant, Ying Pao-shih. These officials reported that they

---

[108] *LWCK Letters*, 4:30b, TC 2/12/7.

[109] *Ibid.*, 5:8a, TC 3/3/16.

[110] *Ibid.*, 5:13a-b, TC 3/4/7.

[111] Li's dependence on merchants is amply evident in his own words both in his
letters and memorials. See, for instance, his tribute to the merchants in *LWCK
Memorials*, 1:40a, TC 1/6/13; 3:28a, TC 2/4/7. His defense of merchants is found
in, for instance, *LWCK Letters*, 4:30b, TC 2/12/7; *LWCK Memorials*, 6:26a, TC
3/2/28.

[112] *Ibid.*

had conferred with the officials in the opium office, and they all were of the opinion that if a license tax were added to the existing tax burden, the merchants would try to evade their taxes. Li added:

In Shanghai each hundred chin of opium usually requires payment of twenty liang for likin, five liang for defense tribute, and certain amounts for local corps and relief respectively. All these taxes are paid by Chinese merchants after the importation of the opium. If one wishes to export opium, a payment of thirty liang for export tax is required for each hundred chin of opium thus re-exported. But this opium has already paid the thirty-liang import tax. This duty is already too heavy. Now we are supposed to add a sixteen-liang additional duty. As a result the merchants feel that the taxes are too heavy, and they find no profit in their business. They must either avoid entering their goods at our port or else have the foreigners sell their goods for them. Consequently, our income will be reduced rather than increased.[113]

It was Li's belief that the idea of the extra tax was introduced by Robert Hart, the English inspector-general of the Chinese Maritime Customs Service. Li spoke to Hart and was informed by him that when he (Hart) had suggested the tax he had understood that no other collections were to be made on the goods.[114] Li did not suggest that the likin or tribute taxes could or should be modified. These he regarded as the essential and primary imposts, for these went largely, if not completely, to him.

Extension of the Military Campaign—1864

After the capture of Soochow, only two important centers of Taiping strength remained in Kiangsu. The first was Nanking, already under siege by Tseng Kuo-ch'üan. The second was Ch'ang-chou, along the Grand Canal, northwest of Wu-hsi. In March, 1864, the combined forces of Kuo Sung-lin, a former Hsiang-chün commander, and Colonel Gordon, moved upon I-hsing and took that strategic city.[115] These forces then moved northward to join other elements of the Huai-chün in a concerted attack on Ch'ang-chou. Ch'ang-chou was taken in May, 1864, when the armies of Ch'eng Hsüeh-ch'i, Liu Ming-ch'uan, Chang Shu-sheng, Kuo Sung-lin, and Gordon, using howitzers and other artillery, bombarded and breached the city walls and attacked simultaneously through the north, south, east, and west gates of the city.[116]

---

[113] *Ibid.*
[114] *Ibid.*
[115] *TWCK Letters*, 24:9b.
[116] *LWCK Memorials*, 6:33a ff., TC 3/3/21; Li deployed his armies as follows: Ch'eng Hsüeh-ch'i's heavy artillery and Gordon's howitzers attacking the South gates,

Nanking was now the only major city in Kiangsu still held by the Taipings. In an endeavor to isolate the Taipings at Nanking, Li Hung-chang now deployed his forces westward and southward over the Chekiang border and sent Liu Ming-ch'uan's army to the southern end of Lake T'ai to capture the large Taiping garrison at Hu-chou in northern Chekiang.

At the same time Li Hung-chang ordered the Huai and Hsiang battalions of Kuo Sung-lin, P'an Ting-hsin, Liu Shih-ch'i, Wang Yung-sheng, and Yang Ting-hsün to surround and take Ch'ang-hsing with the assistance of the T'ai Lake Corps of Li Ch'ao-pin and elements of the Huai-yang water troops. On July 3, 1864, Ch'ang-hsing, one of the two remaining major strongholds of the Taipings in northern Chekiang, fell to the combined armies of Li Hung-chang.[117]

As the campaign in Kiangsu drew to its climax and the early fall of Nanking became almost a certainty, the calls upon Li Hung-chang for funds and military rations increased. Tseng Kuo-fan requested him to send 330,000 liang, which Li was supposed to be holding for the Ministry of Foreign Affairs, in addition to the 40,000 liang monthly payment that Tseng had ordered Li to provide during the previous year, 1863. He wrote Li expressing the hope that Li would continue sending the funds so that he could pass the next three critical months without the danger of mutinies.[118] As Tseng began to demobilize his war-weary Hunan armies, his financial situation became critical. In a letter to Li Hung-chang he complained of the failure of several of his sources to provide their expected income, and asked Li's help because of the inadequacies of his own revenues from salt.

As for the tribute collected in Shanghai, I know it is difficult to raise. But you are well aware of the shortages my camp suffers because of the bandit activities in Kiangsi. In the fourth month I only collected 20,000 from the Kiangsi likin . . . and since then the situation has worsened. The likin in Hunan and Kwangtung does not even come to 70 per cent of the expected total yet, and the salt offices in Kiangsu and Hupeh have not been able to find profitable outlets. As for the Anhwei likin, the same lack of outlets for salt has made it even less than the others.

In view of this situation, the likin and tribute from Soochow and Shanghai are my only reliable sources. You have merits and a strong army . . . and

---

Liu Ming-ch'uan's artillery attacking the North gates, Kuo Sung-lin attacking the West gates, and Chang Shu-sheng's army attacking the East gate. *LWCK Memorials,* 5:33a ff., TC 2/11/17; J. C. Cheng, "Some Aspects of the Taiping Rebellion in China, 1850-1864," p. 291.

[117] *LWCK Memorials,* 6:56a-58b, TC 3/5/17; 61a-64b, TC 3/5/30.

[118] *TWCK Letters,* 23:39a.

I do not mean to make your army thin and my army fat. But my situation is so desperate that I am compelled to appeal for your assistance. I have requested 80,000 per month from you. I hope you can fill this request in full.

You should not feel that the revenue belongs exclusively to the Kiangsu army.[119]

The regions in Anhwei and Kiangsu north of the Yangtze River and bordering the Huai River, commonly called Liang-Huai, were famous salt-producing areas. The salt tax income from Liang-Huai had been fixed at a quota of 200,000 liang per year in 1857. Since 1863 the salt likin had been increased, and together with the salt tax the total yield had doubled. Li's own figures showed that the income from the salt tax was something more than 10,000 liang per month, and the total yield from salt likin came to approximately 10,000 liang and 12,000 strings of cash each month. This sum was distributed and spent as follows:

Ten thousand liang to the army headquarters at Lin-huai, Anhwei; 10,000 liang to the North Kiangsu army depot, commanded by Wu T'ang; 7,000 to 10,000 liang to the headquarters of the Kua-chou water troops; 7,000 to 10,000 liang to the Chinkiang land force headquarters; 8,000 strings of cash to the various mentioned headquarters and other revenue offices, and to the gunboat crews.[120]

In later years the salt income on which Tseng's Hsiang-chün now relied so heavily was to become a major source of support for Li's own Huai-chün.[121]

In mid-1864 Li received repeated edicts from Peking directing him to send troops immediately to assist Tseng Kuo-ch'üan in the attack on Nanking. Li delayed, claiming that his armies must first capture and clear the area around Hu-chou, to eliminate the possibility of a major Taiping break-through, which might open the way for a strong attack on the flank of Tseng Kuo-ch'üan's besieging armies.[122] It is generally believed that Li avoided taking part in the final attack on Nanking because he feared such a move might be interpreted as an attempt to share in the glory of a victory for which Tseng Kuo-ch'üan had been battling alone since 1862.[123] The real reason was that Tseng Kuo-fan

---

[119] *Ibid.*, 24:1b.

[120] *LWCK Memorials,* 2:57a-58a, TC 1/12/7.

[121] Chou Shih-ch'eng, *Huai-chün p'ing-nien chi,* 11:18b.

[122] See, for example, *LWCK Memorials,* 6:67a ff., TC 3/5/30, and 7:1a-3b, TC 3/6/17. Other evidence will be presented subsequently.

[123] Hummel, *Eminent Chinese,* p. 465, states: "Tseng ordered Li to join forces with Tseng Kuo-ch'üan at Nanking, but fearing that jealousies might be aroused if he shared with Tseng the honor of taking Nanking (which fell on July 19, 1864), he refrained on the ground that his forces were needed elsewhere."

very pointedly discouraged Li from taking an active part at Nanking, and Tseng's position was determined by financial considerations.

As early as 1862 Tseng had discussed the question of whether the Ever Victorious Army, undoubtedly Li's most powerful division at that time, should be sent to the assistance of Tseng Kuo-ch'üan, who was then besieging Nanking. Tseng gave his opinion as follows:

As for the collaboration of Ward in the Nanking campaign, I think this is acceptable. But the rations of his army are many times higher than those of the Hsiang-chün, and this treatment will arouse the jealousy of the Hsiang-chün. I think we should first order them to attack Chia-t'ing and Ch'ing-p'u in order to let them experiment with their guns.[124]

Here, it is true, the question of having a foreign, or at least foreign-led army as far inland as Nanking was involved, and Tseng was notoriously against such a policy.[125] More important was Tseng's fear that to have highly paid soldiers serving side by side with Hsiang troops would destroy the morale of his own forces.

Later in the year, Tseng Kuo-ch'üan, whose siege of Nanking had taken a turn for the worse, had been forced to call upon Ch'eng Hsüeh-ch'i and other Huai troops for assistance. When he heard about this, Tseng Kuo-fan had dispatched a letter to Li saying:

If Ch'eng has not yet been sent, do not send him. If he has gone, please call him back after one or two battles. He must not stay long at Nanking. Chang Shu-sheng has recently enlisted five battalions, and I have ordered him to garrison Wuhu and not press further. After half a month you must recall Chang Shu-sheng to Shanghai, ordering him to travel along the northern bank of the river.[126]

This letter would seem most curious unless the circumstances surrounding it were fully understood. When Tseng Kuo-ch'üan had originally sought assistance, he was being besieged by troops of the Taiping general Li Hsiu-ch'eng, and thus had to fight with his back to the walls of Nanking. By one of the most magnificent feats of endurance in the war, Tseng Kuo-ch'üan had managed to survive the assault, and after forty-six days the attacking Taiping army had retreated, leaving Tseng free to resume his attack on Nanking. Once this immediate peril had passed, both Tsengs were reluctant to have outside aid.

---

124 *TWCK Letters,* 19:14b.
125 Tseng voiced his opinion on foreign participation in a letter: "To co-operate in guarding Shanghai is acceptable, but to permit co-operation in suppressing the bandits at Nanking, Soochow, and Chang-chou is impossible. These places are the heartland . . ." *TWCK Letters,* 18:18a.
126 *Ibid.,* 20:6b.

The fundamental consideration from the first had been the Hsiang-chün's dire need of funds; the looting of Nanking was one solution for the problem of paying troops. Tseng had stated to Li:

My brother repeatedly writes me to halt Ch'eng Hsüeh-ch'i, lest his movements hurt you. As for having Burgevine go [to Nanking], that is not my intention. It is you who initiated this move and he is willing to do it. We cannot stop it now. But before we accept this I have two conditions: (1) Since my brother was previously embarrassed in long trenches, the Ever Victorious Army should not go into the trenches. They can attack from the lower or upper river in a joint assault with my brother. (2) If Nanking is captured, the wealth and property of the city can never be plundered by Burgevine. After the fall of Nanking, the wealth should be preserved there. Half will go to the capital and half will be equally distributed among the troops. Burgevine's army can also enjoy a share, even a double share. If we do not state this clearly, then at the time of distribution Burgevine's army will quarrel with ours. We must have an agreement in advance on this point.[127]

Before Burgevine and Tseng reached the required agreement, Burgevine had quarreled with Yang Fang and been dismissed. When Li Hung-chang soon after appointed Gordon to command the Ever Victorious Army, the entire plan had been dropped.

The question of Huai-chün assistance at Nanking did not again arise until just before the final assault upon the city in July, 1864. Tseng needed the superior artillery and firing power of the Huai-chün, but feared the presence of large bodies of Li's troops. He wrote to Li in somewhat ambiguous terms:

I have received your letter saying that you will order your brother to aid in the assault at Nanking by the middle of the seventh month. I cannot fully express my gratitude. The emperor has asked that you send artillery to co-operate in the attack on Nanking and has also ordered you to go personally to Nanking. I also agree that you should come to Nanking. Do not wait until the middle of the seventh month but come early in the sixth month. Hung Hsiu-ch'üan [the Taiping "Heavenly King"] is stubborn and his forces are not yet exhausted. My brother has mined under the walls in more than ten places, but in vain. The use of mines and guns alone cannot be successful, but if we use your foreign cannon in addition to foreign guns, it should be possible. I have heard that the mines will be completed by the middle of the seventh month.

I will order my brother to wait patiently for you. The officers and soldiers well know that our brothers have been on intimate terms for years, and no one will suspect or fear you. But I have two fears. First, your army is rich and mine is comparatively poor. This comparison will reduce the morale of my troops. Second, your armies are in high spirits and more

---

[127] *Ibid.*, 20:34b.

arrogant after their repeated achievements. Even in times of peace, quarrels could arise between the two armies; how much more so at the time of the fall of the city when they will be tempted to quarrel over the spoils. I think you should discuss these points with my brother. When rations are distributed, I hope that they will be issued equally.[128]

Li Hung-chang apparently concluded that Tseng, although forced to comply nominally with the orders of the court, was not anxious to have the Huai-chün present in force under Li's personal command. Dispatching a force of artillerymen under the command of his younger brother, in accordance with Tseng's request, he himself refrained from participating in the assault. He ordered his major army, the Ming-chün (under Liu Ming-ch'uan), to remain around Hu-chou, although it could have easily moved northwest to Nanking. He also deployed his other forces in such a manner as to prevent an attack on Tseng from the rear. Thus Li permitted Tseng Kuo-fan and Tseng Kuo-ch'üan to solve the problem of paying their armies by leaving to them the lion's share of the plunder of Nanking.[129]

With northern Chekiang and western Kiangsu heavily guarded by Li's troops, Tseng finally forced open the gates of Nanking. Amidst great slaughter he brought the Taiping capital under control on July 19, 1864. Li Hung-chang immediately dispatched his various battalions to cut off the escape of any remnants of the great Taiping armies, while divisions of all his major forces converged upon Hu-chou. Shortly afterward, Liu Ming-ch'uan, Kuo Sung-lin, and others retook that city. Mopping-up operations were still required, but with the fall of Nanking and the collapse of strong resistance in northern Chekiang and western Kiangsu, the Taiping Rebellion was virtually at an end.

Li and the Huai-chün after the Fall of Nanking

The fall of Nanking seemed to increase rather than decrease Li Hung-chang's financial responsibilities. An immediate problem was the rehabilitation of Nanking itself. Tseng had described to Li the

---

[128] *Ibid.,* 24:4b.

[129] Hsiao I-shan, *Tseng Kuo-fan* (Shanghai and Nanking, 1946), p. 191, claims that the Huai-chün was partly responsible for the sack of Nanking. According to him, "When Nanking fell, the Huai-chün commanders seized the rice stores as spoils. Then Li Hung-chang bought this rice from the commanders with public funds. Therefore the Huai-chün commanders became rich." I have found no substantiation of this claim either in Hsiao I-shan's work or in other sources. The conduct described by Hsiao, however, conforms well with the behavior of the Huai commanders and of Li on other occasions. Nevertheless, the absence of most of Li's major commanders and armies from the scene makes it unlikely that Li's army could have taken any significant share of the booty at Nanking.

devastation of the former Taiping capital upon his triumphal entry on the twenty-fifth day of the sixth month:

. . . In the city the palaces of the bandits, their offices, and the civilian dwellings have been completely razed. The bodies of the dead have piled up like mountains. I do not know how we can even start the task of rehabilitation.[130]

As governor of Kiangsu, it was part of Li's work to assist Tseng in putting the capital of Liang-Chiang in order. Still paramount, too, was the problem of military rations. In addition to supporting his own troops, he had to find means of financing what was practically a wholesale demobilization of other large armies. Tseng Kuo-ch'üan had suggested that Li should obtain loans at Shanghai which would be used to provide demobilization funds for the Hsiang-chün. Li was unwilling to entertain this proposal because of the complications it would lead to and because the interest rate on loans in Shanghai was, in his opinion, exorbitant.[131]

Tseng Kuo-ch'üan had been able to demobilize some 10,000 of his soldiers immediately after the capture of Nanking, with the help of the Nanking loot, but Tseng Kuo-fan was contemplating even larger reductions in his own army. During the winter of 1864 and the spring of 1865, he hoped to demobilize between 40,000 and 50,000 men. But to do this he would have to pay them in full, and he admitted that large sums were owing to his men. Li Hung-chang had already offered to send Tseng 30 per cent of the likin income from Shanghai and Soochow, feeling that this could be spared, since some 800,000 liang had been raised by his own generals and assistants, Liu Ming-ch'uan, Ting Jih-ch'ang, P'an Ting-hsin, and Ch'ien Ting-ming. Tseng welcomed the suggestion but cautioned, "It is up to you what percentage can be spared. This tribute business must be brought to a successful conclusion. I hope you can help me because I need this tribute in order to pay my soldiers when they are disbanded."[132] If he could successfully demobilize his troops as planned, Tseng believed his remaining forces would be self-sufficient.[133] During the ensuing months Li provided Tseng with funds, but apparently never the amount he had promised and never enough to satisfy Tseng's needs.[134]

[130] *TWCK Letters,* 24 :9b.
[131] *LWCK Letters,* 5 :30b, TC 3/8/3.
[132] *TWCK Letters,* 24 :16b.
[133] *Ibid.*
[134] See, for instance, *TWCK Letters,* 24 :18b, 27b, 29b.

With southern Kiangsu fairly clear of disturbances, Li soon found
that officials in less fortunate areas, such as those where the Nien rebels
still held out, were looking to him for assistance. In a letter he appealed to Tseng Kuo-fan to intervene against such demands, accusing
the other officials of attempting to "squeeze" him officially and complaining that their "appetites were too great."[135] Now that the Taiping
Rebellion was over, pressure was also being put on him by the gentry
of Kiangsu to abolish or at least reduce the likin. Li insisted that unless the likin was maintained at its existing rate he would have to
demobilize his entire army.[136] He said that in 1863 his troops had been
paid only eight months' rations and in the following year had received
only half the rations due them. He described his army as "on the
borderline of starvation," and stated in a memorial to the throne that
he planned to disband his army, retaining only 30,000 men to man the
Western guns and artillery for coastal defense. But even this measure
was impossible since he was unable to pay off his troops.[137]

Li's statement to the court that he intended to demobilize the Huai-
chün was evidently a move in his struggle to hold revenues back from
the central government. However, little demobilization actually took
place. Rather, Li reorganized the army, numbering some 70,000 men
in all,[138] in preparation for new campaigns against the Nien. Table 3
shows the commands under which the forces were organized.

By 1865 the Huai-chün was composed of 104 battalions. Each
battalion was supposed to include 505 fighting men and 180 laborers.
With all battalions at full strength the Huai-chün would have numbered
52,520 fighting men, a figure confirmed by the *Huai-chün p'ing-nien chi*,
which states that the Huai-chün had "more than 50,000 men."[139] Counting the laborers assigned to the various battalions, the total number of
men whom Li commanded for military operations was about 71,200.
This confirms Li's report to the throne, which numbered his forces at
70,000 men.[140] Allied closely with these forces were various elements
of the Hsiang-chün. The most closely integrated of these was the Sung-

---

135 *LWCK Letters*, 6:5b, TC 4/2/14.

136 *Ibid.*, 6:27a-b, TC 4/5/17.

137 *LWCK Memorials*, 7:28a ff., TC 3/8/23. Hsiao I-shan, *Tseng Kuo-fan*, p. 191,
remarks on this point: "The Huai-chün commanders were always rich and the soldiers
were always poor. Only nine months' rations were paid to them each year."

138 Chou Shih-ch'eng, *Huai-chün p'ing-nien chi*, 11:3a.

139 *Ibid.*, 11:3b.

140 In TC 3/5/8, Li reported that although the Shanghai Customs income of the
previous month had dropped to only 70,000 *liang*, his troops at that time numbered
70,000 men. *LWCK Letters*, 5:16b, TC 3/5/8.

TABLE 3
HUAI-CHÜN COMPONENTS IN 1865

Name of Unit (if given)	Commanders	Number of Battalions	Type of Force (if indicated)
Ming-chün	Liu Ming-ch'uan	24	The combined armies of Liu Ming-ch'uan and Chou Sheng-po, and the detachment of Li Chao-ch'ing†
Sheng-chün	Chou Sheng-po	. . .	
Chung-po-ying	Li Chao-ch'ing	[4]*	
K'uei-tzu-ying	T'ang Ting-k'uei	3	*ch'in-ping* (guards)
Ting-tzu-ying	P'an Ting-hsin	10 1	. . . Water forces
. . .	Liu Ping-chang	12 1	Water and land forces *K'ai-hua-p'ao* platoon (cannoneers)
K'ai-tzu-ying	Wang Yung-sheng	10	. . .
Hsün-tzu-ying	Yang Ting-hsün	6	. . .
. . .	Huang Chung-yuan	2	*ch'in-ping*
Shu-tzu-ying	Chang Shu-shan	6	. . .
. . .	Chang Shu-sheng	1	*hu-chün* (guards)
Hua-tzu-ying	Wu Yü-fen	6	. . .
Sheng-tzu-ying	Wang K'e-sheng	2	. . .
. . .	Chang Chao-t'ang	6	*lu-chün* (land troops)
K'uei-tzu-ying	Ch'en Kuo-pang	2	. . .
. . .	Ts'ao Jen-mei	1	*hu-wei* (guards)
. . .	Lo Ying-kuang Liu Yu-lung	2	*p'ao-tui* (cannoneers)
. . .	Yü Tsai-p'ang	1	*p'ao-tui*
. . .	Yuan Chiu-kao	1	*p'ao-tui*
Chi-tzu-ying	Liu Shih-chi	7	. . .

TOTAL   104 *ying*, battalions

* The figure for the Chung-po-ying has been bracketed because it is part of the total of twenty-four battalions of the Ming-chün.

† Liu Ming-ch'uan and Chou Sheng-po were designated as *ts'ung-t'ung*, or commanders, of several detachments (or of an army, i.e., the Ming-chün, or Ming Army). See Chou Shih-ch'eng, *Huai-chün p'ing-nien chi*, 11:3a.

Li Chao-ch'ing, the younger brother of Li Hung-chang, served as a *t'ung-ling*, or detachment commander, within the Ming-chün, leading his own detachment of four *ying*, known as the Loyal and Plain Battalions. His biography, recorded in *CSK*, 433:5a, reveals that he first served under Tseng Kuo-fan and that when the Huai-chün was being organized, he established five battalions, recruited at Lu-chiang in Anhwei. In 1862 he followed Li Hung-chang to Shanghai, participating in the subsequent battles of Chia-hsing and Ch'ang-chou, among others. He later led units of the Huai-chün against the Nien.

Another younger brother of Li Hung-chang also played a prominent role in the Huai-chün. This

tzu-chün, commanded by the Hunan leader Kuo Sung-lin.[141] This Hunan army, which was now part of the regular Huai organization, comprised eight battalions, or some 4,000 men.[142]

The complex story of Li Hung-chang's effort to pay for an army of his own was summarized in his reports to the throne. Because of war conditions he followed Tseng Kuo-fan's practice of submitting abridged, or "realistic" accounts.[143] These reports ignored the categories for expenditures established by the Board of Revenue and did not comply with the government's requirement that expenditures be made only on the basis of budgets previously approved by the board. Li excused his deviations on the grounds that military expediency and extraordinary requirements rendered the traditional form of report obsolete. Behind this, however, lay the fact that by submitting only brief accounts, Li evaded close scrutiny of his accounts and could exercise greater independence in disposing of his funds.

Li's second formal report on income and expenditures was returned to the throne one year after the capture of the Taiping capital. It covered the period from the fall of Soochow to the fall of Nanking, or the middle of 1863 to the middle of 1864:[144]

Second Report, T'ung-chih 2/7 to 3/6

Received:

Balance on hand from first period	9,931	silver taels
	24,926	strings of copper coins
New income	4,124,596	silver taels
	20,000	strings of copper coins
Total assets	4,134,527	silver taels
	44,926	strings of copper coins
Paid out:	4,125,419	silver taels
	43,264	strings of copper coins

---

[141] Lo Erh-kang, *Hsiang-chün hsin-chih, chüan* 13; Chou Shih-ch'eng, *Huai-chün p'ing-nien chi, chüan* 11, *passim;* LWCK *Memorials,* 1:24a-28a, TC 1/5/27 provides a fair example of an early battle report by Li. In this report he mentions the role played by various commanders serving under him, including Kuo Sung-lin who had been assigned to him from the Hsiang-chün.

[142] Chou Shih-ch'eng, *Huai-chün p'ing-nien chi,* 11:9a.

[143] *LWCK Memorials,* 7:62a-b, TC 3/12/27.

[144] *Ibid.,* 9:12a-13a, TC 4/6/1.

---

was Li Ho-chang. In *CSK,* 433:4b-5a, it is said that Li Ho-chang followed Li Wen-an and Li Hung-chang in organizing local corps in the villages in Anhwei. For his conspicuous role in the taking of Anking in 1861 he was made a *hsien* magistrate and given a feather decoration. He followed Li Hung-chang to Shanghai in 1862, taking command of the *ch'in-ping,* or personal guard detachments, and participated in many important battles. He fought together with Ch'eng Hsüeh-ch'i in the early stages of the Kiangsu campaign, and co-operated with Liu Ming-ch'uan and Kuo Sung-lin in the later stages of the campaign. In 1865 he was ordered to serve in Kansu but retired on the grounds of illness. He died in 1880. *TWCK Memorials,* 22:45a-b, TC 4/5/13. Li Ho-chang's outstanding role in the organization of local gentry resistance in Ho-fei, Anhwei, was given recognition in an imperial edict issued in the ninth month, third year of Hsien-feng.

The report on expenditures for the Ever Victorious Army and certain other "foreign" items was made in a separate memorial to avoid confusion on the part of the Boards of War and Revenue, which were unaccustomed to coping with the kind of materials that appeared as items of expenditure. This report covered the expenses of the Ever Victorious Army from T'ung-chih 1/10 (1862) to T'ung-chih 3/4 (1864), as well as all other expenses on foreign items. These items were arranged under five categories: rations for local militia under foreign instructors; salaries for foreign instructors; expenses for the purchase of foreign steamships; expenses for the purchase of foreign munitions and weapons; expenses for the manufacture of Western-type munitions at Shanghai. The total of all such foreign expenditures for the entire period up to the fall of Nanking was 2,788,388 liang.[145]

The pattern of Li Hung-chang's development in the period from 1862 to 1865 is clear. Establishing Shanghai as his military base, he had quickly moved to bring under his own control the revenue offices of the city. Because the growth of trade had made customs and likin taxes important new sources of revenue, Li and his followers developed them thoroughly and made them the basis of support for the Huai-chün. In the past, Chinese armies had been supported principally by the return from agriculture. Li's reliance on customs and likin was typical of the new basis that regional leaders like Li and Tseng established for military survival. Trade was replacing agriculture as the primary source of available wealth. Equipped with Western weapons and trained by Western officers, both easily available at Shanghai, the Huai Army and its auxiliary, the Ever Victorious Army, within two years had brought all of Kiangsu under Li's control. As Li's forces recovered new areas, he widened his network of revenue collection and entrenched his bureaucratic machine more firmly in the region. Within the few years since the first Huai troops had disembarked in Shanghai, Li had grown to be one of the strongest governors, and his Huai-chün one of the most powerful armies, in China.

---

[145] *Ibid.,* 8:11a ff., TC 4/2/17.

IV. The Huai-chün
and the Nien Rebellion

THE fall of Nanking and the collapse of the Taiping movement left the government armies free to deal with other insurrections that had developed during fifteen years of bitter warfare and hardship. Dissident elements in Fukien province had joined forces with remnants of the great Taiping armies and resisted with some success the efforts of government forces to subdue them. In the north, mounted rebels were active around Honan; Moslem rebels were on the march in Kansu; but most serious at the moment was the activity of the Nien. The earliest activity of the Nien was a general resistance movement which spread among the mud-wall-protected villages in the Huai valley. With the influx of Taiping leaders and troops into Nien ranks in 1864, the Nien movement became stronger. Positional warfare, characteristic of the earlier stage when mud-walled villages were the basis of resistance, gave way to mobile warfare. Cavalry had been introduced into the Nien armies, and the Nien now struck swiftly at ever-widening areas, eluding government forces and swinging the war-wearied populace to their support.

Reduction of the Hsiang-chün

During the Taiping period government armies of various kinds, including the Hsiang and Huai forces, had been sent against the Nien. Li's own early experience had been in local fighting against them. The Nien had been no less a threat to the government and gentry than had the Taipings, and by 1864 and 1865 they were an even greater threat than before. The central government still needed the regional forces which had played the decisive role in crushing the Taipings, but it was also anxious to reassert its own political and military power. For twelve years the court had watched the growth of Tseng Kuo-fan's power, unable in self-interest to curtail it to any great extent. Now secure from the Taipings, the central government could worry whether it was equally secure from Tseng. Tseng was aware of the government's fears and extremely sensitive to pressures exerted upon him to reduce his strength.[1] In 1864, while the attack on Nanking was in progress, he wrote to Li:

Along the three thousand li of the Yangtze River almost every ship hoists my flag. Therefore the outsiders suspect that my power is excessive. They think that the likin of four provinces is concentrated in my hands, and that the military camps accept my orders.

The suspicions of these people are not entirely groundless, because daily we are growing too proud. But actually our paltry strength and shortage of revenue is not fully known. I plan after finishing everything to return my seal as governor-general to the throne. This does not mean, however, that I will keep aloof from everything. At that time I may need only some ten thousand men and confine myself to one route.[2]

It is idle to speculate on the basis of Tseng's own writings whether or not he was sincere in his protestations. Tseng was a consistently cautious man, and even had he entertained hopes of greater power for himself, it is unlikely that he would have confided them to Li. For his part, Li was anxious to assure Tseng of his support and to encourage him to remain firm for the time being. He answered Tseng's doubts in the following words:

I have learned that in view of recent troubles you have been exceedingly perturbed. Why should this be? You should never have asked to be relieved of your seals of imperial commissioner and governor-general. After the recovery of Nanking it would be in keeping with correct procedure for high officials if you should then offer your resignation. This would conform with the proper practice of retirement. To the ignorant outsider it may seem wrong to hold too great military powers and financial responsibilities, but the throne surely must comprehend the circumstances.[3]

Tseng felt increasingly uneasy in his power as the Taiping campaign came to its conclusion. Matters became even worse after the confessions of various captured Taiping leaders were received, for it was rumored that they had approached Tseng to request his co-operation.[4]

---

[1] See, for instance, *TWCK Letters,* 23:39a.

[2] *Ibid.,* 23:36b.

[3] *LWCK Letters,* 5:15a-b, TC 3/4/24; Cheng, J. C., "Some Aspects of the Taiping Rebellion in China, 1850-1864," pp. 293-94.

[4] Some credibility is lent to these suspicions by the fact that Tseng Kuo-fan edited and expurgated whole sections of the confession of the Chung Wang, Li Hsiu-ch'eng (subsequently published in English by the *North China Herald*), deleting some twelve thousand words for fear of offending the throne. Although approaches to Tseng by

Well-founded or not, such rumors could be used to great advantage by Tseng's enemies and rivals.

The brunt of the attacks upon Tseng was borne by his younger brother, Tseng Kuo-ch'üan. Scarcely had the smoke cleared from the battlegrounds of Nanking when voices arose maligning the younger Tseng. He had erred in reporting to the throne the death of Hung Fu, successor of Hung Hsiu-ch'üan to the Taiping throne. It was a simple case of mistaken identity, which had little importance in itself, since all the important Taiping leaders including the youthful Hung Fu were rounded up shortly afterward. But it seemed to give credence to the rumors that the Tsengs were not above making a deal with the Taipings and was sufficient to cause the impeachment of the victorious Hsiang-chün commander. Furthermore, the rampant looting of Nanking, which had been planned by the Tsengs as a means of paying their troops, had aroused ire and perhaps envy in high circles. Undoubtedly the prestige of the Tsengs was high enough to enable them to withstand such charges. Their valiant efforts on behalf of the dynasty gave them some immunity. Their personal armies, exhausted and depleted though they were, could not be lightly dismissed from mind. In addition, some of the most important commanders still in the field, such as Li Hung-chang, were personally devoted to Tseng Kuo-fan and capable of exerting considerable influence on behalf of the Tsengs. Nevertheless, in the face of criticism, Tseng Kuo-ch'üan requested permission to retire from office, and the court hastily consented.[5] The conqueror of Nanking was stripped of power at the moment of his triumph, and his armies were demobilized on a large scale.[6] Including men released from Tseng Kuo-fan's own escort forces, over sixty thousand men were released from the Hsiang-chün within the space of one year.[7]

---

the Taipings did not necessarily reflect on Tseng's own loyalty, he was anxious to avoid even the appearance of collusion between himself and his foe. The historian Hou Wai-lu considers it quite possible that the Kan Wang, Hung Jen-kan, entertained a scheme to compromise with Tseng Kuo-fan, and Hou condemns Tseng for this "reformist tendency." See Hou Wai-lu, "Hung Hsiu-ch'üan and Hung Jen-kan, Ideologists of the Taiping Rebellion," *Hsin Chien She*, April, 1952; reproduced in translation by Hu Chang-tu in the *Soviet Press Translations* (University of Washington), VII, No. 15 (1952), 329.

[5] *TWCK Letters*, 24:18b; Hummel, *Eminent Chinese*, p. 750. Tseng Kuo-ch'üan remained in retirement for two years, emerging in 1866 to accept the post of governor of Hupeh province.

[6] Immediately after the fall of Nanking, Tseng informed Li that the number of disbanded Hsiang troops totaled twenty thousand. (*TWCK Letters*, 24:18a.) Shortly afterward, he mentioned that an additional seven thousand men had been mustered out.

[7] *TWCK Letters*, 24:35a.

Outside pressure alone cannot account for the retreat of the Tsengs from power in the wake of victory. Had their forces been strong enough they might possibly have ignored criticism, but after thirteen years of fighting, the Hsiang-chün had reached its limit of strength. By 1864 it was on the decline.

The incidence of mutiny, which before the fall of Nanking had caused Tseng to demand funds from Li, increased after victory.[8] Immediately after the fall of Nanking, Tseng described to Li the ebbing morale of the Hsiang-chün forces and revealed that he was disarming some of his troops.[9] Serious uprisings were occurring among his men, and Tseng noted with consternation: "Even the officers co-operate with the soldiers in the mutinies. Nevertheless we cannot yield to the soldiers, for should we do so even once, the mutinies will become incessant."[10] It was therefore not only politic but necessary to reduce the Hsiang-chün, weeding out the undesirable battalions and bringing it down to a size at which its payroll could be met with some degree of certainty.

The retreat of Tseng Kuo-fan, through reduction of his military forces and the retirement of his brother, was not an abdication of his unique position as the leading provincial figure in China. He had prepared for this moment carefully and had already provided another means for maintaining the power he had heretofore derived principally through personal and family command of the Hsiang-chün. The new means was indirect control, and that control was to be exercised through Li Hung-chang.

The court had not dared to go so far as to deprive Tseng of his office when the Taipings fell. He remained posted at Nanking as governor-general of Liang-Chiang. Similarly, Li Hung-chang stayed on at Soochow, the capital of Kiangsu, as governor of the province. Both men still regarded Liang-Chiang as the most important region in China so far as military revenues were concerned. But the passing of the danger from the Taipings, which had brought about the rise of Tseng and Li as regional leaders, now made it more difficult for them to tax freely the resources of the region. When the rebellion was at its height, Li Hung-chang had contended with local officials, with other provincial leaders, and even with the central government itself for control over revenues. He had usually been able to count upon the support of the local mer-

---

[8] Ibid., 23:39a.
[9] Ibid., 24:27b.
[10] Ibid., 24:35a.

chants and gentry, who looked to him and his armies for protection, but when the emergency passed, both merchants and gentry sought relief from the heavy tax burden. In 1864 Li had subjected several new items to likin, but under the pressure of merchant and gentry complaints he removed the new excises and a few of the older ones in the following year. The continuing exodus of merchants from Shanghai, according to a memorial by Li, had at that time also reduced his general customs and likin income.[11] Because of this decline in income Li began to prepare for the demobilization of parts of the Huai-chün, planning to reduce its size by 10 per cent. But even this small reduction did not take place, for by this time Tseng Kuo-fan had convinced the court that the Huai-chün was indispensable if the Nien Rebellion was to be crushed.

Plans to Use the Huai-chün

As early as 1862 Tseng Kuo-fan had considered the particular fitness of the Huai soldiers for campaigning against the Nien. In advising Li on how to train his newly formed army, he had written:

During this first year you should always be in close contact with your officers. Endure hardships with them from morning until night. Instruct and train them so that the army of the Huai will become a strong force of good reputation. Such a reputation will induce the strong boys of Ho-fei to abandon their bandit life and come to you. And in the future we can rely on the Huai-chün as the main force to suppress the Nien bandits.[12]

Tseng's plans for the Huai-chün, it can be seen, took into account the tendency toward lawlessness among the people of Ho-fei, Anhwei. By recruiting the local population of Li Hung-chang's district into an army loyal to the government, he hoped to raise new troops and buy off potentially dangerous bandits at one stroke. The bandits who joined Li's forces would be loyal Huai-chün soldiers; those who did not were potential or actual Nien-fei.

The Huai-chün was to be more than an outlet for the unruly youth of Ho-fei; it was also intended as the means by which the lawless Nien in areas other than Ho-fei would be suppressed. Tseng considered the Huai-chün an indispensable adjunct to his own army, as he had revealed shortly after the capture of Nanking:

We should celebrate the granting of titles to us for merit in accomplishing

---

[11] *LWCK Memorials,* 8:5a ff., TC 4/1/29. See also *LWCK Letters,* 6:3a-b, TC 4/1/26; 28b, TC 4/5 int./27.

[12] *TWCK Letters,* 18:27a. See also Hummel, *Eminent Chinese,* pp. 632-34, for a concise account of Seng-ko-lin-ch'in's campaigns against the Nien.

the fall of Nanking.... You know that I created the new army of Huai volunteers in order to make up for the weakness of my Hsiang volunteers. I want it to compensate for many of my deficiencies.[13]

It was with this idea in mind that Tseng at that time had suggested to Li that units of the Huai-chün be deployed north of the Yangtze River to "pacify" the Huai valley. Such an action, he told Li, would simultaneously protect Li's native place in Anhwei and safeguard the border of Kiangsu, over which Li then ruled. Standing by his fundamental principles of military operation, Tseng pointed out that his own Hsiang Army could not be as effective in the Huai valley as Li's Huai volunteers.[14]

Perhaps Tseng Kuo-fan's most explicit statement on his plans for the Huai-chün after the suppression of the Taipings was the following:

In northern Anhwei the Hsiang Army has become but the end of a strong arrow. Their vitality has melted away, and they are not strong enough to deal with the Nien-fei. The future pacification of the Huai valley will depend on the Huai volunteers. It is a matter of record that I have had this plan in mind from the first. Military affairs are not yet over; we should preserve our morning freshness and shake off our evening fatigue. The Huai Army is at its zenith in morale, and it will never be disbanded. On the other hand, most of the Hsiang Army should be disbanded.[15]

Tseng proposed that Liu Ming-ch'uan's army, known as the most vigorous force in the Yangtze and Huai regions, should undertake the burden of the Nien campaign.

He should not decline. I have written a memorial to the throne on this matter yesterday. I do not think that the Huai Army should fear more service, for only thus will their actions suit their reputation. If you really love your army, you must keep them at work as does a father his son.[16]

Li Hung-chang, without himself moving from Soochow, ordered Liu to move northward with his forces. In addition to Liu's Ming-chün, he dispatched two other major forces, the armies of Chou Sheng-po and Chang Shu-shan, to counter the Nien.[17] Thus gradually the burden of suppressing the Nien Rebellion passed to the Huai-chün.

Liang-Chiang Remains Li's Revenue Base

The new responsibilities assumed by the Huai-chün gave Li the excuse, opportunity, and strength to hold out against new outside de-

---

[13] *TWCK Letters,* 24:12b.
[14] *Ibid.,* 24:9b.
[15] *Ibid.,* 24:16b.
[16] *Ibid.,* 24:22b.
[17] *Ibid.,* 24:29b.

mands for a share of the Kiangsu revenues. As in the past, he used the
dependence of the government upon his forces to strengthen his own
army and position at the expense of other officials. He declined an imperial order to provide funds for the troops of Tso Tsung-t'ang, then
fighting rebels in Fukien, on the grounds that the money was needed
for his own troops. He went on to suggest that the government order
Tso to follow his own practice of supplying his troops with only half
their pay during periods of difficulty.[18] In another instance, Yang
Yüeh-pin, governor-general of Shansi and Kansu, sent an emissary to
press Li for 30 per cent of his likin revenues. These funds were badly
needed for campaigns against the Moslem (Hui) rebels in the northwest. Li received Tseng Kuo-fan's support in refusing the request.[19]

Shanghai continued to be the most important source of Huai-chün
revenues, despite the fall of trade which Li had attributed to the return
of merchants to their prerebellion trade centers. He attempted to foster Shanghai's prosperity artificially by preventing the revival of competing trade areas. The restoration of peace in the Yangtze valley had
made it possible to reopen customhouses along the river. Li objected to
this, because ships destined for upriver ports would not be required to
pay full customs duties at Shanghai, and because the opening of additional customhouses threatened Li's likin income. In a memorial to the
throne, Li pointed out that many classes of goods that would be subject to customs excises at the new houses would thereby be exempt
from likin collections. Consequently, the revenue of the many likin
bureaus Li had established along the river would decline. The implica-
tion of all this was clear. If the central government expected Li to keep
his armies in the field against the Nien, the Huai-chün revenue sources
would have to be protected.[20] Since a good share of customs revenues,
in contrast with likin, was remitted to the central government, this
meant that Li was continuing to protect local, that is, likin, income
at the expense of the central government.

In the middle of 1865 Li informed the central government that the
customs revenue of Shanghai, which once had amounted to 200,000 to
300,000 liang per month, had dropped to little more than 100,000
monthly.[21] In an effort to hold the line, Li would have to continue his

18 *LWCK Memorials,* 8:5a ff., TC 4/1/29; see also *LWCK Letters,* 6:3a-b, TC
4/1/26; 28b, TC 4/5 int./27.
19 *TWCK Letters,* 24:29b.
20 *LWCK Memorials,* 8:23a, 26a, TC 4/4/14.
21 *Ibid.,* 8:43a ff., TC 4/5/6.

practice of holding back from other customhouses funds collected on their behalf at Shanghai. This applied particularly to the important silk taxes Li levied at Shanghai. Li defended his actions on the grounds that it was costing him over 500,000 liang per month to support the Huai Army and other troops for which he was responsible. At this time, he claimed, his monthly revenue, including money from the land tax and likin of Kiangsu province and Shanghai, did not amount to even 300,000 liang.[22] Li explained his acts of appropriation as desperate measures essential for the survival of the Huai-chün. Each new call upon the Huai-chün by the government made his case stronger.

Li's frequent complaints that his military expenditures far exceeded his income eventually raised questions in the minds of members of the Board of Revenue. In response to an inquiry in mid-1865, Li explained his system of "deficit financing." He informed the board that from the beginning he had called upon his soldiers to make "contributions." These "contributions" were raised by withholding a portion of the soldiers' rations and giving them instead certificates entitling the bearers to official titles. The soldiers did not themselves receive the titles, but sold the certificates to civilians and thus received compensation for the rations they had "contributed."[23] This, it may be remembered, was the same kind of manipulation for which Li Hung-chang had condemned Wu Hsü three years earlier. In commenting on his system of paying his troops, Li compared the Huai soldiers with those of Tseng Kuo-fan. He drew a distinction between the expectations of the Huai and Hsiang troops. The Hsiang troops from the beginning had always received their pay in full, and when they were not paid they mutinied. The Huai troops expected less, and therefore did not grow restive when they received less. Li went out of his way to emphasize that Tseng's Hsiang troops, despite increasingly frequent mutinies, were essentially loyal, a strong indication that Peking was already aware of the fact that the morale of Tseng's troops was ebbing.

Tseng Assumes Command Against the Nien

In May, 1865, Prince Seng-ko-lin-ch'in, the Manchu commander-in-chief of operations against the Nien, was killed in an ambush. His death, so far as the campaign was concerned, may have proved to be a blessing in disguise for the government. Prince Seng-ko-lin-ch'in had been in command of a campaign in which elements of the Hsiang-chün

[22] Ibid., 8:40a-42b, TC 4/5/6.
[23] Ibid., 8:27a-29a, TC 4/4/14.

and Huai-chün were supposed to co-operate, but he had been unable to control either of these regional armies. The Hsiang troops listened only to Tseng, and the Huai troops only to Li. It is doubtful whether either Hsiang or Huai commanders followed any decisive orders that were not first cleared through their own leaders. Furthermore, the main body of older provincial troops directly under Seng-ko-lin-ch'in were discredited and had inspired little confidence among co-operating forces. Finally, the Manchu commander had failed to develop an effective strategy and seemed to be leading his forces on a wild and pointless chase against the now highly mobile and elusive Nien.[24]

Once again the court called upon Tseng Kuo-fan to cope with rebellion. Tseng was ordered to put aside temporarily his duties as governor-general of Liang-Chiang and proceed immediately to Shantung province to assume over-all command of the embattled government armies. In appointing Tseng High Commissioner for Bandit Suppression, however, the court had overlooked the fact that the Hsiang-chün's star was on the wane.

Tseng delayed his trip northward in order to await the arrival at Nanking of the new acting governor-general of Liang-Chiang, Li Hung-chang. At the same time, contrary to regulations, he succeeded in obtaining the appointment of Li Han-chang as governor of Kiangsu. That the two Li brothers could share the two top posts in the same province was an unusual situation, underlining the urgency felt by both Tseng and the court. The reason for Tseng's delay would have surprised the court. Unwilling to trust his own Hsiang troops any longer, Tseng was counting on the arrival of three to four thousand Huai troops, which he had requested Li to bring with him as a personal guard for Tseng.

Tseng's earlier calculations now bore their full fruit. The imperial order calling him to the front had caught him on the verge of demobilizing virtually the entire Hsiang-chün. He planned to retain a limited force, partly because he could not raise sufficient funds to muster them out and partly because he needed some troops as a labor force for river works. Attempting to rally the remains of his once high-spirited army to their new assignment he discovered, "As soon as they heard of the imperial order for the northern expedition, they became so timid as to be unwilling to go. If we compel them to go, they will still be nothing but the tail of a strong arrow."[25]

---

[24] Siang-tseh Chiang, *The Nien Rebellion*, pp. 84-86.
[25] *TWCK Letters*, 24:30b.

The alternative to relying on the Hsiang-chün was to lay even further responsibility upon the newer and more vigorous Huai-chün. Yet, as Tseng put it, ". . . although your Huai armies [the Ming, Sheng, and Shu chün] belong to my family, I wonder whether, if they leave Kiangsu and go to Shantung, they will be harmonious with me in heart and character."[26]

Tseng's solution for the dilemma was in keeping with his whole approach to the problem of military organization. He suggested that Li Hung-chang's brothers, Li Chao-ch'ing and Li Ho-chang, accompany him, and urged Li to persuade his brothers to assist Tseng.[27] The years of guidance that Tseng had devoted to Li, the old relationship with Li's father, and his patient teaching of "sincerity" and "loyalty" were now put to the test. Li's position was pivotal for the success and future of Tseng Kuo-fan.

The direct connection between the Huai commanders and Tseng was to be the Li family. Their authority among the Huai troops was guaranteed by family right, and yet they would be amenable to Tseng's control. Tseng needed particularly the loyalty of the Ming-chün of Liu Ming-ch'uan, the Sheng-chün of Chou Sheng-po, and the Shu-chün of Chang Shu-shan, which he described as his "heart and stomach," his "city wall and spears."[28] He later paid perhaps unconscious tribute to his own success in planning when he described the path to victory in a couplet:

Without the Huai volunteers, the Nien rebels cannot be exterminated. Without the Li family, the Huai volunteers cannot be controlled.[29]

Tseng had his own plans and strategy, however, and did not want interference, even though he might be holding power, indeed his very command, only by remote control. He pointedly asked Li to keep aloof from military affairs as long as his armies remained under Tseng's command. In spite of Li's co-operation and the assistance of his brothers, Tseng was never able to control completely the Huai troops upon whom his power had come to rest. He had become a Huai-chün commander but was not himself a Huai man. No one knew better than Tseng that he was bound to fail, for the very basis of the military organization which he had created was personal ties with the troops based on common regional background. When the Huai-chün succeeded the

[26] Ibid.
[27] Ibid.
[28] Ibid., 24:31b.
[29] Ibid., 25:23a.

Hsiang-chün as Tseng's principal source of strength in 1865, Li Hung-chang had in effect succeeded Tseng Kuo-fan as China's principal regional leader.[30]

Li, the Provider

As acting governor-general of Liang-Chiang, Li's primary responsibility was to support with food, equipment, and funds the armies that Tseng Kuo-fan had taken over in Shantung province. The appointment of Li had been recommended by Tseng himself, for the aging commander was unwilling to see control of Liang-Chiang pass into less trustworthy hands.[31] Li jealously held on to his post in Liang-Chiang, refusing to leave Nanking, despite imperial orders directing him to move northward with his armies. Late in 1865, in declining a command that he direct campaigns around Lo-yang, Honan, Li outlined his ostensible reasons for refusing to move. His first reason was based on the regional character of the Huai-chün. Because of the special composition of his Huai-chün, which was mainly drawn from the region around Lu-chou in central Anhwei, it would be difficult to acclimate his army to the northern regions. Not only would the natives of the Huai valley find the climate intolerable, but differences in customs and diet would discourage the soldiers and lessen their effectiveness.

Second, although he realized the seriousness of the Nien incursions to the north and the dangers posed by the Moslem Rebellion in the northwest, he believed that to remove himself and the remainder of his army from Liang-Chiang would increase rather than decrease the burden on the other armies at the front. His army as a whole depended almost entirely on the financial sources of Kiangsu, and withdrawal from that province would weaken the provincial defenses and cut off the sustenance of his army—the Kiangsu revenues.[32] At the same time he would not get sufficient support from other provinces to make up the resulting deficit. Li gave as his third reason for declining the order the importance of maintaining and increasing the supply of foreign weapons for his army. This material was obtainable only at the coast, and Li's presence was essential for the assurance of a continuous supply.[33]

Like Tseng, Li distrusted other officials. As long as he remained at

---

[30] Lo Erh-kang, *Hsiang-chün hsin-chih, chüan* 13, section 2.

[31] *TWCK Memorials,* 25:21a ff., TC 5/11/2.

[32] *LWCK Letters,* 6:41b (to Ying Pao-shih), TC 4/8/22, aptly summarizes Li's evaluation of the benefits he derived from Kiangsu: "The foreign guns, the likin, and the tribute are the lifelines of my army."

[33] *LWCK Memorials,* 9:53a-57a, TC 4/10/8; *CSK, chüan* 411.

Nanking there was little likelihood that he would be supplanted as governor-general of Liang-Chiang. He was committed, moreover, to the support of Tseng's troops at the front as well as his own. A victory by Li and his forces over the rebels at Lo-yang might help his prestige and protect the central government, but it would not guarantee the revenues which only direct control of Liang-Chiang brought in.

Meanwhile, Li's unrelenting efforts to squeeze additional funds from the Liang-Chiang region brought him into open conflict with his erstwhile supporters, the gentry. Li's growing power and the extension of his jurisdiction throughout the Liang-Chiang region had made him less dependent upon the gentry of eastern Kiangsu. By 1865 his bureaucratic machine was well ensconced in the area, and he had brought into it many of the local leaders from Kiangsu. There remained no significant opposition to him within the local bureaucracy with whom his critics might safely conspire. It was no longer necessary for Li to cater to the gentry or to any other group. On the other hand, the gentry, now safe from the Taipings, no longer depended upon Li for restoration of their position and lands. The gentry noted with alarm that Li was no longer responsive to their calls. A clash between Li and the gentry seemed almost inevitable. When it came, it was at the instance of the gentry, and the point of contention, as might be expected, was Li's tax policies.

Immediately after the collapse of the Taipings in 1864, Li and Tseng had inaugurated a land tax reform which, while easing the burden of the gentry, did not greatly affect their own income. Finding himself unable to impose new exactions in the form of likin, Li determined to hold the line. The new calls upon the Huai-chün gave Li ample excuse to resist pressure for further tax relief, and he ignored the swelling chorus of complaints against his financial administration. When their protests to Li went unheeded, the gentry of Kiangsu used their influence at court to instigate charges against their oppressor. They may have hoped to discredit the entire likin system and so secure its eventual abolition, or perhaps they merely hoped to forestall any new levies Li may have been contemplating.

In the middle of 1865 Li was impeached in a memorial that besought the court to put him to death for corruption in administering the likin in Kiangsu province. The impeachers claimed that the yearly income from the Kiangsu likin amounted to forty million liang, more than enough for his needs but not enough for his insatiable desires. In his quest for more revenues, they charged, Li placed intolerable burdens upon the merchants by establishing likin collection stations every five to ten li (two to three miles approximately) along the roads of trade. Li was alleged to have levied imposts at 30 per cent of the total value of commodities and to have taxed shipments from Shanghai to Soochow as many as eight or nine times en route. They accused Li of placing no bounds upon potential revenue sources. According to them, tea shops, gambling houses, pastry stalls, barber stands, brothels, and night soil, all furnished their likin toll. Added to this, the incompetence and cruelty of Li's collectors made it obvious, they felt, that Li deserved harsh punishment.[34]

Sending on a copy of the charges, the court ordered Li to respond in detail to them and commanded him to reduce the likin in Kiangsu. Fortified by the wholehearted support of Tseng Kuo-fan, Li answered the charges against him.[35] Launching into a financial history of Kiangsu province since the beginning of the Taiping Rebellion, he explained why it had been necessary for the former governor, Hsüeh Huan, to establish the likin bureaus in Shanghai. The subsequent expansion of military forces in Kiangsu under Li had made the likin absolutely indispensable as a source of income:

Whenever I retook any place I established a new likin bureau. Each bureau is usually fifty to seventy li from the next.... At Shanghai we taxed at a rate of 3 or 4 per cent in accordance with the regulations, and not at 30 per cent as reported. Between Shanghai and Soochow cargoes were usually taxed three or five times, not eight or nine as reported.... The gentry have reported that I placed a tax on tea shops, gambling shops, pastries, barber stands, night soil, and prostitutes. Although I have instituted many different taxes, there are none on the above-mentioned items.[36]

Li attempted to disprove the statement that his likin income was 40,000,000 liang by pointing out that only in 1795 had the total annual revenue of the entire empire reached that figure, and that subsequently it had declined by some 30 or 40 per cent. If that were the case, how was it possible, he asked, for him to raise 40,000,000 a year from Kiangsu alone? Rather, in the two-year period between 1862 and 1864 he had collected a total likin income of 6,400,000 liang, only a small fraction of the amount alleged. But the fact that this income was six times more than that collected in either Kiangsi or Hupeh prov-

[34] *LWCK Memorials,* 9:1a-7a, TC 4/6/1.

[35] Tseng Kuo-fan advised Li, "Pay no attention; we are at the pinnacle of power and others are jealous. They will calumniate not only your brothers but the very spirits." *TWCK Letters,* 24:39a.

[36] *LWCK Memorials,* 9:3a-b, TC 4/6/1.

ince proved that his Kiangsu collectors were far from incompetent and inefficient. Having thus disposed of the charges, Li went on to explain the military commitments of his troops which justified his retention of the likin taxes at their existing level.[37]

The Soochow gentry also claimed that Li's tax collectors "squeezed" in exacting the land tax and grain tribute, principally through false measurements of land and illegal registration of households. To these allegations Li replied by describing what he claimed to be the actual practices followed by his subordinates and demonstrating that they were in accordance with the legal regulations.[38]

The question of how factual Li's reports were and how justified the complaints of the gentry cannot readily be answered. While a few of the most exaggerated charges, such as the collection of forty million a year in likin, are open to question, there can be little doubt that Li was not above engaging in the practices he disavowed. It is probably not without reason that a popular pun plays on words as follows:

> *Tsai-hsiang Ho-fei*
> *T'ien-hsia shou*

which may be translated literally as:

> The Prime Minister is entitled to be fattened,
> While the Empire goes lean.

but may also and with more point be rendered:

> If the Prime Minister is Ho-fei [Li Hung-chang of Ho-fei]
> The Empire will be lean.[39]

A Western observer, personally acquainted with Li Hung-chang, writing at the close of the century stated, with perhaps understandable enthusiasm:

Li Hung Chang is said to be the richest man in the world. . . . The foundations of his enormous wealth were laid during the Tai-ping rebellion, where by his shrewdness he obtained the glory for "Chinese" Gordon's victories. Since that time he has gradually widened his influence and increased his power in the empire, and has used his official power to add to his wealth; so much so that a popular Chinese proverb of the time runs: *"Every dog that barks for Li is fat."* The family owns hundreds of thousands of acres of land, numerous silk stores, and pawnshops all over the empire.[40]

---

[37] *Ibid.,* pp. 4a-7a.

[38] *Ibid.,* 9:8a-11a, TC 4/6/1.

[39] I am indebted to Dr. Hu Chang-tu for bringing this popular rhyme to my attention.

[40] J. Martin Miller, *China: Ancient and Modern* (Chicago, 1900), p. 321.

Whatever Li's private and official gains from his heavy taxes may have been, and however justified the complaints of the gentry, the real significance of their opposition to Li is that for the sake of his likin Li permitted the coalition, which had existed since 1862, to break down at last. With Kiangsu safe from rebels and bandits, and with the gentry returned to their homes, the gentry's enthusiasm for the man who had freed their territories had considerably diminished. The man who had given a military force and unity to the rallying local gentry now became for them just another powerful official who stood in the way of vested gentry interests and prerogatives and attempted to take the lion's share of the commercial revenue.

Li, secure in power, gradually assumed more and more the unsympathetic attitude of an official intent on exploiting his territory to the utmost. Kiangsu and all of Liang-Chiang were officially his, and he could maintain tight control through the presence of part of his army within the regional borders. He was openly acknowledged as the favorite of Tseng Kuo-fan, a prestige factor not to be overlooked. His men infested the local bureauracy and owed their allegiance to him alone. In the four and a half years that had elapsed since his entry into Kiangsu, he had discovered new opportunities to increase his power and new groups to depend upon. He held what amounted to a monopoly in both the production and acquisition of foreign arms. The customs were under his control. Indeed, all the facilities the West offered at Shanghai seem to have passed into Li's hands. If the gentry who had moved back to Soochow from Shanghai with the collapse of the Taipings no longer supported him, the rich and rising coastal merchants and shippers were still dependent upon him and could be drawn upon for services and revenues.[41] Thus Li could afford to ignore the enmity of one particular gentry group and pursue a policy of enriching his own armies at the expense of the Liang-Chiang region.

The arrangement between Li and Tseng, whereby Tseng led the Hsiang and Huai armies at the front while Li held the Liang-Chiang base as a source of income, benefited both men. One of Li's first tasks as governor-general had been to straighten out the accounts of the Hsiang-chün. Despite Tseng's efforts to reduce expenses by demobilizing his troops, he had been forced to turn over to Li responsibility for

---

[41] See, for instance, Li Hung-chang's memorial recommending tax exemptions for shippers of tribute rice; *LWCK Memorials,* 9:67a-68a, TC 4/12/3. Also see his recommendations for rewarding tea merchants, *ibid.,* 10:21a-b, TC 5/3/9, and his memorial requesting a monopoly for bean-shippers, at Shanghai, *ibid.,* 7:36a ff., TC 3/9/10.

meeting a deficit of some three million liang, which Tseng owed to his troops as back pay. Li eventually succeeded in meeting this deficit.[42] While Li was governor-general of Liang-Chiang, he had allotted two-thirds of the total income from the Kiangsu customs and likin, as well as the salt tax from Huai-nan, to the Huai armies engaged in suppressing the Nien. On one occasion, when the Board of Revenue demanded that part of the salt tax be sent to the capital, Li Hung-chang responded by demanding immediate approval for an increase in the likin and taxes of Kiangsu.[43]

Li and Tseng operated on the basis of an agreed division of funds. Upon leaving for the front, Tseng had enjoined Li to observe it faithfully. The income from the salt trade, the likin, and the tribute from the region north of the Yangtze River, or Chiang-pei, was to be placed directly at the disposal of Tseng, who agreed to use part of this income to pay the Huai-chün troops serving directly under him. The income from the rest of Liang-Chiang was assigned to Li Hung-chang.[44] This was no great change for Li. His hold upon the Chiang-pei, or northern Kiangsu, income had always been tenuous at best, and he had always relied much more heavily on Kiangnan, with its wealthy centers of Shanghai, Soochow, and Chinkiang. Now, for the first time, he had authority to manage the revenues of the entire Liang-Chiang viceroyalty, and this enabled him to extend his control over the regional bureaucracy and tie the fiscal administration of the region more closely to his own needs.

Li Assumes Command against the Nien

Tseng Kuo-fan remained in command of the Nien campaign for eighteen months. When no victory appeared imminent, an impatient court queried Tseng on his delay in bringing the struggle to a successful conclusion. The aged commander was unable to provide a satisfactory answer. It was difficult to explain that his basic strategy by its very nature could only yield gradual results. Nor could he reveal that he was hampered by his lack of adequate control over the Huai-chün,

---

[42] Chou Shih-ch'eng, *Huai-chün p'ing-nien chi,* 11:18b.

[43] *Ibid.; LWCK Memorials,* 10:18a-19a, TC 5/3/9.

[44] In urging Li Hung-chang to carry out faithfully the financial responsibilities thus assigned to him, Tseng remarked, "If you manage well the two likin offices in southern Anhwei and along the Yangtze River, I think your income will be increased and plentiful for the payment of the soldiers. From now on the soldiers will be grateful for your merit in paying them in full, and if they complain of former shortages they will not lay the blame upon you. You will be their benefactor and I will be the target of their complaints. . . ." *TWCK Letters,* 24:34a.

which had become the nucleus of his combined force. Instead, on the pretext of illness he offered to resign his command. In December, 1866, Tseng was ordered to Peking for an audience, and Li Hung-chang was designated to succeed to his command.

The appointment of Li as Commissioner for Bandit Suppression was the result of Tseng's recommendation to the court. Tseng informed Li of this action in a letter, in which he expressed considerable misgivings over withdrawing Li from the Liang-Chiang region. He feared that in the absence of Li, the Liang-Chiang revenues would fail to reach the troops in the north and that as a result both the Huai-chün and the Hsiang-chün would "immediately starve."[45]

Li himself was not unwilling to go north, and proposed that Tseng return to his old post at Nanking, as governor-general of Liang-Chiang, so as to assure the continued support of the armies in the field. Tseng, however, was not a man easily moved, particularly when a question of "face" was involved. He instructed Li to appoint either his brother or his follower Ting Jih-chang as governor of Kiangsu and to memorialize the throne to reserve the salt income and likin exclusively for the Huai-chün. He wrote:

You must entrust foreign negotiations, administration, and salt affairs to a reliable man . . . . But despite your concern over these affairs, after you leave, because of my sickness and the widespread jealousy of me I can never replace you as governor-general of Liang-Chiang. I hope you will understand . . . .[46]

Li apparently read between the lines, for he immediately memorialized the throne, requesting that Tseng be ordered back to Nanking to assure his troops a steady and full income. He pointed out that although he had always paid the Hsiang-chün troops their twelve months' rations, he had only paid the Huai-chün troops for nine months of the year, since they were a smaller force. Because of their personal attachment to him, the Huai-chün troops did not revolt despite their short rations, but he warned that if their income were further jeopardized, he could not predict the consequences. For this reason, Li argued, Tseng should once more take over the administration of the rich Liang-Chiang region.[47]

Tseng did what he could to save his pride before his former subordinate when the court accepted Li's recommendation. Embarrassed, he wrote to Li:

45 *TWCK Letters*, 25:37b.
46 *Ibid.*, 25:40a.
47 *LWCK Memorials*, 11:6a-7a, TC 6/1/19.

People will laugh at me. When the emperor wanted me to continue at the front as Imperial Commissioner, I became ill. Now that I have been appointed governor-general of Liang-Chiang, I become well again. But you thoroughly understand the situation.... Although I have accepted the seal of office, I do not intend to hold the post more than three months. After that I hope never again to occupy a high office.[48]

His protestations notwithstanding, Tseng returned to Nanking, and except for a year's absence while he served as governor-general of Chihli, remained there for the rest of his days. By permitting himself to be pushed back to his old post he avoided an appearance of ambition, and by his actions he seemed to deny that he had a vital stake in Liang-Chiang and its revenues and that he was a partner with Li in the maintenance of the Hsiang-Huai armies.

The actual exchange of posts between Li and Tseng took place at Hsü-chou, Kiangsu. There, fresh from his field experience, Tseng briefed Li on strategy and armaments, while Li brought him up to date on the financial situation in Liang-Chiang and thus assured once more a smooth turnover of office.[49] As a result, policy and administration in Liang-Chiang were carried on as in the past, and the armies in the north continued to receive their supplies and funds without delay or interruption.

In making way for Tseng to reassume his former post as governor-general of Liang-Chiang, Li moved into a new regional office. Shortly after his appointment as Commissioner for Bandit Suppression he took over the post of governor-general of Hu-Kuang (Hunan and Hupeh). But Li did not go to Wu-ch'ang, his new regional capital. Rather he proceeded north to take over personal command of the Huai and Hsiang armies.

The force Li headed in 1867 had changed in some respects from what it had been during the Taiping Rebellion. New elements had been added by Tseng Kuo-fan when he first moved north to Shantung. At that time he had stopped at Hsü-chou, in northern Kiangsu, and, apparently with Li's assent, had strengthened his Huai-chün guard with new recruits. The Hsü-chou soldiers were taken into both infantry and cavalry. Describing them to Li, Tseng wrote:

The tradition of vigor at Hsü-chou is like that of Ho-fei. If we convert that arrogance into loyalty, I believe that the Hsü-chou volunteers will increase the strength of the Huai-chün. It will be like adding more waves

---

[48] *TWCK Letters,* 26:3b.
[49] *Ibid.,* 26:3a.

to the sea and adding more branches to the trunk. Your Huai-chün will be like a large tree with plentiful leaves and branches.[50]

At Hsü-chou the "arrogance" Tseng noted was apparently nothing short of banditry, which at that time was often the first step to rebellion. If Hsü-chou were like Ho-fei, Tseng hoped that the Huai-chün would offer sufficient attractions to lure its young men to the government side.

The selection of Hsü-chou as a source for new volunteers was determined by other considerations as well. Like Ho-fei, Hsü-chou was an area where rice and noodles were of about the same importance as staples of consumption. The great division between the rice-producing and the wheat- or kaoliang-producing areas in China results in entirely different dietary habits in north and south. The farther north one moves, the greater the dependence on noodles and other wheat products. For the Chinese of one area, a shift to the other means some discomfort, if not hardship, in meeting dietary requirements. Individuals moving from region to region can make the shift gradually, and can usually find some rice or noodles in any area. But for an army the problem is different. Food must be shipped and prepared in quantity. An army in the north cannot be fed in the same manner as an army in the south. When the southern armies from Hunan moved northward, hundreds of thousands of catties of rice had to be shipped for them. Even so, their needs could not be met. The problem was not so much one of health as of morale. Tseng Kuo-fan had been keenly aware of this problem in moving his troops to various areas. Indeed, he had admitted that the problem of finding enough rice for his troops prevented him from moving the Hsiang-chün into northern regions for extended periods.[51] This had seriously hampered him in extending the Hsiang-chün's sphere of influence.

Li Hung-chang was more fortunate than Tseng in the food habits of his army. Lu-chou, the prefecture in Anhwei from which the major part of his army was drawn, is a borderline area. Although its people are principally rice-eaters and prefer rice, they are able to subsist without too much difficulty on wheat noodles.[52] North of Ho-fei there

---

[50] *Ibid.*, 24:31b.

[51] *Ibid.*, 24:40a. Tseng also recommended that Li supply the Huai-chün with one meal of rice and one of noodles daily. This reduced the Huan-chün rice requirements by 50 per cent. Tseng did not favor a complete noodle diet for the Huai-chün. Thus his suggestion is in perfect accordance with the observation of Dr. Wu (see note 52).

[52] This fact was particularly brought to my attention by Dr. Wu, of the Department of Animal Husbandry, Oregon State College, Corvallis. Dr. Wu is himself a native of Ho-fei and a specialist in problems of agriculture and husbandry.

is an increasing dependence upon wheat foods. This made the Huai-chün more mobile than the Hsiang-chün and made it possible for Li's armies to be stationed in the north for considerable lengths of time. In expanding the Huai-chün through additional recruiting at Hsü-chou, which borders both Shantung, a wheat-consuming area, and Anhwei, where consumption is mixed, Tseng and Li brought into the Huai-chün another more easily adaptable group of soldiers. Thus the Huai-chün was not subject to one of the major limitations on the movement of regional armies into new territories for long-term occupation. This made it easier for the Huai-chün to serve comfortably in the north and simplified the problems of logistics. It also made possible the successful prosecution of the war against the Nien and opened the way for the later stationing of part of the Huai-chün in Chihli and its environs.

Development of Cavalry Organization

Li and Tseng also adapted the Huai-chün to campaigning in the north, particularly against the mounted Nien rebels, by adding cavalry units. The organization of the cavalry closely resembled that of the foot battalions. Each battalion, or *ying*, was commanded by a battalion commander, or *ying-kuan*. The *ying-kuan* had at his disposal one *pang-pan*, or manager, as well as a *tzu-shih*, one who could read characters. This last was apparently necessary because of the intricate bookkeeping involved in supporting cavalry battalions.

The cavalry battalion was divided into five companies, designated as the forward company, the rear company, the right company, the left company, and the middle company. This seems to contrast with the foot battalions which had four regular companies, but the difference actually is not great when the personal guard or *ch'in-ping* of the foot-battalion commander is taken into account. The principal distinction appears to be one of nomenclature, for the *ch'in-ping* may be considered as equivalent to the middle company of the cavalry battalion.

The middle company was commanded directly by the cavalry battalion commander and his two special assistant company commanders, while the forward, rear, right, and left companies were each commanded by one regular company commander, or *cheng shao-kuan*, and one assistant company commander, or *fu shao-kuan*.

Each company comprised 50 mounted soldiers and 5 *p'eng* of foot soldiers, or *hsi-yung*. Each *p'eng* consisted of 10 foot soldiers, of whom 9 were privates *(hsi-yung)* and 1 a sergeant, or *shih-chang*.

The total number of soldiers in a battalion, including the battalion commander, 4 company commanders, 6 assistant company commanders, 250 mounted soldiers, 25 sergeants, and 225 foot soldiers, was 511 officers and men.

Servants and porters, or *chang-fu,* including cooks were assigned to the officers and to each *p'eng* of soldiers, a total of 81 in each battalion. Thus each battalion of cavalry consisted of 592 men,[53] almost 100 men more than the foot battalions of the Huai-chün.

Horses were assigned as follows within each battalion: The battalion commander was entitled to 4; the manager to 1; the *tzu-shih* to 1; the regular and assistant company commanders to 2 each; the sergeants and cavalry men to 1 each. This made a total of 276 horses for each battalion. Each battalion was allowed to report (for replacement) 36 horses dead out of every 100 horses in the battalion. However, the general practice in the event of a high number of casualties among horses was to reimburse the battalion in cash rather than in horses.[54] This system afforded opportunity for graft, yet the difficulty of procuring mounts through central government agencies allowed no alternative.[55]

In addition to adding cavalry units, Li and Tseng strengthened the Huai-chün by continuing to modernize old battalions and raise new battalions, which were furnished with Western-style arms. A few examples will give some idea of the changes that took place within the Huai-chün during the Nien campaign.

In 1865, even before Tseng or Li had personally taken command of the campaign, the armies of Yang Ting-hsün were augmented by 8 battalions of soldiers, or approximately 4,000 men, using foreign small arms. Although Yang himself and, presumably, many of his troops were from Szechwan province, he was a long-time follower of Li and was considered a principal Huai-chün commander. The foreign weapons he received came from Li Hung-chang, who made a continual effort to modernize the equipment of his forces.[56] In the same year

---

[53] Chou Shih-ch'eng, *Huai-chün p'ing-nien chi,* 11:2b-3a.

[54] *Ibid.*

[55] I have found no evidence of attacks upon the Huai-chün commanders or Li Hung-chang for fraudulent practices relating to cavalry management. This is somewhat surprising as attacks were leveled upon virtually every other aspect of his military and financial management, and the opportunities for receiving cash reimbursements for lost horses were so frequent. It is possible that the various commanders and the central government had an understanding that the loss of thirty-six out of one hundred horses would not be questioned but that no allowance would be considered beyond that.

[56] Chou Shih-ch'eng, *Huai-chün p'ing-nien chi,* 11:5a, 3a.

Wang Yung-sheng, another Huai commander, increased his force from 10 to 11 battalions, the exact type being unspecified.[57] Shortly afterward, 6 new battalions of troops, totaling some 3,000 men, were raised and put under the command of the Anhwei soldier Wu Ch'ang-ch'ing.[58]

In the following year, 1866, further additions to the Huai-chün were made. Chang Shao-t'ang, who already commanded 6 battalions of foot soldiers, formed 2 or 3 battalions of cavalry, a total of 1,200 to 1,800 men.[59] At the same time Wang Yung-sheng used some of his new recruits to create his own cavalry detachments. At Hsü-chou, the Ho-fei brigade commander, Tung Li-kao, created 7 battalions of mounted and unmounted soldiers, adding another 3,000 to 4,000 men to the swelling Huai-chün ranks. Later, Li Hung-chang's brother, Li Chao-ch'ing, recruited and trained additional men, whom he attached to his former 4 battalions, making a total of 12 battalions, known as the Wu-I-chün (Resolute Army). Subsequently this force was increased to 19 battalions, comprising some 9,500 men.[60]

Changes in the Huai-chün continued in 1867. At the time, when Chang Shu-sheng inherited the command of the Shu-tzu-ying from his recently deceased brother, Chang Shu-shan, 2 battalions of cavalry were added to that army. Likewise, Liu Ming-ch'uan had begun to add cavalry platoons to various battalions in the Ming-chün.[61] Also, during the same year, several battalions of Hsiang-chün forces serving under Li Hung-chang's command were reorganized as a cavalry division.[62] Li's brother, Li Chao-ch'ing, also converted 7 of his battalions into cavalry units.

The total mounted force of the Huai-chün at the conclusion of the Nien campaign has been estimated at 28 or 29 battalions, or roughly between 16,800 and 17,400 men, possessing at maximum strength some 7,000 horses.[63] Although the cavalry performed notable, even decisive, service in tracking down the Nien and other mounted rebels, its usefulness diminished with the closing of the campaign. Since Li now intended to use the army mainly in his own regions where cavalry was less effective, the expense of these units was no longer justified. Almost immediately after the conclusion of the Nien campaign in 1868,

---

[57] *Ibid.*, 11:5b.
[58] *Ibid.*
[59] *Ibid.*, 11:6a.
[60] *Ibid.*
[61] *Ibid.*, 11:6b-7a.
[62] *Ibid.*, 11:10a.
[63] *Ibid.*

Li Hung-chang sharply reduced the number and size of his mounted units. The Wu-I-chün eliminated its 7 cavalry battalions entirely; the Ming-chün abolished 1 battalion; the Sheng-chün 2 battalions; the Jen-chün 3; the Hsün-chün 3. Other similar reductions took place during the course of the year, leaving at the end only 3 cavalry battalions of Li's personal guard and 4 battalions under Liu Ming-ch'uan.[64]

At the close of the Taiping Rebellion, the Huai-chün had numbered some 70,000 officers and men. After several moves toward reduction in 1864, the army was again increased to meet the needs of the Nien campaign. Under the successive commands of Tseng Kuo-fan and Li Hung-chang some 16,000 to 17,000 cavalrymen and at least 15,000 infantrymen had been added to the Huai-chün.[65] Taking into account earlier reductions in force and the fact that some of the new troops may only have been replacements, it is probable that the Huai-chün force under Li in the Nien campaign numbered not less than 82,000 men.

Tseng, the Provider

This huge force was supported, as we have seen, principally on the revenues of Liang-Chiang, which were administered throughout the period by either Tseng or Li as they alternated with each other in the posts of governor-general of Liang-Chiang and commander of the troops at the front. While Li was at the front and Tseng was supplying the troops, a clearly specified arrangement for the support of Li's troops was observed. Tseng established four principal offices for the collection of revenues needed by the Huai-chün: (1) the Shan-nei (within Shantung) office, situated at Ch'i-chou, Anhwei; (2) the Chiang-wai (outside Kiangsu) office, situated at Anking, Anhwei; (3) the Chin-ling (or Nanking) office, at the capital of Liang-Chiang; and (4) the Hsing-ying (mobile battalions) office, apparently a field quarter-master's headquarters. To each of these headquarters specific sources of revenues were assigned as indicated in Table 4. Although the figures given are sketchy and incomplete, it has been estimated that the total income derived from the sources shown in the table came to approximately 5,000,000 liang each year.[66]

---

[64] *Ibid.*, 11:10b.

[65] The foot-soldier figure is derived as follows: Yang Ting-hsün's new small-arms battalions, 11; Wang Yung-sheng, 1; Wu Ch'ang-ch'ing, 6; Tung Li-kao, probably 4 or 5; Li Kao-ch'ing, 8; also unspecified additions to their forces by Liu Ming-ch'uan, Chou Sheng-po, Chang Shu-sheng and additional Hsü-chou recruits. Allowing for some overlapping, we reach a total of more than 30 battalions, or 15,000 men. These figures do not include cavalry units.

[66] Chou Shih-ch'eng, *Huai-chün p'ing-nien chi,* 11:18b.

TABLE 4
Revenue Sources for the Suppression of the Nien

Office	Source of Revenue	Amount
Shan-nei Office	Jao-chou, Ching-te-chen	20,000 strings of cash per month
	Anhwei tea license tribute and likin	20,000 liang per month
	Southern Anhwei branch, opium	No record
	Southern Anhwei land tax	No record
Chiang-wai Office	Hupeh salt likin	736,000 liang per year
	Kiangsi salt likin	647,000 liang per year
	Anking customs bureau	No record
	Ta-t'ung *chao-shang-chü* salt likin	448,100 liang per year
Chin-ling Office	Hsia-kuan salt likin, customs bureau	4,700 liang, 30,000 strings of cash
	Ta-sheng-kuan salt likin, customs	No record
	Chin-ling rehabilitation tribute	200,000 liang per year
	Hunan salt likin	Of the 680,000 liang per year income, 30% to 40%, or between 204,000 and 272,000, was given
	Shanghai contributions	33,800 liang per month, or 405,600 per year
Hsing-ying Office	Chiang-pei likin	16,000 liang per month 36,000 strings of cash
	Liang-Huai transportation office levies, Huai-nan salt tax, etc.	300,000 liang per year
	Huai-pei salt tax and salt likin	232,000 liang per year
	Wu-ho and Cheng-yang salt likin	400,000 strings of cash
	Chihli and Honan	No record
	Shantung subsidy	50,000 liang per month
	Shanghai Foreign Customs subsidy	No record
	Liu-an opium likin bureau	No record

Source: Chou Shih-ch'eng, *Huai-chün p'ing-nien chi,* 11:17a–18b.

In addition to this income, after 1867 Li Hung-chang also had clear authority, as well as the means, to collect 20 per cent of the Liang-Chiang customs receipts for the support of the Huai forces fighting the Nien.[67] He obtained full title to these funds only by causing the throne to overrule vetoes of the Board of Foreign Affairs, which had objected to such diversion of funds to the Huai-chün. This was a signal victory in Li's long struggle to legitimize his raids on the central government revenues. Although Li did not specify the amount of revenue that the Huai-chün acquired as a result of this political victory, we may estimate it to have been approximately 1,600,000 liang annually, using as a base the reported customs income for the year 1867, which was 8,000,000 liang.[68]

On the basis of the two financial sources mentioned above, the Huai-chün was able to remain in the field equipped and provisioned through revenues which came to not less than 6,600,000 liang each year.[69]

Collapse of the Nien

Li remained in direct command of the armies fighting the Nien for almost two years, holding the title of Imperial Commissioner for Bandit Suppression and, concurrently, the office of governor-general of Hu-Kuang. The campaign was very complex, owing to the great mobility of the Nien. The Nien avoided large battles, forcing the government armies to pursue them until the government troops were exhausted and their supply lines overextended. Then with lightning rapidity and sudden ferocity the Nien turned upon their pursuers. Time and time again this strategy had worked. Li met this problem by relying essentially upon the plans worked out by Tseng—plans which he had helped Tseng to formulate. He planned to hem in the Nien contingents and exterminate them one by one, isolating the Nien communities in turn. By following this procedure and not permitting the Nien to divide their forces, he forced them into two major blocs. Then, using natural barriers and man-made walls, he wedged his armies between the Nien blocs, cutting them off from each other, from food, and from the communities from which they had drawn manpower and sustenance. He then closed in for the kill.[70] His policy has been

---

[67] *LWCK Letters,* 7:2a, TC 6/4/28.

[68] *LWCK Memorials,* 10:4a-5a, TC 5/2/25.

[69] Hsüeh Fu-ch'eng, "Tai Li Po-hsiang ni-ch'en tu Cheng-chung hsün-shih shih-shu," in Tso, *Shih tzu-liao,* I, 188-97. Siang-tseh Chiang, in *The Nien Rebellion,* p. 116, gives the monthly expenses of the Huai-chün as 500,000 liang, which would be 6,000,-000 liang per year, corresponding closely with our own estimates.

[70] This is described succinctly in Li's biography in *CSK, chüan* 411.

aptly described as one of pardon, pursuit, and defense, which took into account and built upon the strategy of his predecessors Tseng Kuo-fan and Prince Seng-ko-lin-ch'in.[71] In the middle of 1868 Li was able to report to the throne the death by suicide of Chang Tsung-yü, the last of the great Nien leaders, and to announce that eastern Chihli had been cleared of the rebels. This signaled the successful conclusion of the eastern Nien campaign.

Li Hung-chang and the Huai-chün participated for a relatively short time in the fifteen-year campaign against the Nien; yet they played a vital part in it. It was not an historical accident that brought Li and his army success where others had failed. The origins, composition, and experience of the Huai-chün and its leaders made the organization particularly suitable for combating the Nien. Familiarity with Western weapons, the assistance of European officers, reliance upon steamships, all gave the Huai-chün great superiority over the other armies of the period, including those of the Nien. The solid control over Liang-Chiang exercised through the partnership and interchanges of office between Li and Tseng made it possible for Li to finance the growth, re-equipping, mounting, and transportation of his army, and permitted him to buy over rebel contingents which then became important elements within the Huai-chün. A large degree of financial independence, personal control over a major regional military force, wide experience in problems relating to Western military technology, and victory in battle carried Li Hung-chang to new heights of power. In fact though not in name, he had replaced Tseng Kuo-fan as the military strong man of China. He came to look upon himself and his force as representative of more than local or regional power. The Huai-chün had moved well beyond its original regional bounds, and to some degree Li's concept of himself and his army had moved correspondingly. Describing the Huai-chün as "an army which fights for the whole country," he now claimed his right to revenues from all regions.[72] Although he still led a regional force, that is, the old troops from Huai-nan (southern Anhwei) and the newer reinforcements from Huai-pei (particularly Hsü-chou), Li was convinced that it deserved national support. Although such support was never fully forthcoming, Li constantly expanded his area of operation and revenue extraction. Every region the Huai-chün penetrated was exploited for Li's greater military strength.

[71] Chiang, *The Nien Rebellion,* p. 213.
[72] *LWCK Memorials,* 16:20a ff., TC 9/3/21.

V. The Huai-chün in Transition

THE suppression of the Nien insurrection brought to a close a twenty-year period of intense civil war, which had threatened to destroy the entire Ch'ing structure. Local warfare continued to drain the energy and resources of the Chinese for another decade, but the major crises had been surmounted. The Manchu dynasty survived, and the political and social structure remained superficially intact. Beneath the surface, however, a process of radical change was under way. While less spectacular than the Taiping bid for sovereignty and the outright defiance of the Nien, the gradual transfer of effective military and financial control from the Manchus and their bureaucracy in Peking to the militaristic governors-general of the provincial regions was the decisive change that brought about the breakdown of the traditional imperial system. The power that accrued to men like Li Hung-chang, Tseng Kuo-fan, and Tso Tsung-t'ang enabled the bureaucracy to repel outright attacks upon the dynasty. By exercising their powers, even over the resistance of the Manchus themselves, these new military leaders extended the life of the dynasty by more than half a century. But they provided only temporary correctives and offered no solution that would enable the Manchu regime and the society it ruled to meet the problems that were engulfing them. Nor were any of these great military-political leaders of the nineteenth century capable of building around themselves power structures extensive enough to sustain a new nation-wide political revival. They could neither strengthen nor replace the Manchus; they could only support them through years of decay and dissolution.

Li Shifts to the North

The termination of the Nien troubles brought Li's career to a new stage. Heretofore, except for a brief period at the Han-lin Academy in

Peking, Li had served in the Huai and Yangtze regions, in territory and among peoples familiar to him. His departure from these areas was a radical change for him, involving problems of personal adjustment as well as bringing him into an entirely new relationship with the central government.

Li's transfer to the north came about as a result of the urgent need of the central government for his military support and experience in foreign affairs. After the collapse of Nien resistance in mid-August, 1868, he had just settled himself in office as governor-general of Hu-Kuang when he was called to leave immediately on a special assignment. Anti-Christian outbreaks had occurred in Kweichow and Szechwan provinces, and representatives of the Western Powers had put pressure upon the court to settle the disturbances and bring the Chinese offenders to account. Making use of Li's good reputation among Westerners, who regarded him as a progressive statesman, amicable diplomat, and vigorous military leader, the court urged him to proceed to the trouble spots at once and take measures to placate the representatives of the Powers. Scarcely had he accomplished his mission in Kweichow and Szechwan when he was ordered to lead forces into Shensi, where serious uprisings had broken out.[1] While he was organizing an expedition for this purpose, the order was countermanded, and he was instructed to lead his strongest contingents to the borders of Chihli immediately, to be held in readiness in the event of an attack upon that province by the French.

The emergency march of the Huai-chün to Chihli was occasioned by the apparent breakdown in negotiations between Tseng Kuo-fan, then governor-general of Chihli, and the French plenipotentiaries over settlement of the "Tientsin Massacre" case. The "massacre" occurred in June, 1870, when in the course of negotiations over the rights and protection of the French Catholic Church and orphanage in Tientsin, the French consul, Fontanier, drew his pistol in public and wounded one of the servants of the Tientsin prefect, Liu Chieh. At this, a mob of Chinese who hovered outside the church set the church on fire and killed the consul, several priests and nuns, and their Chinese servants. Ch'ung-hou, Superintendent of Trade for the Northern Ports, who was stationed at Tientsin, was assigned to make a settlement.

When it became apparent that the French were intent on making a major international issue of the incident, Tseng Kuo-fan was sum-

---

[1] *LWCK Memorials,* 16:1a ff., TC 9/1/2; 4a ff., TC 9/1/13; 8a ff., TC 9/1/13; 9a ff., TC 9/1/13; 14a ff., TC 9/2/30; 18a ff., TC 9/3/21; pp. 26a ff., TC 9/4/22.

moned from his official residence at Pao-ting to take part in the negotiations. The French soon found the procedures of the Chinese negotiators tedious, repetitive, and seemingly lacking in sincerity. Although
Tseng was conciliatory, the French decided upon a show of force in
order to achieve full and immediate satisfaction. The appearance of
a fleet of French men-of-war off the coast near Tientsin threw the
court into a panic, and Li was ordered to the scene. The arrival of
Li and his troops on the borders of Chihli possibly caused the French
to accept Tseng's settlement more readily. They had seen in the Tientsin case an easy opportunity to exact concessions from the Chinese
with little risk. The approach of the Huai-chün, prepared to fight,
gave the French cause to reconsider their position in China. At that
moment in Europe the armies of France and Prussia were wheeling
into position for war, and the French could ill afford to engage in hostilities in Asia. Even before Li Hung-chang appeared at Tientsin,
where he had been ordered to complete the negotiations, the French
had agreed in substance to Tseng's proposals.[2]

It is possible, too, that the arrival of the Huai-chün at Chihli in-
duced the court to take a more favorable view of Tseng's conciliatory
efforts with the French. Having summoned the Huai-chün, the court
soon had misgivings over the presence of Li's personal army in force
near the capital. Like the Roman Senate, the court feared the appearance of a provincial military hero and his legions at its doorstep. An
attempt was made to dissuade Li from bringing too many of his troops
into Chihli, and in an apparent *volte-face* the court recommended that
the Huai-chün take up positions south and west of Chihli. Li, however,
had little difficulty in convincing a frightened and hesitant court that
the security of the northern coast, hence of the capital itself, depended
upon the presence of the Huai-chün in the vicinity.[3]

In its haste to forestall any precipitate French action, the court
had permitted Tseng to retire unceremoniously from the governor-
generalship of Chihli and appointed Li to the post even before his arrival in the metropolitan province. Li, as the principal military and
diplomatic trouble-shooter of the empire, had reached great heights.
The governor-generalship of Chihli was the highest provincial post in
the country, and the confirmation of Li in that office was one means of
assuring the French and other Westerners that a relatively progressive
and tolerant official would safeguard their treaty rights. Li's associa-

---

[2] Hummel, *Eminent Chinese,* pp. 754, 209-11.
[3] *LWCK Memorials,* 16:48a-49b, TC 9/8/4.

tion with Gordon, Admiral Hope, and Protet in Shanghai, his adoption of Western armaments for his armies, and his years of friendly, though stiff, negotiations with diplomats had earned him the favorable regard of the French. His recent victories over the Nien had heightened his prestige among the foreign diplomats and officers, one of whom later described him as "by all degrees of comparison the ablest and most progressive statesman in the Empire."[4] Quick settlement of the Tientsin negotiations after the appointment of Li as governor-general and the appearance of the Huai-chün in Chihli gave the court reason for satisfaction in its selection of Tseng's successor.

Li took office in Chihli with a large army standing behind him. He ignored the regulations that limited governors-general to a small personal guard when removing to a new post. Time and again during the nineteenth century the court had warned high provincial officials that violations of this regulation would not be tolerated.[5] But faced with the emergency the court assented to, and at first encouraged, the entry of the Huai-chün into the metropolitan province. The threat from the West had driven the court to tolerate a potential threat from its own provincial bureauracy.

Li Hung-chang's Followers Remain in Liang-Chiang

The hold that Li Hung-chang's followers had secured over many of the important posts in Liang-Chang, and particularly in Kiangsu, by no means ended with the transfer of Li to the north and the return of Tseng to Nanking. Li Hung-chang therefore had not merely the support of his old teacher and commander in central China but the direct assistance of his own machine, whose members continued to look to him for patronage.

Perhaps the most striking example of the way Li and Tseng managed to keep vital posts in the hands of their own protégés is the case of Ting Jih-ch'ang. After having served under Tseng Kuo-fan and Li Han-chang in Canton, Ting was brought to Kiangsu by Li Hung-chang to supervise production at the Shanghai and Soochow arsenals in 1863 and 1864.[6] In 1865, when Li Hung-chang became acting governor-general of Liang-Chiang, he promoted Ting to the position of customs in-

---

[4] Consul Denny to Secretary of State, U.S. State Department, *Despatches from United States Consuls in Tientsin*, Aug. 12, 1879, hereafter cited *Tientsin Consular Despatches*.

[5] See, for instance, Chang Shou-yung, *Huang-ch'ao chang-ku hui-pien* (1902), 1:63-64.

[6] *CSK, chüan* 448.

tendant at Shanghai.[7] Later that year Ting became salt controller of
the Liang-Huai region, and in the following year was appointed financial commissioner of Kiangsu province.[8] By this time Li was in the
north fighting the Nien, and Tseng was again governor-general of
Liang-Chiang.[9] Both Li and Tseng recommended Ting in 1867 for the
post of governor of Kiangsu, which Li Hung-chang and Li Han-chang
had previously held. Ting remained in this post for over five years.
During the Tienstin massacre negotiations he was brought to the
north, where he assisted Tseng and Li in concluding the settlement. In
later years he rose to be governor-general of Fukien and Chekiang,
and, as shall be seen, collaborated closely with Li in planning over-all
defenses for coastal China.[10] Once he had attained a high independent
position, he was no longer a subordinate member of the Li machine,
since he no longer depended upon Li's patronage. Nevertheless, his
rise had taken place under Li's protection, and his fortunes were inti-
mately tied to Li's. As a strategically placed colleague he supported
Li in Liang-Chiang for many years and stood by him loyally throughout his lifetime.

Li established a succession to office that allowed for the promotion
and transfer of his key men. When Ting Jih-ch'ang was advanced to
the office of salt controller of Liang-Huai in 1865, he was immediately
replaced by Ying Pao-shih, who had assisted him for several years and
now took office as circuit and customs intendant.[11] Ying, one of Li's
earliest followers, was relied upon by both Li and Tseng to keep funds
moving to their headquarters while they were in the north. His success at this job was given recognition by his later promotion to the office of judicial commissioner of Kiangsu province.[12]

---

[7] Hummel, *Eminent Chinese,* pp. 721-22; *Shanghai-hsien-chih,* 12:24a; Chou Shih-
ch'eng, *Huai-chün p'ing-nien chi,* 11:16a ff.; *Shanghai-hsien hsü-chih,* 15:1b.

[8] Hummel, *Eminent Chinese,* pp. 721-22; *LWCK Memorials,* 10:42a ff., TC 5/9/7.

[9] During the latter part of the Nien Rebellion, Tseng listed for Li the three things
he considered necessary for their continued control over affairs in central and north
China: (1) the Kiangsu revenue, (2) the manpower of Honan and the Huai region,
and (3) sufficient ability on the part of Tseng. *TWCK Letters,* 26:15a. Tseng was
usually prompt to supply Li Hung-chang with funds when requested. See, for instance,
TWCK Letters, 26:20b, 27a, 32a, where Tseng finances demobilization of certain elements of the Huai-chün. Much of the credit for Tseng's success in meeting Li's financial requirements must be given to Ting Jih-ch'ang, who supplied a continuity of efficient revenue administration, and to other members of Li's machine who remained in
Liang-Chiang and co-operated closely with Tseng.

[10] Hummel, *Eminent Chinese,* pp. 721-22.

[11] *LWCK Memorials,* 9:39a ff., TC 4/8/1; *Sung-chiang-fu hsü-chih* (1884),
20:20a-22a; *LWCK Letters,* 6:41b, TC 4/8/22.

[12] *Shanghai-hsien hsü-chih,* 15:1b; *LWCK Memorials,* 5:46a ff., TC 2/11/28;
9:73a ff., TC 4/12/19; 71:50a, KH 17/4/15.

The vacancy created by the promotion of Ying Pao-shih was then filled by T'u Tsung-ying, a Huai man from Liu-an, Anhwei.[13] In 1872 Shen Ping-ch'eng, a *chin-shih* from Chekiang, was appointed to replace T'u.[14] Two years later, in 1874, Shen was replaced by Feng Chün-kuang,[15] who was one of Li's most important assistants, his specialty being foreign affairs, particularly industrialization. As a native of the Kwangtung coastal region, he was one of the first of the several Cantonese upon whom Li came to rely as he sought to westernize China.[16]

In 1877 the post of Su-Sung-T'ai circuit intendant was turned over to Liu Jui-fen, who held it for seven years.[17] Liu was an Anhwei man from Kuei-ch'ih prefecture, who had served with Li since the first days of the Shanghai expedition.[18] He later became financial commissioner of Kiangsu, and still later rose to become governor of Kwangtung province.[19] The strategic circuit intendancy of Su-Sung-T'ai continued to remain exclusively in the hands of men from Hunan and Ho-fei until as late as 1894, when it finally was assigned to an official from Kiangsi province.[20]

These men were sources of strength to Li wherever he was. It is clear that they were placed in Liang-Chiang because Li and Tseng wanted them there. They monopolized the wealth of the region for the Li-Tseng clique, while their military counterpart could be relied upon for faithful support, because, among other reasons, they were practically all from Hunan and Anhwei.[21]

Li Hung-chang Consolidates His Power in Chihli

Li Hung-chang formally accepted the seal of office as governor-general of Chihli on the sixth day of the eighth month of the ninth year of T'ung-chih (1870).[22] This marked a decisive transition in Li's

---

[13] *Shanghai-hsien-chih*, 12:24b; *CSK*, 448:3a; *Shanghai-hsien hsü-chih*, 15:2b; *LWCK Memorials*, 9:22a ff., TC 4/7/22.

[14] *Sung-chiang-fu hsü-chih*, 20:20a-22a; *Shanghai-hsien hsü-chih*, 14:1a ff.

[15] *LWCK Memorials*, 19:51a ff., TC 11/4/15; *Sung-chiang-fu hsü-chih*, 21:26a; Hummel, *Eminent Chinese*, p. 722.

[16] *Shanghai-hsien hsü-chih*, 15:3b.

[17] *LWCK Memorials*, 74:41a-43a, KH 18/6/13; *Sung-chiang-fu hsü-chih*, 20:20a-22a.

[18] *CSK*, 446:9a.

[19] *LWCK Memorials*, 74:41a-43a, KH 18/6/13.

[20] *Sung-chiang-fu hsü-chih*, 20:20a-22a; *Shanghai-hsien hsü-chih*, 14:1a ff.

[21] *Sung-chiang-fu hsü-chih*, 20:15a-18b; 20:21a-22a; *Shanghai-hsien hsü-chih*, 14:2b-4a. The records of military command posts for the late Ch'ing dynasty show that even as late as 1905 the commanding officer of the battalions garrisoning the Kiangnan region was a native of Li's birthplace, Ho-fei. *Shanghai-hsien hsü-chih*, 14:14a.

[22] *LWCK Memorials*, 16:50a-b, TC 9/8/6.

career. Heretofore he had been established in the Yangtze and Huai regions, where he had developed his personal army and bureaucratic machine. His distance from the capital and from the watchful eyes of the central government had enabled him to act with minimal interference from Peking. He had extended the already considerable powers enjoyed by a governor-general until, together with Tseng, he exercised almost unchecked dominion over the Liang-Chiang region. In Chihli, he encountered an entirely different situation. The metropolitan province harbored the court and the central government, and for the first time since his rise to high provincial office Li was thrown into close contact with the center of imperial power. Any decisions he made in Chihli, any action he undertook, could now be readily scrutinized by the central administration. And the first concern of central government bureaucrats was always their own positions and the security of the central establishment in which they served. In Chihli the distinctions between central and provincial administration were blurred, for the metropolitan province, besides being the vital center of national government, was an important provincial unit. This was no bailiwick over which Li could exercise undisputed control in building his fortunes. Surrounding him were the servants of an administration that had been ensconced in the region for more than two centuries, whereas he, despite his phenomenal rise, was still a newcomer, whose army was now far removed from its regular sources of revenue, supplies, and manpower.

The governor-generalship of Chihli offered a challenge that Li had no choice but to accept. He could become the virtual prisoner of the central government, carrying out its bidding without question, or he could establish his ascendancy over it, using its authority to gain greater power. For the next twenty-five years Li moved steadily toward establishing his ascendancy in national affairs by taking over control of foreign affairs and customs, as well as the production and supply of armaments, and by securing complete command over the military forces in the north.

Li's underlying objective, independent control of his new region, gave direction to his decisions from the moment he entered office in Chihli. Saddled with a host of new responsibilities, he gave primary attention to administrative and military reorganization.[23] Li had noted

23 A clearer understanding of Li's immediate problems and the measures he took to meet them may be gained from the listing of his memorials as they appear in *LWCK Memorials* for the period between TC 9/8/6 and TC 9/10/6. The following list is

that in the past Tseng Kuo-fan, as governor-general of Chihli, and Ch'ung-hou, as Commissioner of Trade for the Northern Ports, had stalemated each other in their attempts to carry out their separate duties. This had become painfully clear to all concerned in the diplomatic proceedings following the "Tientsin Massacre," when conflicting lines of authority prevented the officials from negotiating effectively. The fundamental question, however, was who would be responsible for defense in the north and who would gain control of the customs revenues of the region.

Traditionally, the governor-general of Chihli was the highest official in the regular provincial hierarchy, responsible for general administration and defense of the province. But at the same time, the Commissioner of Trade was responsible for diplomacy, observation of treaty terms, including guaranteeing security of Western residents, all matters relating to foreign customs, and the defense of northern ports. Ch'ung-hou had held his post as Commissioner of Trade for some time before Tseng arrived in Chihli, and had so impressed the foreigners with his power that the United States consul at Tientsin had made special note of him in a report to the Secretary of State:

quoted from *Guide to the Memorials of Seven Leading Officials of Nineteenth-Century China,* edited by Chang Chung-li and Stanley Spector (Seattle, 1955), "Li Hung-chang," *chüan* 16 and 17.

"TC 9/8/6	Expresses gratitude to the Throne for appointing the memorialist Governor General of Chihli.
TC 9/8/6	A Note. Reports the memorialist's temporary stay at Pao-ting and his defense plans.
TC 9/8/9	Reports the memorialist's departure for Tientsin, and discusses his ideas for settling the case of the murder of the French clergy.
TC 9/8/19	A Note. Reports the transfer of one thousand camels to Tso Tsung-t'ang's troops.
TC 9/9/19	Requests the demobilization of cavalry stationed at Ku-pei-k'ou [in Manchuria] in order to save rations.
TC 9/9/19	A Note. Requests an interview with the Throne for Provincial Commander in Chief Liu Ming-ch'uan.
TC 9/10/3	In compliance with an Imperial edict, discusses the appointment of Provincial Commander in Chief Liu Ming-ch'uan to command troops in Shensi.
TC 9/10/3	A Note. Requests registration of a recommendation for Expectant Prefect Shen Pao-ching.
TC 9/10/24	Reports the distribution of part of Liu Ming-ch'uan's troops to Shensi, Hupeh, and Hsü-chou.
TC 9/10/24	A Note. Requests the Throne to order financial assistance for Liu Ming-ch'uan's troops in Shensi.
TC 9/10/24	A Note. Requests that Lin Chih-wang and Lü Yao-tou be transferred to serve with Liu Ming-ch'uan's troops.
TC 9/10/26	In compliance with an Imperial edict, discusses foreign affairs and the coastal defense of Chihli, following the abolition of the office of Foreign Trade Commissioner at Tientsin."

The chief Mandarin in this port, his Excellency Chung-how, has been engaged during the past six years in raising a corps of foreign drilled troops—infantry, cavalry and artillery—known as Chung-how's Corps, and as the corps has already increased to over 12,000 efficiently drilled and armed men, the ruling powers at Peking are feeling every day more confidence in their ability to preserve tranquillity in the north of China.[24]

When Tseng Kuo-fan took over the governor-generalship of Chihli in 1869, he was apparently able to use his own great prestige and personal following to reduce Ch'ung-hou's position drastically. No more was heard of "Chung-how's Corps," and indeed one writer has absolved Ch'ung-hou completely from any responsibility during or following the Tientsin Massacre of 1870 because, as he put it:

> ... although he [Ch'ung-hou] was a man in authority, it was only as super-intendent of trade, having no control whatever over the hierarchy of territorial officials, who were under the orders of the viceroy, Tseng Kwo-fan. ... it is not probable that Chunghou could move a corporal's guard in Tientsin. ... He dared not, in fact, move a finger against officers who owed allegiance to the viceroy [governor-general].[25]

There is no evidence that Ch'ung-hou ever regained control over the military forces in Tientsin. When Li Hung-chang established himself in Chihli he further undermined Ch'ung-hou's position. Taking advantage of the latter's temporary absence from China in 1870, he took steps to abolish the office of trade commissioner as an independent and separate post.[26] Seeking to acquire full control over the customs revenues, and aware of the growing importance of foreign affairs, Li acted to bring the responsibilities of the Commissioner of Trade for the Northern Ports under his own jurisdiction as governor-general of Chihli. This was no new maneuver for Li, since he had effected the same arrangement in the past at Shanghai when he had set aside first Wu Hsü and then Hsüeh Huan in order to enjoy undisputed control over revenue, military, and foreign affairs. Once before, this had been the crucial administrative step taken to assure the permanence of the Huai-chün. Now in Chihli he did not hesitate to repeat it. Such a drastic measure, which so greatly strengthened Li's position in Chihli at the outset, was a setback for the central government, which had

---

[24] Consul L. Meadows to Secretary of State, *Tientsin Consular Despatches,* December 31, 1868.

[25] Alexander Michie, *The Englishman in China* (Edinburgh and London, 1900), II, 242.

[26] *LWCK Memorials,* 17:10a-13a, TC 9/10/26.

always deliberately used conflicting lines of authority in the bureaucracy to guarantee its supremacy.

According to Li Hung-chang's proposal, which was accepted, the independent office of foreign trade commissioner was to be abolished. Instead, the governor-general of Chihli would always concurrently hold an appointment as Superintendent of Trade for the Northern Ports. Since this involved additional heavy responsibilities, the routine affairs were to be handled by a circuit intendant responsible to the governor-general.[27] Li pointed out that this would facilitate such important tasks as the training, financing, and equipping of the special modernized regiments, or *lien-chün*, which had recently been developed for the protection of the areas around the capital.[28]

In a supplementary note Li presented his choices for the post of circuit intendant of customs at Tientsin and offered to the throne the names of two men whom he hoped would serve in succession. The first nominee was Ch'en Ch'in, an assistant secretary of the Board of Punishments. Ch'en had been acting prefect in the Tientsin area and had been highly recommended by Tseng Kuo-fan. His particular importance lay in his years of experience on the staff of the Tsungli Yamen (Board of Foreign Affairs), where he had specialized in problems of international relations. At the time of Li's recommendation, Ch'en had been on leave owing to illness and had been ordered to report for duty once more with the Tsungli Yamen. Li requested that, instead, Ch'en be temporarily assigned as customs intendant at Tientsin to apply his experience to drafting customs regulations and working out a system for the conduct of foreign affairs. When this business was completed, Li promised, he would send Ch'en Ch'in back to the Tsungli Yamen at Peking.[29]

Li Hung-chang's second choice for the customs intendancy at Tientsin, Shen Pao-ch'ing, appears to have been a special favorite of his. Shortly before recommending Shen for the job of customs intendant at Tientsin, Li had taken pains to have him promoted so that he would be in line for the office. Li had insisted on this promotion despite the objections of the Board of Civil Offices, which attempted to punish Shen for having served in office during a period of mourning. Li Hung-chang admitted that Shen had indeed served in his own headquarters during a mourning period, but pointed out that this service had taken

[27] *Ibid.*
[28] *Ibid.*, 17:12a-b, TC 9/10/26.
[29] *Ibid.*, 17:14a-b, TC 9/10/26.

place under the emergency conditions of the Nien Rebellion and was therefore worthy of praise rather than blame.[30] Depending heavily upon Shen Pao-ch'ing in planning the administrative reorganization of Chihli, Li planned to have him succeed Ch'en Ch'in in office as soon as Ch'en's specific assignments had been completed. Meanwhile he wished Shen Pao-ch'ing to gain detailed knowledge of his future duties through training on the job. After one year Shen's acting appointment was to be reviewed, and at that time it was to be decided whether he should be given a regular appointment or dismissed.[31]

The new customs intendancy which Ch'en and Shen were to fill successively differed from the regular circuit intendancy centering in Tientsin; it was an intendancy based on specific duties rather than on the circuit area. The new customs intendant was to be in charge of everything connected with foreign affairs. Local officials were to be subject to his jurisdiction whenever they became involved in any such matters. He was to be specially charged with the negotiation of treaties, a matter in which, according to Li, "what is most important is not the method but the negotiator."[32] Since, however, many civil and military officials refused to regard a circuit intendant as their superior, it was necessary for Li, as governor-general and Superintendent of Trade, to have over-all jurisdiction in matters of foreign affairs. Li added that the customs intendant was to be concurrently in charge of the Tientsin Machinery Bureau, the principal arsenal in northern China, and recommended that Shen Pao-ch'ing immediately superintend the work of the machinery bureau preparatory to receiving the regular intendancy the following year.[33]

Two months later, in reporting to the throne the final regulations that he and Ch'en Ch'in had worked out for the new customs intendancy, Li mentioned that Ch'en Ch'in's new authority was not limited to Tientsin alone but extended throughout the province of Chihli. In addition to responsibility for diplomacy and customs collections, the new customs intendant was also granted charge of the coastal defenses of the Tientsin area.[34] This meant that a single circuit intendant, solely responsible to Li Hung-chang, now controlled the largest local source of revenue and used it directly to satisfy Li's military re-

---

30 *Ibid.*, 17:5a-b, TC 9/10/3.
31 *Ibid.*, 17:14a-b, TC 9/10/26.
32 *Li Wen-chung kung i-shu han-kao* (hereafter cited as *LWCK Foreign Office Letters*), 1:9a, TC 9/10/ int./7, in *LWCK Collected Works*.
33 *LWCK Memorials*, 17:16a-18a, TC 9/10/26.
34 *Ibid.*, 17:31a-32a, TC 9/11/16.

quirements. A single line of authority and responsibility had been established which formally gave Li the same elements of power he had seized in the south under the emergency conditions of the Taiping and Nien rebellions.

The new powers that Li Hung-chang acquired through his reforms in the organization of the office of Commissioner of Trade put him in a position to influence strongly the conduct of national affairs. The authority for deciding questions of foreign policy rested with the Tsungli Yamen, or Board of Foreign Affairs, which had been established at Peking in 1860. The board was only a deliberative body with no executive power, and it was the responsibility of the provincial authorities to carry out its policies. But even the limited responsibilities of the board were gradually usurped by Li. From the very beginning he insisted that his recognized residence should be at Tientsin, rather than at Pao-ting, the official residence of the governor-general of Chihli. This choice was legally possible because of his concurrent position as trade commissioner. In Tientsin Li came in contact with the representatives of the foreign powers and came to be regarded as China's leading diplomat. Working in Tientsin, Li short-circuited foreign communications with the capital and to a significant extent intruded himself between the Westerners and the Tsungli Yamen. Since from time to time Li served as a member of the Tsungli Yamen, he was frequently able to act in the name of that body as well as in his own capacity as Superintendent of Trade for the Northern Ports.

Tientsin was ideal as Li's principal headquarters. Controlling the waterways to the interior of north China, it protected from outside attack both the national capital, Peking, located eighty miles to the northwest, and Pao-ting, the provincial capital, some ninety miles to the southwest. Under the domination of Li Hung-chang, Tientsin became the main military, naval, commercial, and, for a while, industrial center in north China. One American observer remarked that Tientsin had become the center of all progressive movements in China solely because "Viceroy Li makes it his home and principal place of business."[35] The American consulate flooded the United States Department of State with letters requesting expansion of the consulate in Tientsin, since Li's presence in that city made it to all intents and purposes the political center of China.[36]

---

[35] James Harrison Wilson, *China: Travels and Investigations in the Middle Kingdom* (3d ed.; New York, 1901), p. 89.

[36] Consul Denny to Secretary of State, *Tientsin Consular Despatches*, August 12, 1879.

LOCATION OF THE HUAI-CHÜN: 1870-1892

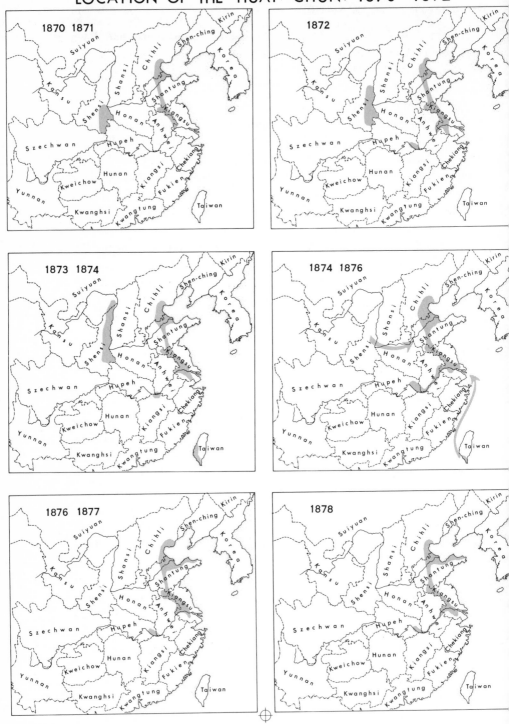

LOCATION OF THE HUAI-CHÜN: 1870-1892

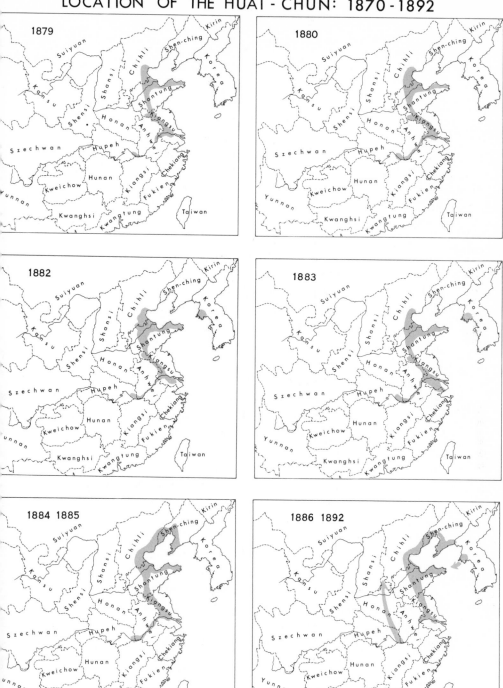

Location of the Huai-chün after 1870

Li's object in reorganizing the administration of Chihli and securing control of the foreign customs was to preserve the Huai Army which had originally brought him to power. Li knew that his power in the north was safe only as long as he maintained his military strength, and this strength, for the time being, was the Huai-chün. No matter what the cost and difficulty of maintaining his personal army in the north might be, he had no intention of relinquishing control of it. Nor was he inclined to depend heavily on the regular government forces in the north.

The Huai-chün had given a good account of itself in the extended campaigns against the Taipings and the Nien and was at this time the most impressive military force in China. If the government needed Li Hung-chang for his skill in handling diplomatic affairs, revenue problems, and general administration, it needed him even more as the one military leader who could control the Huai-chün. In developing his army and planning its location, Li sought to enhance its value to the central government. This meant keeping it strategically placed in the northern coastal region, and at the same time using it to guarantee as much control as possible over the area, extending as far south as Liang-Chiang, upon which his strength had originally been based. During his twenty-five years in Chihli Li's interests and those of the central government coincided insofar as the forces in the north were concerned. But Li's own self-interest also required him to hold Huai troops in regions under the jurisdiction of other governors-general. How well Li succeeded in satisfying both his own needs and those of the government can be partly seen through the movements of the Huai-chün between the years 1870, when it entered Chihli in force, and 1892, just three years before its disastrous defeat in the Sino-Japanese War.

In 1870 and 1871 part of the Huai-chün followed Li into Chihli, while a second contingent moved into Shensi to assist in the campaign against the Moslems. In addition several battalions maintained their positions in Kiangsu and on the Anhwei border.[37] The year 1872 saw no important change, although elements of unspecified size were reported to be stationed in Hupeh,[38] possibly because Li had only recently vacated the governor-generalship of Hupeh and his brother Li Han-chang had succeeded him there.

Between the years 1873 and 1874 Li dispersed the Huai-chün over

---

[37] *LWCK Memorials,* 21:27a-29b, TC 12/4/1.
[38] *Ibid.,* 25:37a-39a, KH 1/7/28.

a wide area, covering the provinces of Shensi, Kansu, and Chinghai in the northwest, Chihli and Shantung in the north, Kiangsu and Hupeh in central and central coastal China, and the islands of Taiwan. Forces were stationed in the northwest because of the continued Moslem disturbances there—and in the south because of the contest with Japan over Taiwan.[39] These forces were subsequently withdrawn, and by 1876 the Huai-chün was confined principally to the provinces of Chihli, Shantung, and Kiangsu.[40]

From 1876 to 1882 the Huai-chün remained in its principal positions in Chihli, Shantung, and Kiangsu.[41] During the year 1882, internal strife in Korea led Li Hung-chang openly to assert China's suzerainty over its traditional vassal by sending six battalions of Huai troops, or some three thousand soldiers, to be garrisoned in Seoul.[42] These troops remained in Korea until withdrawn by agreement with the Japanese in 1885.

Beginning in 1884 and for a decade thereafter, the Huai-chün gradually moved into strategic locations along the Liaotung Peninsula and within Manchuria. At the same time the army spread more broadly over the coasts of Chihli and Shantung. Among the points taken over were Shanhaikuan in northern Chihli, Mukden and Chinchow in Manchuria, and Dairen (Port Arthur) on the Liaotung Peninsula.[43] The outbreak of war with Japan in 1894 occasioned major movements of the Huai-chün into Manchuria and Korea, as well as the relocation of various components along the northern coasts. The collapse of the Huai-chün in the face of the Japanese assault led to a complete reorganization of the northern defenses and was the beginning of a new phase of China's military history.

The Huai-chün remained for over two decades a bulwark of China's northern defenses, responsible not only for China proper but also, in later years, for the homeland of the reigning Manchu house as well. That the Manchus should have permitted the Huai-chün to dominate the defenses of Dairen, Chinchow, and Mukden is striking proof of the decline of their own power in contrast with the growing strength of Li Hung-chang and his army.

[39] *Ibid.*, 27:13a-16b, KH 2/5/14.

[40] *Ibid.*, 29:30a-32a, KH 3/6/19.

[41] *Ibid.*, 32:31a-33a, KH 4/8/29; 34:22 ff., KH 5/4/16; 33:17a ff., KH 4/9/26; 37:50a-b; KH 6/7/14; 40:4a-6a, KH 7/1/18; 42:54a-56a, KH 7/12/20.

[42] *Ibid.*, 48:15a ff., KH 9/10/29; 52:35a ff., KH 10/12/1.

[43] *Ibid.*, 55:42a ff., KH 11/12/13; 58:48a, KH 12/12/16; 63:50a-51b, KH 14/11/27; 66:35a-36b, KH 15/12/3; 69:35a ff., KH 16/11/16; 73:29a ff., KH 17/11/30; 75:31a ff., KH 18/10/28; 77:40a ff., KH 19/10/26.

Later Development of the Huai-chün

The operations against the Moslems in Shensi during the years 1870 to 1874 had required the services of several of Li Hung-chang's crack divisions. At the beginning of 1870, various infantry and mounted battalions of the Wu-I-chün and the Sheng-chün, led by Kuo Sung-lin and Chou Sheng-ch'uan respectively, were shifted westward to Shensi. Later in the same year Liu Ming-ch'uan was given over-all command of operations in Shensi, and departed for that province with an additional 28 battalions of his own Ming-chün troops, 10 battalions of Wu-I-chün foot soldiers, and 2 battalions of Hunan cavalry—a total of 40 battalions, or approximately 20,000 men. By the end of 1870 well over 20,000 Huai troops were engaged in operations in Shensi. To sustain this army, quartermaster depots were established at Wu-ch'ang and other places in Hupeh, demanding the services of additional Huai troops.

Meanwhile, Li Hung-chang had led another force of 8 battalions, or 4,000 men, to protect the area around the capital. There remained in Kiangsu 8 battalions of the Ch'ing-tzu-ying, commanded by Wu Ch'ang-ch'ing, an artillery battalion under Liu Yü-lung, and 2 battalions of cavalry under Hsü Tao-k'uei, a total of 11 battalions comprising some 5,700 men. Units of the Huai-chün were also assigned to protect transportation routes, particularly those used for the shipment of grain tribute to the capital. On the basis of these figures, as reported by Li personally, in the year 1870 the Huai-chün numbered no less than 30,000 soldiers. But several major armies, such as that of T'ang Ting-k'uei, were not mentioned in the report.[44]

Between the years 1873 and 1874 major changes in the Huai-chün assignments were made. T'ang Ting-k'uei's forces, numbering 13 battalions, were moved first into Hsü-chou, in northern Kiangsu, and subsequently transferred southward to Kua-chou, Kiangsu, where they occupied a commanding position overlooking the Yangtze River. Thus the total Huai-chün force in Kiangsu, including the garrisons of Wu Ch'ang-ch'ing and Liu Yü-lung mentioned earlier, rose to 22 battalions, or over 10,000 men, exclusive of an unspecified number of troops from the Wu-I and Ming armies reported to have been sent into Kiangsu between 1873 and the middle of 1874. These changes were in preparation for operations against the Japanese, who had effected a landing on Taiwan, and during the course of the year some 2,000 men of the Kiangsu garrison were shipped to Taiwan. At the same time Li

---

[44] *Ibid.*, 21:27a-29b, TC 12/4/11.

Hung-chang ordered 3,000 of his "westernized" Huai troops to Taiwan and covered their absence by recalling a considerable number of
troops from the Ming-chün, the Sheng-chün, and the Wu-I-chün, to
the coast. These forces took up posts principally in Chi-ning, on the
Shantung coast, and in Hsü-chou, which had been evacuated by T'ang
Ting-k'uei. Such widespread shifts and exchanges demonstrate something of the extent to which the Huai-chün served in the over-all
defense mobilization at a time of crisis.[45]

In the middle of 1874 Li wrote to the governor-general of Liang-
Chiang, giving the size of his army in Kiangsu as 10,000 men, and
commenting that not only in Kiangsu but in other areas as well the
Huai-chün was serving the general interest of the nation rather than
Li's own private interests.[46] Chang Shu-sheng, to whom Li addressed
the remark, had been one of the original Huai-chün commanders and
undoubtedly took it for granted that the Huai-chün was a personal
army which Li used, at least partly, for his own benefit.

Li Hung-chang's task of establishing permanent lines of northern
defense was facilitated by the conclusion of the Shensi campaign and
the return of the Huai forces in 1875. Seventeen battalions of the
Ming-chün, led by provincial commander-in-chief Liu Sheng-hsiu,
moved from Shensi to Chi-ning, Shantung, and took up positions as
the southern branch of the North China coastal defense organization.
In the south, T'ang Ting-k'uei, who had led several battalions from
Kiangsu to Taiwan, returned to the mainland and stationed his troops
at Nanking to assist in the defense of Kiangsu. Additional troops
from Wu Ch'ang-ch'ing's personal guard, an artillery battalion, 5 battalions of Wu-I Army foot soldiers, and 5 battalions of cavalry completed the Huai-chün rolls in Kiangsu. This force was essential for
the security of the area, at least in the opinion of Shen Pao-chen, governor-general of Liang-Chiang during the years 1875 to 1878. According to Shen, Kiangsu was defended by 17,000 local volunteers
stationed in garrisons at Soochow, Sung-chiang, Chiang-ying, Yang-
chou, and Hsü-chou. These he had found scarcely sufficient to rely
upon for the defense of the whole area. At the same time many of the
remnants of the old Hsiang-chün in Kiangsu had either been disbanded
or transferred elsewhere. He found the Huai-chün components in
Kiangsu to be his only additional source of military support. These

---

45 *Ibid.*, 23:27a-29a, TC 13/6/10; 27:13a-13b, KH 2/5/14.

46 *LWCK Letters,* 14:25a-26a, TC 13/8/7. Li's report on the size of his Kiangsu
armies completely confirms our own estimate presented on the basis of battalion
movements.

troops, Shen held, were veterans serving under seasoned commanders, and without their presence it was feared that difficulties would arise in maintaining order in the province.[47]

Shen Pao-chen was provoked to comment on the importance of the Huai-chün in Kiangsu by a recommendation of the Board of Revenue that called for an over-all reduction of the Huai-chün in 1878. His own conclusion was that as far as Kiangsu was concerned no reduction in the Huai-chün was possible. The memorial that Li Hung-chang himself addressed to the throne on this question provides the most complete survey of his force that can be found for this period.

According to Li Hung-chang, the Huai-chün up to 1877 totaled 78 battalions and 20 independent companies of water, foot, and mounted troops, or 39,800 men (the equivalent of 82 battalions). Of these, 5 battalions guarded the port of Shanghai, and 21 battalions were divided among Chiang-yin, Ch'ing-chiang, Chiang-ning, P'u-k'ou, and other sites in Kiangsu. To the north were 14 battalions of the Ming-chün guarding the area around Ch'ang-ch'iu, Shantung. These forces, Li remarked, were to be at the disposal of both the southern and northern defense organizations. Tientsin, which Li described as "the gateway to the Pei-yang (Northern Sea) region," was protected by 16 battalions of the Sheng-chün rifle corps. The remaining 22 battalions and the independent companies were not specifically referred to in the report.

Li Hung-chang proposed to disband 14 battalions, consisting of 11,800 men, to meet partially the requirements of the Board of Revenue. He declined to order further reductions on the ground that the Huai-chün, as distinguished from other armies on the periphery of the defense system, was defending the vital coastal ports and the very center of the empire. He anticipated that after the reduction the Huai-chün would still muster something over 28,000 men.[48]

In the regular financial account that Li Hung-chang rendered for the year 1877, he noted that he had at his direct command in Chihli 31 battalions but did not mention his forces in other areas.[49] No change

[47] *Ch'ing-ch'ao hsü-wen-hsien t'ung-k'ao*, 203:9507.

[48] *LWCK Memorials*, 32:21a-23a, KH 4/8/18. Additional details on the location of troops are to be found in *ibid.*, 32:31a-b, KH 4/8/29. The figures given in these two memorials are slightly different because they cover different periods. The first covers the period to KH 3/10 (1877), whereas the latter covers the slightly earlier period of KH 2/1-2/12 (1876). In his report for 1876, Li mentioned a total of 81 *ying*, distributed as follows: Chihli, 33; Shantung, 17; Kiangsu, 31. This would have been a total of 40,500 men, if we allow 500 men per *ying*.

[49] *Ibid.*, 34:22a-23a, KH 5/4/16.

at all was indicated for the following year,[50] but by 1879 the Huai-chün had been somewhat reduced. Li Hung-chang's report for that year gave the total strength of the Huai-chün as 66 battalions distributed as follows:

Chihli	Tientsin, Pao-ting, and other strategic points The governor-general's guard; transport guards and supply depots directly under Li Hung-chang	27 battalions
Shantung	In the area around Ch'ang-ch'iu, Ming-tzu-chün foot and cavalry battalions under Liu Sheng-hsiu	13 battalions
Kiangsu	Along the northern and southern banks of the Yangtze, Ming and Wu army foot soldiers; Wu Ch'ang-ch'ing's personal guard (16 battalions) Woosung and Shanghai, the Wu-I Left Army; Hsü-chou and Hsien-ch'ien, cavalry (5 battalions)	26 battalions

The total of 66 battalions for 1879 represents a decrease in strength from 1877 of 12 battalions, or 6,000 to 9,000 men, depending on whether the battalions demobilized were foot or cavalry and whether or not laborers are counted.[51] This was nevertheless two battalions less than Li had promised to demobilize.

During this period the Huai-chün came close to being evenly distributed, with an almost equal number of battalions at the northern and southern extremities of the defense zone, Chihli and Kiangsu, and half the number in the center at Shantung. The thirteen Shantung battalions represented a 50 per cent potential reinforcement for either the northern or southern branch of the Huai-chün at any time Li commanded.

The size of the Huai-chün appears to have remained stable during the following year, 1880, but significant changes in the assignment of troops took place. In Chihli, Li Hung-chang placed more of his troops in coastal regions, and transferred two battalions of cavalry from Hsü-chou, Kiangsu, to the. northern coast. At the same time he withdrew Wu Ch'ang-ch'ing's six battalions from the Yangtze River banks in Kiangsu and assigned them to protect the coastal regions adjoining Teng-chou, in Shantung, bringing the army in Shantung to a total of

---

[50] *Ibid.*, 37 :50a-b, KH 6/7/14.
[51] *Ibid.*, 40 :4a-6a, KH 7/1/18.

nineteen battalions. He thus destroyed the balance that had previously existed between his forces in Kiangsu and Chihli, reinforcing
the Chihli region at the expense of Kiangsu.[52]

It is possible that this rearrangement was undertaken because of
growing tension between China and Russia over the Ili territory in the
far northwest, and the fear of a Russian attack upon the Chinese
coast. Yet when amicable Sino-Russian relations were resumed, the
movement of the Huai-chün northward and along the coast continued.
This change in the disposition of troops reflects a growing awareness
on the part of Li Hung-chang and his contemporaries of the constant
opportunity for foreign aggression that military weakness invited.
Although it is difficult to conclude that Li Hung-chang ever actually
believed that Chinese armies could withstand foreign troops, it is
entirely within reason to surmise that he was anxious to make an impressive show of strength in the areas where it would be properly
appreciated by the foreigners, that is, near the principal ports of entry.

The new alignment of troops also seems to have been part of a
broader plan to bring the Huai-chün under closer control and to place
its major components in areas where Li could directly oversee the command and personally guarantee the military revenues. Of the sixty-
six battalions that comprised the Huai-chün in 1880, only eighteen
remained in Kiangsu, while the remaining forty-eight were distributed
between Shantung and Chihli, much closer to Li's headquarters.[53]

The system of reporting Huai-chün financial accounts underwent a
significant change after 1882. Previously Li Hung-chang had assumed
responsibility for the financial statements of his entire army, although
the detailed accounts for the forces in Kiangsu had also been submitted
separately to the central government boards by the responsible local
officials of Kiangsu. In reporting on accounts for the years before
1882, Li Hung-chang had often given the actual number of battalions
maintained in Kiangsu and other areas outside his direct jurisdiction
together with a general statement of their financial accounts. For the
years after 1882, the financial reports of Huai-chün units outside Li's
area were submitted only by the local provincial officials, and Li no
longer had responsibility for even the over-all accounting of his more
distant armies.[54] Unfortunately, the regular detailed statements made
by the local provincial officials for the Boards of War, Revenue, and

---

[52] *Ibid.*, 42:54a-56a, KH 7/12/20.

[53] *Ibid.*

[54] This does not mean that he did not receive the accounts of his armies in Kiangsu
and other "outside" areas. The local officials had customarily submitted their state-

Works were not submitted in the form of memorials, and Li Hung-chang's memorials have had to be relied upon as practically the sole source for a statistical survey. As his memorials no longer contained information on his armies in Kiangsu and other areas outside of Chihli and the north, it is difficult to obtain the same detailed information for the Huai-chün after 1882 as for the previous period.[55]

In October, 1881, Tso Tsung-t'ang, Li's greatest rival, was appointed governor-general of Liang-Chiang, and after assuming that post in February, 1882, he sought actively to counter Li Hung-chang's growing power. Although the court had several reasons for removing Tso from Peking and sending him to the south, it has been observed that Tso Tsung-t'ang competitive actions were often encouraged by the central government in order to maintain some equilibrium within the provincial government system.[56] By granting Tso Tsung-t'ang the governor-generalship of Liang-Chiang, the court had summoned to the original base, now the secondary source, of Li Hung-chang's military power, the only man in China who then rivaled Li Hung-chang in military prestige and national fame. The granting to Tso of responsibility for reporting the accounts of the Huai-chün elements within his territorial jurisdiction was a first step in the attempt to limit Li Hung-chang's military power. This attempt will be seen more clearly later when financial sources of the Huai-chün during Li Hung-chang's period in Chihli are analyzed in detail.

It is evident that in the decade before the 1894 war with Japan, Li Hung-chang concentrated increasingly upon the development of his northern armies. However, he did not abandon the posts occupied by the Huai-chün in Kiangsu. As late as 1890, there were references to the importance of maintaining the military supply depots of the Huai-chün at Wu-ch'ang in Hupeh, at Yang-chou and Ch'ing-chiang in Kiangsu, and at Chi-ning in Shantung.[57]

---

ments on the Huai forces in their areas on a quarterly basis, both to Li Hung-chang and to the responsible boards (Revenue, War, and Works) in Peking. Li Hung-chang used these statistics for compiling his annual report on the entire Huai Army, referring the boards to the quarterly reports for more detailed information. After 1882, Li continued to receive the quarterly reports but no longer referred to them in his general account. Rather they formed part of an over-all report submitted by the local provincial officials on the general financial status of their own areas.

[55] The quarterly reports are very likely still preserved in the various archives of China, which unfortunately are inaccessible.

[56] Alicia (Mrs. Archibald) Little, *Li Hung-chang: His Life and Times* (London, 1903), p. 53, points out that Tso Tsung-t'ang was encouraged to develop the Foochow Arsenal as a "counter plot" against Li Hung-chang and Tseng Kuo-fan, who, the central government feared, "together could become masters of Central China."

[57] *LWCK Memorials,* 67:27a-b, KH 16/3/21.

In 1882 the forces directly under Li's command numbered 39 battalions. The army in the north continued to increase; by 1884 Li had 6 battalions in Chin-chou and Fengtien (now Mukden), Manchuria, 19 battalions newly enlisted in Tientsin, and 40 regular battalions covering the coastline and defense perimeter of the capital, as well as the military supply routes of the north.[58] This makes a total of 65 battalions in Chihli and Manchuria alone. Li had felt it necessary to raise 19 new battalions for the defense of the Tientsin area, and there is no evidence that he had withdrawn any forces from Shantung or Kiangsu. Had such a withdrawal been undertaken, those troops could have been transferred to Tientsin and used in place of raw recruits. This increase in force was intended to meet the war situation of 1884, when France and China were engaged in limited hostilities over rights in Annam.

The international situation having returned to normal by 1886, the justification for continuing the heavy payments for an augmented Huai Army around the capital vanished. A new reduction in the Huai-chün took place in the north, at the end of which the total battalion strength was only 49 battalions or approximately 25,000 men.[59] This reduction in the north was slightly offset in 1888 by the shifting of 2 battalions of Wu-I-chün troops, previously stationed at the supply depot in Hupeh, to Chihli, bringing the total strength back to 51 battalions.[60] By this time the Huai-chün was spread over the entire northern coast from southern Chihli up around the Liaotung Peninsula to Dairen.

The size of the Huai-chün in the north remained stable, at 51 battalions, from 1888 until 1893, the last year in which Li Hung-chang made a regular report on the Huai-chün finances, size, and disposition.[61] This figure does not include troops in Shantung, for instance those at Weihaiwei, the presence of which was on occasion briefly noted.[62] Comparing the number of Huai-chün battalions in Chihli and Manchuria in 1892 and in 1882, we note that the Huai-chün forces in these areas had increased over the decade by 12 *ying*, or more than 30 per cent. It has not been possible to establish whether corresponding or contrary changes occurred in Kiangsu or even in Shantung, although

---

[58] *Ibid.*, 55:42a-44a, KH 11/12/13.

[59] *Ibid.*, 63:50a-51b, KH 14/11/27.

[60] *Ibid.*, 66:35a-36b, KH 15/12/13.

[61] *Ibid.*, 69:35a ff., KH 16/11/16; 73:29a ff., KH 17/11/30; 75:31a ff., KH 18/10/28; 77:40a ff., KH 19/10/26.

[62] See, for instance, *ibid.*, 67:27a-b, KH 16/3/21.

it is likely that the Huai-chün's importance in these areas diminished somewhat, particularly in Kiangsu.

So long as the Huai-chün was strong and was solidly maintained by Li, he firmly held power as governor-general at Chihli and was unquestionably the most influential official in the north. Yet in the quarter of a century following Li's arrival at Chihli considerable changes had taken place in the army. It was smaller by half than it had been during the Taiping and Nien rebellions. It was spread over a larger area, and was no longer based mainly in its own homeland, the Liang-Chiang region. This does not necessarily mean, however, that the Huai-chün had become weaker. It was better equipped than in the past, and after its drastic reduction immediately after the Nien Rebellion, the Huai-chün had remained quite stable in size while the armies of other commanders were continually reduced, if not completely demobilized. The expansion of the Huai-chün over a larger area was not accompanied by loss of control on Li's part or by any notable decrease in its fighting strength. Rather, it provided for Li a wider area of authority than he had ever enjoyed before, extending from the coastal garrison on the Liaotung Peninsula to the heart of the Yangtze valley.

The maintenance of the Huai-chün in the north was in itself a major accomplishment. In order to achieve it Li had found it necessary to keep open his lifeline to Liang-Chiang, to develop new arsenals for his armies wherever they were, to resist calls by the central government for reduction of forces and expenses, and to enlarge and consolidate his political and military machine. None of these tasks differed markedly from those he had successfully carried out in his first year as governor of Kiangsu. There was, however, one basic difference. Liang-Chiang, where Li had started his rise, was his native region, and it was only there that he had been able to establish his strength. Now on the basis of that strength he had succeeded in moving himself and his organization into Chihli, where he had set himself up as the protector of the dynasty and strong man of the north. In spite of this drastic shift, the Huai-chün not only survived but became an integral feature of military power and national defense in the north.

VI. Li Hung-chang and the Problem of "Self-Strengthening"

NATIONAL security ranked first among the problems that faced China's leading officials after the impact of the West had been felt. Even before the catastrophic rebellions had turned China into a vast battlefield and focused attention upon the need for military reform, China's humiliating defeats in the Opium War had alarmed those who were charged with resisting foreign aggression.[1] It had become evident that British ships were capable of reducing Chinese towns to rubble, and that well-equipped Western troops could effect landings and limited occupation on Chinese soil. The experience of the provincial military leaders Tseng, Li, Tso, and others, who learned through bitter trial the value of equipping their own troops with Western weapons and denying them to the enemy insurgents, provided a fresh and material background for the movement in China which came to be known by the concise but adequate name of "self-strengthening."[2] The self-strengthening movement was not a great concerted effort or a wide popular program, but rather it was a continued and accelerating series of attempts by various government leaders and groups to increase China's military strength by emulating the military, and to a lesser extent, the industrial techniques of the West.

Li Hung-chang was famous in his time as being the most advanced proponent of self-strengthening. He has been praised for his unswerving attention in the face of conservative opposition to the creation of

---

[1] Ssu-yü Teng, John K. Fairbank, and others, *China's Response to the West, A Documentary Survey, 1839-1923* (Cambridge, 1954), pp. 28-42. See also Fang Hao, "Ming-mo hsi-yang huo-ch'i liu-ju wo-kuo chih shih-liao," *Tung-fang tsa-chih*, XL, No. 1 (January, 1944), 49-54.

[2] Mary Clabaugh Wright, *The Last Stand of Chinese Conservatism: The T'ung-Chih Restoration, 1862-1874* (Stanford, 1957), p. 14.

modern military forces in China. He has also been ridiculed for the lame showing his forces made when finally put to the test against those of another power. Like other men of great achievement, Li is often either praised or damned too much. He did not originate the idea of self-strengthening, nor was he alone in attempting to achieve its goals. On the other hand, he cannot be assigned all the blame for the failure of an effort for which the Chinese government and society were not yet ready, and which was additionally hampered by adverse conditions of foreign relations.

The most striking aspect of Li Hung-chang's endeavor to transform China's weakness to strength was the way in which he identified the nation's interest with his own. It is not accidental that the movement for self-strengthening was promoted by regional leaders like Tseng Kuo-fan and Li Hung-chang, who found in the military techniques of the West the means of strengthening their own forces. While Tseng's protestations of loyalty to Confucian civilization and the Ch'ing dynasty may seem to indicate that he strengthened his own forces in order that he might better serve his imperial masters, the same cannot be said for Li Hung-chang. When Li Hung-chang spoke of self-strengthening, he discussed generalities; when he engaged in self-strengthening, he was strengthening himself. Taking over leadership from Tseng in Chihli, Li Hung-chang promoted an approach to public affairs which was essentially regional rather than national. Although certain central government officials also took great interest in self-strengthening and virtually all Chinese officials were united in opposition to the West and to Chinese insurrectionists, their objectives and ideals must be judged in the light of actual achievements. The self-strengthening movement failed to strengthen China, but gave wide powers to Li Hung-chang and a few leaders like him at the expense of the central government and its forces.

Early Efforts at Reforming Military Technique

The first in the line of outstanding officials who saw the need for using techniques imported from the West in order to hold back Western imperialism was Lin Tse-hsü. Lin has become widely known outside China for his uncompromising stand against the British opium trade at Canton, which led to the Anglo-Chinese War of 1839 to 1842, or as it has come to be known, the Opium War. The initial hostilities between the Chinese and British forces soon showed Lin that Chinese forces using traditional weapons were no match for modern troops and ships.[3] Lin employed a staff to translate material from Western sources and wrote several letters on this subject; these provided the basis for Wei Yüan's important study of Western military affairs. The works of Wei, a famous historian and geographer, soon engaged the attention of prominent leaders, among them Tseng Kuo-fan.[4] But despite this interest on the part of a few leaders, Western manufactures and techniques remained almost unknown in China, and only a few sporadic attempts were made to introduce Western machinery or armaments.[5]

It was only under the nearly disastrous circumstances of the Taiping Rebellion that Tseng and others were forced to begin using Western weapons and ships in order to gain superiority over the rebel armies. Tseng at first confined himself to purchasing Western arms through the port of Canton but later, in 1862, he established an experimental factory, employing only Chinese personnel, at Anking, where a steam engine for naval use was constructed.[6] Although this plant produced only a few model pieces, its establishment was a tremendous step toward westernization. It was an entirely Chinese plant and its output proved, at least to Tseng's satisfaction, that China could produce modern implements of war without relying upon untrustworthy foreigners.[7] But despite his interest in Western arms, Tseng made no strenuous efforts to modify even the Hsiang-chün until the very close of his career. Most of his Hunan troops retained their traditional Chinese weapons.

Li Hung-chang undoubtedly was familiar from the first with Tseng's experiments at Anking, and like many of his colleagues did not fail to recognize the obvious advantages of using Western weapons. He was more fortunate than most, since he had been able to acquire firsthand knowledge of Western military techniques at the beginning of his independent command in Shanghai. During his first year there his attitude changed decidedly from open hostility to foreigners and

---

[3] Hummel, *Eminent Chinese*, pp. 511-14; Ch'i-t'ien, Ch'en, *Lin Tse-hsü, Pioneer Promoter of the Adoption of Western Means of Maritime Defense in China* (Peiping, 1934), *passim;* Teng and Fairbank, *China's Response to the West*, pp. 28-29.

[4] Wei Yüan's *Hai-kuo t'u-chih* first appeared in 1844, in 60 *chüan*, and was later expanded to 100 *chüan*.

[5] Ch'i-t'ien Ch'en, *Lin Tse-hsü, passim; Tseng Kuo-fan, Pioneer Promoter of the Steamship in China* (Peiping, 1935), chaps. 1 and 2, *passim*.

[6] *TWCK Memorials*, 3:7a, HF 4/7/11, discusses the purchase of foreign guns at Canton for Tseng's forces to the north; 14:9a, HF 11/7/18, deals with the purchase of war vessels from France; 14:13a, HF 11/7/18, refers to the rental of two American vessels to be used as gunboats.

[7] Ch'i-t'ien Ch'en, *Tseng Kuo-fan*, p. 40.

grudging tolerance of their military methods, to a grudging tolerance of foreigners and open admiration of their military methods.[8]

Li Hung-chang's Early Arsenals

Li was deeply impressed, as we have seen earlier, by the performance of the Ever Victorious Army, and he attributed its success to the excellence of its arms. In the hope of freeing himself from a growing dependence upon foreign sources for new weapons, in 1862 Li Hung-chang ordered the establishment at Shanghai of a small experimental arsenal. At the same time he urged Prince Kung in the north to establish a similar plant at Tientsin for the armies in that area.[9] The Shanghai plant was set up under the supervision of Dr. Halliday Macartney, an English medical officer who had resigned from the British forces to enter Li's service.[10] When Li moved from Shanghai to Soochow in 1863, he insisted that the arsenal be moved also. Li was not dissatisfied with Macartney's direction of the arsenal but did not like to rely completely upon a foreigner. With the consent of Tseng Kuo-fan and in consultation with Ting Jih-ch'ang, an expert recommended by Tseng, Li ordered the establishment of two more small arsenals, one to be managed by Ting Jih-ch'ang and the other by an army colonel, Han Tien-chia.[11] Ting Jih-ch'ang's plant employed Western technicians under Chinese supervision, but Han Tien-chia's establishment employed no Westerners at all. Although the arsenals were intended as trial grounds and the crude weapons and munitions they produced were used by the Huai-chün, Li was disappointed in the results of his experiment, commenting that "although the shells we have produced are comparable with Western products, I am ashamed to say that we have not yet attained mastery over the new, changing methods of production."[12]

Soochow was hardly a suitable location for the arsenals, since materials had to be brought there from Shanghai; but Li was unwilling to have the arsenals at Shanghai in operation during his absence from that city until he felt that he had complete control over the local ad-

---

[8] *LWCK Letters,* 2:46b, TC 1/12/15. See also *ibid.,* 1:46b, TC 1/7/19; p. 5a, TC 1/8/15; and 2:26b, TC 1/10/6.

[9] *CSK,* 146:1a; *LWCK Letters,* 1:58a, TC 1/8/24.

[10] Hummel, *Eminent Chinese,* p. 721; *LWCK Letters,* 1:57b-58a, TC 1/8/24; Demetrius Boulger, *The Life of Sir Halliday Macartney* (London and New York, 1908), *passim.*

[11] *LWCK Letters,* 3:16b, TC 2/3/17; *LWCK Memorials,* 7:17a-19a, TC 3/7/29; Ch'uan Han-sheng, "Ch'ing-chi ti Chiang-nan chih-ts'ao chü," in *Bulletin of the Institute of History and Philology,* Academia Sinica, XXIII (Taipei, 1951), 147.

[12] Ch'uan Han-sheng, *loc. cit.*

ministration. Although he was often discouraged, he was more than ever convinced of the importance of industrial enterprises. In 1863 he wrote to Tseng expressing the hope that "the poisonous vapors of rebellion will soon be dispelled so that we may turn our efforts to the production of foreign machines."[13] With the fall of Nanking in 1864 and his own appointment the following year as governor-general of Liang-Chiang, Li Hung-chang was free to carry out his stated ambition.

Li Hung-chang's appointment as governor-general made it necessary for him to take up residence at Nanking, the regional capital. Reluctant to be at a distance from all his arsenals, he ordered that the factory under Macartney—the most modern and efficient of the three—be moved to Nanking, where it was relocated on the bank of the Yangtze.[14] Thus he was able to supervise his major project directly. The Nanking arsenal guaranteed Li sufficient munitions for his own *ch'in-ping*, or personal troops. Under the skillful direction of Macartney, the staff carried on experiments in productive techniques aimed at introducing China into the machine age. Li realized nevertheless that the single arsenal at Nanking would not be sufficient for his needs and would be handicapped by its distance from the port of Shanghai. Having no further direct interest in Soochow except as a source of revenue, he dismantled the two Chinese-operated arsenals there and had their equipment shipped to Shanghai.

In the middle of 1865 Li Hung-chang divulged to the court the plan he and Tseng had agreed upon for the establishment of a large arsenal at Shanghai, which later became famous as the Kiangnan Arsenal. Even before presenting his first memorial on the subject in 1865, Li had taken the first steps in setting up the projected establishment. The machinery and materials formerly housed in the two plants at Soochow were used as the basic plant of the new arsenal. Previously Tseng Kuo-fan had sent Jung Hung (also known as Yung Wing), an American-educated Cantonese, to America and had commissioned others to go to England to purchase materials for the production of ships and machines. Li now planned to use these materials for his new arsenal. He had ordered Ting Jih-ch'ang and Han Tien-chia to make discreet inquiries in Shanghai with a view to purchasing suitable sites and, if possible, any existing foreign plants. Ting Jih-ch'ang reported to Li that there was an excellent possibility of purchasing "in Hung-k'ou,

---

[13] *LWCK Letters,* 3:19b, TC 2/4/4.

[14] Hummel, *Eminent Chinese,* p. 721; Boulger, *The Life of Sir Halliday Macartney, passim.*

Shanghai, a foreign factory with the necessary equipment for the repair and production of both large and small steamships and cannon and guns," and that this factory was "the largest among the foreign factories in the foreign bund of Shanghai."[15]

The Kiangnan Arsenal, as the Shanghai plant came to be known, remained under the watchful eyes of Li Hung-chang's lieutenants for many years after his departure from Liang-Chiang. During the period when Li was active in the Nien campaign and throughout his occupancy of the governor-generalship of Hu-Kuang, he continued to exercise over-all control of the establishment, though it was by then beyond his area of official jurisdiction.[16]

By 1875 the Kiangnan plant had grown to comprise some thirty-two buildings, including workshops, warehouses, special factories for the production of boats and munitions, map shops, architectural shops, translation rooms, and business offices, in addition to dockyards and outdoor works.[17] The daily output of gunpowder reached 1,000 pounds, and the daily output of Remington shells was 5,000 rounds.[18] In founding the Kiangnan Arsenal Li and Tseng had provided the model for the later renovated Nanking and Tientsin arsenals, as well as for the Foochow, Kuang-chou, and Han-yang arsenals. To strengthen their own forces they had constructed one of the largest Western-style enterprises established in China during the nineteenth century.[19]

Li's six years of experience in initiating and directing arsenal works in Liang-Chiang before his arrival at Chihli in 1870 had convinced him that Chinese workmen and directors alone could not successfully produce modern machines and armaments. This does not mean that his suspicion of foreigners had abated. He was wary enough to cause the Kiangnan Arsenal to be moved from the foreign bund at Shanghai to a new site on the outskirts of the city, thereby removing it from the influence of the foreigners.[20] Li realized, however, that it would take a long time to develop a body of skilled Chinese technicians, and he was also aware of the tremendous strides being made by military

---

[15] *LWCK Memorials*, 9:31a-35b, TC 4/8/1.

[16] *LWCK Letters*, 9:9b, TC 8/4/2; *LWCK Memorials*, 19:51a, TC 11/5/15.

[17] Ch'uan Han-sheng, *loc: cit.*

[18] *LWCK Memorials*, 26:13a ff., KH 1/19/19; Ch'uan Han-sheng, *loc. cit.*

[19] Ch'uan Han-sheng, *loc. cit.;* Chang Po-ch'u, "Shanghai ping-kung-ch'ang chih shih-mo," *Jen-wen yüeh-k'an,* Vol. V, No. 5, pp. 1-14; *LWCK Memorials*, 26:13a ff., KH 1/19/19; Sheng Hsüan-huai, "Shang-hai tsou chien chuan-tz'u shu," in *LWCK Collected Works,* Introductory *chüan,* pp. 49b-50a.

[20] *LWCK Memorials*, 9:31a-35b, TC 4/8/1.

industry in the West. Yielding to what he considered to be expediency, he employed an increasing number of foreign managers through the years. By insisting upon absolute loyalty from his foreign advisers and managers and by refusing them any measure of independent control, he believed that, unlike Tso Tsung-t'ang, he had avoided the pitfalls of foreign domination over his enterprises.[21]

The Kiangnan Arsenal played an important part in China's economic history and in Li's development as a statesman and reformer.[22] By the time he arrived at Chihli, Li was equipped to push self-strengthening in the north and prepared to promote arsenal development to meet the requirements of his forces at their new base.

Together Li and Tseng had laid the basis for the production of modern armaments in China. Li's forces were the first to benefit from this development. The products of the Soochow, Nanking, and Kiangnan arsenals were used mainly to rearm the Huai-chün and give it unquestioned superiority in ordnance over other Chinese armies. But Tseng, although a pioneer in developing arsenals and shipyards, was slow to use them to equip his Hsiang army.

Tseng's Attempts to Modernize the Hsiang-chün

In Chihli Tseng actively pushed the modernization of the forces assigned to protect the capital. These troops were already organized along the lines of his Hsiang-chün and had been trained in the use of Western firearms. Their resemblance to Hsiang-chün forces was not accidental, since Liu Ch'ang-yu, the initiator of the earlier military reform in Chihli, was himself a Hsiang-chün man.[23] The forces which Liu Ch'ang-yu began to modernize as early as 1864, and which Tseng reorganized and strengthened in 1868, were known as *lien-chün*, literally, "trained troops," or troops drilled along Western lines. The development of *lien-chün* will be discussed presently; for the moment it is sufficient to note that Tseng was active in this development, which was a basic part of the self-strengthening movement.

When Li Hung-chang replaced Tseng as governor-general of Chihli

---

[21] *LWCK Letters*, 12:2b, TC 11/1/21. Shortly after the establishment of the Kiangnan Arsenal, Tso Tseng-t'ang established an arsenal and shipyard at Foochow. Li Hung-chang was severely critical of Tso's project, although in the interest of modernization he was forced to defend it. Partly motivated by personal rivalry and jealousy, Li attacked Tso's project for being "too expensive and too much under the control of the Frenchmen."

[22] Ch'uan Han-sheng, *op. cit.*, pp. 155 ff.

[23] Liu Ch'ang-yu was a native of Hsin-ning, Hunan. See *CSK*, 419:1a ff.; also Lo Erh-kang, *Hsiang-chün hsin-chih*, sections 1 and 2, *passim*.

in 1870, the court was faced with the problem of finding a suitable post for the venerable elder statesman and military leader. This was solved when the governor-general of Liang-Chiang, Ma Hsin-i, a protégé of Tseng, was assassinated, and the post which Tseng and Li had monopolized for almost a decade was once more vacant.[24] Tseng was reappointed and proceeded to Nanking, where he spent his last days in the governor-generalship of the area in which he had enjoyed his greatest power. It was here that he made his final efforts to revitalize his military organization.

Liang-Chiang, with its good revenues and ports—particularly Shanghai—was for Tseng an ideal region in which to undertake the organization of *lien-chün* and other projects for self-strengthening. The reassignment of Tseng to the Liang-Chiang region was of decided advantage to him as well as to the court, which was by now interested in self-strengthening. Whatever the court may have felt about Tseng earlier, there is little reason to doubt that by 1870 it was convinced of his loyalty and devotion. The assignment of Tseng, the acknowledged leader of the provincial officialdom, to the vital Liang-Chiang post was a wise and cautious decision. Liang-Chiang was still the "stomach land" of China and controlled the major section of the water route connecting the central regions with the capital. Tseng could be expected to safeguard tax and tribute en route to the capital and to exert a favorable influence upon other provincial leaders in neighboring areas.

After Tseng's dismissal from Chihli, his assignment to Liang-Chiang meant less loss of face than any other possible appointment. The governor-generalship of Liang-Chiang was second in importance only to that of Chihli; it afforded control of central, or as the Chinese called it, southeast China, and offered ample opportunities for pressure upon the court. Tseng had never been enthusiastic about going north to an area for which his Hunan troops were ill suited in habit and temperament. He was probably quite satisfied to be called upon to govern Liang-Chiang again, and his preference was well indicated in the comparison of the two regions which he drew for Li:

In the north there is weakness in the armies while now the southeast has emerged from rebellion. The armies in the southeast are not scanty and we have there a good foundation for manufacturing [war material]. Our policy of self-strengthening can therefore be carried through by using the southeast as our base.[25]

[24] Hummel, *Eminent Chinese*, pp. 554-56.   [25] *TWCK Letters*, 32:18a.

Tseng's conversion to the use of modern weapons was reflected in the names which he gave his forces. The remnants of his old armies he referred to as the "old Hsiang-chün" (*lao Hsiang-chün*); the new forces he began to enlist while in Liang-Chiang were called by him the *lien Hsiang-chün*. Thus he used Liang-Chiang as the base for creating in central China a *lien-chün* comparable to that of the north.

Li, who had learned so much from Tseng, now helped to teach his former master how to modernize his forces. After Tseng returned to Liang-Chiang, he wrote Li requesting him to place at his disposal an expert familiar with Western military techniques and weapons. He disclosed to his former student: "In the future the military organization of my Hsiang-chün will follow in the footsteps of the Huai-chün. Then I will be satisfied."[26]

Tseng at the same time depended upon Li Hung-chang's brother, the governor-general of Hu-Kuang, Li Han-chang, to co-operate with him and his own younger brother, Tseng Kuo-ch'üan, by mustering new recruits in Hunan. Tseng hoped in this way to recover the ground lost through the disintegration of the "old Hsiang-chün."

Though there were many skilled Western technicians in Shanghai, Tseng, who never trusted the "barbarians," did not take advantage of their services. Rather, he looked to Li and his own followers for the requisite specialized skills, sacrificing ability for dependability. Although his new army did not have to be large, Tseng insisted that it be completely reliable as well as carefully disciplined and trained. Thus, toward the end of his career, with the support of the Li brothers and his own younger brother, Tseng again set about raising a new type of army to meet a new period of crisis. This work was cut short by his death in 1872, and the *lien Hsiang-chün* was divided among Tseng's Hunanese followers. From beginning to end, whatever Tseng's loyalties may have been, his armies and his attempts to give China military strength had been limited by their regional basis and by Tseng's own regional outlook.

The Tientsin Arsenal under Li

While Tseng was striving to bring his forces up to date in Liang-Chiang, Li Hung-chang in Chihli was giving considerable attention to the development of a suitable source of armaments in the north. Through administrative reorganization he had brought the Tientsin Arsenal, built in the 1860's, under his personal control, for he en-

---

[26] *Ibid.*, 33 :39a.

visaged it as the principal and most reliable source of ready equipment for his troops at their northern base. In the past, wherever Li and his Huai-chün had been, he had established an arsenal, and had even dismantled and moved entire plants. During his long stay in Chihli, not wishing to depend upon the Huai-chün alone, Li extended his control over existing local forces and developed new forces, all of which he attempted to dominate by controlling their source of supplies. By demonstrating the superiority of Western arms and at the same time making his own military and bureaucratic machine the channel through which these weapons could be obtained, he could practically dictate to the central government the location, size, and organization of the forces in the north which the central government regarded as its own.[27]

When Li took over the arsenal at Tientsin he was already familiar with its history and development. He had been instrumental in establishing it almost a decade earlier, lending his support to Prince Kung, who saw the arsenal as a means of strengthening the central government armies around the capital by providing them with superior equipment.[28] The first technicians at the Tientsin plant had been trained by Li's own men at the Shanghai and Soochow arsenals in the early 1860's.[29] At that time, characteristically, Li had cautioned against rapid expansion of the Tientsin works, arguing that it would be better to move forward slowly, taking account of the trial-and-error methods of his Shanghai project.[30] Now as Li himself took over control of the Tientsin Arsenal, he pushed its development vigorously, and attempted to model it closely on the lines of his previous projects by

---

[27] Li Hung-chang's memorial collection has many references to his control of firearms and other supplies for various types of government forces in the north. He helped decide the location of military stations and supply headquarters, the size and armament of forces, and decided on what basis priorities were to be assigned among the armies. See particularly the following examples: *LWCK Memorials*, 17:38a, TC 9/11/5; 44a, TC 9/11/11; 18:8a, TC 10/2/6; 16a, TC 10/4/23; 20a, TC 10/4/23; 26a, TC 10/5/10; 63a, TC 10/9/15; 19:1a, TC 11/1/19; 20:46a, TC 11/12/19; 21:40a, TC 12/4/23; 22:8a, TC 12/6/20; 23:48a, TC 12/11/19; 25:10a, KH 1/4/9; 21a, KH 1/5/17; 22a, KH 1/6/16; 27:3a, KH 2/3/7; 28:5a, KH 4/6/29; 32:13a, KH 4/7/23; 33:30a, KH 4/10/18; 38:24a, KH 6/9/4; 40:40a, KH 7/4/23; 41:45a, KH 7/7/15; 42:44a, KH 7/12/2; 43:15a, KH 8/1/25; 45:6a, KH 8/9/29; 46:21a, KH 9/2/16; 51:36a, KH 10/9/4; 52:1a, KH 10/10/15; 75:44a, KH 18/2/23; 77:6a, KH 19/6/6. These examples include such items as reports concerning the shipment of firearms from the Tientsin Arsenal to troops in Sinkiang; discussions of standards established by Li for the purchase of Western weapons for all northern armies; the delivery of rifles and ammunition to troops in Kirin, Manchuria; discussions of the demobilization of troops at Kulun; and scores of similar cases.
[28] *Ibid.*, 7:17a ff., TC 3/2/29; 9:31a-35b, TC 4/8/17; 17:16a-18a, TC 9/10/26.
[29] *Ibid.*, 7:17a ff., TC 3/2/29.
[30] *Ibid.*, 9:31a-35b, TC 4/8/17.

appointing Shen Pao-ch'ing as its manager.[31] Shen had managed the Shanghai Arsenal under the direction of Li Hung-chang and Ting Jih-ch'ang for several years and was familiar with the administrative problems of arsenals. Li also considered him to be an especially well-qualified personnel director. He noted of Shen:

While he was in Shanghai, I relied upon him in everything. I depended upon his initiative, particularly in employing foreign technicians. He never permitted foreign pressure to sway him in the employment or dismissal of foreign workmen, but always relied on his own judgment. Never were the foreign consuls able to sway him.[32]

Li planned eventually to promote Shen to the position of customs intendant of Tientsin because he saw the problems of coastal defense, revenue collection, and arms production, all of which fell under the jurisdiction of the customs intendant, as inseparable.

Li's first steps in expanding the Tientsin Arsenal were to construct greater storage facilities for gunpowder and to provide new machinery.[33] In the following years, according to Li, the arsenal grew slowly but steadily. Li described its growth in a report on the accounts of the Tientsin Machinery Bureau for the years 1876 and 1877, parts of which are translated below:

In recent years, aside from the purchase of raw materials and the payment of wages, the most important expenses have been for the purchase of machinery and the construction of factories. Since 1875 we have increased the number of our machines, worksheds, and warehouses on a small scale. The various types of shells and ammunition produced compare favorably with those we have imported from abroad.

Water mines are most important for our coastal defenses; therefore in the fourth month of the second year of Kuang-hsü, I invited Western technicians to instruct some of the students at the factory in the production of mines, and I added an Electric Mine Office to the Bureau. They have produced various types of mines, and the experiments have turned out well.

... In the second year of Kuang-hsü [1876] the following was produced:

Gunpowder	643,000 pounds
Caps, copper	40,200,000 pieces
Bullets	948,000 rounds
Explosive cannon shells	68,000
Rifled cannon shells	2,000
Grenades	170,000
Cannon mounts	40

---

[31] *Ibid.*, 17:17a-b, TC 9/10/26.
[32] *Ibid.*
[33] *Ibid.*, 17:16a-b, TC 9/11/6.

... In the third year of Kuang-hsü [1877] they produced the following:

Gunpowder	580,000 pounds
Caps, copper	35,000,000 pieces
Bullets	1,000,000 rounds
Explosive cannon shells	58,000
Rifled cannon shells	4,000
Grenades	187,000
Remington breech-loading guns	200
Water mines	500
Cannon mounts	20

During these two years the Bureau produced over 400,000 pounds of copper plating, constructed more buildings, repaired ships, and added more instruments and machine parts, numbering 70,000 pieces....[34]

This report reflects Li's increasing interest in naval warfare and coastal defense. The attention given to modern Remington breech-loaders indicates a serious attempt to bring Chinese arms production up to contemporary Western standards.

Most promising of all Li's innovations, however, was the inauguration of a school at the arsenal for instruction in the production of electrically detonated mines, which marked the first attempt of the Chinese to produce and use electricity in their own installations. To direct some two hundred Chinese soldiers at the arsenal in the use of electricity, Li appointed Major Manneck, of the United States Army Engineers, to the arsenal staff. Assisting Manneck in the supervision of the Torpedo and Electrical School of the Tientsin Arsenal were fifteen Chinese lower officials who had previously been sent by Li and Tseng to America for technical education. It was anticipated, at least by one British observer, that the Torpedo School would prove to be the first step towards the establishment of a modern school of war in north China.[35] This prediction was proved correct when Li later founded the Tientsin Military Academy. The success of the Tientsin Arsenal stirred the hopes and ambitions of Li and other proponents of self-strengthening, and the arsenal later came to be the principal source of supplies for the modern navy and the new land forces developed in north China at the turn of the century.

Arsenal Control and Military Power

The development of the Tientsin Arsenal was an attempt to strengthen Li's control of the north and was characteristic of the pattern of action that he followed for over thirty years. Up to 1895,

[34] *Ibid.*, 33:25a ff., KH 4/10/18.
[35] Mark S. Bell, *China,* II, 60.

when he at last fell from power in the north, Li always kept at least one major arsenal under his direct control at his place of residence. First Shanghai, then Soochow, then Shanghai again, then Nanking, and finally Tientsin became the scenes of Li's efforts to build up for his forces closely controlled sources of the best available war material. Li did not quickly abandon his old arsenals, even after he was removed from their neighborhood. Although he eventually had to relinquish some of his power, he was usually able to retain at least partial control over his older establishments for varying periods, while creating new ones. The importance of the arsenals was increased by the fact that they frequently served as the agencies through which arms and munitions were ordered from Europe and America. If the arsenals did not always, or even often, produce the best materials available, they still served as important channels of procurement. In Shanghai, Li Hung-chang's arsenal had produced and procured materials almost exclusively for the Huai and Hsiang forces. So closely were the early arms and munitions factories connected with the Huai-chün organization that their accounts were submitted as part of the military accounts of the Huai-chün.[36] After the formal establishment of the Kiangnan Arsenal, a separate budget was set up for the new plant to indicate its independence, but its production remained geared to Huai Army needs and demands. The superiority of the Huai-chün weapons, which made the Huai-chün the strongest fighting force in the land, was largely a result of Li's control over the arsenal.[37]

With the passing of years and Li's continued absence from Liang-Chiang, his control over the Kiangnan Arsenal appears to have diminished, particularly when China's defense system was broken into northern and southern blocs in the mid-1880's.[38] Nevertheless, as late as 1893, Li still exercised enough influence over the arsenal to recommend promotion for its personnel.[39]

---

[36] *LWCK Memorials,* 8:9a-13a, TC 4/2/17.

[37] Shen Pao-chen, governor-general of Liang-Chiang, claimed that the guns and munitions manufactured at the Kiangnan Arsenal (which was then under his jurisdiction) "supply the governor-general of Chihli and the provinces of Kiangnan." Shen Pao-chen's memorials, *chüan* 7, KH 4/3/14, quoted in Ch'uan Han-sheng, *op. cit.,* p. 148. The importance of the arsenal in the defeat of the Nien is stressed in the special appendix on Huai-chün weapons, in Chou Shih-ch'eng, *Huai-chün p'ing-nien chi,* 12:1a-11b, *passim.*

[38] *LWCK Memorials,* 19:51a, TC 11/5/15; *LWCK Letters,* 9:9b, TC 8/4/10; *LWCK Memorials,* 17:16a, TC 9/10/26; *TWCK Letters,* 33:35a. Sir Halliday Macartney, perhaps the best informed Westerner in his time on the subject of Chinese arsenals, pointed out in 1876, "That [arsenal] of Shanghai is directly under the Taotai and Viceroy of Kiangsu." Boulger, *The Life of Sir Halliday Macartney,* p. 250.

[39] *LWCK Memorials,* 77:1a-3a, KH 19/6/16; 4a-5a, KH 19/6/16.

The Nanking Arsenal, five hundred miles to the south of Li's center at Tientsin, remained for a long time the special depot of Li Hung-chang and the Huai-chün. Even after the death of Tseng Kuo-fan, the governor-general at Nanking, in 1872, the Nanking Arsenal continued to be directly under the control of Li, and its products were entirely at his disposal. Sir Halliday Macartney, who had played a prominent role in the establishment of the arsenal, made the following comment as late as 1876, a decade after Li had left Nanking and six years after he assumed the governor-generalship of Chihli: ". . . [the arsenal] of Nankin . . . though its revenue comes from Kiangsu, acknowledges only the Viceroy of Chihli. Very little of its manufacture goes to Kiangsu, the main part going to Chihli, but orders have been received from the Imperial Government to supply other provinces such as Kansuh."[40]

Macartney's observations were borne out by Captain Trotter, who made an extensive survey of military encampments, fortresses, and arsenals along the Yangtze on behalf of British Military Intelligence. He was surprised to see at Nanking what appeared to be two entirely separate plants for military production. After describing the buildings and products of the first of these plants, the Nanking Arsenal which had originally been constructed by Li, he added the following note:

There is also said to be a small powder manufactury and a small arsenal, entirely under native management, lying to the west of the town, subject to the control and under the orders of the Governor-general of Nanking [Shen Pao-chen], who has nothing whatever to do with the larger arsenals, which are entirely in the hands of Li-Hung-Chang, the Imperial Commissioner, and are in no way subject to the local authorities.[41]

Li Hung-chang was able to maintain his control over the Nanking Arsenal until at least 1884. Until that time the expenses and production of the arsenal were conspicuously mentioned in Li's reports, indicating that he had a direct interest in it.[42] But in 1882 the governor-general of Liang-Chiang took over the responsibility for reporting the accounts of the Huai-chün battalions in his region, and this change

---

[40] Boulger, *The Life of Sir Halliday Macartney,* "Letter on the Military Forces of China, 1876," p. 250.

[41] Captain R. E. Trotter, "Report on the Nanking Arsenal," in Bell, *China,* II, 85.

[42] The reports appear in *LWCK Memorials* as follows: 1872-73—25:45a, KH 1/7/28; 1873-74—27:13a, KH 2/5/4; 1874-75—29:30a, KH 3/6/16; 1875-76, '76-77—32:31a, 34a, KH 4/8/29; 1877-78—34:22a, KH 5/4/16; 1878-79—37:50a, KH 6/7/14; 1879-80—40:4a, KH 7/1/19; 1880-81—42:54a, KH 7/12/20; 1882-83—48:15a, KH 9/10/29; 1883-84—52:35a, KH 10/12/1. These accounts of the Huai-chün receipts and expenditures all include reports on the Nanking and Tientsin arsenal payments.

was evidently followed by a change in the reporting of the Nanking Arsenal as well, for in Li's periodic reports covering the years after 1884 no mention of the arsenal appears.[43]

There is no indication that this change in accounting procedures diminished Li's interest in Nanking or interrupted arms shipments to Chihli. Li remained governor-general of Chihli and Commissioner of Trade, responsible for central government interests as well as his own forces, and was in an excellent position to demand continuance of the supply. Yet he had been absent from Liang-Chiang almost twenty years, and many of his old followers there had long since gone. He was increasingly dependent upon his position as protector of the court in the north and upon his influence with the central government for aid from the south. In the absence of details concerning Li's relationship with the Nanking Arsenal after 1884, no conclusions can be drawn as to the extent of his control over it after that year. It seems likely that his control was strongly challenged after 1882, when Tso Tsung-t'ang became governor-general at Nanking. Although Tso retired after serving there only two years and died a year later, he had already taken vigorous steps to combat Li's control over Nanking's munitions. In 1883, British Intelligence noted:

Powder works are about to be started at Nanking on a large scale. The plant for six incorporating mills has arrived at Shanghai and is being transported to Nanking. A European supervisor has been engaged to superintend the work.

Tso Tsung-t'ang, the Viceroy of the Province, under whose auspices these works are started, is anxious to establish others of a like nature in the interior of South and Mid China for the defense of which he is Chief Commissioner.[44]

Tso's efforts to produce armaments were undertaken to supply his own forces with munitions and weapons. His aim, apparently, was to expand and strengthen his own forces in Liang-Chiang in order to thrust aside the Huai armies still entrenched there and still receiving supplies from Nanking. Tso's death prevented any conclusive struggle of this sort. It is clear, however, that by the mid-1880's Li was at a disadvantage in the Yangtze valley and had lost, at the least, his old monopoly over the production of arms and munitions in Liang-Chiang.

---

[43] From 1884 (KH 10) onward there are no further references to the Nanking Arsenal, although mention is made, as before, of payments to the Tientsin Arsenal. See *LWCK Memorials*, 55:42a, KH 11/12/13, for accounts of KH 10; 58:48a, KH 12/12/16, for KH 11; 63:1a, KH 14/7/27, for KH 12-14.

[44] Bell, *China*, II, 84-85.

The provincial organization and division of power under the Manchu dynasty were maintained in part to prevent such monopolies and power formations, and even Li could not completely evade the obstacles imposed by the system. He was hampered even more by his distance from his former center of power and by the slow but inevitable deterioration of the bureaucratic machine which he had so skillfully developed there during and after the Taiping Rebellion. That he was able to retain a large measure of control over the region after two decades had passed shows the vitality of his own regional organization and the weakness of the central government. Li's gradual loss of control in Liang-Chiang was not a surrender of power to the central government. Rather he was being supplanted by other regional leaders using the same techniques that Li had employed there in his time. Like Li they saw self-strengthening in the concrete terms of the struggle for position and power, both within the bureaucracy and between the regions in which they exercised their growing strength.

The Adoption of the Lien-chün by Li Hung-chang

The responsibilities that Li assumed as governor-general of Chihli were wider than those he had held in the past. Although he had served as governor-general in both Liang-Chiang and Hu-Kuang, his major efforts at that time had been confined to meeting immediate emergencies, and he had used his powers as governor-general to serve the urgent needs of the Huai-chün on the field of battle. His first concern had been the suppression of rebellion, and the army he had founded and led was designed for that task. At the same time he was well aware of the importance of his army in supporting his own political aspirations. As an instrument of Chinese power politics its superior training and armament made it indispensable to the central government for the maintenance of internal security, while its loyalty to Li himself, or to his own Huai officers, made it unusable by others. As long as the Huai-chün was needed and feared by the government, Li Hung-chang enjoyed a measure of security unknown to most Chinese bureaucrats, either central or provincial. To the end the Huai-chün remained Li's primary source of strength, but in Chihli, where Li was responsible for the defense of the capital from external as well as internal threats, he had new problems to deal with and new military forces to take into account.

The traditional military forces in the north were the Manchu Banners and the Chinese Army of the Green Standard, or Lü-ying. Neither of these forces had made a good accounting during the Taiping Rebellion; both had been outshone by the militia forces of the Hsiang-Huai type. At the close of the emergency, however, the central government, unwilling to trust its defense solely to the personal, regional armies of men like Tseng, Li, and Tso, insisted on retaining the discredited older Banner and Lü-ying forces. Some compromise was attempted, however, as the government, recognizing the superiority of the militia forces, tried to combine the two types into a single force under central government control. This attempt was unsuccessful, and the result was that in the closing years of the nineteenth century a patchwork of militia, Lü-ying, and varying mixtures of the two dominated the Chinese military scene.

Yet military affairs in the north were more orderly than in other parts of the nation, because the central government had a vital interest in the protection of that region, and because it had already permitted partial adoption of the Hsiang-chün battalion organization, modern drill, and equipment. As early as 1864, a follower of Tseng Kuo-fan, Liu Ch'ang-yu, who had been appointed governor-general of Chihli, set about reorganizing and re-equipping the government troops around the capital. These troops, it will be recalled, were known as *lien-chün*. Li Hung-chang was interested in these forces from the beginning, and in 1864, when they were first reorganized, Li ordered his assistants in Soochow and Shanghai to instruct officers and soldiers from the Peking lien-chün in the manufacture and handling of modern weapons. These lien-chün, organized for the protection of the capital, represented the first attempt of the government to combine militia, Lü-ying, and certain Banner force men into a new, superior, central government army.[45] Although not entirely unsuccessful, the attempted reform did not go far at the time. Liu Ch'ang-yu himself did not possess a powerful army, and he did not develop the fledgling lien-chün into a force of any real size or significance. It was, in fact, hardly an army but rather a small conglomeration of scattered, specialized battalions.

The first real effort toward shaping the lien-chün into an effective army was made by Tseng Kuo-fan when he became governor-general of Chihli late in 1868. Tseng, rigid in his approach and objectives, molded the lien-chün battalions into the Hsiang-chün pattern and ap-

---

[45] The basic pattern of lien-chün development has been shown by Franz Michael. See, for instance, his article "Military Organization and Power Structure of China During the Taiping Rebellion," *Pacific Historical Review,* XVIII, No. 4 (November, 1949), 481.

parently succeeded in placing his own officers in command posts.[46] Yet
Tseng was not the ideal man to effect modernization. He had not
transformed the Hsiang-chün into a modern force, partly because
he held fast to the rule that "good men are more important than good
weapons."[47] In fact, his antipathy to foreign weapons (though not to
ships) was so strong that he had criticized a request by his younger
brother for Western cannon and rifles during the siege of Nanking in
1864.[48] It was only after his return to Liang-Chiang in 1870 that
Tseng began to re-equip and modernize the new Hsiang-chün forces
along the lines of the Huai-chün.

Aside from Tseng's own limitations, however, there was a more fundamental obstacle to the development of a successful lien-chün. A
modern army has a highly integrated command system, and its officers
are replaceable and transferable, but the Hsiang-Huai army system
was based on a rigid relationship between officers and men, and everything depended on personal loyalty. The armament of the lien-chün
changed, but its spirit and organization never went beyond the militia
stage.

When Li Hung-chang took over his seal in Chihli, he inherited lien-
chün battalions which had already been organized by Tseng. At his
disposal from the beginning, therefore, were a number of battalions
organized precisely along the lines of the Huai-chün. Without too
much reorganization he was able immediately to set about bringing
them within the framework of the Huai-chün. The lien-chün were im-
perially designated for special duty, and Li could not have disbanded
them, even if he had wished to do so. He tried to strengthen them and
at the same time to make them a branch of his own Huai-chün. In time
he was to find them an extremely important adjunct to his military
power in the north.

The lien-chün were technically under the command of the provincial
commander-in-chief of the province in which they were stationed. The
majority of the lien-chün battalions were within Chihli province, and
one of Li Hung-chang's first moves in Chihli was to place a reliable
Huai commander of his own choice in the post of provincial commander-in-chief of that province. Kuo Sung-lin, Li Ch'ang-lo, Chou
Sheng-ch'uan, Chou Sheng-po, and a number of other Huai-chün men
monopolized the post, assuring Li actual as well as nominal control of

---

[46] *TWCK Memorials,* 28:17a-21a, TC 8/5/21 ; 34a-37a, TC 8/8/27.
[47] *Ibid.*
[48] *TWCK Letters,* 20:34b.

the lien-chün throughout his governor-generalship in Chihli.[49] In addition, Li himself established the regulations for lien-chün battalions developed outside Chihli, in Ying-k'ou and other areas along the Manchurian coastline.[50] He was responsible for the stationing of lien-chün battalions in Shantung and outside the Great Wall, and he controlled most of their sources of supplies.[51]

Li did not attempt to impose the Huai-chün organizational system rigorously upon the lien-chün but rather used the system as a rough guide in setting up the new battalions. Whereas in the Huai-chün organization a battalion at full strength consisted of 500 foot soldiers, the lien-chün battalions varied considerably, at times consisting of 100 men, and sometimes, as at Ying-k'ou, of 300 foot soldiers and 100 cavalry soldiers.

Li eventually gave the lien-chün particular responsibility for the maintenance of coastal forts, mobile artillery units, and modern rifle companies. By combining lien-chün and Huai-chün detachments he was able to use the lien-chün to compensate for deficiencies in the Huai-chün, very much as Tseng Kuo-fan had originally used the Huai-chün to give additional firing power and mobility to the Hsiang-chün.[52] By supplying the lien-chün with instructors and commanders from the Huai-chün and by controlling the employment of foreigners assigned to the lien-chün as drillmasters, Li succeeded in establishing in Chihli and other areas of the north a second army subject to his personal command alone.

Li Hung-chang's efforts to develop the lien-chün grew from his desire to displace the old Banner forces and Lü-ying guarding the ap-

---

[49] *LWCK Memorials*, 17:1a-4a, TC 9/10/3; 37:14a, KH 6/4/26; 16a, KH 6/4/26; 43a ff., KH 6/6/11; 51:3a, KH 10/7/5; 53:1a, KH 11/1/18; 54:26a, KH 11/7/6; for Yeh Chih-ch'ao, who became provincial commander of Chihli in 1889 after being in command of lien-chün forces at Hsin-ch'eng, Chihli, see *CSK*, 462:2b-3a. Li Hung-chang acknowledged his responsibility for over-all command of all military forces in the north in a memorial dated KH 1/5/10 (1875); see *LWCK Memorials*, 25:18a.

[50] *LWCK Memorials*, 46:45a-48b, KH 9/6/21.

[51] See, for example, *ibid.*, 38:18a, KH 6/8/22, discussing the Tientsin defense arrangements; 40:50a, KH 7/4/27, in which Li Hung-chang vigorously opposed the handing of command of the lien-chün forces at Ying-k'ou and Shanhaikuan to a Banner officer, and proposed instead that command be given to the customs intendant of Shanhaikuan, Hsü Ch'ang, who was directly responsible to Li himself; 51:19a-21a, KH 10/7/27, on the withdrawal of lien-chün from the area outside the Great Wall; 53:15a, KH 11/3/3, on the stationing of lien-chün at Dairen; and numerous memorials on the expenses of the lien-chün in Tientsin.

[52] Major Bell of British Intelligence was struck by the fact that, "The Lien-Chun and the Hwei-Chun may be brigaded together. Thus, at Tientsin there are three battalions of the former and one of the latter, under the command of one general." Bell, *China*, II, 58.

proaches to the capital and substitute for them modern, well-trained units subject entirely to his own command.[53] The lien-chün provided the basis for an important interest that Li could share with the central government; as part of Li's expanding personal army these troops strengthened his position within the Ch'ing bureaucracy, and they were at the same time the core of the central government's defense system.

Was it possible for Li to serve his own interests and the interests of the central government simultaneously? The history of his efforts at self-strengthening seems to indicate that compatibility of interests meant for Li the adaptation of central government needs to his own purposes. The conflict between central and regional interests, short of outright insubordination or at worst rebellion, had to remain implicit. It is possible that Li himself was not aware of its full dimensions, nor is it likely that he anticipated the consequences which were to come— collapse and warlord terrorism. But the conflict of interests was none- theless present, dictating his military policies. This fact is perhaps partly obscured in the case of Li Hung-chang (and even more in the case of Tseng Kuo-fan) because no clear line could be drawn between his central and regional functions, and he therefore appeared to repre- sent central and regional power and interests simultaneously. If Li is considered solely as commander of the Huai-chün, he is seen depend- ing upon an army which grew from a local, then regional, background, and rested upon the foundations of regional loyalty and wealth. But he received authority for his command of the lien-chün in Chihli di- rectly from the central government and exercised it over forces raised specifically for the central government. Combination of the two armies brought into being a force which was both regional and central. Li, as commander, was forced into a dual role: where at one moment for his own security he must consider his new army as personal and at another moment must use it as a quasi-national force. This contradic- tion limited his own development on the one hand and the rejuvenation of central power on the other.

During Li's lifetime the problem was not resolved. Li was unable to develop his personal forces to the point where he could usurp cen-

---

[53] *LWCK Memorials*, 33:17a, KH 4/9/26; "Report of Captain Gill," in Bell, *China*, II, 43, in describing Li Hung-chang's armies around the capital notes: "This force is composed chiefly of the natives of Honan and Ngan-Hwei; some of them are said to be recruited from the Luh-Ying or Green Standard troops. Many served under Li Hung Chang during the rebellion of the Taipings, and some come from the ranks of the rebels."

tral power; yet he did not give unqualified support to the government's weak and sporadic efforts to establish national defense. He accepted in large measure the system in which he had been reared and though he changed it in fact, he gave no evidence that he was aware of so doing. His goals were greater control and power within the structure as it stood. Thus he failed to see the anomaly, which was obvious, for instance, to the British Intelligence agent, Captain Gill, who recorded: "It is a strange illustration of the anomalous state of things that exists in the Chinese army that we find the Governor-General of the province in which the imperial capital is situated, in possession of a large army which is the only force worthy of the name in this huge empire."[54]

The military organization—or disorganization—of the later nineteenth century reflected, and in part determined, the direction of the transition which the Chinese political organization was undergoing. Weakened and discredited by foreign pressures and internal social and economic changes, the Manchu rulers were forced to rely more and more upon the local, provincial, and regional political-military leaders, who had contributed to this weakening and then offered themselves as the only bulwarks of strength. Even the special forces which the court had originally relied upon as its own direct source of military power became part of the personal armies of the regional leaders.

Coastal Defense and Naval Development

Protection of China from outside attack was primarily a matter of coastal defense. This required adequate land forces (represented by the Huai-chün and the lien-chün), the maintenance of coastal fortresses, and the development of a modern navy. When Li Hung-chang rose to the governor-generalship of Chihli, China possessed no modern fleet, although some progress in that direction had been made. Li was only one of a number of influential leaders who fully realized the importance of naval development for China's security. Lin Tse-hsü had vainly attempted to produce mechanized ships for China in the decade following the Opium War.[55] Tseng Kuo-fan, equally conscious of the need for first-rate ships-of-war, sought to acquire them through purchase from abroad as well as construction at home. In 1861 Tseng had purchased two American steamers, which he brought to Anking as

---

54 "Report of Captain Gill," in Bell, China, II, 43.

55 Ch'i-t'ien Ch'en, Lin Tse-hsü, Pioneer Promoter of the Adoption of Western Means of Defense in China, passim.

convoys for his more unwieldy Chinese transport boats.[56] Tseng's attitude toward development of a Chinese navy is evident in the following excerpt from a letter he addressed to Li Hung-chang in 1865:

Guns are of course important and are urgently needed, but steamships are of equal importance and should be built as soon as possible. Such an accomplishment will demonstrate to the foreigners that we are strengthening ourselves and will stabilize the morale of our own countrymen.

At my headquarters we have been trying to build steamships for three years, but nothing has come of it. . . . When you manufacture both guns and steamships, you should appoint a man with at least the rank of circuit intendant to manage these affairs. I wonder if Yü-sheng [Ting Jih-ch'ang] is not the man to supervise this work at the same time that he carries out his other duties.[57]

Li Hung-chang concurred in Tseng's opinion on the importance of steamships, and agreed upon the suitability of Ting Jih-ch'ang to manage the necessary construction work. Under the sponsorship of Tseng and Li, Ting rose to be one of China's outstanding experts on westernization. He was the guiding spirit behind the Shanghai Arsenal and supported similar projects during his later years as governor of Kiangsu, director of the Foochow Arsenal, and governor of Fukien province.[58]

Although steamship construction was not attempted at the Kiangnan Arsenal in 1865, when it was opened, Li Hung-chang, Tseng Kuo-fan, and Ting Jih-ch'ang from the outset planned eventually to use the arsenal as a base for developing a modern fleet.[59] In the same period Tso Tsung-t'ang, also originally a protégé of Tseng Kuo-fan, took steps to develop an arsenal and dockyards at Foochow, Fukien. In 1866, Tso purchased machinery, hired European workmen and supervisors, and established foundries, docks, and buildings, all of the Western type. He invested approximately three million liang in his effort to produce Chinese-made weapons and warships. This enterprise was supported by the central government and southern provincial leaders in an effort to counter the growing power of the Li-Tseng clique, but in 1867 it fell into the hands of Shen Pao-chen, a loyal follower of Tseng and close colleague of Li, and later it was put under the direction of

[56] CSK, 142:1a-b (translated by Fang Chao-ying for the Chinese History Project, Columbia University and University of Washington). See also Ch'i-t'ien Ch'en, Tseng Kuo-fan, Pioneer Promoter of the Steamship in China, p. 40.

[57] TWCK Letters, 25:15b.

[58] Hummel, Eminent Chinese, pp. 721-22; CSK, 448:1a ff.; LWCK Memorials, 4:44a-b, TC 2/8/20; Shanghai-hsien-chih, 12:24a.

[59] LWCK Memorials, 9:31a, TC 4/8/1.

Ting Jih-ch'ang.[60] Li was therefore closely connected with the work of all the major arsenals concerned with shipbuilding, although he did not directly control in any way the operation of the one at Foochow.

During the decade after 1865 great strides were made toward the development of a technological foundation for a modern naval force in China. In the middle of 1867, while Li Hung-chang was engaged in the Nien campaign, Tseng Kuo-fan and Ting Jih-ch'ang succeeded in having 20 per cent of the revenues from the Shanghai customs assigned to the Kiangnan Arsenal. It has been estimated that during the remaining years of the T'ung-chih reign, that is, from 1867 to 1874, the Kiangnan Arsenal spent approximately 400,000 liang annually on the production of weapons and boats. After 1875, owing to a rise in the revenue receipts of the Shanghai customs, the income of the arsenal rose still further, and by 1897 it was receiving and spending on production over one million liang each year.[61] While the Kiangnan dockyards were not so extensive as those at Foochow, they were equally important as training grounds for technicians and provided the first successful undertakings in Chinese naval construction. The first steamship built there was launched in 1868, and six more were completed by 1876. After that time production declined. Only one more vessel was produced, and it was not completed until 1885.[62]

Li had first become interested in Western technology during his years at Shanghai, and it was there that he gained experience in these matters. His interest in the development of naval forces, however,

---

[60] Alicia Little, *Li Hung Chang, His Life and Times*, p. 53; Hummel, *Eminent Chinese*, pp. 721-22. Sir Halliday Macartney believed that the Foochow Arsenal and dockyard was "more imperial than any of the rest," since it was directed by a commissioner (Shen Pao-chen and Ting Jih-ch'ang, at different times) appointed directly from Peking. See Boulger, *The Life of Sir Halliday Macartney*, pp. 248-51. This statement perhaps supports Mrs. Little's conclusions regarding the encouragement of the Foochow Arsenal as a balance to the Tseng-Li Kiangnan Arsenal but fails to take into account the close personal ties existing between the imperial commissioner and Tseng and Li.

[61] Ch'uan Han-sheng, "Ch'ing-chi ti Chiang-nan chih-ts'ao chü," *Bulletin of the Institute of History and Philology*, XXIII, 148.

[62] *Ibid.*, p. 154.

Name of Vessel	Horsepower	Displacement	Year Launched
Hui-ku	392	600	1868
Ts'ao-chiang	425	640	1869
Ts'e-hai	431	600	1869
Wei-ching	605	1000	1870
Hai-an	1800	2800	1873
Yü-yuan	1800	2800	1875
Chin-ou	200	‑‑‑‑‑‑	1876
Pao-min	1900	‑‑‑‑‑‑	1885

As can be seen from this listing, only three of the ships constructed were of the class of larger warships, the others being small gunboats useful for river and coastal patrols.

went back to an earlier period when, under the direct command of Tseng Kuo-fan, he had organized the Huai-yang water troops. The water forces were a marine force in the fullest sense. They not only were responsible for river and lake campaigns, fighting both on land and water, but also manned their own vessels, and were therefore a navy as well as an army. The Huai-chün always maintained its own water corps and in effect had its own naval auxiliary. Li Hung-chang realized, however, that traditional water troops were no substitute for a modern navy, and supported efforts to secure such a naval force. In 1874, less than four years after his arrival at Tientsin, he addressed a memorial to the throne, reviewing in detail the defense problems confronting China and supporting proposals made by Ting Jih-ch'ang for their solution. This long memorial of over thirty pages expressed most of Li's principal ideas in the field of military defense.

Li began with a statement of five basic objectives to be attained before China could achieve a measure of security. These were: (1) the training of troops in the use of modern weapons; (2) the production of modern weapons; (3) the building of modern ships; (4) the securing of funds for these purposes; and (5) the development of a corps of bureaucrats capable of dealing with these and other problems arising from China's new relations with the Western powers. It had to be recognized, Li said, that the entire picture of Chinese defenses had been changed by the opening of rivers and seaports to foreigners and the establishment of treaty relations with them. As he put it, "All the gateways to China have become places occupied in common by both parties [China and the Western powers]."[63] In Li's opinion it had become almost impossible for China to set up a completely adequate system of defense.

The foreigners yielded only to power and not to reason, Li said. China therefore had no alternative but to strive to attain maximum military strength. This was becoming increasingly difficult owing to the recent technological advances of the foreigners, which made their steamships better than ever and gave them such wonderful aids as the telegraph and new weapons. Indirectly pointing to himself and his group as the only men prepared to cope with the emergency, he attacked those statesmen who wished to deal with new conditions in the traditional way, describing them as "those who talk about defense when they understand nothing of the situation and have no concrete proposals to offer."

---

[63] *LWCK Memorials,* 24:10b, TC 13/11/2.

Li proposed that the training of capable personnel should be the first step toward an adequate defense program. Once a body of officials with the knowledge and skill required for the production of modern implements was available, it would be possible, he hoped, to gain the military strength and economic foundation that would be necessary for China to take the initiative in the future.

The memorial continued with a discussion of the measures Li considered immediate and practical. His comments under the subheadings he assigned may be summarized as follows:

(1) *On the training of troops:*

Li believed that it was much more difficult to resist the foreigners than to suppress internal rebellions. The Taipings, Nien, and other rebellious native elements were at a great disadvantage since they had almost no modern weapons. Furthermore, rebels could be defeated and annihilated, but even if the foreigners were defeated, they could withdraw beyond reach only to return with additional strength when they chose. To meet this threat Chinese troops had to be trained in the use of foreign weapons. However, more than a change in weapons was needed: new drill techniques and strategy had to be employed, and therefore the old military regulations should not be continued at the expense of the quality of the army.

Acknowledging Tseng Kuo-fan's previous estimates on the minimum military strength needed to defend the seven coastal provinces, Li pointed out that the provinces had proved unable to sustain armies of this size. Li recommended that the provincial armies be reduced and that the funds thus saved be used to provide modern military equipment. The result would be a smaller but stronger and more mobile defense force. The entire land army should be reorganized into foreign rifle and cannon platoons, and heavier artillery concentrated at the strategic coastal ports.

(2) *On the improvement of weapons:*

Li listed the leading makes of weapons employed by the various European armies, discussing their advantages and disadvantages and the prices at which they could be obtained from the West. He then discussed the arms produced at his arsenals and at the Foochow Arsenal under Shen Pao-chen. Although the weapons produced at the arsenals were far superior to the traditional Chinese weapons, they were inferior to those produced in the West. To manufacture effective weapons in China the mining industry had to be modernized and the basic machinery produced. As important as the production of arms was the manufacture of torpedoes and water mines, which were absolutely necessary for coastal defense. More arsenals and factories were needed in China. In Li's words: ". . . to rely on foreigners for our supplies is suicide."

(3) *On shipbuilding:*

The shortage of warships in China, Li felt, precluded the adoption of the best means of naval warfare—blockading the enemy. The great length of China's coastline and the financial condition of the country made it impossible to build up a uniform coastal defense system capable of holding the enemy at bay. The defense system for the coast would therefore have to be developed gradually, and attention given to the relative importance of the various areas. The most important area in Li's judgment was that encompassing Tientsin, Pei-t'ang, and their environs, the gateway to the capital itself. The second most important area was that stretching from Woosung to Chiang-yin, in Kiangsu, which he described as the gateway to the Yangtze River, also an area of considerable wealth. As long as those two strategically vital areas were defended, military setbacks in other regions would not be fatal. To illustrate this, Li recounted the highlights of the Opium and Franco-British ("Arrow") wars, demonstrating how China had been defeated in the first war through penetration of the Yangtze region, and in the second war through penetration of the Tientsin—Pei-t'ang region.

Li recognized that China was not sufficiently advanced in technology to build enough ships for her needs. Moreover, as the cost of producing ships in China was extremely high, Li concluded that it was too expensive to build a fleet in China, and recommended that ships be purchased in England. He suggested that competent cadets be sent abroad to select the vessels in order to prevent the acquisition of large but useless ships. Meanwhile, Chinese shipbuilding yards should be encouraged to expand and improve.

Li recommended that for the present and the immediate future six more cruisers were needed to defend the northern (Tientsin, Pei-t'ang, etc.), eastern (Woosung, Chiang-yin, and the Yangtze region), and southern (Fukien, Kwangtung) coastal sectors. The long-range objective should be set at forty-eight large warships and many additional small swift craft. In order to help support such a fleet he suggested that funds be saved by demobilizing the old water-force ships.

(4) *On fund-raising:*

Li proposed that as an economy measure Chinese forces should be withdrawn from Sinkiang and the western regions. Next, the provinces should be ordered to transfer whatever funds they had available to the central government for defense expenditures. Since the provinces were not likely to have enough funds for this purpose, Li advised that the initial expenses be met by drawing on the various customs bureaus. (The Maritime Customs divided their revenue into two categories, the so-called 60-per-cent fund and the 40-per-cent fund. The 60-per-cent fund was usually held by the customs office pending instructions as to disposal, while the 40-per-cent fund was supposed to be sent directly to the Board of Revenue.) Li proposed that the entire 40-per-cent fund of the Tientsin and Shanhaikuan customhouses be delivered to the Tientsin Arsenal, and that half of the Shanghai customs 40-per-cent fund be given to the Kiangnan Arsenal. The 40-per-cent funds of the other customhouses and 40 per cent of the annual income of the Board of Revenue were to be made available to the Tsungli Yamen (Board of Foreign Affairs) and the officials responsible for coastal defense.

Li proposed intensified mining, manufacturing, and commercial activity on the part of both the government and the merchants as one way of producing the wealth necessary for an adequate defense program. He also suggested the slackening of government restrictions on the planting of opium in China, in order to discourage importation of opium from the foreigners. (Li pointed out, incidentally, that native opium was milder and not so harmful and habit-forming as the "foreign medicine.") It would also be worth while to impose a uniform rate of taxation on imported opium in all provinces, in order to get the maximum revenue yield and at the same time discourage smuggling and thus further reduce expenses. Li summarized his proposals in this field with the plea that new sources of income should be opened and unnecessary expenses cut.

(5) *On the development of personnel:*

Competent military leaders had to be selected, Li said. In addition there was the important problem of uniting the seven coastal provinces. The Chinese coastline was too large an area to be given to the command of a single person. In fact, Li doubted that it was feasible even to divide the whole area into a northern *(Pei-yang)* and a southern *(Nan-yang)* command. He therefore concurred in Ting Jih-ch'ang's earlier suggestion that the defenses be divided into three areas (namely, northern, eastern, and southern).

He further advised that the examination system for entry into the bureaucracy be modified, with the subject of foreign affairs appearing as one branch of study. In addition, schools of European studies offering instruction in such subjects as mathematics, physics, geography, and engineering should be established in those provinces where coastal defense was important. The graduates of such schools who proved themselves to be competent in these branches of learning should be given the same opportunities to rise within the bureaucracy as those who followed the "regular examination route." In addition, Li suggested that a greater number of students should be officially encouraged to go abroad to study.

Li closed his memorial with a general observation on the need for perseverance in the tasks at hand. The powerful Western nations had risen from weakness. China could do the same.[64]

Although Li's discussion went far beyond the problem of naval development, particular attention should be given to the context within which Li made his proposals for a modern navy as outlined in his third point, *On shipbuilding*. Li apparently not only realized that security depended on economic and political factors but also recognized the limitations imposed on the development of a modern fleet by tradition, geography, and other temporarily insurmountable obstacles.

Regionalism and Centralism in Coastal Defense

Li's own observation had convinced him that China could not become a first-class naval power in the near future. He felt that the best means of naval defense was the establishment of a blockade against the enemy. Believing that China could not yet develop a navy capable of blockading and thus subduing potential enemies, he saw the navy only as a deterrent to aggression and as a means of forestalling an immediate collapse in the event of hostilities. Obviously he had little hope that China could win a war through military action alone. This did not preclude the possibility, however, of the long-range development of naval strength along with reform in other fields. Yet even here, Li was willing to admit that only second- or even third-best solutions were possible. Li understood that China needed unified coastal defenses, which meant a single, well-integrated fleet of warships under

[64] *Ibid.*, 24:10a-25a, TC 13/11/2.

centralized control. Yet he was willing to endorse Ting Jih-ch'ang's proposal to establish not only two, but three, defense sectors with complementary fleets.

Li chose to back what he himself acknowledged to be a third-best arrangement because of his concern with his own position. A two-sector defense would have meant the establishment of a Pei-yang (North Coast) and a Nan-yang (South Coast) regional division. These divisions were fairly well accepted at the time, the Pei-yang section covering the coast from the Liaotung Peninsula through Chihli to Shantung, and the Nan-yang section the coastal region from Kiangsu through Chekiang and Fukien to Kwangtung. Li Hung-chang as the outstanding leader in the north would have officially controlled only the little developed northern regions, with Tientsin as his only direct source of naval production and supply. The Nan-yang sector would have included Shanghai with its ports and arsenal, Fukien with its great arsenal and dockyards, and Canton with its ports and foreign and native factories.

By 1874 the Foochow yards in Fukien were the largest and most productive in China. Tso Tsung-t'ang was still in effective control of the entire Fukien-Chekiang region, and was in a position to exert influence further south. Kiangsu alone would have remained in the middle, with an officialdom sympathetic to Li but attached to the Nan-yang organization. A two-sector arrangement threatened to pull Kiangsu out of Li Hung-chang's power orbit and isolate Li in the north. In contrast to this, unification of this eastern sector with Li's northern area would have brought under one command the two strategic areas which Li himself had described as the "gateways to China." According to his own statement, as long as those areas were held, it did not matter what other areas might fall.

The three-sector arrangement proposed by Ting Jih-ch'ang and so strongly endorsed by Li served the purpose of interposing between north and south an eastern or *Tung-yang* zone, covering northern Kiangsu and Shanghai. The local officials of this region (such as Ting Jih-ch'ang) were closely connected with Li. It was, too, the site of his Kiangnan Arsenal and dockyard. In effect Li would thus attain a balance of two against one, the northern and eastern defense zones against that of the south. To counterbalance the Foochow and Kwangtung dockyards and arsenals, Li would retain control over the Tientsin and Shanghai facilities. In this way Li hoped to accomplish in naval and coastal defense organization results very similar to those he had already achieved in the military field through the extension of Huai-chün influence and the development of the lien-chün.

The three-sector plan was not accepted, however. Despite Li's recommendations, in the following year, 1875, the defense system for coastal China was organized on a two-sector basis, and Li Hung-chang was appointed Commissioner of Northern Coastal Defenses. This did not prove to be an immediate setback for Li, although it was far less than the power he would have had under a three-sector arrangement. Probably with assistance from Li, Ting Jih-ch'ang was appointed governor of Fukien and concurrently director-general of the Foochow Arsenal.[65] Meanwhile, Li Tsung-hsi, Liu K'un-i, and Shen Pao-chen, old colleagues of Li and former fellow staff members of Tseng's Hsiang-chün, were successively appointed governor-general of Liang-Chiang. Thus Li's counterparts in the south were, for the most part, men friendly to his interests and not likely to oppose his dominating influence in coastal and naval affairs. However, because from the beginning Li was remote from Foochow and never directly controlled the development of the Foochow naval staff, he was never able to engage directly the loyalties of the Foochow naval commanders. For the moment the atmosphere was favorable, and in 1879 it improved further when Ting Jih-ch'ang was given charge of all defense affairs for the southern coast. But in time Li's dissociation from the southern sector lost him support that he vitally needed.

The organization of coastal defenses in 1875 and the appointment of Li Hung-chang as northern commissioner were the first steps leading directly to the creation of a modern navy in China.[66] But despite his recognition of the advantages of a unified system, the naval organization that Li promoted remained on a regional basis.

The Huai-chün Fleet

Li did not abandon his old Huai-chün water-force fleet after taking charge of the Northern Coastal Defense Bureau in 1875. The Huai-chün water force remained independent of other fleets and kept its separate identity as long as the Huai-chün remained a distinct mili-

---

[65] Hummel, *Eminent Chinese,* p. 722.

[66] *LWCK Memorials,* 25:18a, KH 1/5/10. Some writers date the beginning of the navy at about 1885, when the *Hai-chün Ya-men,* or Office of Naval Affairs, was established at Tientsin. This is misleading, since most of the important steps in naval development actually took place in the preceding decade, and the establishment of the new office led to no significant change in the organization or leadership of the northern navy itself.

tary force. It was assigned to the protection of internal waterways, taking special responsibility for safeguarding the transportation of grain to the capital and of military provisions for the Huai-chün. It also assisted in the transportation of Huai-chün troops, although special steamers were often hired or purchased for this purpose as the need for swifter means of conveyance increased.

According to the special accounts of the Huai-chün fleet that Li rendered to the throne, he had eighty-seven vessels attached to his army in the year 1884. Of these, four were of the *chang-lung* ("long dragon") type and eighty-three were sampans. It appears that Li was content to employ ordinary Chinese vessels for his water forces and did not associate them with his plans for a modern fleet. They were part of the coastal defense organization, however, since they served water troops assigned to the protection of the interior coastal waterways in Chihli, Shantung, and Kiangsu, patrolling the Grand Canal at such important points as Chi-ning, Ch'ing-chiang, Kua-chou, and Yang-chou. After 1884, however, the vessels in Kiangsu, being attached to the Huai-chün forces in that region, were no longer accounted for by Li, but were sustained, like the land forces, by the local provincial officials.[67] In 1886, for instance, Li reported only on the thirty-two water-force craft that were attached to his personal guard in the north.[68] This does not mean that Li had lost control over the rest of the Huai-chün fleet, but rather that the fleet itself had been divided into two sections. The section in the south remained as a convoy and patrol fleet, protecting the fleet that transported grain to the capital, an extremely important function, and guarding against smuggling. The section in the north served Li's personal guard and therefore received closer attention from him than before. He gradually abandoned the use of sampans for his northern Huai-chün water-force fleet and employed instead ten gunboats which were fitted and kept in good condition at the Tientsin Arsenal and dockyards.[69] The negligible sums given for the upkeep of this fleet indicate, however, that Li Hung-chang considered it of only minor importance in his defense organization.[70]

---

[67] *Ibid.*, 50:24a-25a, KH 10/5 int./25.

[68] *Ibid.*, 58:51a, KH 12/12/16.

[69] *Ibid.*, 63:53a-b, KH 14/11/27; 66:38a, KH 15/12/13; 69:39a, KH 16/11/16; 73:32a, KH 17/11/13. Li Hung-chang discussed the necessity of replacing sampans with modern gunboats for adequate coastal defense and successful naval warfare in a memorial written in 1884. See *ibid.*, 52:29a ff., KH 10/9/24.

[70] These expenses varied between several hundred and at the most five thousand liang per year.

Despite its dwindling importance the Huai-chün fleet is worthy of note as the precursor of Li's modern navy. That Li did not abandon it entirely demonstrates once again how carefully he kept the Huai-chün intact as a separate and complete force. This it remained, even after an integrated system of defense for the capital and the entire northern region grew up around it.

In his memorial of 1874 Li had advocated the purchase of six new cruisers from abroad and the eventual acquisition of forty-eight modern Western war vessels in addition to auxiliary and lighter craft. To meet the heavy expenses entailed in such a program of ship-purchasing, he had recommended the disbanding of various water-force fleets. While he was careful to preserve the Huai-chün water force, he did not hesitate to demobilize the fleets of the central government's Banner forces on the Manchurian coast.[71] It is apparent that Li's program of naval reform involved more than modernization of the existing forces. In carrying out the program he took every opportunity to dismantle the fleets of the central government's old regular forces, thereby increasing his own relative strength.

The Acquisition of Modern War Vessels

Li Hung-chang turned first to England for his new naval vessels. In 1878 four gunboats were acquired, of which two were assigned to the Northern Coastal Defense Bureau and two were put at the disposal of Shen Pao-chen and Ting Jih-ch'ang in the south.[72] The following year four more gunboats constructed at English shipyards were brought to China and attached to the slowly growing Pei-yang and Nan-yang fleets.[73] Realizing that these vessels would be extremely vulnerable in the event of sea warfare, Li began to search for means of adding ironclad vessels to his fleet. He placed his orders for these vessels in Germany through the agency of Li Feng-pao, a trusted assistant who was then Chinese minister to Germany.[74]

In 1880, Li dispatched Ting Ju-ch'ang, provincial commander in chief of the Huai-chün water forces, to England to bring back two cruisers previously ordered there.[75] The return of Ting and his junior officers on board the newly purchased vessels was regarded at the time as a landmark in Chinese naval history. Actually, the only thing distinguishing this purchase from others of the period was that although English officers and an English crew were aboard the vessels,

---

[71] *LWCK Memorials*, 42:22a ff., KH 7/10/11.
[72] *Ibid.*, 32:1a, KH 4/6/17.
[73] *Ibid.*, 35:22a ff., KH 5/10/16.
[74] *Ibid.*, 36:3a, KH 6/2/19.
[75] *Ibid.*, 39:16a ff., KH 6/11/26.

delivery was made by Chinese officers.[76] The successful voyage greatly enhanced the prestige of Li Hung-chang and his navy and paved the way for Ting Ju-ch'ang's subsequent appointment as commander of the Pei-yang Coastal Defense Bureau fleet.[77]

By 1882 the Nan-yang and Pei-yang fleets together possessed twenty-two comparatively modern vessels, some of which had been constructed in England and Germany, and others at the Shanghai and Fukien arsenals. Seven of these vessels were at that time assigned to the Pei-yang coastal defenses at Tientsin and other bases. The remaining fifteen vessels were part of the Nan-yang defense system and were distributed as follows: three in the Chiang-ning sector, three in Woosung waters, two in Chekiang, five at Taiwan, and two farther to the south.[78] The vessels at Taiwan were for a while subject to Li Hung-chang's orders, since they were operating in conjunction with the Huai-chün water and land forces stationed on that island.

Li considered this fleet too small and its vessels too light to provide adequate coastal defense. In 1882, when trouble was brewing with Japan over rights in the Liuchiu Islands, Li compared the strength of the Chinese and Japanese navies, and warned against any actions on the part of China which might precipitate war.[79] Although in the following decade Li and his colleagues in the south continued to purchase war vessels from abroad, the purchases were insufficient in number and quality to improve China's standing as a naval power. Li realized this, and for this reason consistently rejected policies which tended to imply an eventual settlement of issues by force. Only in 1894, when the so-called war party at the capital finally forced Li either to make a show of strength or lose all standing, did he venture upon an openly antagonistic course against Japan. The result, as Li had anticipated, was a crushing defeat for China, in which the entire Pei-yang navy was lost. As Liang Ch'i-ch'ao described it: "In the Sino-Japanese War the fleet was destroyed and the Huai-chün constantly defeated. . . . and the thirty years' work of the Chihli *Pei-yang Ta-ch'en* [Li Hung-chang] was dispersed like a cloud and became a dream of the previous night."[80]

---

[76] *Ibid.*, 42:17a ff., KH 7/10/11. At about the same time two gunboats ordered by the Shantung provincial authorities through Li Hung-chang and his agents were delivered from England.

[77] *Ibid.*, 42:22a-b, KH 7/10/11.

[78] *Ibid.*, 44:17a-20b, KH 8/8/16.

[79] *Ibid.*

[80] Liang Ch'i-ch'ao, *Chung-kuo ssu-shih nien-lai ta-shih-chi* in *Ying-ping shih ho-chi, chuan-chi san*, p. 38.

Li Hung-chang made little effort to create a unified naval force during the ten years following his first memorial on coastal defense in 1874. Such unification as he attempted was limited to the northern region, where one of his major objectives appears to have been either to displace the local central government forces or to bring them under his own control. It was more, however, than a play for personal power. Despite the presence at the capital of a few relatively enlightened officials, such as Prince Kung, the bureaucracy had little understanding of the world around them and showed little interest in devising a practical plan of action to meet the threatening pressures from the outside. Li Hung-chang was therefore acting for the central government as well as against it when he took over much of its military power and tried to introduce a modicum of reform in the military establishments he had set up or brought under his command. He made no secret of this when, for instance, he memorialized the throne in 1881:

One naval fleet is more useful than several thousands of militia, and one army of militia is more useful than several tens of thousands of Lü-ying [the central government's Armies of the Green Standard] .... I propose therefore to decrease the Lü-ying by 20 to 30 per cent and use the funds thus saved for the promotion of a navy.[81]

Had Li been able to establish and retain control over a single, centralized naval fleet, his personal power interests might have coincided at this point with the national, or central government, interests. But opposition was too great and political jealousies were too widespread. Kuo Sung-tao, who was aware of Li Hung-chang's position and aims, and whose wide experience in both China and Europe permitted him to comment on the relation between the power structure of China and the development of naval strength, interpreted the situation to Li Hung-chang in the following terms:

The purpose of the navy in former days was merely to make maneuvers and frighten off the foreigners. But your critics do not know that the foreigners of today are not the Japanese of the Ming period. The method of the foreigners today is to single out key points to attack and not merely rely on the vigor of their troops [in defense]. If we attempt mere maneuvering, the foreigners will select our weak points to attack and leave other places intact.

It is proposed that a high-ranking figure be selected to lead the navy, but in my opinion a high-ranking figure without a provincial position leads an isolated navy and has no base.[82]

[81] *LWCK Memorials,* 39:30a-36a, KH 6/12/11.
[82] Kuo Sung-tao, *Yang-chih shu-wu ch'üan-chi* (1892), *wen-chi,* 12:13a-15b.

Kuo Sung-tao's suggestions were obviously aimed at encouraging Li to establish a unified navy under his own provincial command. Certainly no official in China had provincial ties comparable to Li's. He had been active as governor-general of Chihli for almost fifteen years. He had the support of a strong personal army and a large measure of command over all other useful armies in the north; his water forces were entrenched along the Grand Canal and on the Yangtze, and he had access to all the major arsenals in China. Moreover, as a military hero in the region stretching from Kiangsu, through Anhwei, Hupeh, Shantung, as far west as Shensi, and up to Chihli, he commanded more respect than any other army leader of the time.[83]

The Establishment of the Admiralty

Once Li was reasonably secure in the north and well on his way to having his own fleet at Tientsin, he proceeded to urge the establishment of a central office of naval affairs. In a letter addressed to the Tsungli Yamen in 1884, he outlined his ideas concerning the unification of the navy. He first made it clear to the Yamen that "in view of the vastness of the seas along our coasts and the many places involved, the entire coastal defense must be vested in the hands of one man; otherwise it will be impossible to co-ordinate the work in all sectors."[84]

Although Li felt that co-ordination by a single high official was necessary to achieve the unity required for the reconstruction of defenses, he saw the difficulties involved. He stated that it was beyond the ability of any one man directing the proposed board from the capital to extend his control over the three thousand miles from north to south, and to overcome provincial barriers from Fengtien to Hainan Island. It appears that Li was anxious to convince the central government that no one high official was capable of competing with its position as arbiter by monopolizing control over the defenses of the entire coastal area. Nonetheless some concentration of power was required for unification of defense. Without a plan to control so vast an area, Li warned, strength would gradually grow in the provinces and decline at the center. This situation could be tolerated for a short time but could not last indefinitely,[85] and Li argued that without his proposed reform the central government would continue to lose power to the provincial officialdom. He appears here in his role as a defender of the

---

[83] Tseng Kuo-fan died in 1872 and Tso Tsung-t'ang in 1885.
[84] *LWCK Foreign Office Letters,* 15:29a-31b, KH 10/2/13.
[85] *Ibid.,* 15:29b, KH 10/2/13.

central order; but in further elaborating his plans, he reveals that what he sought was power for himself.

Li's status as an expert in Western affairs and as a successful "modern" military leader gave the necessary weight to the radical proposal he then laid before the Tsungli Yamen:

It is my understanding that the Western powers have foreign affairs ministries and naval ministries which are located at their capitals and which enjoy the same prestige as the other ministries. The naval ministries all have exclusive control over military matters, supply and personnel, and are not subject to interference by the other ministries. Furthermore, the Minister of the Navy, as a rule, also serves as a State Counselor [member of the cabinet]. In this manner the orders emanate from the core [of the government], and the naval administration is not unduly hampered.

In view of this I repeat that it is my belief that we should adopt this institution. We should not be bothered by an aversion to learning from the barbarians, even though we Chinese do not like to have our opinions trail in the dust of others. . . .

Moreover, the two words "coastal defense" signify no more than self-defense. They are therefore inadequate to express the aspirations of our nation. . . . It is therefore my opinion that a Board of the Navy should immediately be established, and for the time being be housed in the building of the Tsungli Yamen.[86]

Li Hung-chang went on to suggest who might be suitable as head of the proposed Board of the Navy:

Furthermore, if Your Excellencies should feel that I am sufficiently familiar with the nature of the work to be undertaken, and find it advisable to appoint me concurrently as Minister of the Navy, it would not be unusual for a provincial official to hold simultaneously a post in a capital office. Thus, in the thirteenth year of T'ung-chih, Shen Pao-chen managed the defense of Taiwan, and in the fifth year of Kuang-hsü, Ting Jih-ch'ang supervised the Nan-yang coastal defenses, and they were given the title of *Ke-kuo shih-wu ta-ch'en* [Minister of Foreign Affairs].[87]

With a similar arrangement made for himself, Li explained, he would be able to consult with the Tsungli Yamen from time to time. Furthermore, since Tientsin, Li's residence as Commissioner of the Northern Ports, was not far from the capital, it would be a good location from which to exercise control over the entire coastal area.

On October 13, 1885, an imperial decree ordered the establishment of the Board of Naval Affairs, or Admiralty. In order to preserve at least the appearance of real central government control over the new

---

[86] *Ibid.*, 15:29a-b, KH 10/2/13.
[87] *Ibid.*, 15:29b-30a, KH 10/2/13.

organization, the court confirmed a Manchu, Prince Ch'un, as the
president of the board. In conformity with the practice observed for
other boards, the vice-presidency was assigned to two men, one Manchu and the other Chinese. In this case the Manchu was Prince Ch'ing,
and the Chinese, Li Hung-chang. They were assisted by Shan-ch'ing,
a Bannerman, and Tseng Chi-tse, the son of Tseng Kuo-fan. The
imperial decree went on to state: "The formation of a northern navy
being at present in the initiatory stage, we commit the special control
thereof to Li Hung-Chang."[88]

The creation of the Board of Naval Affairs and the appointment of
Li Hung-chang to co-manage it brought no change in the actual naval
organization. Li Hung-chang, being the only one of the three ranking
members with any knowledge or experience in naval matters, was, in
fact, in complete charge of this new central government board. Nevertheless, he was subject to the veto of his Manchu colleagues, and in
this way his control was indirectly but effectively circumscribed. The
board was only a paper organization at the outset, for as Li himself
suggested, a real navy could not be established until the "steel ships"
ordered in Europe arrived to form the basis of a fleet.[89]

Li's designation as the official to handle the management of a *Pei-
yang* (North Sea) fleet was merely a confirmation of the authority he
had possessed as manager of the Pei-yang Defense Bureau.[90] Nevertheless, he evidently placed great importance on his new post, for he
cautioned the Tsungli Yamen against appointing an official who he
suspected was being considered instead of himself.[91]

In his new position as actual manager of naval affairs, Li Hung-
chang could report to the Naval Board on the affairs of all naval
vessels and fleets in China and participate in the allocation of all
materials to and from the various arsenals. What had been only customary practice in the past now became legal procedure.

The crises growing out of the constant threat of war with the European powers and Japan had finally forced the central government, in
order to strengthen itself, to create a new board, run by a powerful

---

[88] James Harrison Wilson, *China: Travels and Investigations in the Middle Kingdom*, pp. 72-73. Hummel, *Eminent Chinese*, pp. 384-85 (Biography of I-huan, the
Prince Ch'un).

[89] *LWCK Foreign Office Letters*, 15:30a-b, KH 10/2/13.

[90] James Harrison Wilson, *China*, p. 73, comments: "The formal decree in this
case, as in many others, followed rather than preceded the march of events, for the
Great Viceroy had been practically in control of the naval defense of the Northern seaboard for ten years."

[91] *LWCK Foreign Office Letters*, 15:31b.

regional official. In some respects the changes that were taking place paralleled those of the immediately preceding period of crisis when the Taiping threat had had to be met. At that time the government had been forced to confirm and legalize the power that military leaders had assumed in the course of struggle, and men like Tseng Kuo-fan, Tso Tsung-t'ang, and Li Hung-chang were given high provincial offices and sweeping authority in exchange for their loyalty and support. Now, more than two decades later, the central government felt it necessary to confirm Li Hung-chang, already the master of northern defense, as the real director of a "centralized" naval organization.

If his new title and responsibility conferred new powers and prestige upon Li, it did not induce him to regard the central government boards, including his own Admiralty, with any more confidence than in the past. More than ever, he regarded the northern defense system as his own. Barely two months after the establishment of the Admiralty, he addressed a letter to his colleagues there complaining of plans afoot to subject the financial system of the Pei-yang navy to their close control:

Recently the Board of Revenue has proposed that the Northern Coastal Defense Bureau funds be turned over completely to the Hai-chün Yamen [Naval Board], and then if the Northern Defense Bureau needs additional funds, the governor-general [of Chihli, Li Hung-chang] can apply to the Naval Board for them. . . . But I have an edict from the throne stating that "if we train a fleet for the northern defenses, we will order Li Hung-chang particularly to handle this matter."[92]

Li was juggling power. As governor-general of Chihli he was stationed at Pao-ting and was responsible for any decisions affecting his province, and in particular the defense of the capital. As Superintendent of Trade for the Northern Ports he was stationed at Tientsin and was responsible for the defense of that port, for customs patrols, and for customs revenues, as well as for the general management of the Tientsin Arsenal. As commander of the Huai-chün he was responsible for all aspects of its management and disposition, for the Huai-chün

---

[92] See, for instance, the following memorials submitted to the throne, the accounts attached to them on many occasions being sent to the Boards of Revenue and Works: *LWCK Memorials*, 55:16a, KH 11/10/18; 58:51a, KH 12/12/16; 59:1a, KH 13/1/5; 62:44a, KH 14/11/27; 63:65a, KH 14/12/10; 65:23a, KH 15/4/22; 78:1a, KH 20/2/25; 78:52a, KH 20/7/29. The following was submitted to the Board of Foreign Affairs: *LWCK Foreign Office Letters*, 17:40a-42a, KH 11/6/19. The more than 115 letters and telegrams submitted by Li to the Board of Naval Affairs, covering the period from 1885 to 1894, are contained in *Li Wen-chung kung hai-chün han-kao, chüan* 1-4, hereafter cited *LWCK Naval Board Letters*, in *LWCK Collected Works*. These letters cover a wide variety of subjects, relating to industrialization, mining, commerce, and foreign affairs, and are a good indication of the extensive responsibilities of that board.

water forces and the Huai-chün fleet, and the protection of inland grain transportation. As Commissioner of Northern Coastal Defenses he was responsible for the security of the entire coast from Fengtien to the northern borders of Kiangsu, including over-all supervision of the fleets within that sector. As manager of the proposed Pei-yang navy his responsibility for the fleets in the Pei-yang area was confirmed, and he was charged wtih welding them into a single unit. As co-adjudicator of the Hai-chün Yamen he was the only experienced member of that central government board, which was charged with supervising all naval affairs and with integrating all phases of naval work, including the purchase of ships, the construction and outfitting of ships, the training of personnel, the provision of rations and supplies, the installation of naval bases and command of naval operations. For each of these positions Li submitted separate reports and accounts to the various central government boards concerned.

The great concentration of power in Li's hands did not produce a corresponding unification of naval strength for China. The establishment of what purported to be a modern admiralty in no way reduced the number of conflicting agencies already in operation, although it lessened confusion by having one man, Li Hung-chang, as their unifier.

Despite his statement that the new naval development would begin from a fresh point of departure, Li was unable to rise above his own provincial biases. When it fell to him to select a commander for the Pei-yang navy, he insisted on the appointment of Ting Ju-ch'ang, former provincial commander-in-chief of the Huai-chün water forces, as acting provincial commander-in-chief of the Pei-yang Coastal Defense Bureau water forces. Undoubtedly Ting was a loyal Huai-chün man, whose devotion to Li Hung-chang was unquestioned. But it was impossible to create a modern, national fleet along the regional lines of the Huai-chün. The same regional loyalties that had so strengthened the command of the regional army now operated to the detriment of the navy. Thus the following comment in the official biography of Ting Ju-ch'ang:

In the ninth year of Kuang-hsü he became naval commander of Tientsin. ... In the fourteenth year of Kuang-hsü he helped fix the regulations for the navy, and became its admiral [hai-chün t'i-tu]. Because there were many officers from Fukien in the navy, Ting Ju-ch'ang, being a Huai-chün man and being placed above them, found that his actions were constantly being circumscribed.[93]

---

[93] CSK, 462 :1a ff.

This difficult state of affairs was also described by an Englishman in a volume published in 1890, scarcely five years after the formal establishment of the Pei-yang navy:

The navy ... was nevertheless unable to withstand the pressure of immemorial heredity. As the first and principal naval school happened to be at Foochow, it was natural that new battleships and cruisers should be officered and manned in the first instance by natives of Fukien province. The admiral [Ting Ju-ch'ang], however, hailed from another province— that of Li Hung-chang. Though brave and capable, Admiral Ting was uneducated, and found it hard to hold his own among the captains and lieutenants who had been to Greenwich and could speak and write English, and some of them French. Neither the Chinese admiral nor the English co-admiral ... were able to repress the intrigues which ran riot among the Foochow officers,—intrigues having for their object the complete control of the fleet ..., and the general determination to subordinate the naval service to their personal and family advantage :[94]

Li Hung-chang had tried to prevent such a situation from developing by establishing a naval academy at Tientsin under the direction of Wu Chung-hsiang as early as 1881. There he had hoped to develop a corps of officers capable of manning his northern ships. In attempting to confine the training of his own naval and military officers to Tientsin, where he could directly supervise them, Li Hung-chang unwittingly gave an advantage to the cadets from the south. These young officers were sent abroad, with Li's encouragement, and returned to China far better equipped to man war vessels than Li Hung-chang's own officers. Consequently, he found himself forced to rely on them in order to fill the junior officer ranks.

With this situation existing within the so-called unified navy of the Pei-yang, it could scarcely be expected that the fleets of the southern provinces were better integrated. They remained very much as described by one Chinese writer:

Now in China the ships, both imported and home-constructed, number over forty, but each province only has its own ships and its own defense. In emergencies we are forced to patch together ships from the various provinces, the vessels having different flags and the sailors different uniforms. In the maneuvers off Korea, the warships of Nan-yang and Pei-yang could not even signal to each other with flags. If Nan-yang and Pei-yang are so different, how then can we expect uniformity among the provinces ?[95]

---

[94] Alexander Michie, *The Englishman in China*, II, 399-400.
[95] *Huang-ch'ao ching-shih-wen t'ung-pien*, 81 :1a.

Even in the wake of naval defeats by France and under the threat of attack by Japan, China was unable to organize a systematic defense. This reflects not only upon the provincial outlook of the southern officials but also upon the limited approach of Li Hung-chang. Although he professed to support military and naval reform and did more for that cause than perhaps any other leader of his time, he defeated his own projects by forcing them into the mold of the Huai-chün and subordinating his own position as manager of a central government unified navy to that of manager of the Pei-yang navy. In doing so he showed that he realized that his central government responsibilities were the result of his unique power hold in the north. The loss of personal control over his own forces would have made him dependent on a ruthless and often blind regime.

Li's membership in the Board of Naval Affairs did little to promote the development even of the Pei-yang fleet. The fleet was organized as a single unit in 1888, yet after that date not a single addition was made to it. In fact, as Li himself pointed out to the court, its vessels had become almost obsolete. The last two vessels purchased, in 1887, for instance, attained speeds of only fifteen to eighteen knots, while the newer vessels of other nations' fleets reached speeds of twenty and twenty-three knots. Despite Li's high hopes for a Pei-yang fleet of large modern vessels, his program came to a halt less than five years after it had been formally sponsored by the central government. This is seen in the following list of the vessels acquired before the Sino-Japanese war.[96]

Two of the ironclads, the *Ching-yüan* and the *Lai-yüan,* were little more than light cruisers. This meant that the entire heavy ironclad force consisted of two vessels of seven thousand tons. Most of the gunboats of light wood, while effective for patrol, were useless when faced by larger vessels, particularly since their ordnance was negligible. This small fleet was responsible for the entire north coast of China, including the Liaotung Peninsula and Korea. As Li himself warned at the outset of the Sino-Japanese War, the Japanese were able to protect their own coasts adequately and venture in strength into the open sea, whereas the few Chinese vessels that were in condition to maneuver at all were urgently needed both on the coasts and on the

---

[96] Liang Ch'i-ch'ao, *Chung-kuo ssu-shih nien-lai ta-shih-chi,* in *Ying-ping shih ho-chi, chuan-chi san,* pp. 35-37. Also compare *LWCK Memorials,* 44:17a-20b, KH 8/8/16; 76:3a, KH 19/1/19, for the years 1885 to 1889; 67:30a, KH 16/4/16; 74:34a, KH 18/5/25; 76:50a, KH 19/5/28.

Date Acquired	Name of Vessel	Type	Tonnage	Service
1865	Ts'ao-chiang	Gunboat	950	Auxiliary
1869	Mei-yün	"	578	"
1871	Chen-hai	"	950	"
1876	T'ai-an	"	1,258	"
1877	Wei-yüan	"	1,300	Training Ship
1879	Yang-wei	Cruiser	1,350	Coast Patrol
1879	Chen-tung	Gunboat	440	" "
1879	Chen-hsi	"	440	" "
1879	Chen-nan	"	440	" "
1879	Chen-pei	"	440	" "
1881	K'ang-chi	"	1,300	Training Ship
1881	Chao-yung	Cruiser	1,350	Coast Patrol
1881	Chen-chung	Gunboat	440	Coast Patrol
1881	Chen-pang	"	440	" "
1882	Ting-yüan	Ironclad	7,335	Battle Fleet
1883	Chin-yüan	"	7,335	" "
1883	Chi-yüan	Cruiser	2,300	Coast Patrol
1886	Chih-yüan	"	2,300	" "
1886	Ching-yüan	"	2,300	" "
1887	Ching-yüan	Ironclad	2,900	Battle Fleet
1887	Lai-yüan	"	2,900	" "
(date not known)	P'ing-yüan	Cruiser	2,200	Coast Patrol

open seas.[97] Li's failure to gain sufficient support for the future expansion and modernization of the Pei-yang fleet was, as he foresaw, a prelude to disaster.

Li's modern navy was sunk by the Japanese in 1894 and 1895, and the pseudo-central government organization that he had created under the name of the Hai-chün Yamen, or Admiralty, failed to survive even that long. In 1893 the Admiralty quietly disappeared. Prince Ch'un, the Manchu director, had been unable to oppose an empress and court which plundered its own navy. The central government not only failed to sustain Li Hung-chang's less than half-hearted effort at naval unification but proved that its only real interest in the Admiralty was to use it as a new channel to provide funds for the amusements of the court.[98]

Li's responsibility for the failure and collapse of the Admiralty and the subsequent destruction of the northern fleet lay in his direct and indirect encouragement of regionalism and sectionalism. With his

[97] LWCK Memorials, 78:52a-53b, KH 7/20/29.
[98] Stanley F. Wright, Hart and the Chinese Customs (Belfast, 1950), p. 482.

limited outlook and his reluctance to give full support to projects that
in any way weakened or competed with his local and regional undertakings, Li was not the man to guide other provincial officials toward
unity, or to counter the distrust, ignorance, and irresponsibility of the
court and those central government officials who followed its dictates.
The spirit at the top was reflected in the ranks. Officers from the
south refused to accept orders from Li's former Huai-chün commanders, and all but a few of Li's closest followers were insubordinate
to Captain Lang, the British officer to whom Li had entrusted working
command of the fleet. So flagrant was the disregard of Li's under-
officers for naval authority that on one occasion in 1890, when Ting
Ju-ch'ang, Li's second in command, was absent, they refused to carry
out Lang's orders and contemptuously hauled down his colors.[99] The
limitations of the Huai-chün system were imposed upon the entire
naval structure despite Li's gestures toward unity under central government leadership.

---

[99] *Ibid.*

VII. Problems of Military Financing

LI HUNG-CHANG faced a new problem in financing his military forces after his removal to Chihli in 1870. Before this time he had directly controlled the regions that had furnished the bulk of his military revenues, or at the very least he had maintained strong indirect control through subordinates in key posts with the co-operation of Tseng Kuo-fan. But after moving to Chihli, and especially after the death of Tseng in 1872, he became more and more separated from his original base region. He was forced to rely more upon officials in other provinces and finally to turn to the central government for assistance in order to finance his forces. We have seen that Li depended heavily upon his military forces and defense program to assure his position of power, but these supports in turn depended upon his ability to raise money. Examination of the financial aspects of Li Hung-chang's military affairs reveals the extent to which he became a prisoner of the increasingly decentralized, almost chaotic, system of fiscal administration during the late Ch'ing period. It was Li himself who earlier had resisted the central government's attempts to control provincial finances and had thereby contributed to its weakness. Now Li's attempts to reform the military administration in the north were frustrated by similar provincial disregard of his own calls for financial help.

Military expenditures claimed a large part of the government's income.[1] One estimate, for 1887, held that 73 per cent of the total expenditures were for military purposes.[2] Although military subsidies were often allocated from one province to another, the military forces

---

[1] *Ch'ing-ch'ao hsü-wen-hsien t'ung-k'ao,* 66:8227-28; 67:8232-33.

[2] Pao-chao Hsieh, *The Government of China (1644-1911),* p. 205. This material is based on the *Ta-Ch'ing hui-tien,* 1887. Hsieh reduces the material on government expenditure to seven categories, of which military ranked first, and salaries for civil officials second (19 per cent).

in any region usually had to be supported mainly by the revenues of the region itself. Li Hung-chang's ambitions for the Huai-chün and for the strengthening of defenses in the north were therefore closely related to the amount of revenue which Chihli itself was able to produce.

Chihli as a Source of Revenue

Chihli, however, seems to have been a relatively poor region. The quotas established by the Board of Revenue fixing the minimum tax collections, although not always followed in practice, give a fairly clear idea of expected revenue yields. An undated document of the Board of Revenue, probably referring to the year 1873 or 1874, furnishes some pertinent figures on the quotas to be collected. The two customhouses in Chihli at Tientsin and Shanhaikuan were expected to yield annually 440,000 liang and 180,000 liang respectively from maritime duties. The total income in Chihli from this source was therefore expected to be 620,000 liang annually. This was much less than the Maritime Customs quota for the Liang-Chiang provinces, where Li had originally nurtured the Huai-chün. There the customhouses at Chinkiang and Shanghai in Kiangsu and at Kiukiang in Kiangsi were expected to yield an annual total of 3,860,000 liang.[3] Though this comparison is only between customs revenues and does not take other sources of income into account, it is still significant that the Maritime Customs (which Li had always relied upon heavily for "Western-type" military expenditures) in Chihli were expected to yield little more than one-fifth of Liang-Chiang's revenue in the same period. In fact, with the exception of the Tung-hai customs in Shantung province, Chihli ranked lowest among all the provinces collecting duties on foreign commodities.

The customs revenues in Chihli apparently became much higher during the next thirty years, as trade in the Pei-yang region increased. An admittedly speculative estimate of the average provincial income from the Maritime Customs for the Kuang-hsü period (1875-1908) shows Chihli's income from this source to have almost reached that of Kiangsu and Anhwei together. The *Ch'ing-ch'ao hsü-wen-hsien t'ung-k'ao* gives the average quota for Chihli as 3,029,644 liang, and

---

[3] China, Board of Revenue, "Summary of Various Cases Under Consideration by the Board of Revenue," section on Kiangsu rice and tribute and transportation allowance; and section on duties at various customhouses collecting on foreign goods. I have used a translation by Chang Chung-li, of the Modern Chinese History Project, University of Washington, filed together with a photostat of the original documents at the office of the Modern Chinese History Project.

the actual collection as 2,200,000 liang.[4] According to the same source, Kiangsu was scheduled to receive 3,277,971 liang, but actually took in only 1,468,000 liang.[5] But the most spectacular growth in China's foreign trade, and therefore in customs revenue, occurred only after the Sino-Japanese War, when Li Hung-chang was no longer engaged in military affairs in the north.[6] Even if the figures for average provincial income given above are accepted, it still appears that the customhouses in Chihli were not of great financial advantage to Li. Moreover, the Tientsin customs were assigned to remit heavy payments directly to the capital.

Provincial likin collections also provided a large part of the funds assigned for military purposes. Here, too, Chihli fared badly. The Board of Revenue document mentioned above lists Chihli as the lowest among the provinces that reported their likin collections. In 1873 or 1874 Chihli reported a collection of likin (on opium) amounting to 79,000 liang. In the same year Kwangtung collected 1,200,000 liang; Fukien, 1,800,000 liang; and Kiangsu, 3,000,000 liang. The Liang-Chiang provinces together reported a sum of approximately 5,000,000 liang from likin alone. Chihli's receipts were less than 2 per cent of the Liang-Chiang total.[7] Unfortunately, owing to the loss of Chihli's likin records through fire, there is less information on likin collection for that province than for any other.[8] The remaining fragmentary records, however, demonstrate Li's financial problem in Chihli. Lo Yü-tung has presented an estimate for the year 1893 which places the Chihli likin collection at 276,299 liang. For the same year he estimates the Kiangsu likin income to have been between 2,100,000 and 2,400,000 liang.[9] Lo also provides estimates for the years 1875 to 1880, during which period he estimates Chihli's highest collection to have been 300,383 liang, and its lowest 139,770 liang, for one year. This was in contrast to a high of 2,281,181 liang, and a low of 1,766,633 liang in Kiangsu province.[10] It can be said, then, on the basis of the figures given above, that the likin collection in Chihli never yielded as much as 15 per cent of the amount collected in Kiangsu. The only other likin figure I have been able to locate for Chihli in this period is for the

[4] *Ch'ing-ch'ao hsü-wen-hsien t'ung-k'ao.* 66:8228-29.

[5] *Ibid.*

[6] Hosea B. Morse, *The Trade and Administration of the Chinese Empire* (London, 1908), p. 285.

[7] Board of Revenue, "Summary of Various Cases Under Consideration," section on likin figures for the various provinces. Compare to Lo Yü-tung, *Chung-kuo li-chin shih,* II, 486, 487. [9] *Ibid.*

[8] *Ibid.,* I, 185. [10] *Ibid.,* I, 180.

year 1885, when Li Hung-chang reported receiving likin from opium amounting to 100,000 liang.[11]

Mention has been made above of the subsidy system whereby the various provinces extended financial help to each other. The Board of Revenue took note of this, and the figures set forth in the Board's documents furnish additional information regarding the potential resources that Li Hung-chang could muster in Chihli. The subsidy records indicate how much outside support a province required and how much support a province could extend. In the light of the figures presented above it is hardly surprising to find that Kiangsu province required, and therefore received, no military subsidy. Nor did Kwangtung, Kiangsi, Fukien, Hupeh, Chekiang, Szechwan, or Shantung. The major recipients were provinces such as Kansu, Shensi, Kweichow, and Yunnan, where, in the 1870's, rebellions raged and there was great need of support for military expenditures and relief. Compared with these provinces Chihli was in a good position; nevertheless, the Board of Revenue allowed Chihli a subsidy of 106,000 liang per month, or a total of 1,272,000 liang per year. Part of this money, at least, was available to Li Hung-chang as governor-general of that province. This subsidy was derived from no less than ten provinces, but indications are that the largest amount came from Kiangsu.[12]

Chihli also rendered limited assistance to other areas. To Mukden in Manchuria, and the territory of Sinkiang, 330,000 liang were paid each year, while to the imperial capital, Chihli rendered 400,000 liang annually during the period around 1873 or 1874. Liang-Chiang, Li's former region of administration, at this time paid out 8,610,000 liang per year.[13] These figures only represent the requirements of the Board of Revenue, and there is no certainty that payments were made in accordance with the Board's schedule. My own survey of the writings of Li Hung-chang and Tseng Kuo-fan indicates that subsidy commitments frequently were postponed or ignored and that the system degenerated over the years. However the system may have operated in actuality, it is clear that Chihli was not regarded as a rich province and, in sharp contrast with Liang-Chiang, was treated as a "have-not" province. Chihli was, of course, the metropolitan province, the protector of the imperial capital, and the central government perhaps lightened the obligations of that province and increased its income

---

[11] *LWCK Memorials,* 54:30a-34b, KH 11/7/8.

[12] Board of Revenue, "Summary of Various Cases Under Consideration," section on military subsidies to and from all provinces.

[13] *Ibid.*

in order to strengthen the military forces most vital for the security of the government.

In his new location Li required outside financial support. Such support could come either from officials in provinces with financial surpluses, from a patronizing central government, or from both. In a previous chapter we have seen how Li worked within the bureaucracy to secure a loyal following and to ensure for himself future financial, military, technological, and administrative support.[14] But the provincial system of the empire and the central government's system for controlling its bureaucrats were substantial counterforces to Li's efforts. Unless he could build rapidly upon his own strength, enlarging his military power, widening his economic bases, and extending his patronage, he would be forced to turn to the central government for support of his position.[15] In attempting to assess the relative positions of Li and the central government, we might ask whether Li's new economic situation reversed his position vis-à-vis the central government, whether his need for the regulatory power of the central government over the fiscal system was greater than the central government's need for his forces. Part of the answer to these questions may be indicated in the details of his military accounts as seen against the background of historic development during the last decades of the nineteenth century.

Financing the Huai-chün

Li Hung-chang's outstanding efforts in the military sphere during his long tenure in Chihli were directed toward the development of the

---

[14] Among the more important colleagues who generally co-operated, though at times competed, with Li, were Shen Pao-chen, Ting Jih-ch'ang, Liu K'un-i, and Kuo Sung-tao, all of whom had served in Tseng Kuo-fan's *mu-fu*. Tseng Kuo-ch'üan had also held top provincial posts and carried on his deceased elder brother's support of Li. Li Han-chang always quietly co-operated with his brother. Newly emerged from Li's own coterie of followers were Chang Shu-sheng, onetime governor-general of Liang-Chiang, and Ch'ien Ting-ming, who rose to the post of governor, as well as Chou Fu, and many others.

[15] In 1874, for instance, Li Hung-chang presented to the central government a strong recommendation that the military campaigns in the west under the command of Tso Tsung-t'ang be abandoned or stepped down and that exclusive attention be paid to coastal defense, particularly in the north. Although broad strategic considerations and larger questions of foreign policy were involved in this recommendation, the basic issue was the struggle by Li for greater control and disposition of military revenues. Tso's armies in Sinkiang and the western territories were receiving large military subsidies from many provinces. To Li, in Chihli, this meant that his own northern area was being sacrificed in the interests of remote border defense. He attempted to prevent the Huai-chün from further losing economic support. Li's loss of direct control over Liang-Chiang made him all the more determined that Tso Tsung-t'ang, his greatest political-military rival, should not entrench himself in Liang-Chiang. See, for instance, *LWCK Memorials*, 24:10a-25a, TC 13/11/2.

so-called "trained armies," or lien-chün, and the creation of the Pei-yang fleet. These undertakings were directly related to his special responsibilities as governor-general of Chihli and Commissioner of Northern (Pei-yang) Defense. While the tasks of maintenance and disposition of the Huai-chün battalions were inseparable from the larger military problem of Pei-yang security, Li never permitted the Huai-chün to lose its separate identity as his own regional army. Although the distinction between the Huai battalions and other battalions raised by Li for Pei-yang defense tended to become obscured in practice, Li took pains to preserve the identity of the Huai-chün by extending his patronage in the appointment of Huai-chün commanders who had been with him over the years. Li also tried to preserve the regional character of the army by favoring Anhwei and northern Kiangsu men in recruiting the ranks. Most relevant to our present inquiry was his practice of keeping the military accounts of the Huai-chün separate from those of the other forces under his jurisdiction.[16] He attempted to maintain distinct sources of revenue for his Huai battalions, and to keep their expenditures apart from the expenditures of his other forces. It appears that in this way he was distinguishing between forces over which he had more limited control, at least nominally, and the Huai troops who were to be recognized indisputably as his own.

Li Hung-chang rendered separate financial reports for the Huai-chün in statements to the Boards of Revenue, War, and Works, and presented the over-all accounts to the throne at regular intervals. We have seen that the financial accounts covering the first few years of the Huai-chün's existence were rendered in a single report at the close of the Taiping Rebellion. Li's collected memorials do not contain any regular reports of the Huai-chün accounts up to the time Li moved to Chihli. It is only beginning with the year 1873 and thereafter that there are regular reports. His report of 1873 covered the twenty-one-month period from the fourth month of 1870 to the twelfth month of 1871. In 1875 he presented another report covering the year 1872-73. His next two reports, presented in 1876 and 1877, covered two periods of eighteen months each, and it is only beginning in 1878 that annual reports were made. The annual report that Li presented in 1878 covered the year 1876-77, and the subsequent annual reports were usually made between twelve and twenty-four months after the year concerned. All of this makes it difficult to reproduce Li's reports in a

---

[16] See Table 5 for a list of Li Hung-chang's memorials reporting military accounts.

systematic manner. But this is perhaps the least of the difficulties of handling financial material of the Chinese empire. H. B. Morse, who spent a lifetime dealing with Chinese statistics as a member of the Chinese Maritime Customs Service, speaks of the financial system as "a subject veiled in obscurity."[17] He admits being bewildered by the confusion resulting from the absence of a common purse when dealing with the so-called official budget. He quotes E. H. Parker, an expert on the taxation and expenditures of nineteenth-century China, in stating that ". . . all accounts in China seem to be so arranged as to present as many anfractuosities, callosities, and complications as possible." Among the factors which made the bookkeeping of the time almost impossible to maintain on a systematic, rational basis were "arrears to be dunned for, advances to be made, loans to other provinces, divertings to meet sudden or unforeseen demands, such as famines, wars, foreign loans, Imperial marriages, birthdays, funerals, etc., etc."[18] It is into this labyrinth that we must descend in order to gain some clue to Li Hung-chang's problems as a military financier. The figures which we shall offer are, unless otherwise indicated, those presented by Li Hung-chang, and it is only with the utmost diffidence that we shall attempt to organize, compare, and synthesize these figures.

In Tables 5 and 6, I have attempted to set down the Huai-chün income, expenditures, and the balances remaining for the years 1871 to 1892, the latter being the last year for which Li rendered an account. For both tables I have employed the term *Gross Income* to indicate newly received income exclusive of the balance carried forward from the previous year. This *Gross Income* was subject to a multitude of deductions, and in some cases additions, made in the process of currency conversion, advance payments and receipts for certain types of goods and services, and many other items. The statistical chart, Table 5, also contains a column designated *Funds Available for Expenditure*. This was a category used by Li to refer to the *Gross Income* plus the balance on hand after all other deductions and additions had been made. It is what Western accounts might designate as net income plus balance on hand, or financial assets. The column of *Remarks* attempts to indicate briefly how many battalions of the Huai-chün were covered in the report. The final column gives the location and date of Li's memorial containing the data presented. Table 5, upon which the linear graph, Table 6, is based, shows reports to be missing

---

[17] Hosea B. Morse, *The Trade and Administration of the Chinese Empire,* p. 118.
[18] *Ibid.,* p. 113.

TABLE 5

HUAI-CHÜN ACCOUNTS, 1871-93 (IN K'U-P'ING TAELS)
(As Reported by Li Hung-chang)

Year	Balance on Hand	Gross Income	Available for Expenditure	Expenditures	Balance Remaining	Remarks	Source: *Li Wen-chung kung tsou-kao,* in *Li Wen-chung kung ch'üan-chi*
1870-72 (21 mos.)		4,071,219[a]	3,505,840[a]	3,348,262[a]	497,656	Forces in Shensi and other provinces	21:27a, TC 12/4/11
1872-73	497,656	3,869,142	3,562,867	3,208,930	353,936	Forces in Shensi, Chihli, and others	25:37a, KH 1/7/28
1873-74 (18 mos.)	353,936	5,542,331	5,300,905	4,825,757	475,148	61 battalions	27:13a, KH 2/5/14
1874-76 (18 mos.)	475,148	5,728,642	5,254,371	4,520,853	733,517	82 battalions	29:30a, KH 3/6/19
1876-77	733,517	3,688,883	3,806,180	3,021,421	784,759	82 battalions	32:31a, KH 4/8/29
1877-78	784,759	3,037,099	3,522,020	2,785,386	736,634	81 battalions	34:22a, KH 5/4/16
1878-79	736,634	2,897,276	3,247,761	2,524,323	723,437	81 battalions	37:50a, KH 6/7/14
1879-80	723,437	3,196,569	3,187,435	2,232,581	954,854	66 battalions	40:4a, KH 7/1/19
1880-81	954,854	3,178,382	3,146,781	2,194,903	951,878	67 battalions	42:54a, KH 7/12/20

See footnotes at end of table.

TABLE 5, continued

Year	Balance on Hand	Gross Income	Available for Expenditure	Expenditures	Balance Remaining	Remarks	Source: *Li Wen-chung kung tsou-kao*, in *Li Wen-chung kung ch'üan-chi*
1881-82	- - -[b]	- - -[b]	- - -[b]	- - -[b]	- - -[b]	- - -[b]	- - -[b] KH 8/12/17
1882-83	1,268,040	2,602,826	3,361,655	1,669,328	1,692,337	63 battalions including forces in Korea	48:15a, KH 9/10/29
1883-84	1,692,337	2,193,590	3,457,482	1,743,504	1,713,977		52:35a, KH 10/12/1
1884-85	1,713,977[c]	1,993,307[c]	3,396,454	2,384,051	1,012,403	65 battalions	55:42a, KH 11/12/13
1885-86	1,012,400[d]	2,954,300	3,552,544[c]	2,468,576	1,083,968	66 battalions	58:48a, KH 12/12/16
1886-87	- - -[b]	- - -[b]	- - -[b]	- - -[b]	- - -[b]	- - -[b]	- - -[b] KH 14/2/2
1887-88	972,288	2,505,560	2,944,649[c]	2,092,234	852,307	49 battalions in Chihli and Manchuria	63:50a, KH 14/11/27
1888-89	852,307	2,426,982	2,860,099[c]	1,926,920	933,178	51 battalions in Chihli and Manchuria	66:35a, KH 15/12/3
1889-90	933,178	2,126,125	2,607,330[c]	1,946,006	661,324	51 battalions in Chihli and Manchuria	69:35a, KH 16/11/16

See footnotes at end of table.

TABLE 5, continued

Year	Balance on Hand	Gross Income	Available for Expenditure	Expenditures	Balance Remaining	Remarks	Source: *Li Wen-chung kung tsou-kao*, in *Li Wen-chung kung ch'üan-chi*
1890-91	661,324	2,426,106	2,704,363^c	2,097,027	607,336	51 battalions in Chihli, Manchuria, and Weihaiwei	73:29a, KH 17/11/30
1891-92	607,336	2,170,577	2,349,716^c	1,976,899	372,817	51 battalions in Chihli, Manchuria, and Weihaiwei	75:31a, KH 18/10/28
1892-93	372,817	2,488,154	2,479,287^c	2,118,240	361,046	51 battalions in Chihli, Manchuria, and Weihaiwei	77:40a, KH 19/10/26

a Average for one year, calculated by S.S.

b Report missing from sources.

c Not given by Li in report.

d Note discrepancy.

for the years 1881 and 1886. These reports seem to have been made by Li, for he refers to them in other memorials as being dated Kuang-hsü 8/12/17 and Kuang-hsü 14/2/2 respectively, and in each case the memorial for the succeeding year refers to the balance brought forward in the missing reports. It would appear that the compiler of Li's collected works was unable to locate the memorials in question. Li Hung-chang was not consistent in his form of presentation, and we have been forced to interpolate some figures for the sake of consistency. Such interpolated figures are indicated by appropriate symbols.

While Table 5 presents the actual figures of income and expenditure found in Li's reports, in attempting to trace their trend over the years it is necessary to take into account the varying time periods the reports cover. This has been done in Table 6, where figures are given on the basis of one-year periods. Thus it has been necessary to present averages for the years 1871, 1873, 1874, and 1875. This distorts the trend slightly by giving the impression that Li's income for those years was completely stable but avoids the greater distortion of showing very high income for some years and not indicating that it was used over a longer time span.

As may be expected, income and expenditure over the twenty-two-year period followed roughly parallel lines, with the declining income exerting almost constant pressure on Li to reduce his expenditures. We see a fall from roughly 4,000,000 liang received for 1871 to almost 2,500,000 liang for 1892, a decrease of approximately 1,500,000, or 37½ per cent. This is partly to be accounted for by the removal of special subsidies that the Huai-chün had enjoyed while campaigning against insurgents in Shensi in the early 1870's. The low points for income were the years 1883 and 1884, when only 2,000,000 to 2,200,000 liang were received. In 1885 Li was apparently able to bring his income close to 3,000,000 liang, possibly owing to military threats from the French and the Japanese, but thereafter his income wavered between roughly 2,100,000 and 2,500,000 liang per year. The third line on Table 6 designated as *Balance Available* shows the surplus funds remaining at the end of each time period. In his reports Li indicated that this balance would be used in the subsequent period; such funds did not revert to the government or to the provinces. It can readily be seen that the large balances accumulated during the period from 1873 to 1884 served as a cushion during the following decade when Li's income had fallen considerably. The depletion of reserve funds made Li increasingly dependent upon his yearly income, and the

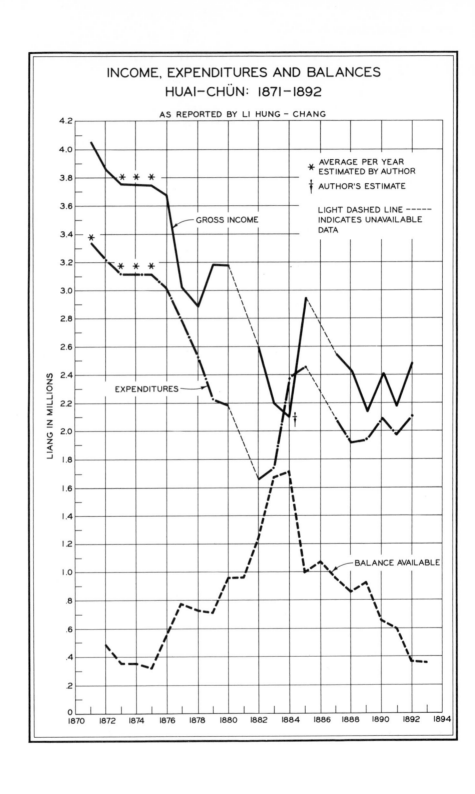

INCOME, EXPENDITURES AND BALANCES
HUAI–CHÜN: 1871–1892

AS REPORTED BY LI HUNG – CHANG

* AVERAGE PER YEAR
ESTIMATED BY AUTHOR

† AUTHOR'S ESTIMATE

LIGHT DASHED LINE -----
INDICATES UNAVAILABLE
DATA

GROSS INCOME

EXPENDITURES

BALANCE AVAILABLE

LIANG IN MILLIONS

Huai-chün was virtually forced to live from hand to mouth. Any interruption or delay in the remittance of funds would have forced Li to curtail expenditures, probably through reduction in the size of the army. Li's own reports to the throne indicate that financial exigencies did in fact drive him to reduce the size of the Huai-chün in the years between 1871 and 1892.[19] Since Li's accounts were not always consistent and data on the exact size of the Huai-chün is fragmentary, we cannot do more than attempt to establish the most general kind of correlation between income and the size of the army.[20] But even this rough survey is illuminating. We see an over-all reduction of the Huai-chün, in spite of sharp increases in the period between 1874 and 1879, when Li's reports covered as many as eighty-one or eighty-two battalions. In the years from 1879 to 1885 Li's reports covered the accounts of sixty-three to sixty-seven battalions. In the year 1887 only forty-nine battalions remained on Li's books. Thereafter Li was able to stabilize the size of the army at fifty-one battalions. (See Table 5.) These figures may in some cases be misleading, since certain units were on occasion assigned to special stations outside Li's sphere of direct jurisdiction and sustained by local provincial allocations. In such instances, where Li did not hold the purse strings, his control over the units may have been somewhat restricted. It is testimony to the strength of the regional army system, regional (Huai) identification, and the personal loyalty of his officers toward Li that such units remained an integral part of the Huai-chün, and could be so regarded in Li's memorials to the throne.

Over the twenty-two-year period from 1871 to 1892 Li's Huai-chün suffered losses in both income and manpower, but such losses were by no means crippling. Li could hardly have hoped to maintain the income or size of the Huai-chün at the same level after the Taiping and Nien emergencies had passed. The central government could not help but take an ambiguous view of regional forces like the Huai-chün. It was apparent that such forces were always a potential threat to the central power and were a drain upon national resources; but in times of emergency it was to these forces that the government turned for protection. From time to time the central government exerted pressure upon Li to reduce the size of the Huai-chün, only to be obliged to sanction additional recruiting at the next emergency. Li resisted demands to eliminate several battalions of the Huai-chün, but was not entirely

---

[19] See, for instance, *LWCK Memorials*, 32:21a, KH 4/8/18; 33:17a, KH 4/9/26.
[20] See Chapter 5 for a discussion of the size and distribution of the Huai-chün.

successful. He had to yield because he had no means of paying the army from local revenues and could not compel officials in other provinces to remit the required funds. The assent and active intervention of the central government were becoming more and more necessary.

Sources of Huai-chün Income

In the years following Li Hung-chang's assumption of the governor-generalship of Chihli, the bulk of the Huai-chün was garrisoned in the north. Nevertheless, the Huai-chün still received the greater part of its income from Liang-Chiang. Next in importance as a source of income were the Hu-Kuang provinces, Hupeh and Hunan, where Li had formerly served as governor-general and had built up useful bureaucratic followings. In the years for which we have been able to obtain detailed data, the relative importance of Liang-Chiang increased, while Hu-Kuang, still second, provided a smaller proportion of the Huai-chün's revenues. For a while Shantung, Chekiang, and Szechwan provinces also made important contributions, while Shensi occasionally made a token payment, but these provinces provided at the most only 17 per cent of the total income of the Huai-chün, more often considerably less. By 1885 Shantung was providing no funds at all for the Huai-chün, and Chekiang in the south and Szechwan in the west were

TABLE 7

HUAI-CHÜN INCOME BY REGION*
(In Liang and Percentage)

Year	Liang-Chiang		Hu-Kuang		Other
	In Liang	Percentage	In Liang	Percentage	Percentage
1871-72	2,156,412[†]	53	1,226,034[†]	30	17[a,b,c,d]
1872-73	2,369,515	61[‡]	1,211,049	31[‡]	8[‡a,b,c]
1873-76	2,402,160[†]	64	1,172,746[†]	31	5[a,c]
1876-77	2,327,600	63	867,947	23	14[a,c]
1885 (quota)	1,340,000[†]	70	400,000[†]	20	10[a]

* See Table 5 for source of data.
† One-year average.
‡ Percentage based on author's totaling of Li's income as reported. Li's totals appear to be incorrect in this case.
a From Szechwan province.
b From Shantung province.
c From Chekiang province.
d From Shansi province.

the only provinces besides Liang-Chiang and Hu-Kuang rendering financial support to Li's army. Table 7 illustrates the relative importance of income from the major regions over a period of fifteen years.

Liang-Chiang and Huai-chün Revenues

While the over-all income of the Huai-chün fell, and receipts from Liang-Chiang declined considerably, by 1885 Liang-Chiang was providing for Li's Huai troops more than three times the support required of any other region. Li Hung-chang had always had special interests in the Liang-Chiang area, and because these interests coincided with those of the central government he could make good his claim upon that region.[21]

Li was able to hold his Liang-Chiang income, although it had diminished to less than 60 per cent of its former total, partly because of the special functions that the Huai-chün retained in the Liang-Huai area. Shipment of the grain tribute to the capital from Liang-Chiang, and particularly the heavy shipments from the Su-Sung-T'ai circuit in Kiangsu, were routed to the north through Shanghai and thence by sea. From the Chiang-pei area (north bank of the Yangtze River), also in Liang-Chiang, came additional shipments, which although routed by sea in 1868 and 1869 were thereafter sent by smaller boats through the inland waterways. Special measures to protect these shipments were undertaken, and it fell to the Huai-chün, as the army under the direct command of the Commissioner of the Northern Ports, Li Hung-chang, to guard the vital freight.[22] Permanent garrisons at Ch'ing-chiang, Yang-chou, Hsü-chou, and other areas in Kiangsu and Shantung were therefore manned by Huai troops. This was ample justification for the maintenance of parts of the Huai Army, under Li's control, in areas south of Chihli. This, added to the connections Li retained with former colleagues and subordinates, gave him an authoritative voice in Liang-Chiang.[23] Thus, although he no longer served

---

[21] *LWCK Letters,* 15:19a, KH 1/6/21, contains remarks to the governor-general of Liang-Chiang, indicating the Huai-chün dependence on the Kiangsu likin and other taxes. Li points out that the funds from Kiangsu are two months late, and reminds Liu K'un-i, the governor-general, that his post and Li's are "like one family." See also Li's letter to his former Huai-chün subordinate, Chang Shu-sheng, who in TC 13 was Liang-Chiang's governor-general. Li reminded Chang that if Tso Tsung-t'ang's army had failed to receive its subsidies from other provinces, "they would have perished from starvation." *Ibid.,* 14:25a-26a, TC 13/8/7.

[22] British Intelligence Reports in Bell, *China,* give ample evidence of the activity of the Huai-chün in guarding the inland waterways of Kiangsu during the 1870's and 1880's. See especially pp. 45 ff.

[23] See note 21 above.

personally in Liang-Chiang, Li was able to preserve some of his important interests in that region. However, the costs of maintaining the Huai-chün in Liang-Chiang were specifically assigned to that region. Governor-general Shen Pao-chen, reporting to the throne in 1876, stated that his likin bureau in Soochow spent more than 177,000 liang, or nearly one-third of its income, for the monthly rations of the Huai-chün battalions in that region. At the same time, he stated, the Huai-chün was drawing an additional 304,000 liang from the Shanghai likin bureaus.[24] Up to 1885 Li reported on the garrisons in Liang-Chiang, stating that the payments were made directly to the Huai-chün quartermaster offices there and that they were also reported upon separately by the local provincial officials. After 1885, however, the accounts for these troops were no longer submitted by Li, although his memorials indicate that he examined them closely. The Huai troops along the Yangtze River and the canals, generally known as *tsao-piao*, or grain transport troops, linked Li directly with his former base. A British Intelligence observer noted this tie in 1876:

It appears that the whole of the defensive works on the Yang-tse are being constructed, and are or will be armed on a tolerably uniform system, which has probably been agreed upon by the Commissioners, and which appears to have been carried out under the immediate supervision of Shen-Pao-Chen [the governor-general of Liang-Chiang], who has been making a tour of inspection, which appears to have embraced nearly all the newly-constructed works. It would appear, however, that when once completed, these works and their garrisons are placed under the order of Li-Hung-Chang, for the almost invariable reply of every soldier in garrison on the Yang-tse, to whom we put the question, was that he belonged to Li-Hung-Chang. . . . thus proving incontestably the connection of these troops with Li.[25]

Making a tour of inspection two years later, the British consul at Chinkiang observed the wide dispersal of Huai-chün troops in the area between Nanking and Chinkiang. His report indicates how well Li had succeeded in preserving his own military interests in Liang-Chiang through protection of the central government's key economic interests:

Thus, the Tsau-Hia channel, with the land and water approaches to Nanking, the Grand Canal and the salt fleet, are now under the protection of the Viceroy Li, and do not concern the Viceroy of the Two Kiang [Liang-Chiang] at Nanking.[26]

---

[24] *Shen Wen-su kung cheng-shu* (1880), 6:34a-b, KH 2/5 int./7.
[25] Bell, *China,* II, 44-45.
[26] *Ibid.,* p. 199.

Shen Pao-chen, the governor-general of Liang-Chiang in the late 1870's, considered the Huai troops in Kiangsu so important that he memorialized the throne to prevent Li Hung-chang from reducing his force in that area. He stated that he relied upon the Huai-chün to make up for deficiencies in the existing local provincial garrisons, and went on to say:

Now Li Hung-chang plans to disband fourteen battalions of Huai Braves, of which five are in Kiangsu. In recent years some of the Hsiang troops in Kiangsu have been either disbanded or transferred. Now if we wish to disband more of our own garrisons this would make it difficult to maintain order. Commanders like Chang Ho-ts'ai and Wu Ch'ang-ch'ing are veterans of a hundred battles, and they are very generous in outlook. In case of shortage of revenue, they request to disband their armies. But I dare not consent.[27]

Despite Shen's protest, Li effected some economies by carrying out his proposed reduction.

In 1879 Li reported that he still maintained twenty-six battalions in Kiangsu, and in 1880 eighteen battalions were still located in that region. British reports vary considerably in estimates of Huai-chün strength in the south. The consuls and military intelligence officers had difficulty in clearly ascertaining which troops were Huai-chün and which were local provincial garrisons. One report in 1876 mentioned the existence of sixteen stockades (mud forts garrisoned by five hundred men) at P'u-k'ou under the command of "General Wu" (probably Wu Ch'ang-ch'ing), twenty-two stockades at Hsü-chou, and twenty at Yang-chou.[28] Captain Trotter of the Royal Engineers more clearly described the distribution of forces as sixteen regiments, which he estimated to comprise eight thousand men, under the command of General Wu, four of which were at P'u-k'ou, two others at Yang-chou, on the Grand Canal, and five more at Wu-lung-shan. He also stated that at Hsü-chou, two hundred miles north of Nanking, another of Li Hung-chang's generals had twenty-four regiments under his command.[29]

Vice-consul Carles described the Huai-chün garrison at P'u-k'ou as follows:

The troops are composed of Ngan-Hway [Anhwei] men by preference, but there is a considerable proportion of Hu-Nan men. The officers come

---

[27] *Ch'ing-ch'ao hsü-wen-hsien t'ung-k'ao*, 203:9507.
[28] Bell, *China*, II, 196-97.
[29] *Ibid.*, p. 45.

mostly from Lü-Chau in Ngan-Hway, Li-Hung-Chang's birthplace. The men that we saw were very favourable specimens of the Chinese lower classes. Few of them were over 35 (for this they accounted by the destruction wrought by the Taiping rebellion), and all were strong, healthy men, of courteous manners and intelligent countenance. . . .

Of the officers, and more especially of the artillery officers, we received a very poor account. When the troops are drilled, it is generally the corporal who gives the word of command, and by degrees the higher officers fall so far behind their men in knowledge of foreign drill, that they are loth to leave their tents. . . . The lower officers are quite unable to preserve any order among their men; but the colonel will have the men bambooed on the slightest appearance of disrespect or insubordination. The officers themselves do not escape scot free, and during a campaign Li has been known to kick a General.[30]

The same account says that the soldiers received 4.6 liang (approximately U.S. $4.50) every forty-five days. From this the equivalent of ninety cents was deducted for rice (which the "general" supplied). As the "general" (probably the provincial commander-in-chief) was able to provide a man's rations at a cost of seventy-five cents at most, the difference that went into his own pocket was considerable. Another source of profit for the officers was the pay owing to deserters who had not been reported. According to the same account, the colonel profited most from this practice, but the general and captain also had a share.[31] The pay of captains, which was fifteen liang per month, was said to have commonly been doubled through these irregular means. Colonels, according to the British observers, were able to make five hundred liang a month, and the "general" was reputed to have received emoluments amounting to three thousand liang a month.[32] During this period one liang was worth approximately one-third of an English pound sterling, or something more than one United States dollar.[33] In a country where the relatively well-paid Huai-chün common soldier received only four and a half liang a month, the pay of Li Hung-chang's officers by regulation and peculation was fabulous. Li's favor through promotion offered substantial monetary rewards, and his control of his officer corps rested on grounds of real economic advantage.

The troops of the Huai-chün in Liang-Chiang, besides garrisoning stockades at strategic points along the rivers and the Grand Canal, were also engaged in incidental tasks required for maintaining the

---

[30] *Ibid.*, p. 197.
[31] *Ibid.*
[32] *Ibid.*, p. 45.
[33] H. B. Morse, *In the Days of the Taipings,* p. xii.

public waterworks.[34] After 1882 when telegraph lines were constructed to the north, these Huai troops were also charged with guarding the lines and keeping them in good repair.[35]

In 1882 six battalions under the command of Wu Ch'ang-ch'ing were transferred to Korea, but Li Hung-chang continued to report their accounts and control their funds. At the same time Li gave notice that the eighteen battalions of the Ming-Ch'ing Huai-chün forces then garrisoning Kiangsu would be paid entirely and reported upon by that province.

In 1890 Li reported on the accounts of only fifty-one battalions of Huai-chün land and water forces stationed on the coasts of Chihli and at Port Arthur and Dairen. These were the Wu-I, Jen, Sheng, Ming, and Ch'u armies and the new Ch'ing army cavalry and fortress garrisons. At that time he complained strongly to the throne that his military funds for the Huai Army were insufficient and that as of the eleventh month of 1890 the unpaid rations due his troops amounted to 1,610,690 liang.[36] In the following year his balance of unpaid rations remained approximately the same. This indebtedness also carried into the year 1893. (See Tables 5 and 6.)

Tax Sources of Huai-chün Income

The Huai-chün derived almost its entire income from four major sources. These were revenues from (1) foreign customs (levied on imports from abroad which entered China at such ports as Shanghai, Hankow, and Chinkiang; (2) likin, principally on the sale and transport of goods and opium; (3) tax, likin, and license fees levied on salt; and (4) subsidies. These subsidies may have been derived originally from any possible tax source, but in all probability they came in large measure from customs, likin, and taxes on salt. A fifth source of revenue for Li's Huai Army were the funds remitted by the provincial treasuries of Hupeh and Kiangsu. Such funds probably originally derived from land tax and a variety of other sources. The Huai-chün received additional contributions, but these were usually negligible sums given as repayment for special services performed by the army. From the time Li moved to Chihli through 1885, only once did the Huai-chün receive as much as 20 per cent of its income from special contributions, and that was in 1876 when Chihli province paid more

---

[34] Bell, *China,* II, 182, 189.
[35] *LWCK Memorials,* 52:25a ff., KH 10/11/21.
[36] *Ibid.,* 69:35a ff., KH 16/11/16.

TABLE 8

HUAI-CHÜN INCOME BASES*

(In Liang)

Year	Customs	Likin	Salt Likin and Tax	Subsidy	Treasury	Other
1871 (one-year average)	1,199,498 (29%)	785,449 (19%)	793,287 (19%)	666,171 (14%)	566,602[h,k] (14%)	60,212 (1%)
1872-73	1,214,298 (31%)	1,000,019 (26%)	766,499 (19%)	679,748 (17%)	240,000[k] (6%)	2,736 (.8%)
1873-76 (average per year)	1,298,962 (35%)	994,123 (26%)	808,642 (22%)	396,513 11%	253,333[k] (7%)	1,343 (.03%)
1876-77	1,163,112 (31%)	1,071,209 (29%)	684,113 (16%)	259,923 (7%)	165,100[k] (4%)	369,022 (10%)
1885 (quota)	800,000+ (40%)	140,000+ (7%)	700,000+ (35%)	200,000+ (10%)	100,000+[k] (5%)	. . .

* See Table 5 for source references.

h Hupeh treasury.

k Kiangsu treasury.

than 365,000 liang to the Huai-chün in return for munitions that the army furnished to the metropolitan province. The only available specific data on the tax sources of the Huai-chün income is given in Table 8.

In addition to the income listed in Table 8, Li's memorials on the Huai-chün accounts indicate that in the year 1878 he received subsidies (amount unspecified) from Kiangsu, Chekiang, Szechwan, and Hupeh, as well as income from salt likin. In 1879 and 1880 he reported that his income was derived from Chekiang, Szechwan, and Hupeh subsidies, Kiangsu customs and likin, and Liang-Huai salt likin. In 1882 and 1883 he mentioned the same sources with the addition of a subsidy from Shantung. In 1884, the last year for which we have specific reference to detailed income figures, only Szechwan and Kiangsu were reported to be providing subsidies. In addition Li reported the receipt of income derived from salt likin in Liang-Huai. In subsequent years Li's accounts provide only total figures, with no indication of the specific sources of income. But in 1885, reporting on the finances of Chihli province, Li referred to a government-approved quota which had been assigned as revenue for the Huai-chün.[37] Although the figures Li specified under the stated quota do not necessarily correspond with the actual receipts of the Huai-chün, there is a rough correlation between the total sum due from the various provinces and the total sum that Li's army actually received; and the 1885 quota may be used as a further indication of the basis of the Huai-chün's income.

During the period under discussion the Huai-chün received more income from customs receipts than from any other tax source. Likin on goods, which in the earlier years had provided substantial funds, eventually declined in importance, to be replaced largely by income from taxes on salt. The two major sources upon which the Huai-chün became almost entirely dependent, customs receipts and salt, remained relatively stable because they were derived by agreement and long-term practice from specific regions and bureaus. The Huai-chün's position as protector of salt transportation to the capital made it possible for Li Hung-chang to supervise the salt monopolies from which both tax and likin were derived. Income from salt was generally the same year after year, and since a specific amount of that income was earmarked for the Huai-chün, it assured the army a fairly definite income relatively secure from appropriation by other provincial agencies.

---

[37] *Ibid.*, 54:30a-34b, KH 11/7/8.

Customs receipts, largely from foreign trade, were also stable. The government's practice was to assign to each of the customs bureaus a quota to be received annually by the Board of Revenue. This was intended to guarantee a fixed minimum income to the government. Certain portions of the quota were assigned, in the same manner, for other purposes. We have noted that during his administration of Kiangsu Li had frequently refused to meet demands of the various provinces and even of the central government for remission of funds due them from the Kiangsu customhouse. The urgency of his own requirements, the importance of his armies to the government, and the strong position of his bureaucratic machine in the various financial offices had made this resistance possible. In his later days in Chihli, Li was able to maintain his military establishment largely through his continuing (though considerably lessened) ability to draw customs revenues for the support of his armies. After 1885 when the quota mentioned above was established for the Huai-chün, he could expect to receive 400,000 liang yearly from the customhouses in Kiangsu, principally Shanghai (see Table 9). The Hu-Kuang provinces, which for a while had been under the successive administration of Li Hung-chang and Li Han-chang, assigned an equal amount from their customs revenues for the Huai-chün. Once this quota was fixed, it appears to have remained constant. Li was apparently unable to increase the customs remissions from either Shanghai or Hankow (Hu-Kuang) to their earlier high level, but at the same time the fixed quota for which

TABLE 9*

ANNUAL QUOTA FOR HUAI-CHÜN REVENUE, 1885

Hankow Customs	400,000 *liang* plus
Kiangnan Customs	400,000 *liang* plus
Liang-Chiang Treasury	100,000 *liang* plus
Shanghai Likin Bureau	40,000 *liang* plus
Kiangsu Opium Likin	100,000 *liang* plus
Liang-Huai Salt License Bureau	700,000 *liang* plus
Szechwan (diverted to Kiangsu, Anhwei, Shantung)	200,000 *liang* plus

* *LWCK Memorials, chüan* 54, pp. 30a-34b, KH 11/7/8.

he eventually obtained central government sanction guaranteed the continued existence of his personal army.

The shift to dependence upon foreign trade and salt production and trade for military revenues localized and redefined the power struggles in late Ch'ing China; for military strength could not be maintained over any considerable period without direct or, at the very least, indirect control over the regions that yielded such reliable and substantial revenues.

Financing the Lien-chün

Owing to his loss of direct control over the regions from which the Huai-chün received the major portion of its income, Li was unable to prevent his army from dwindling and was handicapped in his ambitions to transform it into an entirely modern land force. But his position in Chihli provided opportunities to develop new forces in the north. These were the "trained armies," or lien-chün. With the support of the central government, which was dissatisfied with the protection afforded by the Banner and Lü-ying battalions drilled and armed in the traditional manner, Li reorganized certain northern forces, building upon the foundations laid down by his predecessor, Tseng Kuo-fan. In all but name, the organization of the lien-chün by Li was an expansion of the Huai-chün. If for his older personal army he could not obtain locally or from other provinces as much revenue as in the past, as governor-general of Chihli and Commissioner of Northern Defense, he could claim them for the new armies. Funds for these lien-chün came to him through two major channels: the Chihli provincial treasury, for which he was responsible as governor-general, and the Pei-yang defense bureau, which he supervised as Commissioner of Northern Defense.

Except for the Huai troops garrisoned in Liang-Chiang, most of Li's old and new forces were merged. Huai-chün commanders took over the command and training of the lien-chün, certain battalions of which were recruited from Anhwei and northern Kiangsu. Battalions and even platoons of Huai soldiers and lien-chün recruits were quartered together.[38] They shared the same modern armaments and manned the same new fortresses. Although financial reports showed the existence of separate forces, the Huai-chün and lien-chün, in fact, constituted one large scattered army which held common allegiance to Li. The lien-chün were of two designations, *chen lien-chün* (former

---

[38] Bell, *China*, II, 58-59.

Lü-ying troops undergoing reorganization) and *hai-fang* [sea defense] *lien-chün,* battalions specially organized to man coastal fortifications. The *hai-fang lien-chün* were generally the more important battalions, well integrated with the Huai-chün and armed with the most modern weapons Li could secure. The *chen lien-chün* were not so clearly distinguished. Certain battalions were throughly reorganized and re-equipped, while others were not. The best of these troops, like the new coastal forces, were thoroughly absorbed into the Huai-chün complex.[39] In 1885 the total number of such lien-chün, both *chen* and *hai-fang,* was forty-five battalions, or approximately 22,500 men, of which fourteen battalions were considered to be crack coastal defense troops. All lien-chün in Chihli were under the command of the provincial commander-in-chief, who was almost always a Huai-chün officer. At this time Li commanded only forty-seven battalions of Huai troops in Shantung and Chihli (another nineteen battalions, the location of which was unspecified in Li's reports, were presumably stationed in Liang-Chiang). Thus the addition of lien-chün compensated for the reduction of the Huai-chün.

The lien-chün, in 1885, received from Chihli provincial funds 1,100,-000 liang paid out to thirty-one battalions of regular lien-chün and "new" river patrol forces, and 370,000 liang spent for fourteen battalions of coastal defense troops. In addition, other forces of Lü-ying and river patrol units, some of which were being reorganized into lien-chün, received part of the 1,610,000 liang paid to the forces in Chihli and the garrisons in Fengtien, Heilungkiang, and Sinkiang. Payments to the lien-chün, therefore, roughly equalled the money spent on the Huai-chün proper. In addition some 390,000 liang were spent on ammunition and fortifications used by the lien-chün and the Huai-chün in common.[40]

The regular lien-chün were paid from regular provincial funds held by Chihli. But the new coastal defense forces had specially designated sources of income. Li arranged to support these troops locally from the so-called 60-per-cent tax on foreign commodities from the Tientsin customs, the revenue from opium likin, a subsidy from the Shantung customs, surtaxes on the salt from Ch'ang-lu, and miscellaneous sources.[41] In 1885 the Shanghai customs supplied 300,000 liang earmarked for lien-chün engaged in river patrols and defense. In addi-

---

[39] Demetrius Boulger, *The Life of Sir Halliday Macartney,* pp. 248-51, distinguishes ordinary troops in Chihli from Li's various battalions.

[40] *LWCK Memorials,* 54:30a-34b, KH 11/7/8.

[41] *Ibid.,* 34:42a ff., KH 5/6/18; 27:34a ff., KH 2/6/26.

tion, Shanghai paid directly part of the 1,100,000 liang that supported the thirty-one battalions of regular lien-chün and river forces.[42]

The local customs administrations were hard pressed by both Li Hung-chang and the Board of Revenue for the revenues they collected. Li depended upon them for his lien-chün, and the Board of Revenue sought funds for rations for the forces of the capital. Li's direct control of the local customs gave him a certain advantage over the Board of Revenue. Following his earlier procedures in Shanghai, Li almost invariably insisted that the first obligation of the customs was to support his own modernized forces.[43] When called upon to pay the interest on loans raised for the central government's Peking Field Force from the Tientsin customs, Li declined on the grounds that the obligations of the Tientsin customs for defense (lien-chün and Li's coastal fortress garrisons) were already too high. He then went on to suggest that the Board of Revenue make good the deficit of the Peking establishment.[44]

The Ch'ang-lu salt merchants were second to the Tientsin customs as providers of rations for Li's coastal defense forces. Li was solicitous of their interests and went out of his way to gain and hold their gratitude. He showed his favor most clearly in 1873, when he attempted to have the past debts of the Ch'ang-lu salt merchants canceled. In the same year he proposed that the central government lend funds to the merchants, who at the time were in difficulty because the government had issued too many licenses for salt production and distribution, and overcompetition had resulted in a depression in the industry:

... to help the salt merchants is to help the government. This is different from our help to the pawn merchants, and we should therefore not require the payment of interest from the salt merchants. The funds should be repaid over a period of four years. . . . but not with interest and not on the rigid period system that applies to the Chekiang pawn merchants.[45]

The salt merchants also received special treatment in the collection of

[42] *Ibid.*, 54:30a-34b, KH 11/7/8.

[43] *Ibid.*, 27:10a ff., KH 2/4/27; 17:55a ff., TC 9/12/1.

[44] *Ibid.*, 66:22a ff., KH 15/11/1.

[45] *Ibid.*, 22:43a ff., TC 12/10/27. It was a practice of the government to lend funds to merchant groups on interest, thus acquiring profits from funds which would otherwise have lain useless in the treasury. The funds collected for the lien-chün in particular were lent out to the pawn merchants of Chekiang, thus increasing the lien-chün revenues. Li's memorial shows a sharp difference in his attitude toward the salt merchants, who were high taxpayers in Chihli, and the Chekiang group, whom he had so despised in Shanghai (e.g., Yang Fang and Wu Hsü).

the salt tax in Chihli, largely for the same reasons. In 1876 the throne ordered the Ch'ang-lu merchants to pay their taxes in full by the fifth month. Because of calamities in preceding years, the merchants had been permitted to pay in the tenth month. At the request of the salt merchants, Li Hung-chang took the postponement of some of their payments in the past as a precedent, and on numerous occasions thereafter petitioned the throne to continue to grant this and similar favors to the Ch'ang-lu merchants.[46]

Pei-yang Financial Accounts

Li provided separate accounting for his Pei-yang forces. He submitted these accounts under various categories. For the years 1873 through 1881 he designated one group of accounts as "Reports on the Tientsin Coastal Defense Contribution Bureau." These reports accounted for funds received from the Tientsin customhouse, opium likin, the Tung-hai customs, and income from certificates issued to the Ch'ang-lu salt merchants. The funds were expended for local defense. In 1881 Li reported that the troops covered in this account were the newly designated Tientsin Coastal Defense lien-chün, the coastal fortress garrisons, the official troops at Ta-ku, and the Yün-tzu-ying. After 1882 this same account was submitted under the title "Report of the Accounts of the Tientsin Coastal Defense Lien-chün." These figures are reproduced in Table 10.

The sources of income, being fixed with the consent of the Board of Revenue and subject to Li's direct control, provided a relatively stable, but often insufficient, yield, as shown in Table 10. These lien-chün forces, paid under separate account, were actually integrated locally with Huai-chün components. In 1882 a British Intelligence observer noted that "The Lien-Chun and Hwei-Chun may be brigaded together. Thus, at Tientsin there are three battalions of the former and one of the latter, under the command of one general."[47] If we count these lien-chün as being for all practical purposes part of the Huai-chün and add their revenues to the Huai-chün receipts, the latter are increased by between 15 and 25 per cent.

The fullest accounts submitted by Li as Commissioner of Defense of the northern coast were given in still another set of memorials to the

46 Ibid., 27:9a ff., KH 2/4/7. See also ibid., 18:4a, TC 10/1/24; 18:34a, TC 10/6/1; 19:33a, TC 11/4/17; 20:22a, TC 11/11/3; 20:27a, TC 11/11/12; 21:23a, TC 12/4/11; 22:20a, TC 12/6/20; 22:23a, TC 12/7/21; 22:43a, TC 12/10/27; and 22:55a ff., TC 12/11/19.
47 Bell, China, II, 58-59.

TABLE 10

TIENTSIN COASTAL DEFENSE REPORTS

Year	Received	Spent	Balance or Deficit (−)	Continuing Deficit (−)
1872	385,000	385,895	−895	
1873				
1874				
1875	388,633	390,406		
1876				
1877				
1878	354,525	354,977	−205	
1879	388,620	389,090	−120	
1880				
1881	390,883	392,554	−1,188	
1882	357,646	359,117	−1,471	
1883				−21,178
1884	414,909	398,704	−4,973	−21,178
1885				
1886	383,141	378,408	31,816	−21,178
1887	402,489	407,809	26,496	−21,178
1888	378,724	377,939	27,283	−21,178
1889	363,155	379,850	10,585	−21,178
1890	396,456	407,873	−830	−21,178
1891	382,536	379,383	2,322	−21,178
1892	408,120	408,760	1,682	−21,178
1893	402,705	378,391	25,996	−21,178

Source: The materials for the table are derived from *LWCK Memorials* as follows: *1872*, 21:42a, TC 12/4/23; *1875*, 30:17a, KH 3/10/4; *1878*, 34:42a, KH 5/6/18; *1879*, 38:35a, KH 6/9/10; *1881*, 45:37a, KH 8/12/17; *1882*, 53:7a, KH 11/1/19; *1884*, 55: 51a, KH 11/12/20; *1886*, 60:35a, KH 13/8/30; *1887*, 63:33a, KH 14/9/13; *1888*, 66:1a, KH 15/8/5; *1889*, 68:34a, KH 16/7/29; *1890*, 72:41a, KH 17/8/19; *1891*, 75:3a, KH 18/7/2; *1892*, 77:19a, KH 19/8/16; *1893*, 79:1a, KH 20/9/1.

TABLE 11

PEI-YANG DEFENSE ACCOUNTS, 1875-91

Year	Income (in liang)	Expenditure	Balance Brought Forward
1875-80	804,436*	494,038*	1,054,300
1881-82 1882-83	1,136,631*	815,088*	1,698,462
1883-84 1884-85	1,262,674*	1,647,541*	928,727
1885 } single	1,908,806	1,473,873*	
1886 } report	953,340	1,473,873*	620,596
1887 } single	993,074	1,297,415*	
1888 } report	1,291,329	1,297,415*	79,721
1889	1,029,939	997,183	80,667
1890	1,464,246	1,426,038	42,506
1891	1,334,339	1,278,047	21,445

Source: The materials for the table are derived from *LWCK Memorials* as follows: *1875-80*, 48:40a, KH 9/12/19; *1881* and *1882*, 58:15a, KH 12/11/4; *1883* and *1884*, 61:11a, KH 13/11/26; *1885* and *1886*, 64:14a, KH 15/1/21; *1887* and *1888*, 71:3a, KH 17/2/16; *1889* (designated as Pei-yang Fleet, First Report), 74:34a, KH 18/5/25; *1890* (Pei-yang Fleet, Second Report), 76:50a, KH 19/5/28; *1891* (Pei-yang Fleet, Third Report), 78:24a, KH 20/5/17.

*Average for each year.

throne, which he usually called "Accounts of the Pei-yang Defense Bureau." They provided data on various items of coastal and naval expense and covered periods of varied lengths. The last of these accounts was designated only as "Reports on the Pei-yang Naval Fleet." For the most part Li used the money designated as Pei-yang Defense Funds for rations, fodder, the upkeep of naval and military academies, payments to cadets and instructors, expenses incurred in sending students abroad, production and purchase of munitions, labor, dockyards, naval supplies, and maintenance of vessels. Table 11, based on Li's periodic reports, provides the basic figures of Li Hung-chang's Pei-yang Defense Accounts over a seventeen-year period ending in 1891.

Fluctuation in both income and expenditure can be noted in the table. Perhaps the most significant tendency is the steady depletion in the balance brought forward for each succeeding time period. This balance was used as a financial cushion in years when income de-

TABLE 12
Sources of Income For Pei-yang Defense, 1875-91*

Year	Likin	Customs	Customs and Likin	Other	Salt Certificates	Total Income
1875	386,667†	396,873†	783,540†	20,895†	. . .	804,436†
1876	386,667†	396,873†	783,540†	20,895†	. . .	804,436†
1877	386,667†	396,873†	783,540†	20,895†	. . .	804,436†
1878	386,667†	396,873†	783,540†	20,895†	. . .	804,436†
1879	386,667†	396,873†	783,540†	20,895†	. . .	804,436†
1880	386,667†	396,873†	783,540†	20,895†	. . .	804,436†
1881	352,500†	747,591†	1,100,091†	36,538†	1,392†	1,136,631†
1882	352,500†	747,591†	1,100,091†	36,538†	1,392†	1,136,631†
1883	170,000†	485,847†	655,847†	606,826†	51,183†	1,262,674†
1884	170,000†	485,847†	655,847†	606,826†	51,183†	1,262,674†
1885	115,000	617,819	732,819	1,175,977‡	. . .	1,908,806
1886	50,000	486,555	536,555	416,785	. . .	953,340
1887	480,000	407,526	887,526	105,548	. . .	993,074
1888	530,000§	698,582§	1,228,582	62,747	. . .	1,291,329
1889	. . .	. . .	965,110	64,827	. . .	1,029,939
1890	. . .	. . .	1,387,880	76,366	. . .	1,464,246
1891	. . .	. . .	1,260,713	73,624	. . .	1,334,339

* This data is derived from Li's periodic reports on Pei-yang defense funds. For sources see Table 11.
† Average per year.
‡ Including special Chihli defense contribution.
§ Includes payment on balance due for 1887 and previous years.

creased or expenditures grew, and as such reserves diminished, fluctuations in yearly income became correspondingly more crucial. For instance, in 1882 the balance of income over expenditures was 1,698,-462 liang. Four years later it had dwindled to 620,596 liang. In 1889 it fell as low as 80,667· liang, and in the two remaining years for which reports are available it diminished by approximately half annually. Li's last report shows that he had on hand only 21,445 liang. If this trend continued, as seems likely, by the time of the Sino-Japanese War of 1894 the navy could not have had sufficient funds for efficient opera-

TABLE 13

SOURCES OF PEI-YANG REVENUE IN PERCENTAGES*

Year	Likin	Customs	Likin and Customs	Other
1875-1880	48	49	97	3
1881-1882	31	66	97	3
1883-1884	13	38	51	48
1885	6	32	38	61
1886	5	51	56	44
1887	48	41	89	10
1888	41	54	95	5
1889	. .	. .	94	6
1890	. . ·	. .	95	5
1891	. .	. .	94	6

* Based on Table 12.

tions, and expansion and improvement would have been totally out of the question. In these last years the expenditures reported were made almost entirely for the maintenance of three cruisers and four destroyer-type vessels. Li was spending approximately 1,000,000 liang solely to keep these ships in operation. Theoretically this left him only between 80,000 and 300,000 a year for all other expenses. But in a letter addressed to the Naval Board in 1886 Li mentioned that aside from expenses for the three cruisers of his fleet, the coastal defense organization actually disbursed over 1,000,000 liang each year.[48] In that same year he estimated the minimum needs for coastal defense at 2,000,000 liang per annum.[49] This financial goal was reached only once, however, when in 1885 a special defense contribution bureau was set up in Chihli because of the imminence of a French attack during the war over Indo-China. The quotas for the Pei-yang naval development had been more or less fixed in 1875, and re-established

[48] LWCK Naval Board Letters, 2: 1a-2b, KH 12/7/4.
[49] Ibid., 1: 14b-15b, KH 12/1/18.

TABLE 14

REGIONAL SOURCES OF PEI-YANG INCOME*

(Yearly Average in Liang)

Year	Region									Miscellaneous	
	Kiangsi	Chekiang	Kiangsu	Hupeh	Chihli	Fukien	Kwang-tung	Honan	Shan-tung	Other	Huai-chün
1875-80	113,333	191,199	125,117	133,333	43,981	33,947	159,511	. . .	. . .	. . .	. . .
1881-82	75,000	226,524	396,838	100,000	30,428	113,419	159,274	20,641	6,116	3,053†	. . .
1883-84	55,000	177,619	197,645	20,000	87,960	88,251	80,553	. . .	22,239	1,755‡	530,534
1885-86	20,000	143,676	299,423	25,000	794,055	51,734	50,000	. . .	12,102	18,881§‖	14,864
1887-88	60,000	309,611	303,852	285,000	100,268	. . .	. . .	. . .	33,113	10,339†‖	23,591

* See Table 11 for sources by year.
† Board of Revenue.
‡ Lien-chün.
§ Pei-yang Coastal Defense Supply Bureau.
‖ Telegraph Bureau.

in 1885, but allowance was never made for the continuously increasing costs of maintaining a navy, and no method of enforcing payments from the provinces was ever worked out.

Sources of Pei-yang Income

The Pei-yang military organization under Li Hung-chang received most of its support from likin and customs revenues, except during the years 1883-86. In those four years special contributions were provided by Li from the Huai-chün funds and from provincial funds of Chihli. (See Tables 12 and 13.)

The responsibility for supporting the Pei-yang forces was laid on all the coastal provinces, with Chekiang, Kiangsu, and Hupeh bearing the largest burdens. While this provided some financial security, the inability of Li and the central government to enforce payment strictly resulted in considerable irregularity in the time and size of remittance. (See Table 14.)

The Naval Board: Regionalism versus Centralism in Naval Financing

When the Naval Board was established in 1885, Li Hung-chang had hoped, in his position as co-director, to be able to increase the income for his Pei-yang fleet and to have a stronger hand in raising funds. He responded eagerly at that time to a request from the Board, probably inspired by him, for his estimate of the cost of naval defense. After describing his small but "excellent" fleet in the north he went on to say:

If we want to train a fleet, for the time being we only have five ships which are suitable for battle and defense on the high seas. I have reported that we have ordered four ships in England and Germany. After they have arrived, we will have a total of nine ships. In the future if our funds increase we should add some shallow, armored, speedy ships and mine-layers amounting to five or six in number.

The funds of the Pei-yang navy come from the provincial customs annual receipts. Formerly the Board of Revenue assigned two million liang annually for the Pei-yang fleet, but recent years have seen most of these funds discontinued. Each year we receive five hundred to six hundred thousand liang. Last year because of the French War we received even less. At that time we retained [in the Pei-yang Defense Bureau] the sea defense contributions which we raised to meet the emergency. But this is not our permanent policy. Recently the Board of Revenue proposed that our Pei-yang Coastal Defense funds all be given to the Naval Board, and then if we need more money for Pei-yang defense the governor-general [Li Hung-chang] can apply to the Naval Board for it.[50]

---

[50] *Ibid.*, 1:1b ff., KH 11/11/29.

Li Hung-chang seemed somewhat reluctant to follow the orders of the court and the Board of Revenue to turn his total Pei-yang Defense income over to the Naval Board, even though he managed the board, at times almost singlehanded.[51] Undoubtedly he distrusted his colleagues at the capital and felt they could only interfere with his management of the Pei-yang funds. If this was so of Li, how much more strongly his fellow governors and governors-general in the various provinces must have felt, for they had no voice in Naval Board administration. In 1886 Li reported what was apparently an exceptional case. He noted with satisfaction in a letter to the Naval Board that the Chekiang customs intendant had forwarded without delay the customs payment for coastal defense from that province. But this intendant was Li's old colleague and follower, his former secretary, Hsüeh Fu-ch'eng.[52] Once again, informal arrangements and personal loyalty seemed to be the essential ingredients in securing interprovincial cooperation. Li had more trouble with some of the other provinces. We find him rather irritably wiring the superintendent of customs at Canton, ordering him to submit his entire customs receipts to Robert Hart, who would collect all funds and manage the indemnity payments. Quoting an imperial edict, Li stated that he wanted no further dissent on the matter.[53] Li hoped that by this means he could be sure to receive his own cut, for though there was little friendly feeling between Hart and Li, Li trusted Hart's enthusiasm for the cause of modernization and centralization in China. In 1889 Li complained that although he had been promised two million liang a year from the various provinces for the support of his defense program in the north, he was not receiving even half this allotment. The situation became worse with the passing years, and in 1891 Li was requested by the boards at the capital to reduce his naval expenditures and demobilize part of his troops in north China.

The Economic Failure of the Pei-yang Program

It is difficult to say how much money Li would have needed to maintain his northern defenses successfully. His most conspicuous failure was not in his land forces but in the navy of which, according to foreign reports, he was so proud. So long as Japan or any other nation kept ahead of China in naval strength, the Pei-yang navy was bound

---

[51] *LWCK Memorials*, 55:9a, KH 11/9/21.
[52] *LWCK Naval Board Letters*, 1:15b, KH 12/1/18.
[53] *Li Wen-chung kung tien-kao* (hereafter cited as *LWCK Telegrams*), KH 13/4 int./9, in *LWCK Collected Works*.

to be a failure, since its only purpose was defense against foreign, not internal, enemies. Huge sums had been spent by Li, raised from special levies upon the customhouses in the various provinces, for the purchase of modern warships. The two cruisers brought back from England by Ting Ju-ch'ang in 1881 had cost 200,000 pounds each. The four gunboats which Li ordered about this time cost about 30,000 pounds each, and the total outlay for the gunboats was to be about 450,000 liang.[54] Li had been able to raise funds for these vessels, but in the following decades he was unable to win support for additional naval purchases. The Board of Naval Affairs was a thin cloak for his ambitions for the Pei-yang fleet, and the provincial officials steadfastly refused to do more than pay part of their annual commitment for maintaining the existing fleet. One of the reasons for their justified suspicion of the board was that its ineffectual Manchu director, Prince Ch'un, and his successor, Prince Ch'ing, were unable to administer its funds properly and could not prevent the empress dowager from. diverting the funds for other purposes. Sir Robert Hart, commenting on Li's humiliation when news of the sinking of the Pei-yang fleet by the Japanese in 1894 reached China, wrote:

This Government now realises the situation and sees what a poor thing the great satrap [Li Hung-chang] has made of his opportunity to create an army and navy; but they still require their eyes to be opened further, and to see that *honesty* must be the rule of the Court itself:—e.g. the Admiralty has had big sums paid to it yearly the last ten years and ought to have a balance of 36,000,000 taels, and lo! it has not a penny, having allowed the Empress Dowager to draw on it for the many whims she has been indulging in.[55]

The provincial officials had been promised steel ships, but the money collected by the Naval Board was used to build a stone boat in the palace gardens. Li shared responsibility with his Naval Board colleagues for failing to prevent this misuse of defense funds. He has been accused of being complacent and unconcerned, but this was not the case. As late as 1894, immediately preceding the Sino-Japanese

[54] Stanley F. Wright, *Hart and the Chinese Customs*, pp. 469-70, 476-77.

[55] *Ibid.*, p. 645. Hart had little personal regard for Li, having been subject to many years of Li's doublehandedness and suspicion in dealing with foreign advisers who rose to, or aspired to, great influence. Hart's own sense of frustration was so great that he was badly torn between his old loyalty to China (particularly the central government) and his desire to see her suffer what he considered to be a badly needed lesson at the hands of Japan. Although he was cold toward China in the Sino-Japanese War, he reversed his views subsequently during the Boxer Uprising and made himself highly unpopular with the Westerners by his justification of the Chinese actions.

War, Li requested funds for the purchase of new guns for the Pei-yang naval vessels. The cost was to be more than 613,000 liang.[56] These funds, so far as we know, were never made available to him. When the first battles with the Japanese had been fought, and Li was ordered to dismiss Admiral Ting Ju-ch'ang, Li came to the defense of his old Huai-chün follower and at the same time defended his own policies. He pointed out that the Chinese vessels were much slower than the newer Japanese vessels. The latter could do between twenty and twenty-three knots, while the Chinese ships could reach only fifteen or sixteen knots at the most. He complained that although Ting Ju-ch'ang and his other officers had tried to get faster vessels, he had not been able to purchase a single boat since 1888. Reminding the court that he himself had also been troubled by the problem of a slow fleet, he commented that with the ships she had China could not win a sea battle.[57]

In trying to establish and direct a unified Naval Board, without sufficient power to control funds at court or compel payment by the provinces, Li dangerously overextended himself. Liang Ch'i-ch'ao considers that Li's overconfidence and hastiness were fatal flaws in his character, leading him to undertake what he could not fulfill.[58] But while Li's own limitations provide part of the explanation, his failure to create the navy he had promised resulted from other factors as well. A few of Li's colleagues, particularly those in the provinces, shared with him the vision he at times possessed—a vision of China defended in a modern and even heroic manner. They had co-operated at first in meeting the demands of the Naval Board for funds, but when they saw how these funds were misused, they decided that the money could be better used for their own regional forces. Li's own experience as a provincial and regional leader warned him, as his memorials of 1874 and 1884 show, that what he was attempting was an impossibility. He regretted the conditions which prevented unity; he complained about the failure of the various provincial officials to give active support to his "national" navy. But his own regional outlook manifested itself clearly, as when, for instance, he refused the central government and the Board of Revenue the use of Chihli funds for the purchase of patrol cutters or troop rations.[59]

---

[56] *LWCK Memorials*, 78:1a-2b, KH 20/2/25.

[57] *Ibid.*, 78:52a ff., KH 20/7/29.

[58] Liang Ch'i-ch'ao, *Chung-kuo ssu-shih nien-lai ta-shih-chi*, in *Ying-ping shih ho-chi, chuan-chi san*, p. 38.

[59] *LWCK Memorials*, 28:16a, KH 2/11/9; 29:52a, KH 3/8/27; 39:56a, KH 13/4/30.

In the twenty years following Li's transfer to Chihli, the Pei-yang defense program served to offset the economic losses incurred by Li in moving out of the Liang-Chiang region. The new land and naval forces which he developed helped to compensate for limitations imposed on the old Huai-chün. Despite the obstacles Li encountered and the ultimate failure of his fleet when tested in battle, Li's Pei-yang program served him well politically, adding to his strength in the bureaucratic councils of the empire and to his prestige in the eyes of the foreign diplomatic corps. The long-term significance of the program was that it was a necessary trial project leading to the gradual reform and reorganization of China's military system at the beginning of the twentieth century.

During his period in Chihli Li achieved greater control over military forces than did any other individual official in the empire at the time. Even after the disastrous Sino-Japanese War, the Huai-chün still remained for a short period the largest regional force in China. Including the lien-chün and other branch armies raised and supported by Li in the north, Li's total force was about twice the size of the nearest similar military grouping.[60] On a national scale the total annual rations allotted to all such regional armies amounted to about twenty million liang.[61] Between 1873 and 1892 more than 10 per cent of this total was drawn and consumed by the Huai-chün alone. Despite the decrease in Huai-chün income in the 1880's, Li was still able to control approximately 15 per cent of the total regional army funds through the addition of Pei-yang and Tientsin lien-chün funds. This gave him probably five times more military income than any other regional leader.

We can make only a very rough guess as to how Li's military income and expenditures compared with those of the government as a whole. The existing estimates of governmental receipts and expenditures are far from reliable. Having no alternative, let us tentatively accept an estimate of the average annual governmental income as being somewhere in the neighborhood of eighty million liang.[62] During this period, according to the calculations we have presented above, Li Hung-chang took in roughly four million liang annually for the combined Huai-chün and Pei-yang forces. (See Tables 15 and 16.) This would mean that his total military income constituted around 5 per cent of all governmental income. It must be emphasized that Li

---

[60] *CSK*, 132:1b-2a.
[61] *Ibid.*
[62] *Ch'ing-ch'ao hsü-wen-hsien t'ung-k'ao*, 66:8227; 67:8232-33.

TABLE 15

TOTAL REPORTED HUAI-CHÜN AND PEI-YANG INCOME, 1873-93*

Year	Huai-chün Income	Pei-yang Income	Tientsin Coastal Defense	Total
1873	3,756,991	. . .	. . .	. . .
1874	3,756,991	. . .	. . .	. . .
1875	3,756,991	804,436	388,633	4,950,060
1876	3,688,883	804,436	. . .	. . .
1877	3,037,099	804,436	. . .	. . .
1878	2,897,276	804,436	354,525	4,056,237
1879	3,196,569	804,436	388,620	4,389,625
1880	3,178,382	804,436	. . .	. . .
1881	. . .	1,136,631	390,883	. . .
1882	2,602,826	1,136,631	357,646	4,097,103
1883	2,193,590	1,262,674	. . .	. . .
1884	1,993,307	1,262,674	414,909	3,670,890
1885	2,954,300	1,908,806	. . .	. . .
1886	. . .	953,340	383,141	. . .
1887	2,505,560	993,074	402,489	3,901,123
1888	2,426,982	1,291,329	378,724	4,096,945
1889	2,126,125	1,029,939	363,155	3,519,220
1890	2,426,106	1,464,246	396,456	4,286,808
1891	2,170,577	1,334,339	382,536	3,887,452
1892	2,488,154	. . .	408,120	. . .
1893	. . .	. . .	402,705	. . .
Total	51,156,709	18,600,299	5,412,542	

* Figures are based on Tables 5, 10, and 11.

did not intend his forces to be huge standing armies, which he believed to be obsolete; he aimed rather at establishing many small crack battalions. In contrast, the "old-style" standing armies of the central government were many times larger and absorbed approximately 20

TABLE 16

HUAI-CHÜN AND TIENTSIN COASTAL DEFENSE
(LIEN-CHÜN) COMBINED INCOME*

Year	Income
1875	4,145,624
1878	3,251,801
1879	3,585,189
1882	2,960,472
1884	2,408,216
1887	2,908,049
1888	2,805,706
1889	2,498,280
1890	2,822,562
1891	2,553,113
1892	2,896,274

* Figures based on Table 15.

per cent of governmental income. The *fang-chün,* including the Huai and Pei-yang forces, are estimated to have received about one-third of total governmental expenditures in the 1880's, and roughly one-fourth of such expenditures in the 1890's. According to these estimates Li Hung-chang's forces received from 15 to 20 per cent of such governmental military expenditures.[63] Although the figures available cannot all be completely reconciled, it seems safe to conclude that Li Hung-chang's Huai and Pei-yang forces together took in not less than 15 per cent and not more than 25 per cent of all funds for provincial and "new-style" defense. This figure in itself is impressive; but it is even more so when we consider that most of the government's expenditures were widely scattered over the various provinces and were made in small payments by many regional and provincial officials, while Li's funds were in the hands of a single regional leader who had forced his entire military command into one mold—the mold of the Huai-chün.

Through some twenty years of power in Chihli, Li did not alter the nature of his military organization in any essential way. It rested on

---

[63] *Ibid.*

the old regional structure which had given shape to the Huai-chün from the beginning. But as Li's direct control over sources of income gradually disappeared, he became more closely tied to the central government. His skill in organization and the untested power potential of his military forces, particularly his naval forces, made him a figure to be reckoned with and even feared by the central government. But the military purse was held by officials in several provinces, and the strings were more subject to central government control, weak as it was, than to Li's. He was therefore at no time in a suitable position for really independent action.

In his later years Li saw the importance of centralization and co-ordination, since the livelihood of his own forces had become subject to the caprice of outside provincial officials. Although he frequently contested jealously for funds with the Board of Revenue, his own interests dictated his striving toward a national military policy and central control over military funds. But because Li realized that no sweeping reform was likely to succeed, and perhaps because he himself was unable to shake off his regional outlook, he made no move that would have jeopardized his personal control over his own regional forces. Unwilling to take the first essential step by merging his own forces in a larger national organization, Li effected only shallow re-forms, as his financial arrangements particularly demonstrate.

In the last quarter of the nineteenth century the Huai-chün and Pei-yang forces, compared with others in China, were relatively unified and modern. Nevertheless, they were only part of a scattered military structure.[64] This fragmented military structure rested upon a similarly fragmented regional economic basis. Under these conditions, despite the primacy of his own military organization, Li could not but fall far short of attempting or achieving a major power synthesis.

---

[64] Liang Ch'i-ch'ao, *Chung-kuo ssu-shih nien-lai ta-shih-chi*, in *Ying-ping shih ho-chi, chuan-chi san,* p. 35, stresses Li's realistic appraisal of the military situation in the following sentences: "Li felt that the military strength of China was sufficient to cope with internal rebellion, but not sufficient for defense against foreign invasion. He put great weight on this point. Such farsightedness is unusual."

VIII. Li Hung-chang's Quest for "Wealth and Strength"

Li Hung-chang played a vital role in the introduction of Western technology and Western ideas to China. His period of official activity covered the half century in which China made her first important strides toward industrialization. Linked with Li's name are such pioneer enterprises as the Soochow, Shanghai, and Nanking arsenals, founded when he served as governor and later as governor-general in Kiangsu; the China Merchants' Steam Navigation Company, inaugurated in 1872; the opening of mines using Western machinery in Shansi in 1875; the development of coal and iron mines in Luan-chou, Chihli, in 1877, and the establishment of a company to operate these mines in 1883; the construction of a three-mile railroad at the Kaiping mines in 1878; construction in 1879 of a short telegraph line from Tientsin to the Huai-chün and lien-chün headquarters at Taku, Chihli; the opening of coal mines at I-hsien, Shantung, in 1879; initiation of construction of a telegraph line from Tientsin to Shanghai (via Chinkiang) in 1880; a proposal to construct a railroad from Chinkiang to Peking in 1880; construction of a telegraph line from Shanghai to Canton, along the coast, in 1882; the opening of the P'ing-ch'uan copper mines in Shantung in 1881; the formation of a company in Shanghai to manufacture textiles using machines in 1882; the opening of the Mo-ho gold mines in Heilungkiang in 1887; the opening of the Shanghai Weaving Mills in 1890; the reconstruction of the Shanghai Weaving Mills in 1893; and the extension of the Kaiping mine railway 175 miles, from Tientsin to Tangshan, Shanhaikuan, and Peitaiho, in 1894[1] The promotion and founding of the Tientsin Military Academy,

---

[1] *LWCK Memorials*, 20:32a ff., TC 11/11/23; 40:41a ff., KH 7/4/23. The development of this railroad was kept secret. Interestingly enough, at the time it was being constructed, the U.S. Consul at Tientsin, in noting the inauguration of the Kaiping

the Torpedo School, and various schools and agencies connected with Li's arsenals have already been noted in a previous chapter.

Although Li was not the only official to encourage such enterprises, he was one of the earliest and most vigorous, following closely in the footsteps of Tseng Kuo-fan and Lin Tse-hsü. Of all the leaders of his time, he was the greatest of the westernizers, being responsible for more innovations than any other official. His attitude toward the development of Western enterprises and the adoption of Western knowledge remained fairly stable once he had taken his first important steps in that direction. A man of action, Li made scant contribution to the discussions of the revolutionary problems which were visited upon China by the West. Rather, through attempt and achievement he paved the way for actual changes in his society. When he was an old man, Li was looked upon by the Chinese youth of his day as a reactionary or, at best, a rather unimaginative reformer, but to the world at large he still appeared as one of China's outstanding progressives. Li's thinking on foreign matters was tied closely to his own struggle for power. What the West offered to him in the way of strength he seized upon; what was not useful for his purposes he ignored. During his early period in Shanghai, when his primary task was to build and equip the Huai-chün, he thought mainly of Western

---

mines some eighteen months earlier, remarked, "The probabilities are therefore that the first railroad built in the North of China will connect these mines with Tientsin." "Annual Report on Trade of Tientsin," *Tientsin Consular Despatches,* Oct. 31, 1879. See also *LWCK Memorials,* 38:16a ff., KH 6/8/12; 47:10a ff., KH 9/7/13; 39:20a ff., KH 6/12/1; 45:32a ff., KH 8/12/8; 40:46a ff., KH 7/4/23; 43:43a ff., KH 8/3/6; 61:45a ff., KH 13/12/5; 77:38a ff., KH 19/20/26. In addition see *Shanghai-shih t'ung-chih-kuan ch'i-k'an* (Shanghai, 1933), p. 1129. Also see Stanley F. Wright, *Hart and the Chinese Customs,* p. 611. *LWCK Naval Board Letters, chüan* 3, under the following dates: KH 14/9/9; KH 14/12/28; KH 15/4/20. James Harrison Wilson, *China: Travels and Investigations in the Middle Kingdom,* p. xvii; Consul Smithers to Assistant Secretary of State Porter, *Tientsin Consular Despatches,* May 21, 1887. The first official sanction for Li's railroad-building in the north came in 1887, when Li decided to incorporate and extend his existing short lines running from the Kaiping mines. The purport of his proclamation as recorded by the American consul at Tientsin was as follows:

(1) The Board of Naval Affairs has presented a memorial proposing the opening of an experimental railroad at Tientsin and other places "in order to benefit the mercantile classes." This memorial has received imperial sanction. (2) The first line of the railway has already been constructed at Kaiping. (3) The railroad company shall be distinct from the Kaiping Mine Company. (4) Wu Ting-fang, the manager, is to draw up regulations and invite merchant participation. (5-7) Discusses distribution of shares and management. (8) Informs people of general benefits of railroads. (9) Officials must protect railroad interests to make them permanent. (10) The company shall follow Western practices. The Board of Directors selected by shareholders shall make all decisions in public meetings. Officials should not interfere with their authority but only guard against the existence of evil practices.

guns and munitions, but later he came to realize that railroads, ships, mines, and general manufacturing were equally important sources of strength, and that the wealth they provided to those who controlled them was an asset of inestimable importance for military and political purposes.

There can be no doubt that at the time Li Hung-chang introduced Western arms into the Huai-chün, in the early 1860's, he was well aware of the superiority and advantages of many aspects of Western military technology, as his early acquisition of gunboats for the Huai-chün and his work in arsenal development testify. Like a few of his predecessors, Li was fully aware of the need for using Western methods to hold back the West. His interest in Western technology, however, went beyond this limited objective, and as early as 1865, only three years after his arrival at Shanghai, he made the following observations regarding the use of the machines which he had ordered for the Kiangnan Arsenal:

> These foreign machines can also produce machines for tillage, weaving, printing, and pot-making. All these things are good for the people's livelihood and have a daily use. They are not merely for the production of arms and munitions.
>
> The wonder of the machines lies in the fact that they save human labor and material by employing the power of fire and water. Their principle does not extend beyond the connection of parts and the movement of gears. If one thing moves, the whole system moves. The form is quite obvious and visible; the theories and methods are also exact and understandable.[2]

In recognizing the advantages of using Western machines to produce consumer goods, Li showed himself far in advance of most of his contemporaries, who believed that Western machines were good only because they provided guns with which to throw out the foreigners. This early interest in using machines to raise the living standard of the people was not, however, repeated by Li later, even though he came to know much more about Western methods and ideas.

Since the arsenals were for military production, there was no question but that some government agency, either central or provincial, would control and operate them. But Li expected that private capital, supplied by farmers or merchants, would one day have an important part in the development of new industrial enterprises. This the government could not or should not prevent, but he maintained that government control of coinage and of guns and munitions must never be relaxed:

---

[2] *LWCK Memorials,* 9:34b, TC 4/8/1.

I anticipate that after several decades there must be some Chinese farmers and big merchants who will want to copy the foreigners in constructing machines, and they will then produce such machines for their own profit. Government regulations cannot interfere with this. But insofar as coinage and the production of firearms are concerned, these, according to precedent, must not be permitted to be privately manufactured. Since the manufacture of guns should be in the hands of the government, the personnel and laborers involved must always be under government control.[3]

In this same memorial of 1865 on the Kiangnan Arsenal, Li attempted to put his proposed innovations in an acceptable framework, and expressed his views on China's whole problem of strengthening herself. He said:

Our Chinese culture and institutions are quite different from the foreign barbaric customs. There must be some reason for the prosperity of our people and the security of our country and for the preservation of our great heritage from destruction. I also do not entertain the narrow opinion that the imitation of foreign machines is all that is necessary to transform danger into security and weakness into strength. In managing national affairs there are the general problems and the particular ones. That is, there are the roots and there are the branches. For instance, in case of critical illness, we have to give immediate treatment, but this does not mean that this is the way to furnish fundamental nourishment and care. Thus, too, when the floods descend, the dikes must be repaired, but this does not mean that we should neglect the dredging of the rivers and the irrigation of the land.[4]

It is not clear how well Li perceived the consequences of westernization or how far in this direction he intended to go. He saw that the changes needed in China would have to go beyond mere technological innovation, but he evidently believed that this could best be done within the framework of Chinese cultural tradition. The topic of the roots and the branches as applied to China's dilemma was much discussed in Li's generation and later by Chang Chih-tung, who strongly believed that China could flourish only if the new "branches" of Western methods and ideas were grafted on the "roots" of Chinese culture and tradition.[5] Li's formulation, made in 1865, is very much the same as that arrived at by Chang Chih-tung at the turn of the century.

Whether Li ever understood the need for thoroughgoing change is uncertain. His frequent references show that he was well aware of

---

[3] *Ibid.*, pp. 34b-35a.

[4] *Ibid.*, p. 35a.

[5] Hellmut Wilhelm, "The Problem of Within and Without, a Confucian Attempt in Syncretism," *Journal of the History of Ideas*, XII (1951), 48-60.

Japan's rapidly growing strength, brought about by the acceptance of Western ideas and practices. Yet he did not work for fundamental changes, but stood by while China became hopelessly engulfed in a morass of contradictions. He may have believed that the time was never right for him to take a decisive lead. Perhaps, unable to extend his power southward beyond the Yangtze, he waited too long; for when the real opportunities came, for instance, during the Hundred Days of Reform after the Sino-Japanese War, his own basis of strength had already been destroyed. Certainly he would never have contemplated thoroughgoing political reforms which would have demanded the weakening of provincial and regional positions unless he could have been absolutely sure of holding power at the center.

The Founding of the Chao Shang Chü: A Pattern is Formed

The pattern of Chinese commercial and industrial development under Li's guidance was set when Li founded the Chao Shang Chü, or the China Merchants' Steam Navigation Company, in 1872. The company was organized by the boat merchants of Shanghai and the local Shanghai officials. From the beginning it was in the hands of a small group of men who had previously been patronized by Li Hung-chang. Li had given them special commercial privileges while he was in Kiangsu, and they in turn had given financial assistance to his armies, a form of co-operation which continued even after Li's transfer to Chihli.[6] Li's presence in Chihli offered an excellent opportunity for the development of a modern commercial steam fleet to operate between Shanghai and Tientsin and participate in the Yangtze River trade.

The idea of encouraging Chinese-operated steamships was not new, having been suggested in the early 1860's by Feng Kuei-fen, one of Li's principal advisers. Although Feng was mainly concerned with the shipment of government revenues and had emphasized the advantages of steamers for the cheap delivery of rice tribute and salt, he had also pointed out that the resultant fall in grain prices would benefit the economy of the Yangtze area.[7] In 1867 Ting Jih-ch'ang, also, had proposed that Chinese merchants be permitted to use steamers to transport the Kiangsi and Anhwei rice tribute to the capital, but the proposal had come to nothing, since it lacked support in the north.[8] Early in 1872 the Grand Council of the central govern-

---

[6] *LWCK Memorials*, 1:40a, TC 1/6/13; *Ch'ing-ch'ao hsü-wen-hsien t'ung-k'ao*, 75:8327; *Shanghai-hsien hsü-chih*, 7:8a.

[7] Feng Kuei-fen, *Hsien-chih-t'ang kao*, 10:14a-15a.

[8] *LWCK Letters*, 12:28b-30a, TC 11/10/10.

ment put pressure on the Board of Foreign Affairs to stop the building of steamships at the Kiangnan and Foochow shipyards, charging that the work was a waste of precious funds. The Board of Foreign Affairs then asked Li if he would consider it advisable to sell the steamships produced by the shipyards to private merchants in order to raise funds. Li replied that shipbuilding must continue. The Foochow shipyard, founded by his rival, Tso Tsung-t'ang, might well cease production after completing a few ships, but the Shanghai shipyard, under Li's own control, could adapt itself to the circumstances. He suggested that the ships could either be used to transport the grain tribute or hired out to merchants. One problem, however, had to be solved: The merchants might hire the ships only for a limited time, since they believed that the ships did not have enough cargo space and that the pilots were not trustworthy. Li directed the customs intendants of Shanghai and Tientsin to summon the merchants involved to discuss the matter.[9]

During the next ten months Li Hung-chang, together with his Tientsin and Shanghai intendants and Chu Ch'i-ang, a boat merchant, worked out a plan for the creation of a company. The plan embodied all the features of previous proposals: the use of steamships by Chinese boat operators, the right to transport the grain tribute of the Liang-Chiang region to Tientsin by steamship, and the furnishing of funds for the ships by the boat merchants. Li Hung-chang was well acquainted with the boat merchant Chu Ch'i-ang and was impressed by his optimism. To those who questioned whether the new firm might not displace the old boat trade and adversely affect the old customhouses, Li replied:

These are weak excuses. . . . they do not realize that the Chinese merchants have already been hiring foreign steamships to carry the grain. The old fleet of *sha-ch'uan,* which once numbered two thousand vessels, has shrunk to a mere four hundred because of this. If on the one hand we do not stop Chinese merchants from hiring foreign steamships, and on the other hand we prevent them from purchasing foreign ships, it will be most unfair.

Furthermore, when Chinese merchants buy ships, according to the regulations we do not charge likin immediately, but after the goods are unloaded and distributed for sale we charge likin according to the inland regulations. They cannot therefore hurt the customs revenue of the old [inland] customhouses.

The Kiangsu and Chekiang grain tribute transported each year by sea exceeds one million tan. The *sha-ch'uan* and *ning-ch'uan* are never suffi-

---

[9] *Ibid.,* 12:1b-3a, TC 11/1/21.

cient to carry this volume. Now if we supplement the *sha-ch'uan* with steamers it will only fill the gap and never steal their business.[10]

Chu Ch'i-ang himself has relatives in the *sha-ch'uan* business, and he has already explained this to them. Chu Ch'i-ang wishes only to share about 200,000 tan, a small portion which cannot hurt the *sha* and *ning* operators. He has told me in person that the warehouses in Shanghai and Tientsin have already been rented. He is extremely enthusiastic, but fears he cannot do it singlehanded. . . .[11]

Chu Ch'i-ang had first proposed that he undertake the venture privately, keeping it as his own business. Li informed him that this was not practical and ordered him back to Shanghai to work out regulations with the customs intendants. Li authorized an agreement whereby the customs intendants would borrow from customs funds originally set aside for lien-chün rations a sum of 200,000 strings of cash "as a token of official encouragement," and Chu provided his own properties as a guarantee of his interest.[12] The ground was thus prepared for a partnership between the government and a merchant and his associates in a new kind of commercial venture. This form of capitalization became a precedent for most later ventures in westernization.

From Li's own accounts it is apparent that the initiative for the enterprise came both from officials within Li's coterie and from merchants with whom Li had had previous connections. After his interest had been sufficiently aroused by Chu's proposals, Li forced government participation upon Chu, an easy matter, since Li directly controlled the port of Tientsin, one terminus of the line, and indirectly controlled the Shanghai customs officials.

Li's memorial officially proposing the Chao Shang Chü (and informing the court of its inauguration) termed the undertaking "an experiment in the navigation of steamships for the purpose of transporting the coming year's grain tribute from Kiangsu and Chekiang, while laying the way for the acquisition of ships now under construction." Li took the opportunity to say again that China must build her own ships, and added that in the future ships should be constructed according to commercial rather than military specifications. The Board of Foreign Affairs, he said, had approved the establishment of the company and had authorized him to proceed with the selection of personnel to man-

---

[10] *Sha-ch'uan* were sea-going junks from the Shanghai area, and *ning-ch'uan* were similar vessels from the port of Ningpo.

[11] *LWCK Letters,* 12:28b-30a, TC 11/10/10.

[12] *Ibid.*

age it. The company would solve two problems: the Chinese merchants' need for ships, and the shipyards' need to sell the ships then under construction in order to cover their deficits. He explained:

If the government sets up a merchant company to invite merchant participation, the merchants will incorporate their ships and capital within it. Thus on the one hand we can satisfy the feelings of the merchants, and on the other we can extend our national prestige. I plan therefore to establish the Bureau for Summoning Merchants [*Chao Shang Chü*] in order to pave the way for harmony between the government and the merchants. . . .

. . . The government should use the regulations of the Board of Revenue which provided originally for the lending of lien-chün funds to the Chekiang pawnbrokers in Shanghai at interest. Now we should have the Board of Revenue provide from the lien-chün funds [actually then in the hands of the customs intendants] the sum of 200,000 strings of cash as an indication of the government's good faith. We should require the merchants to pay interest in advance toward relief work, however.

Once the business is under way, the gains and losses will be those of the merchants and it will have nothing to do with the government. Chu Ch'iang [the proposed manager] has been engaged in sea transport for over ten years. He is familiar with the situation of the merchants and is a competent man. After I sent him back to Shanghai to create the company, he sent back frequent reports indicating that he had reached unanimous agreement with the customs intendants . . . and the rich merchants.

Now they have purchased three solid, swift ships, and arranged for warehouses, docks, etc., in Shanghai and Tientsin and the quotas of grain they will carry. They wish me now to communicate with the governors of Kiangsu and Chekiang to allow them to transport 200,000 tan next year. The rates will be in accordance with the *ning* and *sha-ch'uan* regulations, and they will pay taxes according to the new customs regulations. . . .

. . . I have received an answer from Chang Shu-sheng, the acting governor-general of Liang-Chiang, who says that in his opinion the difficulty of sea transportation has been in the securing of adequate ships. . . . He is going to order the Shanghai customs intendant to exert his utmost efforts without pausing halfway in the business. This indicates that both the south and the north are devoted to this undertaking. . . .

I think the management of ships by Chinese merchants will be successful. . . . In the future both the inland rivers and the open seas will no longer furnish their benefits to foreigners alone. The Chao Shang Chü is concerned very deeply with the national wealth and the living conditions of the people. Together with the commissioner of trade in the south [Chang Shu-sheng] I will repeatedly instruct the various customs intendants to supervise it, and I shall instruct them and the gentry to look into the opinions of the merchants, so that it can be managed honestly. I have warned them not to monopolize or open the road to corruption.[13]

---

[13] *LWCK Memorials,* 20:32a ff., TC 11/11/23.

A striking aspect of the Chao Shang Chü was its reliance on the interregional tie between Tientsin in the north and Shanghai in the south. Chang Shu-sheng, Li's old Huai-chün follower and a native of Ho-fei, was then serving as governor-general of Liang-Chiang and Commissioner of Trade for the Southern Ports. Li Hung-chang made full use of his connections and influence to set up an organization that, despite his denials, was intended to monopolize the transport of grain tribute over which he exercised the right of protection. He put the management of this firm in the hands of a Shanghai merchant, while using his control over lien-chün funds to start operation of the line. In explaining this arrangement to the central government Li stressed the importance of guaranteeing the shipment of grain tribute and retaining all projects vital to the national interests in Chinese hands.

In Li's opinion, economic resistance to the foreigners was of the utmost urgency. Between 1862 and 1867 at least three foreign steamship lines in China had come to exercise almost complete control over ordinary steamship trade. Although some of these firms were actually Chinese-owned, they were incorporated at the foreign consulates and their vessels sailed under foreign flags. Thus they gained privileges not available to ordinary Chinese merchants.[14] Li Hung-chang firmly believed that the country's military strength rested on the achievement of national wealth, and therefore he saw the Chao Shang Chü not merely as an aid to Chinese prosperity but as a powerful economic weapon against the foreigners.

After the company was established, Li Hung-chang gradually extended its monopoly of the grain tribute transporation, which was the surest source of profits, since the grain tribute system was the life line of the Ch'ing court. In 1873 Li proposed that more of the tribute be allocated to the sea route, suggesting that if the sha-ch'uan, or junks, could not carry the additional load, the Chao Shang Chü would do so.

---

[14] Examples of such foreign steamship firms are Russell and Company's I-Ch'ang Company, established in 1862; the Provincial Hong Kong and Macao Steamer Corporation, established in 1865; and the Chinese Shipping Company, organized by the English T'ai-ku Company in 1867. See Pai Shou-i, Chung-kuo chiao-t'ung shih, in the series Chung-kuo wen-hua shih ts'ung-shu, edited by Wang Yün-wu (Shanghai, 1937), p. 214. An American consul described the prospects of one of these firms as follows: "The only American firm at present [1868] established at this port is a branch of the ...firm of Messrs. Russell who besides doing the other usual business of merchants are also agents for the steamship navigation company known under the name of 'the Shanghai Steam Navigation Company,' which has had during the last seasons from 4 to 5 large steamers running on the Shanghai and Tientsin line; and which have been obtaining very profitable freights for the cargoes brought to this port during the greater part of the season." Consul Meadows to Secretary of State, Tientsin Consular Despatches, Dec. 31, 1868.

The money thus saved could be used for the sea defense program. In Li's words: "This is a measure designed to strengthen the root and also take care of the branches. It is my opinion that wealth and strength can thus be secured."[15]

Li's frequent intercessions, as well as the real economic advantages provided by the company steamers, were to make a radical change in the transportation of tribute. The *Shanghai-hsien hsü-chih* ("Revised Local History of Shanghai") described the change as follows:

In the twelfth year of T'ung-chih the government permitted the grain shipped by sea from Kiangsu and Chekiang to be carried on board the ships of the Chao Shang Chü. It was entitled to 20 per cent of the total as compared with 80 per cent allowed to the *sha-ch'uan*. Then the proportions changed to 40 per cent and 60 per cent. Then because the *sha-ch'uan* decreased in number by the day, in the winter of the twenty-sixth year of Kuang-hsü, the entire tribute went to the Chao Shang Chü. At that time only fifty *sha-ch'uan* remained. . . .[16]

The effect of the new company was soon felt by the foreigners as well. Montalto de Jesus has recorded the success of the Chinese company and its triumph over foreign competitors:

[After the shift of the tea trade from Canton to Shanghai in 1861] An important trade soon developed, and steamers came into such demand that, as early as 1862, Russell & Co. floated the Shanghai Steam Navigation Co. with a capital of one million sterling, the first local concern in which the Chinese were associated with foreigners as shareholders. Surviving a keen rivalry, the company more than doubled its capital in eight years, and owned a first-class line of eighteen steamers. By subsidising Chinese merchants, however, the Chinese government gradually created such a powerful opposition that in 1877 the whole concern was bought over and merged in the Chinese Merchants' Steam Navigation Company.[17]

An American consul mourned the great decrease in American tonnage entering Tientsin, blaming it upon the success of the Chao Shang Chü. He went on to say, "It is a remarkable coincidence that the date of this falling off in tonnage is also the date that ushered in the growing demand for American cotton goods at all the ports in China."[18] Between 1872 and 1880 the Chao Shang Chü increased its fleet from two vessels, totaling 1,168 tons, to twenty-nine vessels, totaling 20,747 tons, not counting vessels lost through sea disasters.[19]

---

[15] *LWCK Memorials*, 22:17a ff., TC 12/6 int./3.

[16] *Shanghai-hsien hsü-chih*, 7:15a.

[17] C. A. Montalto de Jesus, *Historic Shanghai* (Shanghai, 1909), p. 237.

[18] "Annual Report of American Trade in Tientsin," *Tientsin Consular Despatches*, Oct. 31, 1879.   [19] Mark S. Bell, *China*, II, 13.

The Chao Shang Chü appears to have been the first really successful enterprise undertaken by the Chinese using Western technological advances, but the faults in its management were various. Disregarding the merchant investment, for the moment, we see that the Chao Shang Chü only took money from one government pocket to put it into another, a shift of funds that was exceedingly profitable to Li Hung-chang and his group. At the beginning of operations Li Hung-chang had requested an official loan of 200,000 strings of cash from the lien-chün ration funds, claiming that the company would need no further government support. Later, however, he secured additional loans for the company, generally on the quite valid grounds that foreign competition had to be thoroughly stamped out before the Chinese merchants could get on their feet. These loans came mainly from the provinces where Li or his agents had influence, especially those in the northern and Yangtze areas.[20] In time, because of the heavy government investment and the obvious mismanagement within the company organization, the customs intendants of Shanghai and Tientsin were appointed as co-managers of the company, sharing responsibility with the merchant managers. The government loans, however, seemed to grow larger rather than smaller, and questions began to be raised in the capital, as well as in other quarters, about official peculation.[21]

The Chao Shang Chü required heavy loans when it bought the steamships belonging to Russell and Company. Later, during the Franco-Chinese War of 1884 to 1885, the company sold its entire fleet to Russell and Company in order to protect it from French attack or seizure. It repurchased the vessels in the following year at a huge loss, which was made up by borrowing funds from foreign sources.[22] How

---

[20] *LWCK Memorials*, 30:29a ff., KH 3/11/15.

[21] *Ibid.*, 30:29a ff.; 56:1a ff., KH 12/1/21; see particularly 41:20a ff., KH 7/2/11, which describes cases of misappropriation and falsification of records, and 36:35a ff., KH 6/3/27, which answers charges that officials in charge of the company were "filling their pockets at public expense." Although the Chao Shang Chü was completely controlled by officials, according to law its organization developed as follows: 1872, established by the government, with government and merchant capital; 1873, reorganized and theoretically totally managed by merchants; 1877, Li promised to have his customs intendants check regularly for corruption; 1885, reorganized under Sheng Hsüan-huai, no real change, but now officially termed government-supervised and merchant-operated; 1908, management shifted from Northern Trade Commissioner to Board of Posts and Communications. Under the Republic it was placed under the Ministry of Communications, but was still merchant-operated. In the 1930's it was still managed by a grandson of Li Hung-chang. Recently, it has been taken over by the Communist government and reorganized as a state bureau. See Pai Shou-i, *Chung-kuo chiao-t'ung shih*, p. 215.

[22] *LWCK Memorials*, 41:20a ff., KH 7/6/9.

much Russell and Company paid in commissions to the officials involved can only be imagined.

The ratio of government to private funds invested in the company was very high. In three years of operation after the purchase of the American line, the division was as follows:

Year	Government Funds (in liang)	Merchant Funds (in liang)
1877	1,900,000	730,000
1878	1,928,000	751,000
1879	1,928,000	800,000

In 1880 Li admitted that only 220,000 liang of the original government loans had been repaid.[23] This does not necessarily mean that the lenders were anxious to obtain quick repayment, for the loans were at regular interest rates. When the company repurchased its ships from Russell and Company, it paid well over 2,000,000 liang for them. Of this sum the provincial governments furnished over one million, and the merchants attempted to raise the balance through additional capitalization. Failing to acquire sufficient capital, however, the company borrowed from foreigners. This was of advantage, as foreign interest rates were generally lower than those of the Chinese government, but the company had abandoned an important principle—namely, to exclude the foreigner at all costs. In the ensuing years the company was able to meet capital and interest payments to Western lenders and at the same time repay the provincial governments some 770,000 liang of their investments.[24]

The Chao Shang Chü's financial manipulations were a source of profit not only to the small group of merchants and officials who managed it directly but also to the revenue and military departments in which Li had a special interest. In the north a so-called Chao Shang Chü tax was levied. This was a tax on the cargoes which Chao Shang Chü vessels brought into the northern ports under Li Hung-chang's jurisdiction. Forty per cent of the revenues gained from this tax went for the support of the Tientsin Arsenal.[25] A similar practice existed in Shanhaikuan, Chihli, where 40 per cent of the Chao Shang Chü's tax payment was forwarded to the coastal lien-chün under Li Hung-chang's command.[26] At the Hankow customs, which also charged duties on

[23] Ibid., 36:32a ff., KH 6/3/27.
[24] Ibid., 56:1a ff., KH 12/1/21.
[25] Ibid., 32:11a ff., KH 4/7/2; 36:32a, KH 6/3/27; 31:10a ff., KH 4/3/13.
[26] Ibid., 33:39a ff., KH 4/12/5.

Chao Shang Chü cargoes, a slightly different system prevailed. Here 52 per cent of the receipts was sent to the Board of Revenue, and 48 per cent was retained for subsidies, which, it will be recalled, went largely to Li's defense forces in the north.[27]

The steamer company was used further by Li to pay directly for several war vessels purchased abroad. This is explained in an interesting memorial written by Li in 1881, which reveals the place of the Chao Shang Chü in Li's complex fiscal activities and illustrates briefly some aspects of the governmental economy of the period.

An edict, which had been referred to Li, quoted a statement by an official that the Chao Shang Chü had borrowed from the river embankment works of Chekiang province the sum of 300,000 liang on the condition that it be repaid at the rate of 60,000 liang per year. The official had then requested the throne to order Li Hung-chang to repay 60,000 liang of the loan that year. In response Li stated:

The Chao Shang Chü has on deposit funds from the various provinces amounting to 1,781,500 liang. Formerly I memorialized, proposing to use the fee collected from the transportation of grain tribute to repay the loans at the rate of 356,300 liang per year. But I fixed this rate upon the ability of the company to transport 660,000 tan of grain each year. Kiangsi, however, has stopped its transportation for this period, and only Kiangsu, Chekiang, and Hupeh entrust their tribute to the company, furnishing 500,000 tan for transportation. This yields a total transportation fee of only 290,000 liang. Therefore, the company can furnish only 49,000 liang to Chekiang and cannot satisfy them with 60,000.

Now we are in the midst of purchasing warships. Last year, in the sixth month, I memorialized for authority to use the *Chao Shang Chü* funds for the repayment this year of more than 1,000,000 liang used to purchase these ships. Your Majesty has already given consent to this. These armored ships concern most urgently the sea defenses of the Nan-yang and Pei-yang areas, and their purchase should be supported by the various provinces. Because of financial difficulty we are now compelled to requisition the Chao Shang Chü funds for the purchase.

I have presented to the throne a detailed accounting of the costs for the two vessels now on order and for two vessels to be ordered in the future. The two ships to be ordered in the future will require 2,400,000 liang. We still do not know where to raise the money to meet this cost. If the company should attempt to repay the provinces, our difficulties will grow still more acute. I therefore believe that we should stand by the edict of the sixth month of last year, and transfer the funds in conformity with the original proposal.

It now appears that the income of the Chao Shang Chü from the transportation of tribute cannot reach 350,000 per period. It will require four

27 *Peking Gazette:* Trans. in *NCH*, Nov. 26, 1886.

periods to raise 1,000,000 liang. Therefore the governor of Chekiang should raise his embankment funds elsewhere. After the 1,000,000 for the warships is raised, Chekiang and the other provinces can be repaid. Then the sharp weapons for sea defense can be bought and the repayment of the various provinces will be accomplished sooner or later.[28]

Li Hung-chang succeeded in making it an established rule that all freight sent to the government through Tientsin would be carried on Chao Shang Chü bottoms. In 1886 the governor of Hupeh apologized in a memorial to the throne for his error in sending a shipment of copper from Yunnan to Peking on a German steamer.[29] The company was a jack-of-all-trades, and Li sometimes envisaged it as the beginning of a trans-Pacific fleet and an auxiliary naval fleet.[30] A history of the vicissitudes of the Chao Shang Chü would fill several volumes, but despite everything it managed to survive and exists even today.[31]

The Chao Shang Chü was an important source of strength for Li, providing funds for defense and a regular income for his arsenals. It often transported Huai-chün troops, before the full development of the Huai-chün water-force fleet and the Pei-yang navy, and was an important communication link between Chihli and the Liang-Chiang and Hu-Kuang regions. Through it, too, Li could reward deserving provincial officials, particularly in the customhouses. Finally, it provided Li Hung-chang with personal income. We can find no direct evidence that he had personally invested in the company's stock (certainly a possibility), but he employed its steamers to carry on a duty-free trade in rice and perhaps opium from his private lands in Anhwei.[32]

Li's Program of Industrialization

Li's success in establishing the steamship company encouraged him to undertake other commercial and industrial ventures, some of which laid the basis for major heavy industries. The Chao Shang Chü furnished the pattern of organization for these new enterprises and so to some extent predetermined their fate. Because most of Li's enterprises eventually fell into foreign hands, some Chinese scholars, especially

---

[28] *LWCK Memorials,* 40:56a ff., KH 7/4/27.

[29] *Peking Gazette:* Trans. in *NCH,* Aug. 24, 1886.

[30] *LWCK Memorials,* 41:34a, KH 7/6/34; 25:4a-5b, KH 1/2/27.

[31] A major scandal involving a grandson of Li Hung-chang who was manager of the *Chao Shang Chü* in 1932 is reported in the *China Weekly Review,* April 30, 1932, pp. 296 ff.

[32] Stanley F. Wright, *Hart and the Chinese Customs,* pp. 602-4. The fact was also mentioned by the U.S. Minister to China in a letter to the Secretary of State. U.S. State Department, *Despatches from United States Ministers to China,* Jan. 18, 1893.

economists, have been understandably harsh in their treatment of Li.[33] While Li himself controlled the companies, they remained undeniably Chinese in both ownership and management. It was only in the general collapse following the Sino-Japanese War, when Li's power had declined and foreigners obtained unprecedented rights of exploitation in China, that many of the companies were mortgaged to foreign capitalists.[34] Some scholars have also held that Li had no real program, and by offering only a patchwork of ideas and projects failed to lay a sound foundation for Chinese commercial and industrial development. Such charges, however, can only be evaluated in the light of Li's real objectives in trying to develop Chinese industry.

It is generally agreed that Li's aim was to strengthen China's defenses against Japan and the West through economic and military improvements. This was one important reason for the founding of the Chao Shang Chü and a prevailing motive for his efforts to establish other new enterprises. For example, in referring to the need for coal and iron mines, Li said:

> Natural resources are the basis of the people's day-to-day living. The Western powers take mineral development as their principal focal point; therefore they can compete for domination. England developed her nation on three islands. Her resources were not too plentiful, but each year she produced ample coal and iron; therefore, her wealth and power became the first under heaven.
>
> Our mineral resources, such as gold, silver, coal, and iron, are much more plentiful than those of the Western countries, but because of the rigidity of our habits and customs, our best elements lie undeveloped, buried beneath the ground. The sources of our wealth become drier and drier, and every month, every year, we expend large sums to buy iron and coal from other countries. This is a big loss from our leaking wine-cup.[35]

Once the various mining projects were under way, Li requested the government to exempt them from the usual taxes, and again suggested that Western methods be used against the Westerners:

---

[33] See, for instance, Liang Ch'i-ch'ao, *Chung-kuo ssu-shih nien-lai ta-shih-chi,* in *Ying-ping shih ho-chi;* Ch'uan Han-sheng, "Ch'ing-chi ti Chiang-nan chih-ts'ao chü," in *Bulletin of the Institute of History and Philology,* Academia Sinica, XXIII, Pt. 1, pp. 147 ff. This attitude has also dominated the thinking of present-day Chinese Communist writers. See, for instance, Liang Ssu-kuang, *Li Hung-chang mai-kuo shih* (Tientsin, 1951), *passim.*

[34] An important factor leading to this general mortgaging of China's interests was the heavy indemnity demanded by Japan. Perhaps even more decisive was the provision of the Treaty of Shimonoseki which for the first time gave foreigners the right to import foreign machines for the manufacture of products to be sold on foreign soil. By operation of the most-favored-nation clauses this right extended to all of the Treaty Powers.   [35] *LWCK Memorials,* 40:41a ff., KH 7/4/23.

The rate of taxation upon foreign goods is extremely light, while upon Chinese goods it is extremely heavy. If this continues, our Chinese merchants will be unable to compete with the foreigners.

I have studied the Western practices with regard to taxation and note that they tax imported goods more heavily than their own exports. This is the method of exacting from foreigners and protecting their own merchants. It appears to be most reasonable. But in China, at the beginning of our treaty-signing, we were deceived by the foreigners, and as a result our imports pay only a light tax while our exports pay heavily. Consequently our taxes injure the Chinese merchant and protect the foreigners. This has been the extremely unfavorable situation which we have faced in the several tens of years since the signing of the treaties. . . .

I therefore request Your Majesty to allow the coal exported from the Kaiping mines to pay a tax of only one-tenth liang per ton . . . to give the Chinese merchants an advantage over the foreign coal producers. . . .[36]

After constructing China's first long-distance telegraph line, between Tientsin and Shanghai, Li Hung-chang encouraged the extension of the line to Canton. In doing so he revealed two of his principal, nonmilitary objectives in developing Chinese industries:

The effectiveness [of telegraphs] is quite obvious. In the tenth month of this year, the acting British minister [Grosvenor] . . . requested the addition of a cable from Shanghai to Ningpo, Wenchow, Foochow, Amoy, and Swatow [to Hong Kong]. I found it almost impossible to prevent this. I therefore wrote the Board of Foreign Affairs and corresponded with them frequently. The conclusion is that we should persuade the Chinese merchants to take over the construction of a land-line along the coast from Shanghai to Kwangtung in anticipation [of possible foreign construction] in order to prevent another encroachment by the foreigners, and in order to protect our own right to manage our enterprises. Then their race will discover that there is no profit to hope for [in constructing a similar line] and perhaps they will reluctantly cease to press us.

Moreover, as a result it will be possible to carry on speedy consultation between the capital and the various provinces in regard to national and military affairs. The revenue deliveries will be speeded up. All will be connected like the flow of air. This will benefit both foreign affairs and sea defense. At the same time both the merchants and the people can use the telegraph for communication on trade and transportation.[37]

The same general theme was present in the memorial which Li presented in 1882, requesting approval of his plan to organize a "machine weaving company" in Shanghai. Discussing the subject of the importance of national wealth as a prerequisite to national strength, he

[36] *Ibid.*, 40:44a-b, KH 7/4/23.
[37] *Ibid.*, 45:32a ff., KH 8/12/8.

pointed with dismay to the rising amount of imports into China each year as opposed to the diminishing exports:

The price we pay for these foreign goods has risen to 79,000,000 liang in recent years, while our export of native goods declines with time. We have not been able to compete with them. The reason lies in the fact that the foreign goods made by machines are one time cheaper than native goods made by hand. When their prices are lower their markets are wider. Unless we gradually imitate their methods of transporting goods to sell [i.e., export] and can sell our goods ourselves in order to take a share in the profits, we cannot fix the leaking wine-cup; the sale of one piece more of native goods means the sale of one piece less of foreign goods by the Westerners. And among the imported foreign goods none is as important as the foreign textiles. In recent years the foreign cloth sold in the various ports has been worth from 22,000,000 to 23,000,000 liang, and foreign cloth has become indispensable for daily needs. . . . I plan therefore to select and invite gentry and merchants to buy machines and establish a bureau in Shanghai to imitate the production of foreign cloth. My purpose is to obtain for us a share of the profits which now go exclusively to the foreigners.[38]

No essential difference can be noted between Li's economic and military arguments. The military need for railroads and telegraphs, although disputed hotly at the time, was the most easily established.[39] Before trying to convince the court and the boards of the advantages of these innovations, Li covertly permitted experimental but practical construction in these fields with the inauguration of a three-mile railroad from the mine head at Kaiping to the transportation canal, and

---

[38] *Ibid.*, 43:43a ff., KH 8/3/6.

[39] *Ibid.*, 39:20a-26a, KH 3/4/29; 39:27a ff., KH 6/12/1. In the latter memorial Li made the following point: "If we can strengthen ourselves . . . the foreigners will not dare make exactions. If, on the other hand, we fail to strengthen ourselves, and our economy wavers, the foreigners will intensify their conspiracy. Let us take Indo-China as an example. They failed to manage their national affairs well, and their living standards fell, and the country became more impoverished and weaker. The French then stole her six provinces." He summarized his military arguments in the sentence: "The military principle is that swiftness comes first." *Ibid.*, 38:16a ff., KH 6/8/12.

Li's opposition was vigorous and persistent. One opponent made the following objections to railroad-building in 1881: (1) China was too poor to build railways, and the resources of the entire nation were not equal to those of the Western countries; (2) There was not enough money for the upkeep and operation of railroads; (3) Railroads would injure the spirits of the mountains and rivers, and their anger would cause drought and floods; (4) Foreign technicians and artisans were not reliable; (5) Chinese staff and personnel were not reliable; (6) China's territory was too great to be closely watched. The stealing of one rail would prevent the train from proceeding; (7) It would be difficult for the customs to be collected from railroad trains, because trains go too fast and cannot often be stopped or slowed down; (8) If the railroad is intended to transport soldiers, it would not be satisfactory for the purpose, since soldiers carry too much loose equipment which could not all be taken aboard the train. *Ch'ing-ch'ao hsü-wen-hsien t'ung-k'ao*, 362:11061-62.

the construction of a short telegraph line from his headquarters to his military camp at Taku.[40] The development of mines was directly related by Li to the needs of the navy and of the Chinese arsenals, as well as to the extension of the services of the Chao Shang Chü.[41]

Owing to his study of the Industrial Revolution in the West, Li believed that industrial and commercial development required a program of orderly growth. He noted that railways had developed from mining and metal fabrication in England and that telegraph lines had been laid in close co-ordination with rail lines.[42] In his opinion the textile industry was a foundation for the development of sea power and further industrialization. Any program of military strengthening that did not rest on a solid industrial economic footing was no more than a facade.[43] Besides the arsenals that had been established earlier in response to immediate military needs, he tried to develop mining, to be followed by the construction of railroads and telegraph lines and the development of weaving mills. He related the Chao Shang Chü activities to all the other industrial undertakings, and hoped that the Chao Shang Chü, together with large trunk and branch railroads, would provide an integrated system of communications for the country.[44] The blueprint was one thing, however, and actual development quite another. His efforts were hampered by opposition at court, the lack of sufficient support from the merchants, and by the whole general attitude in China toward Western innovations.

Regional Limitations on Industrial Development

The most limiting aspect of Li's program, however, both in concept and execution, was its regional nature. With the exception of the

---

[40] James Harrison Wilson, *China*, p. 40; *LWCK Memorials*, 38:16a ff., KH 6/8/12.

[41] *LWCK Memorials*, 47:10a, KH 9/7/13. *Ibid.*, 40:41a ff., contains the following concise summary of mining advantages: "From now on the Chinese merchants [the *Chao Shang Chü* and others], warships, arsenals, and other factories will not need to buy coal from afar. In case of war the enemy cannot cut off our coal supply. In general, we will not need to spend too much abroad. This, then, is the foundation of wealth and strength."

[42] *Ibid.*, 39:20a ff., KH 6/12/1.

[43] Li made no secret of his admiration for Western technological development, and most of his important memorials to the throne and letters to the Board of Naval Affairs have pointed and sometimes extended references to the evolution of Western industrial power. By the latter half of the nineteenth century an influential body of opinion in China had come around to this point of view, and the principle of strength through wealth was enunciated and re-enunciated by friends and foes alike.

[44] "The two [railroads and the *Chao Shang Chü*] can parallel each other without hampering each other.... After several years, when the volume of transportation increases, the *Chao Shang Chü* and railroads can assist each other." *LWCK Memorials*, 39:27a ff., KH 6/12/1.

Shanghai-Canton telegraph, undertaken to forestall foreign building, all Li's major undertakings were limited to the area under his direct control, extending only as far south as Liang-Chiang.[45] The small mining operations he had sponsored in Hupeh had been carried on only while he was governor-general there in the late 1860's. Li guaranteed to a sceptical court that the Chao Shang Chü would be protected by the presence of Huai-chün gunboats on the Yangtze and the customs and naval patrols along the coast. The gold mines at Mo-ho were to be operated by special lien-chün battalions under his command.[46] The railroads and telegraphs were to be guarded by special units of his crack Ming-chün, Liu Ming-ch'uan's branch of the Huai-chün.[47] The mines and mills, and the rail, telegraph, and shipping lines were all to

---

[45] In the only instance where Li attempted to build outside his sphere of regional influence, namely, the construction of the Shanghai-Canton telegraph, the following was noted by J. G. Dunn, of the Eastern Extension Telegraph Company, in a letter to the Director, John Pender, dated August, 1882: "I can also say that Hao, the banker, whose name is familiar to Mr. Samuel, had asked Tso [Tsung-t'ang], the Nankin [Liang-Chiang] Viceroy, for permission to make the semi-Imperial lines to connect Nankin with Canton via the Eastern Coast. The land lines would first strike the coast at Hangchow, and there thread southward. *If Li [Hung-chang] proposed the line it would meet with opposition in Fohkien [Fukien province]. But Tso does not excite opposition, or at the least does not do so to any equal extent, and it is possible the Fohkien government might agree to Tso's request and withdraw all opposition.*" (Italics mine, S.S.) British Foreign Office, Papers Relating to Telegraphs in China, F.O. 17/1008, Public Record Office, London.

Li Hung-chang, in the end, managed to secure the building of the line and the purchase of the existing Woosung-Shanghai land line in the manner described as follows by the British consul, Hughes, to Grosvenor: "His Excellency [Li] wished the arrangement, which would afterwards be sanctioned by him, to appear local and spontaneous, and that his name should not be mentioned in the matter.... Speedy settlement likely since the Chinese have already invited Eastern Telegraph Co. to send tenders for materials of proposed land line to connect with Southern Ports." F.O. 17/1009, Shanghai, Feb. 28, 1883.

In a letter to Earl Granville, Thomas Wade, one of the British negotiators, attributed Tso Tsung-t'ang's objections to the arrangements being worked out by Li and the British to his "jealousy and disgruntled attitude." He hinted that Tso had directly or indirectly been bought out by a rival Danish firm. (F.O. 17/1009, March 13, 1883.) Wade's suspicion seems unfounded. Fortunately for British interests, most other officials and agents accepted the personal and regional rivalries of Chinese leaders as a fact of life, and as can be seen above, used them to their own advantage. The manuscripts of unpublished British State Papers in the Public Record Office, London, contain numerous references to similar situations, and prove that the British of the period, as we have seen clearly in Bell, *China*, had made an extremely realistic appraisal of the power factors operating in China. See, for instance, the files of F.O. 17/380, 1007-9, 1011, which contain numerous letters, telegrams, copies of Chinese provincial and imperial documents and maps, all concerning the development of telegraphs in China.

[46] *LWCK Memorials*, 61:45a ff., KH 13/12/5.

[47] British Foreign Office, Papers Relating to Telegraphs in China, F.O. 17/1008, Jan. 21, 1883; *LWCK Memorials*, 45:32a ff., KH 8/12/8; James Harrison Wilson, *China*, pp. 122-26, contains the memorial of Liu Ming-ch'uan advocating railways and mentioning use of his armies in constructing and guarding them. See also *LWCK Memorials*, 39:20a ff., KH 6/12/1.

be supervised by personal aides of Li Hung-chang, often from the customs offices or previously established commercial enterprises. Li made no effort to extend these enterprises below Liang-Chiang, and declined to take any responsibility for the development of railroads in such areas. With the exception of Shanghai, where he apparently had large vested interests and a strong following among the local merchants and officials, he favored development in the north. As he had stated in his memorial on railways submitted in 1880:

> In the present day in a world where every country has its own railways and China alone has none, it is like living in the ages shortly after the ancients, and if we leave aside our boats and wagons we would even be behind them. From my own study I have found that the construction of railways has nine advantages.
>
> The first is as follows: North of the Yangtze and Huai rivers the land routes exceed those of the southern provinces. Every year the income from foreign customs and likin, totaling some twenty to thirty millions, comes 90 per cent from the south and only 10 per cent from the north. If railways can be built like a framework in the north, the region will be transformed from indolence to industry; its natural resources will not be wasted; its manpower will not be wasted; and at key points along the railroad, likin and customs stations can be erected. The income of such stations can be comparable to that of the south. This is the first advantage to the national economy to be gained from railroads.[48]

Li recommended that Liu Ming-ch'uan direct the proposed railway, an arrangement that would have kept it within the Li political-military machine. The entire proposal failed to materialize, however, because of court opposition, frequent emergencies, and economic difficulties. To secure capital for constructing the railroad, Li would have been willing to permit foreign loans, but he would not permit any mortgages to be given, and refused to sacrifice any control over the management. Under these terms foreign capital could not be obtained.[49]

The first Chinese railroad of any size was built in conformity with

---

[48] *LWCK Memorials*, 39:20a ff., KH 6/12/1.

[49] Consul Smithers, writing to Assistant Secretary of State Porter (*Tientsin Consular Despatches*, May 21, 1887), describes the failure of Chinese "gentry and capitalists" to offer to purchase railroad shares from Li. Li himself remarked: "I know that to build a railroad is a very difficult thing. But it is beneficial to the people and the country. The court should resolve to create this new thing in order to accustom the people of the country to it. I cannot, however, assure its success, because it is hard to raise funds and hard to secure foreign loans. Even if the funds can be secured, other difficulties still occur. Yet this is a large undertaking, and we must sweep aside every empty criticism and break with rigid traditions. However, if the foreign loans cannot be collected, then even if the court is willing, we still may not be able to start at once." *LWCK Memorials*, 39:20a-27a, KH 6/12/1.

Li's own regional requirements. After 1878, the Kaiping mine road was gradually extended by his agents, so that by 1894 it covered a total of 174 miles. This railroad connected Tientsin with other ports and with the mine fields, and served as a quick method of transportation for Huai-chün and lien-chün troops and as a feeder to the Pei-yang navy and Chao Shang Chü ships.[50] It was a local rather than a regional system, but not because Li wanted it so. He drew no limit on the extension of railroads within his own orbit of direct control, though he opposed the vast railroad schemes, intended to unite north and south, put forth by Chang Chih-tung.[51]

Li's enterprises increased his authority and prestige within the central government and in the provinces, and at the same time strengthened his regional power base. They served his own military forces and increased his influence over other military forces wishing to use the services he controlled. His private profits cannot be estimated, although it was rumored that he had invested heavily in the Shanghai Weaving Factory.[52] His subordinates drew large incomes, legally and illegally, from the businesses that Li appointed them to manage, and Li himself was generally known to have been one of the wealthiest men in .China.[53] As his diplomacy became enmeshed with his own economic undertakings, it is not surprising that in his foreign policy he sometimes put his immediate regional interests before the general interests of the country.[54]

Li Hung-chang and Bureaucratic Capitalism

Though by the turn of the century the Western powers had absorbed, destroyed, or taken control of most of China's large enterprises, new ones continued to spring up, and a few managed to limp

---

[50] James Harrison Wilson, *China*, p. xviii. Wilson noted, "Its most important service is to carry coal to the Chinese fleet and merchant steamers."

[51] LWCK *Naval Board Letters*, 3:26a-31b, KH 15/4/20; 3:31b-38a, KH 15/5/2.

[52] Alicia Little, *Li Hung Chang, His Life and Times*, p. 210.

[53] Stanley F. Wright, *Hart and the Chinese Customs*, p. 604; Little, *Li Hung Chang, passim.;* J. Martin Miller, *China: Ancient and Modern*, p. 321, stated flatly, but with some exaggeration: "Li Hung-chang is the richest man in the world," at a time when the Rockefeller, Carnegie, Gould, and Vanderbilt fortunes had already been made.

[54] Li's diplomacy with the British on the opium question was largely influenced by his concern over the effects of new regulations upon Huai-chün income. His purchase of Russell and Company ships was attributed to his desire to drive American cottons off the Chinese market. The whole course of his negotiations with the British, Danish, and other interests over telegraph lines particularly reflected his interest in maintaining his own control over telegraphs in China. Elaboration of this point can only be attempted in an adequate study of Li Hung-chang as a diplomat.

along, always failing but somehow surviving. They set the pattern, which started with the Chao Shang Chü, for the organization of many Chinese industries of that time and later. Li's stipulation that government supervision was to be imposed on merchant management in every organization he promoted worked hardship on the great majority of merchants. In each company there was a nucleus of merchants who, together with Li's bureaucratic assistants, actually put the business into operation. These men controlled the management, the stocks, the profits, and the salaries. Their power was great, since they usually were given a monopoly in the industry or service they represented. The influence of officials predominated, substituting bureaucratic mandates for meetings of boards of directors. Opening the way for corruption and coercion, this way of managing the enterprises inevitably tied them to the immediate needs of the officials in control. Li Hungchang stated this bluntly in a memorial on the Chao Shang Chü:

We are uncertain whether business will be good or bad. Even if business should not be good, the only ones who will suffer will be the merchant stockholders. I plan to make the repayment of official loans a steady practice and to exhaust the capacity of the merchants to support the company.[55]

In 1881, one year later, he reiterated this point with equal candor:

Why do we now want to repay the official loans? In order to protect the interests of the government at the expense of the merchant stock.[56]

Most Chinese accounts do not agree with Li Hung-chang's statement, made in a memorial written in 1880, that the managers of the Chao Shang Chü were both fair and honest:

The stocks of the Bureau are managed by these two circuit intendants, and each year the accounts are reviewed by the merchants themselves. Should these two managers attempt to misappropriate funds or become extravagant, the merchants will act in their own interest without waiting for an official impeachment. Yet since the day of the establishment of the Bureau no merchant has ever come to me with such an impeachment. I beseech Your Majesty not to heed such rumors.[57]

Later observers have tended to support the critics of Li and the Chao Shang Chü management, pointing out that the attacks were wellfounded and were, if anything, too weak. Thus, for example the attack

---

[55] *LWCK Memorials,* 36:32a ff., KH 6/3/27.
[56] *Ibid.,* 41:20a ff., KH 7/2/11.
[57] *Ibid.,* 36:35a ff., KH 6/3/27.

by Censor Teng Chün-han upon Li in 1877 was commented upon as follows:

What Teng said was all true. We only regret that he said too little. He should have said more. If at that time Li Hung-chang could have really carried out a reform, today the Company's wharves, warehouses, and land-holdings would be several times larger than they are and would have exceeded those of T'ai-ku and I-ho [foreign firms]. Unfortunately the officials regarded the Chao Shang Chü as a pool of profits. Then the Chao Shang Chü became a servant of the government. Officials crowded in and the merchant stockholders dared not approach.

This situation contradicted the defense offered by Li Hung-chang in the sixth year of Kuang-hsü that the *Chao Shang Chü* was managed by the merchants themselves. We regret, too, the later managers who even made matters worse.[58]

Perhaps the most penetrating criticism of the Chao Shang Chü and the other companies Li established, as well as of others which used his pattern of government supervision and merchant management, was made by Ts'ao Tsai-ch'un. In an essay, "On the Use of Officials to Supervise Commercial Affairs in China," he wrote:

Because our merchants are now exhausted, the officials now turn to borrow from the foreigners. But these Westerners laugh at such persons, because they are neither officials nor merchants. They give the appearance of officials yet behave like merchants; however, they are not merchants and they are not officials. Therefore the foreigners do not like to lend them funds.[59]

Ts'ao went on to explain why Chinese merchants failed to compete successfully with the Westerners. Even if China were to import machinery and utilize cheap labor in order to undersell the West, the problem of official-merchant relations remained:

The merchants look to the officials as heaven, and the officials look down upon the merchants as earth. When they collect taxes from the merchants, they are rough. In lawsuits they exact bribes and practice graft. Therefore they oppress the merchants. This is the first reason for the rottenness of our commerce.[60]

Aiming his remarks obviously at Li, his followers, and men like them, Ts'ao remarked that the very men who talked of reform were those who used their official power to control commerce. Among them

---

[58] *Ch'ing-ch'ao hsü-wen-hsien t'ung-k'ao*, 361:11044.
[59] *Huang-ch'ao ching-shih-wen t'ung-pien*, 57:29a.
[60] Liang Ch'i-ch'ao, *Chung-kuo ssu-shih nien-lai ta-shih-chi*, in *Ying-ping shih ho-chi, chuan-chi san*, p. 39.

were men who, as merchants, bought official positions and then used their official positions to cheat other merchants. Then although the ordinary merchants had contributed all their property in order to buy shares in the companies, the companies all finally belonged to the officials. Having attained a new status as officials, the newcomers adopted the air of the official and no longer cared about the problems of merchants. As a result merchants had become increasingly reluctant to invest in the companies. The use of machines for production meant increasing need for capital, and no one or two merchants, "official" or otherwise, were in a position to sustain the enterprises alone. When the Chinese merchants hesitated to invest, the way was open for the seizure of Chinese enterprise by the foreigners. This, Ts'ao claimed, was the second reason for the decay of Chinese commerce.

He closed his remarks with a strongly worded paragraph:

> Some official-merchants even use our country as security in order to raise foreign loans. First they take over commercial interests, then they take over official interests, and finally they steal our national interests. But still they cannot compete with the foreigners, and still they bind the Chinese merchants like cattle and send them to the foreigners.[61]

Liang Ch'i-ch'ao, the greatest of the late nineteenth- and early twentieth-century pamphleteers and a leader of the reform movement, similarly described the enterprises created by Li Hung-chang and held him responsible for their failure: "If we should say that Li Hung-chang's principle of government supervision and merchant operation caused their ruin, we would be correct."[62]

In a society dominated by a bureaucracy which traditionally regarded merchants with suspicion and hostility, government supervision and domination of new, possibly lucrative, enterprises was perhaps inevitable. This was all the more true of the enterprises sponsored by Li. He was interested in strengthening his own economic and military position, and used the industrial enterprises for his own purposes in his struggle to maintain his position in an unstable political period.[63]

---

[61] Ibid.

[62] Ibid.

[63] Certain Chinese writers believe that Li's system was eminently successful in spurring Chinese industry. Thus the Huang-ch'ao ching-shih-wen t'ung-pien, 63:9, notes the observations of an unknown writer: "Since the opening of the ports there have been some cases of the imitation of the foreigners in collecting stocks. The Chao Shang Chü first set the precedent in collecting merchant stocks and inaugurating that type of enterprise. The merchants also enthusiastically bought stocks. Then the Jen-Ho Insurance Company followed the Chao Shang Chü's example and also made great

profits. Today, the Kaiping Coal Mines, the Ping-ch'uan Copper Mines, the Chi-Ho Insurance Company, the cloth machine mills, the paper mills, the milk factory, the Ch'ang-lo Copper Mines, and the Tientsin-Shanghai telegraph lines all use stocks and are therefore prosperous. Even the companies owned by Westerners are invested in by Chinese stockholders.... The original price of Chao Shang Chü stock was 100 liang per share, now each share is worth 250 liang. The Ping-ch'uan Copper stock has increased from 100 to 200 liang. The Ch'ang-lo Copper Mines stock rose from 100 to 160 liang. The Kaiping Mine stock rose from 100 to 237 liang per share."

Whatever the drawbacks, Li's system of government-merchant partnership helped keep industry in Chinese hands. This is shown in the cotton mill industry as follows:

First mill: started by Li Hung-chang; government-supervised and merchant-operated; second mill: started by Li Hung-chang; government-supervised but later changed to entirely merchant management; third mill: entirely merchant but encouraged by Li Hung-chang; fourth mill: entirely merchant; fifth mill: entirely merchant.

The last four either collapsed completely or passed into foreign hands. Only the first survived. *Ibid.*

IX. The Disintegration of Li Hung-chang's Power

THE Manchu rulers of China, like their Chinese predecessors, gave highest priority to the protection of the power of their dynasty. As alien conquerors, faced with the problem of maintaining their rule over the vast Chinese population and of using and controlling the Chinese bureaucracy, the Manchus were perhaps even more rigid in their restrictions than earlier Chinese ruling groups had been. Since they aimed at preventing the growth of power blocs or any coalitions which might threaten their position, it was their policy to keep their officials as isolated as possible and dependent upon the mercies and discretion of the court.[1] Although the crises which arose in the nineteenth century created new conditions under which the court was obliged to overlook certain violations of the regulations, and more power accrued to certain officials than would have been permitted in the past, the views of the court did not change. It continued to suppress, whenever possible, any practices that might lead to the growth of personal power among members of the bureaucracy.[2]

---

[1] Karl August Wittfogel, *Oriental Despotism* (New Haven: Yale University Press, 1957), offers a detailed analysis of the techniques employed by Chinese and other despotic rulers to control their bureaucrats. Dr. Wittfogel's advice in the early stages of my research was influential in the formulation of my basic hypothesis regarding Li Hung-chang and his significance.

[2] For example, in 1887 a decree took to task Liu Ping-chang, governor-general of Szechwan, for improperly requesting permission to keep one of his officers with him when he transferred from Chekiang to Szechwan. The decree stated: "A practice has of late prevailed among provincial high officials of applying for the personal services of these officers [generals of divisions] because they have earlier recommended them for advancement, while the officers themselves subordinate all appreciation of the important interests of the state to their feelings of private gratitude, and this renders nugatory the intent with which they are invested with special commands by the court. This cannot be allowed for a moment and provincial high authorities are warned

In his rise to power and during his exceptionally long term as governor-general of Chihli, Li Hung-chang frequently violated the government regulations directed against factionalism within the bureaucracy.[3] This could never be done with complete impunity, but Li was powerful and astute enough to escape any serious consequences.[4] Until 1894 he suffered no political reverses, for he had become practically indispensable in the conduct of all affairs in the north. The government never lacked grounds upon which to dismiss him, but so long as he commanded strong support it was unable and perhaps even unwilling to do so. Li's support was derived from his bureaucratic and military machines, and although Li often found it expedient to play politics with court officials, he was generally able to rely upon his own strength rather than upon maneuvers to maintain his position.[5] It was

against making similarly ill-advised applications in the future." *Peking Gazette: Trans.* in *North China Herald,* Mar. 6, 1887.

In 1875 one of the charges against Ying Han which caused him to be removed from the office of governor-general of Liang-Kuang was that he took his own officers with him to Kwangtung. He was further chastised for the conduct of these officers who had no authority to be there, yet pretended to have authority and even asked for salary. The officers were ordered to return to their original posts in Anhwei. This denunciation was based originally upon charges made by the Manchu general of Kwangtung and the governor, who wished to get rid of the governor-general. *Ibid.,* Sept. 2, 1875.

The Manchu Court was always alert to opportunities for unseating officials who overreached themselves. In this case, Ying Han was the victim of both local and central government competition, for the memorials originally denouncing him stressed principally his efforts to establish his own separate Board of Military Supplies in Canton. *Ibid.,* Sept. 13, 1875.

[3] See Chapters 3 and 5 above. In 1881 Li was denounced strongly by a censor for calling to his own services several men who were above the rank of *chang-ching* (secretaries of the Grand Council. There were sixty of these in all). The censor charged that the regulations of the Board of Rites prohibited Li from calling them, and that the appointments made by Li should be canceled. Furthermore, it was stated that Li was illegally employing one of these men who was from Anhwei. Li defended himself by saying that he had called men of similar rank from the capital in the days of the Taiping Rebellion, and he reminded the court that no one had objected when he had summoned Feng Kuei-fen, Liu Ping-chang, and Wang K'ai-t'ai to his headquarters. Li added: "But today I am getting older and weaker while my affairs are becoming more complicated. This is why I call still more people to my staff. . . . I insist upon having them." *LWCK Memorials,* 42:1a, KH 7/8/2.

[4] Alicia H. Little, in *Li Hung Chang, His Life and Times,* p. 159, relates that on one occasion Li was worsted by a censor who memorialized the throne against a cashiered officer whom Li was employing. The officer's record was so bad that the censor carried his point and the emperor ordered the defaulter to be dismissed. Li then applied for the services of Sheng Hsüan-huai, then a cashiered judge from Fukien. Sheng subsequently became one of the most powerful men in China, and Li's special protégé. See below.

[5] Li was not always completely successful in thwarting the government's attempts to isolate bureaucrats. However, other officials fared much worse. An interesting case occurred in the spring of 1894, when Liu K'un-i recommended Li Ch'ing-ts'u, the son of Li Han-chang and nephew of Li Hung-chang, as a high-ranking circuit intendant

just this kind of personal power that the Manchus wished to prevent their bureaucrats from acquiring; but Li Hung-chang had built his organization at a time when the government was unable to interfere, and he later became too strong for the government to challenge.[6] Only a major shift in the national power structure or a spectacular defeat for Li and his organization could have displaced him.

Li's regional structure was finally broken by an outside force—the military power of the Japanese. For more than twenty years Li had recognized Japan as a menace to China. He had watched the Meiji Restoration progressives in Japan systematically carry out a program of reform, not dissimilar to his own, which stressed military prepared-ness and economic development. His policy had been to oppose Japa-nese encroachments as much as possible by all means short of war. Adhering to the traditional *I-i chih-i* ("Use the barbarians to control the barbarians") he relied heavily upon the Western powers, particu-larly Russia, to maintain the status quo in the Far East. For this humiliating but realistic policy he was roundly criticized by his politi-cal enemies in government and court circles. As tension mounted in 1894 over Japanese activity in Korea, Li found himself propelled toward a war which he deeply wished to avoid.[7] Knowing the weak-

---

because of his knowledge of foreign affairs and government administration. He was thereupon appointed Salt Commissioner of Hupeh. In his audience with the emperor the young Li failed to display any unusual knowledge. In addition, a censor charged that he was related to Li Han-chang and Li Hung-chang, and the emperor suspected that family influence had been at work. The emperor said that Liu K'un-i had not been up to the mark in this instance, and canceled the appointment. A similar fate befell a man, recommended by Li Han-chang, who had been Li Hung-chang's secretary. Little, *Li Hung Chang*, pp. 211-12.

From about 1894 on, Li Hung-chang seems to have been a particular target of the young Kuang-hsü emperor. The emperor was apparently not strong enough to do much about Li, who in local politics supported the empress dowager. The emperor took these opportunities to vent his antagonism upon Li. The emperor's attitude was probably influenced strongly by Weng T'ung-ho, his tutor and a man extremely jealous of Li's position. Moreover, the emperor was increasingly influenced by men such as K'ang Yu-wei, who in advocating reform, which the emperor favored and tried to bring about dramatically in 1898, sought to re-establish central power in China and thus opposed nepotism on the part of regional leaders such as Li. See Kung-chuan Hsiao, "Weng T'ung-ho and the Reform Movement of 1898," *Tsing Hua Journal of Chinese Studies,* N.S., I (1957), 127-79, *passim.*

[6] The strength of Li's position in 1894 is described by an American observer in *Tientsin Consular Despatches,* Feb. 16, 1894; see also James Harrison Wilson, *China: Travels and Investigations in the Middle Kingdom,* pp. 6, 116, 117.

[7] Kung-chüan Hsiao, *op. cit.,* pp. 117, 128, 134, *et passim,* mentions some of the circumstances of Li's relations with his contemporaries and also indicates the personal and factional aspects of the "War Party's" challenge to Li. Their success in dis-crediting Li after the defeat of his forces left the way open for Weng T'ung-ho to replace the aging governor-general of Chihli as a policy-maker and diplomat. See also *ibid.,* p. 201, note 48.

ness of China's defense organization, both military and civil, he anticipated defeat unless foreign intervention forestalled the Japanese. But Li could not ignore the challenge of the so-called War Party at Peking, without admitting that his leadership over a twenty-five year period had produced little result. He could not publicly admit that the fleet was inadequate and that he could not trust his "modernized" troops to the fortunes of war, without destroying military morale and losing the confidence of the Manchu government and of his own followers. Against his better judgment Li was forced to make a show of strength and send reinforcements to Korea.

On July 25, 1894, the British transport *Kowshing* carrying 1,120 Chinese troops to Seoul was sunk by a Japanese man-of-war with a loss of over one thousand lives. China was at war in the north, and the Pei-yang fleet and the entire Pei-yang defense organization were summoned to battle. The results are curtly described in the *Ch'ing-shih kao (Draft History of the Ch'ing Dynasty)*:

In the Sino-Japanese War the Huai-chün was completely overturned. . . . After Sung Ch'ing's and Ma Yü-k'un's early and later defeats they were never able to recover their strength. The lien-chün of the Three Eastern Provinces [Manchuria] as a whole never came back in the end. . . .[8]

The reaction to Li's defeat was not long in coming. Once the tide of battle had turned decisively against China, Li was blamed for the entire catastrophe. Li was deprived of his honors, the Peacock Feathers and Yellow Jacket bestowed upon him for his victories against the Taipings and the Nien, and was then permitted to "take leave" from his post as governor-general of Chihli. He was not immediately set aside, however, for the government was aware of his prestige abroad and hesitated to lose a veteran diplomat whose experience might soon be required.

The war had been in progress only two months when it was reported that the emperor had been threatening to deprive Li of his honors for some time. He had issued several decrees to that effect, but on each occasion, reportedly, the empress dowager had destroyed them. It was rumored too that Li, at that early stage, might have saved himself had he offered 400,000 taels to the young emperor so that "there could be peace and friendship between them." But Li had stated that he would not give even four cash.[9] The American consul at Tientsin, who had sent this intelligence on to Washington, interpreted these developments

---

[8] *CSK*, 448:6a.
[9] *Tientsin Consular Despatches,* Sept. 17, 1894.

as a sign of serious internal disruption and predicted the early downfall of the dynasty.

Li meanwhile began to make provisions for the future by dividing his property among his children and converting a good part of it into cash.[10] His position worsened daily as he faced mounting criticism of his conduct of campaigns and management of supplies. His enemies demanded the removal of his faithful Huai-chün follower, the Pei-yang Fleet Commander Ting Ju-ch'ang. But Li stood by Ting, who soon afterward committed suicide when he lost the naval fortress at Weihai-wei to the Japanese. Charges of corruption and secret dealings with the Japanese blackened Li's name, and his continued efforts to induce the Western powers to intervene on China's behalf only served to confirm any doubts of the weakness of his position. The increasing attacks against Li, the well-founded charges of corruption and ill-founded accusations of treason, were damaging;[11] but even more disastrous were the destruction of his military organization, the loss of his navy, and the complete demoralization of his military ration and supply bureaus. Exposed to the public gaze, his followers in these organizations faced purges and censure; and although some of the stronger men such as Sheng Hsüan-huai survived, most of the others were cast aside. Li and his organization had been charged with malpractices before, but until his military machine was crippled by the Japanese, Li had had sufficient strength to protect himself and his organization. Now he was at the mercy of court enemies and public opinion.

Perhaps the final blow to Li's prestige was Japan's refusal to negotiate for peace except with Li himself. Although this was an acknowledgment of his former high standing, it may also have been a way of punishing the statesman who had from the beginning warned his nation against the Japanese threat and tried to ward it off by diplomacy and bluff, as well as by the development of military and naval defenses. With China lying helpless before the guns of the Japanese fleet and the advancing Japanese armies, Li Hung-chang was dispatched to Japan to accept the humiliating terms of the Treaty of Shimonoseki. To carry on negotiations, Li was once more given the title of governor-general of Chihli and was appointed Minister Plenipotentiary.[12] Japanese plans for taking Manchuria were blocked by the intervention of the Western powers at the instigation of Russia, but Li Hung-chang

---

[10] *Ibid.*

[11] *LWCK Memorials,* 79:25a-27a, KH 20/9/26; 28a ff., KH 20/10/26; 30a ff., KH 20/10/26; 37a ff., KH 20/11/14.

[12] *Tientsin Consular Despatches,* June 13, 1895, and July 21, 1895.

returned to China bearing the onus of the concessions he had been forced to make, and receiving little credit for his efforts to make them as light as possible.[13]

After returning to China, Li, a tired old man, suffering from a facial wound received at the hands of a Japanese fanatic, was removed from the scene of his former power at Tientsin and transferred to Peking, where, under the eyes of the central government and isolated from Western diplomats, he remained without real position although he still held the nominal title of Grand Secretary.[14] It was speculated at the time that he might be appointed to one of the central government boards, but some thought it more likely that he would be retired to Anhwei.[15] In Li's place at Tientsin was the new governor-general of Chihli, Wang Wen-shao, who, according to diplomatic observers, was only an average bureaucrat and much weaker than Li. The American consul Read apparently perceived the real meaning of the change when he noted that he expected future diplomacy to be carried on directly with the Board of Foreign Affairs and the Ministers rather than through Li. He added, "A weaker man at Tientsin means undoubtedly greater centralization of power at the capital."[16] The consul noted great uneasiness in Tientsin, for it was generally assumed that with Li gone his subordinates would soon be on the way out.[17]

In 1896 Li Hung-chang was sent to Russia to represent the Manchu throne at the coronation of the new tsar. Li was selected because the Russians would accept no other representative. Behind this move was the desire of the Russian minister, Cassini, and the Russian Foreign Office to isolate Li from China long enough to exact concessions from him as repayment for Russia's help in restraining victorious Japan, and to impress upon him that his sole source of support and strength in the future would be Russia. It is generally agreed by diplomatic historians that the Russians were extremely successful in this strategy and that when Li left Moscow he had laid the foundation for future concessions at the expense of the integrity of North China and Manchuria.

Li proceeded from Russia to Europe, where he called on the important heads of state and then embarked for America, where he toured parts of the United States and Canada. His round-the-world

[13] Stanley F. Wright, *Hart and the Chinese Customs*, pp. 643-50.
[14] *Tientsin Consular Despatches*, Sept. 5, 1895.
[15] *Ibid.*
[16] *Ibid.*
[17] *Ibid.*

trip made the headlines of the world, but what seemed to be the triumphal tour of China's leading statesman was actually a year in exile, enforced by a court and government which availed itself of his absence to reorganize political alignments, separate Li from any remaining sources of power, and at the same time persuade the West that the presence of its great reformer abroad heralded great progress for China in the future. Li took advantage of his enforced journey to re-establish himself in the eyes of the Westerners as a vigorous and enlightened proponent of Westernization. Apparently the tour did much to satisfy his curiosity about the Western world, and he greatly enjoyed his meetings with prime ministers, royalty, presidents, bank clerks, and even tobacco salesmen.[18] Armament-makers and would-be concessionaires in every field flocked to him in quest of orders but received only smiles and questions, for Li was in no position to buy anything.[19] He no longer had an independent source of official income or the forces and enterprises for which to buy.

When he returned to China late in 1896, Li found himself relegated to comparative obscurity. The court appointed him to the Board of Foreign Affairs as a gesture of courtesy to the kings and prime ministers with whom Li had consorted rather than out of respect for Li himself. According to General Wilson, who saw him not long after:

. . . he was outranked and overshadowed by all the princes and several of the members [of the Board of Foreign Affairs]. He was daily subjected to espionage, and as a matter of fact was regarded as an object of imperial disfavor with whom anyone might safely differ in opinion. His influence was but slight, and after submitting to insults and indignities from even the court eunuchs, he was banished from the imperial capital.[20]

In 1898, under the influence of the great reformer K'ang Yu-wei, the young Kuang-hsü emperor made a dramatic bid for power, attempting to assert his own strength and reassert the failing influence of the central government through the famous Hundred Days of Reform. Li's status sank lower than ever as he was dismissed from his Board post by the reformers, even though there was gossip at Tientsin that he had finally won the favor of the emperor and might be returned to the governor-generalship of Chihli.[21] Those who had dismissed Li were

[18] *Scribner's Magazine,* CXX (1896), 656.

[19] *Illustrated London News,* "Li Hung-chang Supplement," Aug. 15, 1896, *passim; Scientific American,* Vol. XLII, No. 1080 (Sept. 12, 1896) ; *Harper's Weekly,* Sept. 12, 1896.

[20] James Harrison Wilson, *China,* p. 116.

[21] Consul Ragsdale to Assistant Secretary of State, *Tientsin Consular Despatches,*

themselves soon turned out of power, as the empress dowager, with
the support of the Manchu general Jung-lu and Li's former protégé,
Yüan Shih-k'ai, regained her regency through a dramatic coup d'état.
More needful of support than ever, the restored rulers of the central
government gave back to Li a small measure of the authority he had
once claimed in his own right. In the fall of 1898 Li was ordered to
supervise the conservancy works of the Yellow River and to recommend measures to be taken against flood and future changes of the
river's course. Although he was not a waterworks expert himself, Li
still had connections and some vestiges of a following, and retained
some influence over many of the managers and technicians who still
held positions in the commercial bureaus and customhouses of the
north. Further, the failure of Li's opponents, such as Weng T'ung-ho,
to cope adequately with diplomatic problems gradually restored Li to
favor. For a few months in 1898 he again held the Superintendency of
Trade for the north.[22] But now the post was not combined with governor-generalship or with command of military forces.

At this time Li's former protégé, Sheng Hsüan-huai, was promoting
enterprises in Hupeh, in collaboration with Chang Chih-tung, and
carrying on private commercial ventures with Westerners in Shanghai.
In Tientsin, Wu Ting-fang, a Li appointee, still held his post as assistant director of railroads, and several other of Li's specialists carried
on as before. But while individuals survived, the basis of Li's machine
was gone.

The court found a means of relieving itself of Li's presence without
too greatly upsetting his Western friends and former Chinese subordinates and the few old colleagues who still felt respect and loyalty
for Li, by appointing him to the governor-generalship of Liang-Kuang
in the remote south. Li's transfer to Canton, the capital of Liang-
Kuang, completed his separation from the remainder of his old military command, from the last vestiges of his machine in Chihli, and
from the diplomatic corps of both the Western powers and China. He
would probably have died in what for him was virtual exile had not the
Boxer Uprising broken out in the north within a few months of his
arrival in Canton. Li was one of the small group of provincial leaders,

July 9, 1898. A scholarly account is found in Kung-chuan Hsiao, "Weng T'ung-ho
and the Reform Movement of 1898," *Tsing Hua Journal of Chinese Studies*, N.S., I,
111-245, *passim*.

[22] *LWCK Memorials*, 79:60a ff., KH 24/10/1, to 85a ff., KH 25/no month/no day;
Hummel, *Eminent Chinese*, p. 470. It was Li who in 1870 started the precedent of
combining the posts of Chihli governor-general and Superintendent of Northern Trade,
and it was he who ended it by holding the latter position without the former in 1899.

which included Chang Chih-tung, Yüan Shih-k'ai, then governor of Shantung, and Liu K'un-i, governor-general of Liang-Chiang, who took vigorous measures against any violent manifestation of anti-foreignism in their territories.

In 1900 an Allied Expeditionary Force was launched to rescue the beleaguered missions in the north and to undertake punitive measures against the Chinese. This threw the court into a panic. In attempting to drive the Boxers from Shantung, Yüan Shih-k'ai had pushed them into Chihli, where they allied themselves with powerful reactionary groups in the government. Nieh Shih-ch'eng, a Huai-chün commander who had been engaged in reorganizing the remains of the Wu-I-chün and had used his army against the Boxers, was killed by the undiscriminating advancing Western troops.[23] The court fled to Sian, abandoning Peking and Tientsin to the foreign armies, and searched frantically for reliable officials who would be acceptable to the Western powers as representatives of responsible Chinese government. It was almost inevitable that the court should turn to Li Hung-chang, the military disciplinarian, progressive reformer, and friend of a generation of "old China hands."

Li's feeling that circumstances had vindicated him was expressed when he discussed his plans wtih the American consul at Canton: "I was Viceroy of Chihli for thirty-four years[24] and in all of that time that place was in peace and prosperity and there was no rebellion. Now it is infested with robbers and I must go to clear them out."[25]

What ambitious thoughts may have crowded Li's mind at this turn of events can only be imagined. Certainly he fully expected that a peace would be concluded with the Western representatives which would lead to improvement of his own position. The American consul, reporting on the latest developments, wrote:

[Li] assured us that his determination is, on his arrival there [Peking] to insist on the adoption by the Chinese Government of such measures as will be beneficial to China and at the same time maintain friendly relations with all foreign nations. He was emphatic in his assertion that above all he desired the friendship of the United States and added that he would do all within his power to promote it.[26]

In response to the imperial summons Li departed for the north, but

[23] Biography of Jung-lu in Hummel, *Eminent Chinese*, p. 408.

[24] This should read "twenty-four years." Consul Wade apparently made an error in transcribing his notes.

[25] McWade to Hill, *Canton Consular Despatches*, No. 23, July 17, 1900.

[26] McWade to Hill, *Canton Consular Despatches*, No. 18, June 26, 1900.

stopped off at Shanghai to await developments.[27] Here he found to his chagrin that several of the Western diplomats, far from favoring him, actually preferred not to restore him to responsibility at all. This was apparently the position of the English and perhaps of the Japanese, who feared that Li was too much under the influence of the Russians and that restoration of Li to power would mean new advantages for Russia.[28] Li also awaited further military developments in the north. He had been urged by the court to undertake the protection of Chihli, but wisely concluded that such forces as he might muster at the last moment would be overwhelmed by the Allied Expeditionary Armies.

Before departing for Shanghai Li had been reappointed as governor-general of Chihli, and now, together with Prince Ch'ing, he was put in charge of all negotiations in the north. He finally arrived at Tientsin on September 20, 1900, and soon afterward proceeded to Peking, where he approached the diplomatic representatives of the powers for terms of settlement. After much wrangling among the various representatives, he was accepted as a plenipotentiary. Li and Prince Ch'ing were handed the notes embodying the unconditional demands of the powers on Christmas Day, 1900. The next eight months saw Li bargaining with the Westerners, attempting wherever possible to modify their demands, and wielding his power in Chihli in ways designed to reassure the occupying powers that he could and did offer security and that their armies could serve no further purpose in Chihli.[29] He had just reached agreements providing for settlement of the Boxer incident and the withdrawal of the expeditionary armies when he fell ill.[30] He

[27] Li may have considered the possibility of establishing a separate government in Canton before departing for the north, but according to recent research his indirect correspondence with Sun Yat-sen never went beyond the stage of seeking information. See Marius Jansen, *The Japanese and Sun Yat-sen* (Cambridge: Harvard University Press, 1954), pp. 86-87, 89, 90.

[28] Stanley F. Wright, *Hart and the Chinese Customs,* pp. 738-39. The American consul at Shanghai was also opposed to Li's resumption of power. He strongly advised against Li's participation in peace negotiations. To this end he presented the Department of State with a petition drawn up by the American Association of Shanghai which attacked Li for representing the "Empress Dowager and the Boxer Party." The Consul could not have been more wrong. What Li seemed to have hoped for was more than an opportunity to negotiate peace. He did not preclude the idea of really taking over power, either with or without the Manchus. The Boxer Party contained many of Li's old enemies, men who had opposed his reform program all along. Consul Goodnow was the same man who in 1915 suggested to Yüan Shih-k'ai that only a monarchy was suitable for China, and influenced Yüan in his ill-starred attempt to found a new dynasty. The consul seems to have been remarkably lacking in understanding of Chinese politics. For Goodnow's report on Li see *Shanghai Consular Despatches,* Sept. 5, 1900.

[29] Stanley F. Wright, *Hart and the Chinese Customs,* pp. 742-43.

[30] On the twenty-second day, ninth month of Kuang-hsü 27 (1901), Li memorialized

died on November 7, exactly two months after signing his final humiliating treaty.[31] His last official action had been the writing of a memorial to the throne wherein he disclosed that he had ordered his still loyal Huai-chün commander, Ma Yü-k'un, to lead his troops into Tientsin to protect the city from disturbances. To the very end Li had looked to the Huai-chün for power, strength, and security.[32]

the empress by telegram: "On the night of the nineteenth, I suddenly vomited half a spittoon of blood; the color was purple black with some lumps in it. Cold sweat appeared and my head became dizzy, and my condition became critical. I immediately summoned a Western physician and took medicine to stop the vomiting. For the past two days I fortunately have not vomited, but at present I cannot rise or sit. When I try to sit up my head immediately becomes dizzy. The doctor says a small blood vessel has broken in my stomach. I must lie quietly and recuperate in a peaceful way for some time. I eat only milk, chicken soup, lotus root powder, and thin gruel. I am forbidden to eat hard and dry foods for fear that the broken blood vessel will not close. Blessed be the Sacred Edict inquiring about my condition of illness, including sleep and food and all details. I am most grateful to the point of weeping. In respectful appreciation of the imperial kindness, I will pay special attention to recuperation, hoping for an early recovery." *LWCK Telegrams*, 40:40b, KH 27/9/2.

[31] Li Shu-ch'un, "Li Wen-chung kung Hung-chang nien-p'u," *Shih-hsüeh nien-pao*, I, (1929), 120. See also Hummel, *Eminent Chinese*, p. 470.

[32] *LWCK Memorials*, 80:84a, KH 27/8/22.

X. The Man and His Influence

So WELL was Li Hung-chang cast in his historical role that it seems dramatically proper that he should have left the stage with the onset of the twentieth century. While China as a whole remained undefinable in terms of Western social and cultural stages, important links with the West had been established in the nineteenth century, and Chinese development was henceforth to take place in intimate relationship with larger outside movements. The Nationalist and Communist movements in twentieth-century China grew out of conditions which Li and his contemporaries had helped to shape. This view of Li may appear as an overemphasis on the role of the hero in shaping history, but it is no exaggeration to say that Li was in the vanguard of his time and that through a shrewd appreciation of institutional forces in China and technological forces in the West, followed by forthright action in developing his own position and projects, he paved the way for the still greater changes to come after his death. The final collapse of the Manchu dynasty, the birth of the Republic a decade after Li's death, the warlord period of the 1920's, the literary renaissance, the consolidation of power by the Nationalists, and the rise of communism mark the beginning of a new chapter in Chinese history. It is a chapter which, while reflecting earlier Chinese traditions and institutions, is marked by the assimilation of Western political and social philosophies, the spirit of science, and above all, Western technology. The triumph of technology has been such that China, with all its vestigial peculiarities, has been pulled out of the cyclical orbit in which its history revolved in past millennia.

No one person can be given credit for changes so vast as those that have occurred in China in the past hundred years. But Li was a leading figure in bringing about the institutional and ideological adjustments, narrow as they were in space and scope, which opened and at the same time limited the paths that China was to follow into the modern world.

On the surface Li's efforts would appear to have ended in a series of failures. By the time he died, his navy had been sunk; his military organization had been in part destroyed and in part taken over and reorganized by others. Few of his bureaucratic, commercial, and industrial enterprises had grown beyond their scant beginnings. While he lived, his broad views on reform were shared by only a few of the important Chinese statesmen, most of whom had not advanced much beyond Li's ideas of the late T'ung-chih period. His diplomacy was branded as a capitulation and sell-out to the foreigners, particularly the Russians. His bureaucratic organization was regarded as a spawning ground for corruption. The legacy that he left included no model of Confucian virtue, no inspirational writings or philosophical guidance.

But Li left behind a living heritage in the models he had created—models of military organization, models of a political machine, and models of military and bureaucratic leadership. Nothing further need be said here of the importance of Li's pioneering enterprises or of his military and political organizations within the larger institutional structure of China. His influence on his contemporaries and successors, however, requires some elaboration.

Li's View on Change

The failure of the majority of Chinese and Manchu statesmen to appreciate the need for radical changes or even moderate technological reform in the post-Taiping period did not leave Li entirely unsupported. He had a coterie of close colleagues, supporters, and followers actively interested in the problem of change. In some cases Li was the student executive, learning and adopting ideas, and using his military and political position to carry them into practice. At the same time he helped to produce a generation of leaders who accepted quite naturally the ideological, institutional, and technological novelties he advocated. It was through men that Li acted and through men that his legacy was passed on.

Never an outstanding scholar or essayist, Li nevertheless made an ideological contribution. It was a contribution picked up and felt by the men he employed and worked with, and many of these held important positions after he had passed from the scene. It was significant and encouraging to those with Western contacts that so high an official as Li should press for fundamental reforms. Some of his attacks on existing institutions were almost revolutionary in terms of the prevailing official norms. In 1875, five years after he had assumed office in the north, he wrote Governor Liu Ping-chang, berating Liu and ridiculing his colleagues:

The public examinations and fine calligraphy have nothing to do with current affairs. There are none who do not know this. You have stated that the literary themes and commentaries derived from the Classics and History can reveal the capacity of a man to manage national affairs and that you regret that the government has failed to reform the examinations in order to achieve this. How true! How true! Recently many people have presented their opinions on the reform of the examination system, but all were rejected by the board. I first introduced this proposal in the hope that the authorities would be awakened and would themselves find the right way.

Someone has argued that the examination system has produced many great figures. Tseng Kuo-fan and you have come through the examinations. But I rejected this argument several years ago. Today, even if we had several tens of persons like you and Tseng, they could never handle Western affairs properly.

You have stated that mathematics is similar to astronomy, which was one of the six arts of Confucius, and that this proves that Confucius himself paid attention to mathematics. But how many precise mathematical instruments have been handed down to us by the Sage?

You have said that studying things to attain knowledge is the only principle of manufacturing. You know that under heaven everything in existence implies the methods and meaning of manufacturing. You cannot despise it!

Again, you have said that the designation "Foreign Studies Bureau" [Yang-hsüeh Chu] is wrong because it means we are adapting Chinese ways to barbarian ways, and you have quoted the words of Confucius, "When the name is not right, utterances will not be consistent." If this point of view is right, our Chinese learning should have checked the barbarians and matched the barbarians. But in fact we have been unable to do so. Therefore, we had better acquire the merits of the barbarians in order to make up for our defects. . . . Now there is no harm in taking this road. Moreover, the barbarians have already come inland and have already stationed their envoys in Peking, but still you hold to the names, worrying whether they are barbarian or Chinese. If you are going to be concerned over such things you had better first have some ability to suppress the barbarians. Only then can you reject this bad policy of adopting the way of the barbarians.

Now I ask you what magic you have to deal with the situation? You merely achieved the clearing of several hundred thousand [liang] in turning over your office, and then you are proud that no one within the four seas can surpass you in the management of finances. I do not believe this.

Li went on to say that although the buying of weapons was not so basic as problems of armament, personnel, and finance, if the government paid attention neither to the basic things nor to the "branches," the enemy would win even before the battle was fought. He continued:

You say that my suggestions are too radical and if put into practice will hurt the country, and if not put into practice will nevertheless hurt my reputation. But I think that if my suggestions are put into practice the life of the dynasty may yet be prolonged several hundred years. If not put into practice, later rulers may take my suggestions as a model. I neither hurt the country nor my reputation. Your opinions on my suggestions are excessively cautious, and I cannot agree with them. Because you look upon me as a critical servant of the country and as a critical friend of yours, I dare to expose my heart to you as if we were talking face to face.[1]

Two years later, answering a letter from Kuo Sung-tao, who was then serving as minister to Great Britain and France, Li showed signs of discouragement in his hopes for change.

Even though I have not visited the Western countries, I have carefully studied their culture and politics for twenty years, and I have some general idea of them. . . . Since the opening of the discussions concerning coastal defense in the thirteenth year of T'ung-chih [1874], I have urged that coal and iron mines must be opened and that telegraph and railway lines must be constructed. The various ports must have Western studies in physics and chemistry added to the curriculum of their official schools in order to produce able persons. But at that time the Grand Councilor Wen Hsiang laughed at me. The conference of the court did not take my proposals seriously. Wang Hsiao-feng and Yü Lien-fang even attacked me bitterly.

In the winter of that year I recall going to the capital to pay homage at the coffin of the emperor. There I saw Prince Kung and presented to him the advantages of railways, requesting him to establish a branch from Ch'ing-chiang to Peking for the purpose of facilitating transportation between south and north. The prince agreed with me, but said that no one dared take the initiative. I requested further that he persuade the two empress dowagers, and he answered that even the two empress dowagers could not decide such a large matter and that in the future he would keep his mouth shut. . . .

The likin in the various provinces should be discontinued, but Tso Tsung-t'ang's western expedition, coastal defense, and the garrisons at various posts all rely on this source of revenue. Everyone knows it should be stopped but the situation makes it difficult to do so. . . .

_____
[1] *LWCK Letters,* 15:3a-5b, KH 1/1/8.

You want me to enlighten the court, to dispel their suspicions, and then you believe the entire country will rise in response to us. I think you are really overestimating me.

Last winter when the Chao Shang Chü bought out the Chi Ch'ang Company's ships, Shen Pao-chen proposed to draw from the various provinces official funds amounting to 1,000,000 liang, and then to collect 1,200,000 merchant stock. But now half a year has passed and not a single Chinese merchant has applied for a share. This indicates that it is hard to unify the peoples' will. . . .[2]

General pessimism did not prevent Li from launching ambitious enterprises, civil and military. But under no illusions as to the response they would meet, he bent them to serve his private interests. He seemed increasingly to absorb the prevailing atmosphere of stagnation and defeat. He adapted himself to existing conditions and did not become unduly alarmed over matters he could not greatly alter singlehanded. He confined his greatest efforts to increasing the strength of his own organization and to using his position in foreign affairs to heighten his own prestige. The failure of his supply organization and the ineptness of his naval commanders, which contributed so heavily to the military disaster of 1894, he viewed as being small matters in comparison with the basic weaknesses for which he held the court and his provincial colleagues responsible. He anticipated a worsening of the situation in the future. Replying by telegraph to an inquiry by the Chinese Minister at St. Petersburg concerning diplomatic affairs, in 1895, he wrote:

Four countries have connived and there is no way to separate them. Future negotiations will be difficult to undertake. Although I have desired reforms and self-strengthening, without talented men, without funds, without supporters, what can we do? In the past we lacked fast ships and good cannon. Thus we have been made to suffer such disaster.[3]

In his later years Li came to depend ever more heavily upon the support of Western powers. At first he had hoped that by adopting foreign methods he could lead the way, growing stronger himself as the country advanced. His disdain for the obstructionism and parochialism of his rivals led him in the end to see little hope for China. Rather than rely upon the central government for any revival of national strength, he could only hope for an opportunity to achieve security for China and power for himself through foreign support. He was not will-

[2] *Ibid.*, 17:13a-b, KH 3/6/1.
[3] *LWCK Telegrams,* 21:44a, KH 21/9/1.

ing to alter the institutional patterns of China, since he was already at the top of the structure.[4] Experience brought him to see China's social structure as clearly as he saw her international position. In 1897 he commented upon its most important aspect as follows:

> It is unfortunately true that suspicion, prejudice, and self-sufficiency are peculiar traits of educated Chinese, especially notable in their estimation of other countries . . . perhaps because of the isolation of China from Western influences for so many centuries. . . .
>
> The social, educational, and official systems of China have tended to give to the educated classes control of the destinies of the nation. Whether such a monopoly of power be good or bad need not now be considered; it exists and the practical question is how to turn it into beneficent and useful channels. . . .[5]

Attempts to Change the Character of the Bureaucracy

Li's attempts to fill the bureaucracy with men capable of handling contemporary problems, that is, problems arising from contact with the West, led to his well-known sponsorship of Chinese student missions to Western countries.[6] Among his ambitions was the creation of a modern officer corps, and to this end he advocated the entry of some of the Chinese students in the United States into the military academy at West Point and the United States Naval Academy at Annapolis. Li's adviser and assistant in this matter, Yung Wing, laid such stress on this proposal that he warned the Americans that if the United States Congress did not agree to accept Chinese military and naval cadets, it was possible that the whole matter of sending Chinese students to America would be dropped.[7]

It is indicative of the ambiguous position of Li as a Chinese official, representing imperial and regional interests simultaneously, that the entire matter of cadet training for Chinese students in America centered on the question of which Chinese interests the United States would be serving if she agreed to Li's plan. The Americans were eager

---

[4] In this respect we are in agreement with Liang Ssu-kuang, who saw Li as desperately seeking to maintain his status at any cost. Liang and other Communist writers go much farther, however, and see Li Hung-chang as selling out China to the foreigners in order to keep the people down and himself on top. It is doubtful whether Li was as worried about the people as he was about his competitive position with the Manchus and the central government, but there is no evidence that he "betrayed" China to the foreigners for personal reasons. See Liang Ssu-kuang, *Li Hung-chang mai-kuo shih, passim.*

[5] Li Hung-chang to the Reverend Gilbert Reid, Peking, Apr. 12, 1897, enclosure in *Tientsin Consular Despatches,* May 17, 1897.

[6] *LWCK Foreign Office Letters,* 1:19b-22a, TC 10/5/9.

[7] *Shanghai Consular Despatches,* Jan. 4, 1872.

for China's favor, but some difference of opinion existed among the American representatives in China as to whether the educational mission sought by Li was provincial or national. The United States Minister at Peking, who observed Li Hung-chang's activities at close hand, felt that the mission was essentially provincial. But Seward, the consul at Shanghai, argued that it was imperial, inasmuch as the students were to come from different sections of China, were to receive expenses from the revenues of the empire, and were to be sent only with imperial sanction. Thus the Americans hesitated, unable to decide what and whom Li's proposals really represented. For the Americans a basic issue existed which cut across the entire problem of diplomacy in China: either one dealt with the central government and regarded it as representing all of China, or else one would have to deal with a number of regional leaders.[8]

As a regional leader, Li's fundamental interest was in the creation of an able body of bureaucrat-technicians, military and civil, capable of handling modern problems and loyal to Li's own bureaucratic and military organization. The central government's view was more conservative. It wished to perpetuate a bureaucracy with the stable values that kept officials loyal to the old way of life and therefore loyal to the dynasty. Because Li Hung-chang's bureaucratic and military machine was created and developed in a partly westernized framework, far from fearing change (within limits) Li saw westernization as a strengthening of his own position and organization. The roots of central government power, however, were deep in tradition; and for the dynasty a change in the mode of the bureaucracy could not be other than a threat. The question of modernization, therefore, was not merely one of cultural tastes; it involved the kind of bureaucracy that China was to maintain, and it was a crucial factor in the struggle between central and regional power, especially as it developed during Li's lifetime.

It was in a similar context that Li sought to develop modern schools and academies within China itself, most notably the military and naval academies at Tientsin. The Huai-chün and lien-chün organizations, the Pei-yang fleet, and their supporting civilian machines required officers and officials with specialized training that the traditional curriculum of the gentry-bureaucrat class could not provide. At the military schools instruction was carried out in the German as well as the Chinese language. The naval academy had two branches, one for naval

---

[8] Seward to Davis, *Shanghai Consular Despatches,* Feb. 17, 1872.

executive officers and one for engineering. The examinations were patterned on those of the United States academies.

In 1880 Li established a telegraph school at Tientsin, where Danish technicians supervised the training of Chinese students. Li had also founded a medical school and hospital, which were specially designed to train men for naval and military medicine and various branches of public service.[9] The men trained abroad and at Li's schools in China eventually found their places in the bureaucracy. To be sure, in many branches of the government, both central and provincial, the services of these heterodox and—from a traditional Chinese point of view—unlettered official aspirants were disdained. Several turned to private business or entered the service of the Western representatives in China, but Li Hung-chang brought as many of these men as possible into his bureaucratic machine.[10] His patronage, while he was powerful, was greatly desired as the key to a successful career.

The infiltration of Western-trained students into the bureaucracy was the beginning of a fundamental change in the character of Chinese leadership. During Li's lifetime, he and others of background and training similar to his own dominated the scene so completely that the new Western-trained men had no chance to rise to leading positions but served instead in secondary capacities.

The enterprises of a Western type, the Pei-yang fleet, the schools and academies, failed for the most part to achieve their objectives. But they were important if only by reason of their existence. Not only did they serve to make commonplace Western devices and words; they also produced a generation of new men of affairs in China. Li Hung-chang left little legacy in prose, no stirring pamphlets or essays. But he created through his enterprises and academies a group of leaders who could handle the technical details necessary to translate his practical program into action. As the new men gradually replaced the old, and as innovations, however sparse, slowly achieved reluctant acceptance all the basic institutions of China almost imperceptibly underwent change. This transition was the dynamic aspect of the legacy of Li Hung-chang.

---

[9] "A Report on Chinese Government Schools at Tientsin," *Tientsin Consular Despatches*, Dec. 31, 1888.

[10] *LWCK Memorials*, 42:28a ff., KH 7/10/26. Li Hung-chang in 1881 noted of these students who studied abroad: "Now they have returned, and I have personally examined the students and find many of them not bad. I have assigned them to work and study at the Tientsin and Shanghai Machinery Bureaus and have sent some of them to the Naval and Telegraph schools. Thus we will reap the fruit of their work."

The Transition in Chinese Leadership

Our evaluation of Li's role must be based on what he and his group accomplished and on the heritage of institutions, ideas, and types of men he left behind. We have seen that despite his failure to produce any major documents he had shown himself to be familiar with the major ideological problems of his time and that his approach to practical problems was more realistic than that of most of his important contemporaries. After 1862, the problems imposed by the West figured largely in his thoughts, and his proposals for reform were issued years before the more famous utterances of K'ang Yu-wei and Chang Chih-tung.[11] Li made fundamental contributions by effecting a transition in the military and bureaucratic organizations of his period, introducing new ideas, new methods, and new types of men to the historical scene.

Our view of Li has been primarily that of a man *in his role,* reacting to institutional situations and to other men. Therefore, in attempting a summation of his career we have looked particularly to the men around him, that is, the men he represented and the men whom he brought upon the scene to play their roles during his lifetime and after his departure from the political stage. The changes which released China from her traditional style of social, political, and intellectual life and carried her to the twentieth century were brought about by a great number of men, some of whom have been identified in large letters, others of whom remain anonymous. Li Hung-chang's role as a leader makes him an inescapable object of historical study, but his significance can be grasped only in terms of the transition occurring around him. It was a transition which he reflected and at the same time speeded up.

Li's Advisers

Before examining the changes which occurred in Chinese leadership as a result of Li's influence, let us examine briefly the ideas and influence of the men upon whom Li relied for advice and support at various times in his career. Their contributions were of fundamental importance in Li's development, and their views helped to shape his decisions and policies. Most of them surpassed Li as writers, and their observations and proposals take an important place in the ideological

---

[11] Ssu-yü Teng and John K. Fairbank, *China's Response to the West,* pp. 205, 269, 147-49, 152-53. See also chapter 5 above. Also Hellmut Wilhelm, "The Problem of Within and Without, A Confucian Attempt in Syncretism," *Journal of the History of Ideas,* XII (1951), 48-60.

history of the late nineteenth century, but to a great extent their plans were realized principally through Li. Thus they are an integral part of Li's own biography, and a description of them is in part a description of Li as well.

Among the earliest of Li's advisers was Feng Kuei-fen, whom Li had known from his earliest days as a scholar of the Han-lin Academy.[12] As a fledgling governor in Kiangsu, Li relied heavily upon Feng for technical knowledge and administrative help. Later he was influenced by him in planning reforms in the land tax and public examination systems.[13] In recognition of Feng's counsel and guidance Li later recommended official promotion for the aged scholar.[14]

Kuo Sung-tao, one of the first men to undertake the reorganization of Kiangsu's revenues for Li Hung-chang during his early years in Shanghai, was perhaps the most eminent of Li's advisers on foreign affairs. While serving as China's first minister in England and France, Kuo acquired a good knowledge of Western social and political institutions and the problems of industrialization. While abroad and after his return, he maintained a regular correspondence with Li that dealt largely with the means by which China could be modernized. Kuo's thinking is amply reflected in Li's own writings and activities. His ideas were available to Li long before they were published, since some of his most important pronouncements were contained in his personal letters to Li. He was frankly critical of many of Li's undertakings and continually urged his colleague and former nominal superior to devote greater attention to fundamental theory and approaches. In one letter to Li Hung-chang he wrote:

In Hunan you emphasized the opening of coal and iron works, the purchase of machines, the operation of steamships, and you also planned to establish a large academy. These are majestic enterprises of great benefit to the people. However, they are not the basic things, nor are they the really urgent matters for the wealth and strength of our country. The wealth and

---

[12] *LWCK Memorials,* 9:24a, TC 4/7/22.

[13] See chapters 2 and 3 above. Mary Wright, *The Last Stand of Chinese Conservatism: The T'ung-Chih Restoration,* 1862-1874, p. 76, states, "He [Li] was greatly influenced by and indebted to his adviser, the penetrating Confucian theorist Feng Kuei-fen; but after Feng's death he chose different advisers and drifted away from Confucian orthodoxy." Perhaps the more fundamental reason, however, was that Confucian orthodoxy was useless in problems revolving around modern military technology and economy. For good outlines of Feng's views on various subjects see *ibid.,* pp. 65-68, 91-94, 163-67, 201-8. See also Teng and Fairbank, *China's Response to the West,* pp. 51-55, 137, 164, 269. Also Feng Kuei-fen, *Hsien-chih-t'ang kao, passim.*

[14] *LWCK Memorials,* 16:24a, TC 9/3/22.

strength of the Western lands are based upon commerce. . . . The state protects the merchants wholeheartedly. Every great labor or military undertaking is undertaken by the people and passed upon by the parliament. The people and nation interlock into one heart and one strength. The people and merchants enlarge their resources in order to safeguard the country.

But in China there is a gulf between the government and the people. Some men talk of wealth and strength. They think that this is a national business which has nothing to do with the people.

Kuo advised Li that the fundamental change required in China was a change in its institutional foundations. China had to be transformed through attention to "law, discipline, institutions, and state of mind, without which talk of wealth and strength will only increase the waste."[15]

Both Kuo Sung-tao and Feng Kuei-fen were mature scholars and leading members of the gentry of their respective provinces, Hunan and Kiangsu. They had served in the central government before the Taiping Rebellion and had been enticed into regional service by Tseng Kuo-fan, and to a lesser extent, Li Hung-chang. As Li grew more powerful, he used his influence to advance their positions. Although Li was five years younger than Kuo, both had attained their *chin-shih* degrees and been appointed to the Han-lin Academy in the same year, 1847. Between the two men there existed a *t'ung-nien* relationship, the same as that between Tseng Kuo-fan and Li Hung-chang's father previously described. After working with Li Hung-chang, Kuo rose to be acting governor of Kwangtung province in 1863, but later he suffered several reverses in his career, a fate not uncommon for bureaucrats who ventured into foreign diplomacy. He was subject to constant attack for his radical views and was finally retired in 1878, thirteen years before his death. Despite Kuo's unpopularity in his later years, Li continually urged the throne to give him adequate recognition in the form of promotion and rewards, and openly advanced Kuo's views.[16]

---

[15] Kuo Sung-tao, *Yang-chih shu-wu ch'üan-chi, wen-chi,* 13:17a-20a. Kuo Sung-tao's principal letters to Li are contained in the *wen-chi* section of his collected works, particularly *chüan* 10, pp. 19b ff., in which are discussed the entire development of English industry, the relative place of China and Japan in the family of nations, the current international situation in Europe and the Near East, and the implications of all of this for China. Kuo also proposed basic reforms in this monumental letter. In *chüan* 12, pp. 1a-4b, he discussed international law and attempted to dissuade Li from contemplating hostilities with France over Indo-China.

[16] Chung-li Chang and Stanley Spector (eds.), *Guide to the Memorials of Seven Leading Officials of Nineteenth-Century China,* p. 187; Teng and Fairbank, *China's Response to the West,* p. 106.

Feng Kuei-fen and Kuo Sung-tao were important to Li initially because of their grasp of problems of local administration and finance, the traditional fields of specialization for government servants in China. Their experience with Europeans dated roughly from the time Shanghai and the rest of Kiangsu were endangered by the Taipings and became of equal and pressing interest to the central government, the foreigners, the local gentry, and the emerging regional organizations of Tseng and Li. In this respect they grew contemporaneously with Li, and like him were rooted in the traditional order. Li did not influence them nearly so much as they influenced him, although he provided substantial support for them and their ideas.

Li was also indebted to his secretaries, Hsüeh Fu-ch'eng and Ma Chien-chung, for many of his advanced views on current questions. These men rose to important positions under Li's auspices. Neither made his mark in the traditional fields of philosophy or letters, as did Li's third outstanding secretary, Wu Ju-lun, but they contributed notable ideas on the practical problems of altering Chinese institutions to meet the challenge of the West.

Hsüeh Fu-ch'eng came to be widely known not only as the secretary who composed some of Li's most important letters and memorials but also as one of China's earliest diplomatic representatives in Europe and as a prolific writer of essays on commerce, mines, railroads, and foreign relations. These writings provided the basis for many of Li's most radical economic and military proposals.[17] Li Hung-chang took pains to keep such a valuable man close to him. In 1878 he supported Hsüeh strongly when the latter declined to go abroad on the orders of the Tsungli Yamen, giving as his reason that he was in mourning.[18] But soon afterward Li memorialized the throne, asking that Hsüeh be summoned to his own headquarters with all possible haste.[19] Li described Hsüeh as "a scholar, determined, possessing high ability and profound knowledge."[20] Hsüeh eventually was sent abroad and later returned to serve on Li's staff as an adviser on foreign policy. As was so often the case with men who were familiar with one aspect of

---

[17] Chao Feng-t'ien, *Wan-Ch'ing wu-shih-nien ching-chi ssu-hsiang shih*, *Yenching Journal of Chinese Studies*, Monograph Series No. 18 (Peiping, 1939), pp. 42-43, 58 ff., 150-51. See particularly Hsüeh's philosophical discussion on westernization written to a student on behalf of Li, in Hsüeh Fu-ch'eng, *Yung-an pi-chi* (1898), *wen-pien*, 2:38b-39b. See also *CSK*, 446:5a ff.; Hummel, *Eminent Chinese*, p. 331; Teng and Fairbank, *China's Response to the West*, pp. 88, 117-18, 124, 140-46.

[18] *LWCK Memorials*, 31:18a, KH 4/4/4.

[19] *Ibid.*, 34:10a, KH 5/3 int./19.

[20] *Ibid.*, 46:36a, KH 9/6/9.

Western culture, Hsüeh soon found himself studying all aspects. At Li's headquarters men were selected and trained for service and study abroad, and were encouraged to increase their store of Western knowledge on the job.

While Hsüeh served in Li's entourage as secretary and personal assistant, he furnished Li with ideas of fundamental importance. On the question of encouraging industry, Hsüeh took a particularly interesting stand, calling for a radical reform in the examination system:

> Once we talk about encouraging the development of various industries we should break up the barrier set up by the examination system. Abolish the distinction between *shih* [scholar] and *kung* [artisan, worker]. Let us not especially respect the *shih* and especially despise the *kung*. In ancient times there never was such discrimination. Now we should recover our ancient tradition with the support of Western methods.[21]

Hsüeh also discussed the problem of technological unemployment, fear of which apparently led many traditionalists to oppose industrialization:

> Machine manufacture will reduce the cost of labor and therefore the price. The goods will therefore be of fine quality and low cost. Some people object that this will throw men out of work. But this is not true, for when we do not use machines, our handmade goods cannot compete and will not be bought. Then the people will think it is useless to work, and only foreign goods will be bought. On the other hand if we build machines we can still feed hundreds and thousands of poor people. Even if the profits go to only a few rich people, still the poor workers will be fed. But if the profits go only to the foreigners, we will suffer a complete loss.[22]

Hsüeh strongly backed Li Hung-chang's mining enterprises, seeing them as especially important for military financing. He felt that certain mines should be opened and operated by the army (Li's Pei-yang forces) as a means of securing a steady income.[23] He was especially concerned about the drain of wealth from China to Europe through commerce and suggested that the government encourage trade by Chinese. His ideas in this field were almost identical with Li's statements on how to repair China's "leaking wine cup."[24]

Another outstanding secretary-adviser who provided Li Hung-chang with valuable ideas on foreign affairs and military development was Ma Chien-chung. Li described Ma as "an expert in French who had

---

21 Chao Feng-t'ien, *Wan-Ch'ing wu-shih-nien ching-chi ssu-hsiang shih*, p. 58.
22 *Ibid.*
23 *Ibid.*, p. 42.
24 *Ibid.*, pp. 89, 90.

also studied to pass the government examinations."[25] He had gained experience in foreign relations while serving as interpreter for Kuo Sung-tao. In 1876, when Li Hung-chang sent a group of students abroad to study ship construction, he appointed Ma as an aide to the group. During that year abroad Ma studied international law, diplomacy, science, government, and literature. Li summoned Ma to Tientsin as soon as he completed his studies in France and Germany. Upon his arrival he presented Li with five diplomas from European institutions. Li was satisfied that Ma was expert in both Chinese and Western affairs and relied on him heavily for diplomatic assignments, pushing him up quickly in the ranks of the bureaucracy.[26] Ma Chien-chung's talents were exploited in many fields including military training, planning political strategies in Korea, and management of the Chao Shang Chü.[27] Li's famous memorial advocating the creation of a united office of naval affairs was composed by this able assistant.[28] Ma's essays on mine opening and commerce are almost identical in word and idea to Li's various memorials on these subjects.[29]

All of these advisers, like Li himself, possessed backgrounds of classical education, although, passing from Feng Kuei-fen to Hsüeh and Ma, we can already note a change in the direction of westernization. All of these men were closer in type to Li than those whom he later employed in large numbers as specialists in his bureaucratic and military enterprises.

Li's Western Advisers

Li relied on occasion upon Westerners, who brought him ideas as well as practical knowledge and whose expert advice gave him an initial lead over most of his contemporaries. Little need be said of them here, for the careers of most of them, such as General Charles Gordon, Sir Halliday Macartney, and Sir Robert Hart, have been amply dealt with in individual biographies. With the exception of Hart, who always liked to consider himself a servant of the central government, these men, when they served China, did so only through Li, and in the course of thirty years provided him with much of the

[25] *LWCK Memorials,* 37:37a, KH 6/6/3.

[26] *Ibid.*

[27] *Ibid.,* 44:48a, KH 8/8/29; 49:52a-b, KH 10/4/17; 51:25a, KH 10/7/23.

[28] "Shang Li Po-hsiang fu-i Ho Hsüeh-shih ju-ch'ang tsou shui-shih shu," in *Huang-ch'ao ching-shih-wen t'ung-pien,* 81:1a-7b.

[29] Chao Feng-t'ien, *Wan-Ch'ing wu-shih-nien ching-chi ssu-hsiang shih,* pp. 44 ff., 89 ff. See also Teng and Fairbank, *China's Response to the West,* p. 95, Document 25, "Ma Chien-chung's Report on His Studies in France, 1877."

basic information he required to start China on the road to industrialization. Many of them, however, were disheartened and disturbed by
Li's reluctance to extend his plans for modernization beyond his own
military forces and beyond the regions he regarded as being of direct
concern to himself.

Perhaps the most important of Li's Western advisers over a long
period of time was the little-known American, William Pethick.
Pethick had gone to China soon after the Civil War in the United
States and had engaged in commercial activities in Tientsin. He
became tutor to Li's children and served as Li's personal secretary
until a short time before Li's death. Pethick also served for many
years as a member of the American consular corps in Tientsin, being
relieved of office when an irate but unrealistic consul discovered him
to be on Li's payroll.[30] Subsequent consuls were chagrined to find that
in the years following Pethick's dismissal from the consulate, orders
for American machinery and requests for American assistance to Li's
modernization program dwindled perceptibly.[31] Pethick obtained for
Li the services of American engineers, mineralogists, and railroad
experts, and assisted him in developing an adequate library in these
fields.[32]

The contributions of Westerners to China's modernization were by
no means slight. The fact that Western help was so readily available
shows that the basic problem of China in the nineteenth century was
not the lack of available knowledge or experts but rather the failure
to make adequate use of them. Except for Pethick, who seems to have
gained Li's fullest confidence, Li was, with reason, suspicious of the
motives of Westerners who came to China to make their fortunes. He
realized the extent of the ambitions of Macartney and Gordon, and
saw Hart as giving service to the central government at the expense of
his own position. He accepted advice from men like Gordon, Hart, and
Macartney only when his own interests and his machine were not
thereby threatened. But even so, Li's failure to meet new conditions
quickly and effectively went beyond any matter of individual will. The
official stamp that characterized Li's whole organization, itself a
notable symbol of the social change at work within the bureaucracy,

---

[30] *Tientsin Consular Despatches,* Mar. 1, 1894; Apr. 2, 1894.

[31] Consul Read, who fired Pethick, warned the Department that he expected Pethick
to "take retribution"; *ibid.* Later consuls wrote letters supporting Pethick and describing him as a "true-blue American" and a good connection for American commerce; *ibid.,* July 9, 1898.

[32] The Tientsin Consular Despatches for the years 1880-96 make numerous references to the growing influence of the American interests in the north.

carried with it centuries of tradition, habits of thought, action, and attitude, which could not easily be shed. Li's bureaucratic machine, for all its innovations, was part of the body of Chinese society and government, representing at once the best and worst of both.

Li's Civilian Staff and the Transition in Leadership

The men upon whom Li relied for the planning and execution of the public and private affairs with which he dealt were for the most part transitional types within the bureaucracy, as can be seen by scrutinizing their origins, functions, and careers. In order to perceive the nature and meaning of the transition in personnel types that was taking place, it is desirable to attempt some form of classification. The problem of classifying the members of Li's bureaucratic machine is difficult, however, because of the characteristics of the machine itself. In the formal system employed by the Chinese government of the time, officials were designated as "civil" or "military" (*wen* or *wu*) on the basis of their degrees and official titles and positions, but such designations do not reveal the actual functions of the officials. Li Hung-chang himself was ranked as a civil official, yet essentially he was a military man. The same is true of Tseng Kuo-fan, Tso Tsung-t'ang, and later of Yüan Shih-k'ai. In the Ch'ing system high provincial officials had always had military as well as civil functions, but the leaders mentioned above—with the possible exception of Yüan— rose to power primarily as military leaders. In the lower levels of the bureaucracy a much clearer delineation of civil and military existed in the traditional bureaucratic order, but in the latter half of the nineteenth century realists like Li tended to ignore the traditional order in their efforts to place the right men in the right jobs. The natural relations between various civil and military tasks made it inevitable that the formal lines of distinction should be cast aside. Gradually there began to emerge a new type of official, experienced in military supply and logistics, and—because all these matters were related to modernization—learned in Western affairs. There were many of these new officials in Li Hung-chang's machine. While Li's various armies and his fleet remained under the immediate command of military men with traditional military titles and ranks, there grew up around his military establishment a bureaucratic group which was simultaneously military and civil.

Leaving for a later section the large group of men who served Li as strictly military officers, or who rose to high *civil* positions through

the military route, we can place the remaining members of Li's bureaucratic machine roughly in two classifications, which often overlap:
(1) men concerned with various aspects of administration, performing
traditional bureaucratic functions as well as servicing Li's military
machine, and (2) men devoted to tasks involving industrialization,
trade, and relations with the Western powers. Although working for
Li usually meant dealing at one time or another with military and
Western affairs, there remained a small group that can be designated
essentially non-Western oriented. Among approximately fifty men who
were mentioned by Li as important assistants, we can find only a few
who were neither military nor Western-oriented.

Functionaries in Traditional and Military Support Services

Most of the officials who did not become primarily concerned with
Western matters were men who had entered Li's service in Kiangsu
during the Taiping Rebellion. These recipients of Li's patronage were
rewarded for able administration of revenue offices and for carrying
on regular administrative tasks loyally and efficiently while Li was
struggling to obtain thorough control of Shanghai and Kiangsu
province.

The most prominent of these men, Feng Kuei-fen, who has already
been mentioned as one of Li's earliest advisers, performed his service
in his local gentry capacity, as did Ch'ien Ting-ming, who first
arranged Li's expedition to Shanghai. Ch'en Nai, who originally helped
Li gain a position at Tseng's headquarters and was repaid when Li
transferred him to his own service, seems to have had a routine bureaucratic career in his later years. Li brought him to Chihli, where he
served as a circuit intendant.[33] Chin Fu-tseng, who joined Li in 1862
and participated in the attack on Soochow, stayed with Li in Kiangsu
and later remained there, helping in the financing of Li's forces while
Li was engaged in the north. In 1881 Li summoned him to Chihli,
where he rose to the rank of expectant circuit intendant and achieved
a reputation as an expert on waterworks.[34] Ho Shen-hsiu was recommended by Tseng Kuo-fan and accepted on Li's staff, where he
handled financial affairs. He had a traditional background, had received the degree of *chü-jen*, and was listed as an expectant Grand
Secretary.[35] Another man highly recommended by Li was the circuit

---

[33] *LWCK Memorials*, 7:35a, TC 3/9/3; 61:62a, KH 13/12/14.
[34] *Ibid.*, 76:47a, KH 19/5/7.
[35] *Ibid.*, 11:18a, TC 6/2/20; 15:30a, TC 8/6/27.

intendant candidate, Kao T'i, holder of a *chü-jen* degree and a native
of Kiangsi. He worked at Li's army encampments and particularly
gratified Li by his skillful handling of relief in the Huai area.[36]
Another early adherent of Li's was K'uai Te-mo, a native of Li's own
province, Anhwei. He assisted Li in the recovery of Soochow and
became an acting prefectural magistrate of that city. Li recommended
K'uai as the holder of a *kung-sheng* degree who "helped the merchants
and farmers, reduced the tribute, and suppressed the local bandits.[37]
We have already mentioned still another early aide at Li's Kiangsu
headquarters, Wang Ta-ching, who served Li as a manager of likin
bureaus, and whom Li used in his efforts to unseat the entrenched
bureaucracy at Shanghai.[38]

All of these men appear to have been degree-holders, traditionally
oriented, who came up as men entrusted with the vital job of raising
funds while Li's organization was still in its formative stage. Their
degrees, together with Li's recommendations, enabled them to rise
through the ordinary routes within the bureaucracy. They represent
the classical type of gentry-bureacrat, the starting point of the
transition.

Western-Oriented Functionaries

The vast majority of Li's civilian followers were men who dealt
largely in affairs that required knowledge of the West. As they are
too numerous to be discussed individually, their composition and background have been given in tabular form in Table 17. The men whom
Li employed to promote and manage the mines, telegraphs, railways
and, most important of all, the Chao Shang Chü, to deal with customs
work and foreign relations, and to modernize military forces were the
products of the new conditions in the coastal areas of China, directly
subject to the influence of the West. They were men who studied the
technical and commercial aspects of Western culture and used their
new knowledge to break into, or advance within, the government
bureaucracy. Few of them, however, attained any positions independently. Except for Li's extensive organization, and perhaps those
of a few other leaders like him, there was no place for such men until
the central government itself belatedly realized the need for central

---

[36] *Ibid.,* 10:42a ff., TC 5/9/7.
[37] *Ibid.*
[38] *Ibid.,* 9:74a, TC 4/12/19; 10:42a-43a, TC 5/9/7.

TABLE 17

WESTERN-ORIENTED FUNCTIONARIES UNDER LI

Name	Birthplace	Background	Function and Career
Chang Hung-chün[1]		Han-lin compiler	Assisted Li in diplomacy. Pei-yang Coastal Defense. Recommended for circuit intendancy
Chang Shih-heng[2]	Anhwei	*Chü-jen* degree	Expert on Western weapons and arms production and lien-chün supplies. Both military and civil merits
Chang Yin-huan[3]	Canton	Failed examinations; purchased title	Foreign relations. Circuit intendant at Chefoo. Minister to the United States
Ch'en Ch'in[4]		Secretary, Board of Punishments; recommended by Tseng Kuo-fan	Customs intendant. Specialized in drafting customs regulations and treaties
Ch'en Fu-hsün[5]	Chekiang	Money merchant; Shanghai United Defense Bureau. Recommended for district magistracy	Employed to help manage Shanghai Machinery Bureau. Responsible for Chinese-Western affairs at Shanghai
Ch'en Hung-chü[6]	Anhwei	*Hsiu-ts'ai* degree Assistant to Tseng Kuo-fan	Military finance for Li's armies. General coastal defense affairs in Chihli. Served in machinery and telegraph bureau, waterworks. Huai army man
Ch'en Lan-pin[7]	Canton	Assistant secretary, Board of Punishments. *Chin-shih* degree	Supervised students in America. Diplomatic and overseas career

See footnotes at end of table.

Name	Birthplace	Background	Function and Career
Ch'en Shu-t'ang[8]			Diplomatic and overseas career
Ch'en Yün-i[9]			Telegraph commissioner
Cheng Tsao-ju[10]	Canton	*Chü-jen* degree	Customs, machinery bureau, and arsenal specialist in Shanghai and Tientsin
Chu Ch'i-ang[11]	Kiangsu	Held no degree but obtained official title. Merchant family	Local-corps leader. Boat operator. Together with Li established *Chao Shang Chü*. First merchant, then official manager. Appointed Tientsin customs intendant
Chu Ch'i-chao[12]	Kiangsu	Probably purchased degree	Expectant circuit intendant. Succeeded his brother, Chu Ch'i-ang, as manager of *Chao Shang Chü*. Founder of various mining enterprises
Feng Chün-kuang[13]	Canton	*Chü-jen* degree. Originally followed Tseng Kuo-fan	Customs, machinery bureaus, shipyards, defense work
Hsieh Chia-fu[14]	Kiangsu	Government student	Managed telegraph affairs. Li assigned him to an official post
Hsü Jen[15]	Kiangsu	Merchant	Circuit intendant in Shanghai. Merchant manager of *Chao Shang Chü*

See footnotes at end of table.

TABLE 17, continued

Name	Birthplace	Background	Function and Career
Hsü Wen-ta[16]			Financial commissioner. Under Li Hung-chang led Huai troops to Shanghai in 1862. Military finance. Entered in Huai-chün shrine
Jung Hung [Yung Wing][17]	Canton	Studied in United States	One of the first Chinese to study in the United States. Later purchased machinery for the Shanghai Machinery Bureau. Supervised Chinese educational mission to America. Railway financier, industrialist. Title of circuit intendant
Ku Chao-hsi[18]			Rose to be salt intendant. Managed flood relief in Tientsin. In charge of commercial affairs, waterworks
Kung Chao-yü[19]			Circuit intendant. Ship bureau, water and land transportation. Pei-yang machinery bureaus for twenty years. Expert in Western technology
Li Chao-t'ang[20]	Kwangtung	*Chin-shih* degree	Customs and foreign affairs. Secretary in Tsungli Yamen
Li Chin-yung[21]	Kiangsu	Military; subprefect	Joined Li Hung-chang in 1862, performing military service. Then in charge of military rations. Concerned with military affairs in Chihli. Became circuit intendant at Mo-ho gold mines

See footnotes at end of table.

TABLE 17, continued

Name	Birthplace	Background	Function and Career
Li Feng-pao[22]	Kiangsu	*Hsiu-ts'ai* degree	Started at Shanghai Machinery Bureau. Ship-building. Foreign affairs. Minister to Germany
Li Hsing-jui[23]		*Hsiu-ts'ai* degree. *Mu-yu* of Tseng Kuo-fan	Served as Li's assistant in Chihli. Foreign affairs. Minister to Japan
Li Shu-ch'ang[24]	Kweichow	*Mu-yu* of Tseng Kuo-fan	Diplomacy. Minister to Japan
Li Yüan-hua[25]	Possibly Anhwei	*Chü-jen* degree. District magistrate. Local-corps organizer in Anhwei	Huai Army affairs. Tientsin coastal defense. Became Shantung financial commissioner. In KH 3 appointed acting governor of Shantung
Ling Huan[26]		Probably held civil degree	Trade affairs and treaty negotiations
Liu Ch'i-hsiang[27]	Probably Anhwei	Relative of Li Hung-chang	Director of Shanghai Machinery Bureau
Liu Han-fang[28]	Anhwei		Followed Li to Shanghai in 1862. Grain transportation. Merits in Nien campaign. Circuit intendant. Personnel director for machinery bureaus. Helped establish navy. Customs and military affairs
Liu Ju-i[29]			Machinery bureau; customs affairs
Lo Feng-lu[30]	Fukien		Naval and personal secretary of Li Hung-chang. Western affairs

See footnotes at end of table.

TABLE 17, continued

Name	Birthplace	Background	Function and Career
Ou E-liang[31]	Canton	*Han-lin* scholar	Foreign affairs; overseas service
She Ch'ang-yü[32]			Telegraph manager
Shen Pao-ching[33]	Kiangsu	*Chü-jen* degree	Served at Li's military headquarters. Shanghai Machinery Bureau, then Tientsin Machinery Bureau. Foreign affairs; customs
Sheng Hsüan-huai[34]	Kiangsu	*Sheng-yüan*: purchased *chu-shih* title	Office assistant in Tientsin; destroyed Woosung railway; helped establish *Chao Shang Chü*; planned construction of telegraph from Tientsin to Shanghai; head of telegraph company; manager of *Chao Shang Chü*; customs intendant of Tientsin; founder of Shanghai Cotton Mill; Kaiping mine administration; railway administration; became chairman of board for Kaiping mines; tried to finance Hankow Lu-kou-ch'iao railway. After 1898 became head of new Board of Trade and Communications. Leading financier of Shanghai. One of the wealthiest men in the country
Tai Tsung-ch'ien[35]	Anhwei	*Hsiu-ts'ai* degree Local-corps organizer	Joined Li at Shanghai in 1862; later became *mu-yu* of Li; promoted to prefectural magistrate. River transportation. Huai and lien-chün management. A principal military and naval strategist

See footnotes at end of table.

TABLE 17, continued

Name	Birthplace	Background	Function and Career
T'ang T'ing-shu[36]	Canton		Manager of *Chao Shang Chü*. Promoter and manager of Kaiping mines
Ting Shou-ch'ang[37]	Anhwei	Military merits	Early follower of Li; later commanded cavalry at Tientsin. Remained in Tientsin to manage military and foreign affairs. Customs intendant. Rose to rank of judicial commissioner
Wu Chia-shan[38]	Kwangtung		Supervised Chinese students abroad. Concerned with Western education and machinery bureaus
Wu Chih-ch'ang[39]	Probably Kwangtung	Spoke Western languages	Connected with *Chao Shang Chü*. Became manager of Kaiping mines
Wu Chung-hsiang[40]		Employed at Foochow shipyards. Expectant circuit intendant	Joined Li at Tientsin in 1880. Director of water-force academy. Naval training. Promoted to circuit intendant
Wu Ju-lun[41]	Anhwei	Civil degree	Li Hung-chang's personal secretary and adviser
Wu T'ing-fang[42]	Canton	Brought up in Singapore; English law degree at Hong Kong	Li Hung-chang's legal adviser and foreign affairs deputy. Promoted railways, co-director of Imperial North Chinese Railways. Director of Tientsin University. Assistant to Li in peace negotiations of 1895. Minister to United States

See footnotes at end of table.

TABLE 17, continued

Name	Birthplace	Background	Function and Career
Wu Tsang-ch'eng[48]	Kwangtung	Expert in Western mathematics	Recommended to Li by Ting Jih-ch'ang. Assisted at Li's headquarters during Nien campaign. Supervisor of arsenals and factories at Shanghai and Tientsin
Yang Chieh[44]	Kiangsu	Nephew of Yang Tsung-lien	Worked as secretary in Li's office. Served at Huai-Ming-Chün arsenal in Formosa
Yang Shou-mei[45]	Kiangsu	Son of Yang Tsung-lien	Assisted father, serving under Li. Official specializing in industrial affairs. Established cotton, oil, telephone, and electric companies in Wu-hsi, Kiangsu
Yang Tsung-lien[46]	Kiangsu	Civil degree-holder	Customs intendant at Hankow. Summoned by Li to establish military academy in Tientsin. Invited members of family to join staff. Circuit intendant in Chihli. Later established arsenals and factories in Shansi. Continued to serve in Shansi and Chihli. Worked with Yüan Shih-k'ai. After death entered in Huai-chün and Li Hung-chang shrines
Yeh T'ing-chüan[47]	Kwangtung		Assistant manager of *Chao Shang Chü*. Specialized in sea transport and Western affairs. Became Kiangsu circuit intendant

See footnotes at end of table.

TABLE 17, continued

Name	Birthplace	Background	Function and Career
Ying Pao-shih[48]	Chekiang	*Chü-jen* degree; lower official in Shanghai	Arranged transportation for Li's army in 1862. Promoted to circuit intendancy. Shanghai defense bureau. Scholar and administrator
Yüan Ta-hua[49]	Anhwei		Commissioner in charge of Mo-ho mines. Expectant district magistrate. Managed lien-chün affairs

1 *LWCK Memorials*, 55:13a, KH 11/9/28.

2 *Ibid.*, 74:16a, KH 18/3/11.

3 Hummel, *Eminent Chinese*, p. 60; Chang Yin-huan originally worked for Ting Pao-chen. Later he served under Li Han-chang at Hupeh. He subsequently was transferred to assist Li Hung-chang in diplomatic negotiations. Hsiao Kung-ch'uan, "Weng T'ung-ho and the Reform Movement of 1898," *Tsing Hua Journal of Chinese Studies*, N.S., I, 111-245, notes that Chang Yin-huan assisted Weng T'ung-ho in the negotiations concerning the Shantung incident in 1897. These negotiations broke down and the government was finally forced to appeal to Li Hung-chang for help. Hsiao believes that Chang was closely enough associated with Li to have deliberately sabotaged Weng's efforts in order to open the way for Li to be recalled (pp. 118, 138-39). See also *CSK*, 442:6b-7b.

4 *LWCK Memorials*, 17:14a, TC 9/10/26.

5 *Shanghai-hsien hsü-chih*, 15:2b.

6 *CSK*, 451:5b.

7 *LWCK Memorials*, 25:13a, KH 1/4/12; Hummel, *Eminent Chinese*, pp. 61, 404.

8 *LWCK Memorials*, 46:59a, KH 9/6/21.

9 *Ibid.*, 54:53a, KH 11/8/15.

10 *Ibid.*, 19:51a, TC 11/5/15; 32:3a, KH 4/6/17; 33:19a, KH 4/9/26.

11 *CSK*, 452:3a-b; *LWCK Memorials*, 25:4a-5a, KH 1/2/27; 31:38a ff., KH 4/5/14.

12 *CSK*, 452:3b; LWCK Memorials, 31:38a ff., KH 4/5/14.

13 *LWCK Memorials*, 19:51a, 11/5/15; *Shanghai-hsien hsü-chih*, 15:3b; *Sung-chiang-fu hsü-chih*, 21:26a. Feng attracted some attention in Ameri-

can circles owing to an unfortunate incident. Feng had arrested the comprador of an American, Hill, for refusing to carry machinery sold by Hill to Feng. Hill testified: "I took my man from there, and took Feng by his cue and brought him back to my place. I was exceedingly angry at the time, so when I got him there I tied him up and took off his jacket and cowhided him until I was tired. That is the cause of his animosity against me; that is the reason he decided against me in my case. Feng refused to permit Hill to operate a small railroad from Shanghai. 45 Congress, 2 session, House Miscellaneous Document 31, pt. 2, p. 80 (Washington, D.C.: Government Printing Office, 1878).

14 *LWCK Memorials*, 54:54a, KH 11/8/15; *CSK*, 451:8b.

15 *LWCK Memorials*, 41:20a ff., KH 7/6/9. Hsü Jen was denounced for corruption, being accused of holding private stocks in a company bought out by the *Chao Shang Chü* at an exorbitant price. Li defended Hsü Jen, but did so rather hesitantly.

16 *Ibid.*, 69:29a, KH 16/10/29.

17 Yung Wing, *My Life in China and America, passim*.; Teng Ssu-yü and John K. Fairbank, *China's Response to the West*, pp. 64, 91-95, 134; Mary Wright, *The Last Stand of Chinese Conservatism*, p. 239.

18 *LWCK Memorials*, 73:11a, KH 17/10/14.

19 *Ibid.*, 79:36a, KH 20/11/12.

20 *Ibid.*, 24:6b, TC 13/10/16; Mary Wright, *The Last Stand of Chinese Conservatism*, p. 230, mentions Li Chao-t'ang as one of the Tsungli Yamen secretaries who rose to an important policy-making position because of his experience with that body. Li Hung-chang seems to have valued Li Chao-t'ang's experience highly, mentioning it prominently in his recommendation of Li Chao-t'ang.

TABLE 17, footnotes continued

21 *LWCK Memorials*, 69:40a ff., KH 16/11/16. Li described Li Chin-yung as being "among the first to open the old-fashioned customs of our country." See also *CSK*, 451:7a.

22 *CSK*, 446:7a; Hummel, *Eminent Chinese*, p. 312; Mary Wright, *The Last Stand of Chinese Conservatism*, p. 230; *LWCK Memorials*, 46:1a ff., KH 9/1/20. In this memorial Li strongly defends Li Feng-pao's conduct and background. Li Feng-pao had been accused of obtaining his position through fraudulent means, of being the son of a peddler, and of immorality. See also *LWCK Memorials*, 55:4a, KH 11/9/5, in which Li wants Li Feng-pao to assist him in dealing with German naval officers.

23 *CSK*, 447:10b; *LWCK Memorials*, 20:41a, TC 11/12/9; 60:23a, KH 13/6/8.

24 Li Shu-ch'ang came to Li from Tseng Kuo-fan's *mu-fu*. See Hummel, *Eminent Chinese*, pp. 65, 483; *CSK*, 446:6a; *LWCK Memorials*, 69:21a ff., KH 16/9/15. He assisted Li Hung-chang in important questions concerning the development of relations with Japan.

25 *LWCK Memorials*, 54:37a, KH 11/7/8.

26 *Ibid.*, 18:73a, TC 10/10/11.

27 *Ibid.*, 77:4a, KH 19/6/16; Hsiao Kung-ch'uan, "Weng T'ung-ho and the Reform Movement of 1898," *Tsing Hua Journal of Chinese Studies*, N.S., I, 128, mentions Liu as being related to Li Hung-chang; Hummel, *Eminent Chinese*, p. 855.

28 *CSK*, 451:4b-5a; *LWCK Memorials*, 71:35a, KH 17/3/19; 73:3a, KH 17/9/16; 77:15a, KH 19/8/16.

29 *LWCK Memorials*, 78:57a, KH 20/8/3.

30 Alicia Little, *Li Hung-chang*, p. 203, writes, "He owed his advancement in the first instance to Li Hung-chang and has done him credit." See also Hsiao Kung-ch'uan, "Weng T'ung-ho and the Reform Movement of 1898," *Tsing Hua Journal of Chinese Studies*, N.S., I, 132 and 206 (n. 121), with Weng T'ung-ho's evaluation of Lo as "a very intelligent man."

31 *LWCK Memorials*, 25:13a, KH 1/4/12; 33:35a ff., KH 4/11/24.

32 *LWCK Memorials*, 65:31a, KH 15/5/22; 74:17a, KH 18/3/11.

33 *CSK*, 452:3a; *LWCK Memorials*, 17:5a, TC 9/10/3; 17:14a, TC 9/10/26; 58:38, KH 12/11/20; 71:38a, KH 17/4/1.

34 *CSK*, 471:1a; *LWCK Memorials*, 43:42a, KH 8/3/6; 29:9a, KH 3/2/24; 49:45a, KH 10/4/16; 54:52a, KH 11/8/15; 74:30a ff., KH 18/5/24.

35 *CSK*, 460:3b.

36 *LWCK Memorials*, 42:27a, KH 7/10/26; 41:20a ff., KH 7/6/9.

37 *CSK*, 451:2a; *Hsü Tientsin-hsien-chih* (1870), 9:7a; *Tientsin fu-chih* (1899), 40:2a; *LWCK Memorials*, 29:22a, KH 3/5/28; 29:46a, KH 3/8/8; 68:37a-38a, KH 16/7/29.

38 *LWCK Memorials*, 42:28a, KH 7/10/26.

39 *Ibid.*, 42:27a, KH 7/10/11.

40 *Ibid.*, 40:47a, KH 7/4/23; 52:9a, KH 10/11/15; 53:29a, KH 11/3/14. Li Hung-chang fought strongly to keep Wu at Tientsin after Tso Tsung-t'ang ordered Wu back to Foochow.

41 Teng and Fairbank, *China's Response to the West*, p. 88. Wu was the compiler of *Li Wen-chung kung ch'üan-chi*.

42 See Wu Ting-fang's biography in a despatch from Consul Read to Assistant Secretary of State Rockhill, *Tientsin Consular Despatches*, Dec. 19, 1896; *LWCK Memorials*, 58:3a ff., KH 12/9/4.

43 *LWCK Memorials*, 22:50a, TC 12/11/19; 19:51a, TC 11/5/15.

44 *Hsi-chin yu-hsiang t'ung-jen tzu-shu hui-k'an*, 1:2a. Yang Chieh also managed a book store at Tientsin for another of Li's protégés, Sheng Hsüan-huai. While working at Li's office, Yang collected all of Li's correspondence for publication. Unfortunately the manuscripts and copies were lost during the occupations of Tientsin by foreign troops.

45 *Ibid.*, chüan *hsia*, pp. 1a-13a.

46 *Ibid.*, chüan *hsia*, pp. 1a-13a; *CSK*, 452:1b; *LWCK Memorials*, 55:48a, KH 11/12/13.

47 *LWCK Memorials*, 32:20a, KH 4/7/23; *Shanghai-hsien-chih*, 12:25a.

48 *Shanghai-hsien hsü-chih*, 15:1b. Ying was noted for having carried on research on ancient music and rites. He established the Lung-men Academy and invited famous scholars and lecturers. He also established a center for vaccination and a poorhouse. He rose to become provincial judicial commissioner. See also *LWCK Memorials*, 5:46a, TC 2/11/28; 9:73a, TC 4/12/28. In describing Ying's efforts to bring the Huai-chün to Shanghai, Li wrote in later years: "When I recall these many incidents I can never forget him." *Ibid.*, 71:50a, KH 7/4/10.

bureaus of trade and communications at the close of the century.[39]
So long as the government did not successfully challenge Li's pre-
eminent rights in these fields, he and his organization were the principal dispensers of official favors for those with interest and ability in
the fields of new importance.

One cannot but be struck by the tremendous scope of the responsibility undertaken by the members of Li's civil machine. Men such
as Sheng Hsüan-huai, Chu Ch'i-chao, T'ang T'ing-shu, Wu T'ing-fang,
and Yang Tsung-lien, in addition to their circuit and customs inten-
dancies, took upon themselves the management of arsenals, mines,
railways, telegraphs, and virtually every other modern enterprise that
Li promoted. The largest enterprise, the Chao Shang Chü, with its
twenty-seven branches throughout China, was the training ground for
many of these men. It was an object of constant interest to them, both
as a source of private profits and as a means of access to all other
types of commercial enterprise. The concentration of control over the
new industries in the hands of so few men, all of whom acknowledged
Li's leadership, shows how little opportunity for advancement in the
new fields existed outside Li's own organization. Li's followers constituted the interlocking directorates of the enterprises, and they used
their positions as officials to bolster their monopoly. The many
branches of the machine brought together the power and capital
necessary for heavy industrial development, but the more ambitious
the enterprise the less sufficient was the organization to operate it.

The career of Sheng Hsüan-huai furnishes perhaps the most striking example of the role played by Li's bureaucratic machine in China's
economic development as a whole, as well as in the extension of Li
Hung-chang's own power.[40] Sheng first served as a minor member of
Li's staff in Kiangsu, where he appears to have served in the financial
and commercial offices connected with customs collection and Huai-
chün provisioning. When Li transferred to Chihli, Shen accompanied
him, and soon afterward, probably on the basis of his connections in

[39] In 1897 the North Chinese Railways were brought under the control of the Imperial Chinese Railway Administration, a fact which an American consul noted as
being of importance only "because it strengthens Taotai Sheng Hsüan-huai's hand."
Tientsin Consular Despatches, Jan. 30, 1897. The only real change that occurred as a
result of the establishment of central government bureaus of trade and communications was that Sheng and his group were now completely entrenched, without Li as
overlord. In addition it proved to be one of the last feeble attempts of the central
government to reassert itself independently of the control of a strong northern regional leader. Ultimately this failed, and Sheng's inability to solve the railroad
problem for the central government was the spark that touched off the Revolution of
1911.
[40] *CSK,* 471:1a ff.

Shanghai, was designated to assist Chu Ch'i-ang in drawing up the regulations for the establishment of the Chao Shang Chü. From that time onward Sheng remained a key figure in the administration of the new steamship line. He gained notoriety in connection with the destruction of the Shanghai-Woosung Railway in 1875 and 1876. This railway had originally been built without authority by British and American merchants in Shanghai. After the road had been in operation for about six months, an accident involving a loss of life occurred, whereupon the Chinese officials in Shanghai protested and took steps to acquire the railroad. The protest was actually inspired from Tientsin, with Li Hung-chang and Sheng Hsüan-huai probably directing from behind the scenes. The apparently "reactionary" Chinese officials who ultimately bought up and destroyed the Woosung railway were Sheng Hsüan-huai, Chu Ch'i-chao, and Feng Chün-kuang, mainstays of the Li machine and three of the principal economic reformers in China. Despite the angry protests of the British and Americans, who accordingly wrote highly colored versions of the incident, there can be no doubt that the destruction of the Woosung Railway by Sheng and his associates was a nationalistic measure, one that was aimed at foreigners rather than at foreign innovations.[41] It is true that operation of the railroad could have been continued under Chinese auspices, but Li apparently believed that it could not long remain clear of foreign control in the foreign-dominated Shanghai port region, and his own distance from Shanghai made him little inclined to engage in contests with the foreigners there. Consequently he employed his most "westernized" men to put an end to the matter once and for all.

Sheng's experience in the negotiations over the Woosung Railway made him Li's choice for the intricate negotiations for the purchase of foreign-constructed telegraphs and the laying of the land line from Tientsin to Shanghai. This involved, among other things, the settlement of the important question of connecting the new lines to the underseas cables of the Western companies. Sheng was then appointed manager of the Chinese National Telegraph Administration, with headquarters in Shanghai and Tientsin. During this period he was also appointed to supervise the opening of mines in Hu-Kuang, a project that Li later abandoned, and served temporarily as customs intendant of Tientsin, again through appointment by Li.[42] A reorgan-

---

[41] See the American documents on the Woosung Railroad Case in House Miscellaneous Document No. 31, pt. 2, 45 Cong., 2 sess. (Washington, 1878), containing a wealth of materials on all aspects of the dispute.

[42] *CSK*, 471 :2a ff.

ization of the Chao Shang Chü in 1885 resulted in Li's appointing Sheng to the management of that enterprise, in which he already had a considerable private fortune invested.[43] Later Sheng was made regular customs intendant of Tientsin and subsequently was designated by Li to promote the sale of shares for the erection of the Shanghai Weaving Mills.[44] When the Kaiping mines and railway were established, Sheng was again a principal director, as were other customs officials and Chao Shang Chü managers.

Sheng's rapid acquisition of such wide powers brought him into quiet conflict with his erstwhile patron-partner, Li Hung-chang. His varied experiences were an asset which other leaders, particularly Chang Chih-tung, were quick to note and call upon. On the basis of his great influence in the fields of commercial and industrial promotion, he became the leader of the merchant groups in Shanghai and other areas who wished to share the economic opportunities afforded by modern enterprise. Sheng avoided any break with Li, however, until the collapse of the Huai-chün and the-Pei-yang navy ended Li's direct power in the north. Thereafter Sheng allied himself with Chang Chih-tung, attempting, with questionable success, to ingratiate himself also with Yüan Shih-k'ai, the new rising military leader of the north. Soon after the Sino-Japanese War a Western writer described Sheng as "for years Li's special protégé, then his decidedly treacherous rival, and now occupying the best posts in China for making money, as Administrator of Railways, Mines, Telegraphs, etc."[45] The same writer relates that Sheng closed his public offices during the Sino-Japanese War and reopened them as gambling houses where men seeking lucrative contracts from him were forced to play—and pay.[46]

In his later years Sheng completely abandoned Li Hung-chang's original principle of borrowing from foreigners only in emergencies and even then only on extremely strict terms. This shows how much more Sheng's interest was purely commercial in contrast to Li's broader concern with the problems of diplomacy and national defense.[47] Li did not hesitate to take profits from his enterprises, but this

---

[43] See review of "First Edition of Drafts of Sheng Hsüan-huai," by Ch'en Ch'i-t'ien, in *Yenching Journal of Social Studies,* Vol. III, No. 2 (August, 1941) ; *LWCK Memorials,* 41 :20a ff., KH 7/2/11; 36 :35a ff., KH 6/3/27. Li admitted that Sheng and other officials had invested in the company.

[44] Ch'en Ch'i-t'ien, *op. cit.*

[45] Alicia Little, *Li Hung-chang, His Life and Times,* p. 159.

[46] Alicia Little, *Intimate China* (London, 1899), p. 613.

[47] See the reference to Sheng's later activities in the biography of Chang Chihtung, in Hummel, *Eminent Chinese,* pp. 27-31. See also the report on Sheng and foreign loans in *Tientsin Consular Despatches,* May 12, 1896.

was clearly secondary to his larger purpose of regional development and support of his military forces, or "wealth and strength" in the classic sense of the preceding period. Sheng therefore represents the end point of the transition in personnel types, from officials who through the existence of new conditions became involved in commercial affairs and westernization to merchants who seized the opportunities offered by the Li machine to carve rich industrial and commercial careers for themselves under the cover of official titles and with the protection of the government itself.[48]

Military Leadership under Li

The character of Li's Huai-chün, his Pei-yang lien-chün, and his Pei-yang fleet can be determined in part by an examination of the origins, training, affiliations, and careers of their commanding officers. A list of these officers, with information about them, drawn mainly from Li's memorials but supported by other available data, is given in Table 18.

The regional nature of Li's military machine is quite evident in the data presented in this list. Forty-eight of the eighty-four commanders were definitely natives of Anhwei, and two others also were probably from Li's native province. Eight of the commanders were from Hunan, and the rest from other provinces. The origins of ten of the men in question could not be determined. Only eight of these military commanders possessed, so far as could be ascertained, civil degrees of any sort. Not all of the men were members of the Huai-chün organization. The three from Fukien were all naval men; two of them served in the Pei-yang fleet, while the third was transferred to Kwangtung. Most of the men from Hunan came into Li's service while Li was under the command of Tseng and the Huai and Hsiang armies were engaged in joint campaigns. These men remained with Li thereafter and were among his most trusted commanders.

Honan province was represented by the members of the Yüan family. This group, too, came into the Huai-chün by way of Tseng Kuo-fan's Hsiang organization, although Yüan Chia-san was actually an independent leader and not a member of either the Hsiang or Huai

---

[48] According to Ch'en Ch'i-t'ien, "First Edition of Drafts of Sheng Hsüan-huai," *Yenching Journal of Social Studies,* Vol. III, No. 2, Sheng spent over one million and several hundred thousand liang on charity alone. This is some indication of the extent of the fortune he made as a bureaucratic entrepreneur.

TABLE 18

Li's Military Officers

Name	Army	Place of Origin	Career
Chang Hai-lung[1]	Huai	Hunan	Recommended for provincial commander in chief
Chang Kao-yüan[2]	Huai	Ho-fei, Anhwei	Under Liu Ming-ch'uan. Brigadier general
Chang Shu-p'ing[3]	Huai	Ho-fei, Anhwei	Local corps; Huai officer. Brigadier general
Chang Shu-shan[4]	Huai	Ho-fei, Anhwei	Followed Li to Shanghai
Chang Shu-sheng[5]	Huai	Ho-fei, Anhwei *Hsiu-ts'ai* degree	Local corps; original follower. Became governor-general
Chang Wen-hsüan[6]	Huai	Unknown	Western-drill expert; recommended for promotion to brigadier general
Chao Huai-yeh[7]	Huai	Ho-fei, Anhwei	Commanded Ming-chün at Dairen. Recommended by Li for promotion
Ch'en Chi-tung[8]	Huai, lien	Unknown	Brigadier general. Supervised Chinese cadets abroad
Ch'en Pen-jung[9]	Huai	Liu-an, Anhwei	Tientsin garrison; recommended for provincial commander in chief
Cheng Kuo-k'uei[10]	Huai	Ho-fei, Anhwei	Managed Pei-yang defense office

See footnotes at end of table.

TABLE 18, continued

Name	Army	Place of Origin	Career
Cheng Kuo-pang[11]	Huai	Ho-fei, Anhwei	Recommended for provincial commander in chief
Ch'eng Hsüeh-ch'i[12]	Hsiang, Huai	Anhwei	Provincial commander in chief. Killed in action
Chia Ch'i-sheng[13]	Huai, lien	Ho-fei, Anhwei	Served with lien-chün. Became provincial commander in chief leading Sheng-tzu-chün battalions
Chou Sheng-ch'uan[14]	Huai	Ho-fei, Anhwei	A principal leader. Local corps. Stationed in Tientsin over ten years
Chou Sheng-po[15]	Huai	Ho-fei, Anhwei	A principal leader. Local corps. Succeeded Chou Sheng-ch'uan in command of Huai and lien forces in Chihli
Chou Shou-ch'ang[16]	Huai	T'ung-ch'eng, Anhwei	Under Chang Shu-sheng and others; promoted to brigadier general
Chu Huan-ming[17]	Huai	Ho-fei, Anhwei	Under Liu Ming-ch'uan and others. Stationed in Shanghai in 1880's. Fought French in 1884
Han Chao-ch'i[18]	Probably Huai	Unknown	Recommended for brigadier general
Hsü Pang-tao[19]	Szechwan, Hsiang; then Huai	Szechwan	Under Liu Ming-ch'uan in Nien campaign; stationed later in Hsü-chou, Kiangsu. Brigadier general. Sino-Japanese War

See footnotes at end of table.

TABLE 18, continued

Name	Army	Place of Origin	Career
Hsü Tao-k'uei[20]	Huai	Unknown	Led Wu-I-chün. Commanded Li's personal guard
Huang Chin-chih[21]	Huai	Ho-fei, Anhwei	Recommended for brigadier general
Huang I-sheng[22]	Hsiang, Huai	Hunan	Commanded Huai-chün water troops under Tseng and Li. Became provincial commander in chief
Huang Shih-lin[23]	Huai	Unknown	Recommended for provincial commander in chief
Kuo Sung-lin[24]	Hsiang, Huai	Hunan	Transferred to Li by Tseng. Served under Li from 1862 until his death. Chihli provincial commander in chief
Li Ch'ang-lo[25]	Huai	Anhwei	Under Kuo Sung-lin; after 1867 replaced Kuo Sung-lin as leader of Wu-I-chün. In Chihli from 1880 to 1889
Li Chao-ch'ing[26]	Huai	Ho-fei, Anhwei	Younger brother of Li Hung-chang. Civil officer. Died 1873
Li Ho-chang[27]	Huai	Ho-fei, Anhwei	Close relative of Li Hung-chang. Wounded in 1865; retired
Li Nan-hua[28]	Huai	Anhwei	Cavalry; led lien-chün in 1896

See footnotes at end of table.

TABLE 18, continued

Name	Army	Place of Origin	Career
Li Sheng[29]	Huai	Ho-fei, Anhwei	Water and land troops commander. Followed Li from beginning
Li Te-sheng[30]	Huai	Ho-fei, Anhwei	Nephew of Li Nan-hua. Raised local corps. Rose to rank of colonel
Lin Kuo-hsiang[31]	Kwangtung navy	Probably Fukien	Appointed to command a Kwangtung ship by Ting Ju-ch'ang
Lin T'ai-tseng[32]	Pei-yang navy	Fukien	Studied overseas. Joined Pei-yang navy. Commanded cruiser
Liu Ch'i[33]	Huai	Kiangsu	Recommended for provincial commander in chief
Liu Ming-ch'uan[34]	Huai	Ho-fei, Anhwei	Military. Led Ming-chün. Changed to civil, and became governor of Formosa
Liu Ping-chang[35]	Hsiang, Huai	Lu-chiang, Anhwei	Civil. Shanghai and Nien campaign under Li. Became Szechwan governor-general
Liu Sheng-hsiu[36]	Huai	Ho-fei, Anhwei	Recommended for provincial commander in chief. Commanded troops in Chihli and Shantung
Liu Sheng-tsao[37]	Huai	Ho-fei, Anhwei	Commanded Ming-chün under Li. Became civil official. Served in Tientsin in the Kuang-hsü period

See footnotes at end of table.

TABLE 18, continued

Name	Army	Place of Origin	Career
Liu Shih-ch'i[38]	Huai	Hunan	Joined Huai in Shanghai. Nien campaign. Chihli coastal defense
Lo Kuo-chung[39]	Huai	Anhwei	Recommended as provincial commander in chief. Died in Shensi campaign
Lo Jung-kuang[40]	Huai	Hunan	Western arms expert. Built Taku forts in Chihli. Brigadier general at Tientsin, 1894
Lü Pen-yüan[41]	Huai and Sung	Anhwei	Huai officer in Taiping and Nien campaigns. Assigned to Sung-chün. Fought in Sino-Japanese War. Commanded Huai and lien-chün against Boxers in Chihli (1900)
Lü Wen-ching[42]	Pei-yang navy	Fukien	Commanded Pei-yang ships on Chihli coast
Lung Tien-yang[43]	Huai and Sung	Probably Anhwei	Organized local corps in Huai-pei and Kiangnan. Nien campaign; garrisoned in Kiangsu. Later served under Sung Ch'ing
Ma Fu-chen[44]	Hsiang, Huai	Anhwei	Under Tseng Kuo-fan, Tso Tsung-tang. Huai-chün fleet. First formed Huai-yung under Tseng. Assisted Li in Huai fleet affairs from 1867 until death. Brigadier general

See footnotes at end of table.

TABLE 18, continued

Name	Army	Place of Origin	Career
Ma Yü-k'un[45]	Huai	Anhwei	Local corps; served under Sung Ch'ing. Shensi campaign. Served directly under Li in Chihli. Leader of the I-chün. Ordered by Li to put down Boxers in Chihli
Mei Tung-i[46]	Huai	Unknown	Recommended for provincial commander in chief
Nieh Shih-ch'eng[47]	Huai	Ho-fei, Anhwei	Originally served under Yüan Chia-san. In 1862 joined Huai-chün under Liu Ming-ch'uan. In 1874 led Taiwan expedition. Later led Pei-yang, Huai, and lien troops. After Sino-Japanese War reorganized army, following German methods
P'an Ting-hsin[48]	Huai	Lu-chiang, Anhwei	Civil. Commanded Ting-tzu-chün under Li for many years. One of original Huai commanders. Became governor of Kwangsi
Pao Ch'ao[49]	Hsiang, T'ing	Szechwan	Commanded his own Szechwan Army. Co-operated closely with Huai-chün until break with Liu Ming-ch'uan. Assisted Li in defense against French
Su Te-sheng[50]	Huai	Ho-fei, Anhwei	Served in Ming-chün division. Recommended for Brigadier general

See footnotes at end of table.

TABLE 18, continued

Name	Army	Place of Origin	Career
Sun Hsien-yin[51]	Huai	Hupeh	Recommended for provincial commander in chief. Served under Nieh Shih-ch'eng leading Sheng-tzu-chün battalions
Sung Ch'ing[52]	Huai, Yü-chün	Shantung	Originally led local corps. Served under Yüan Chia-san in Anhwei. Later commander of the I-chün. Joined army of Liu Ming-ch'uan in 1861. After forming Honan Yü-chün in 1865, joined Li's staff. Fought under Li's command and was promoted by Li to provincial commander in chief. Assisted Li in defense against French. Under Li, assigned to Dairen. Joined forces with Ma Yü-k'un in 1894 against Japanese. Became assistant to Li. Reorganized northern armies in 1898 as Wu-wei-so-chün with assistance of Ma Yü-k'un, thus combining Shantung and Huai forces
T'ang Jen-lien[53]	T'ing-chün, Huai	Hunan	First attached to Pao Ch'ao's army. Then became brigadier general. In Huai Army. Munitions specialist
T'ang Tien-k'uei[54]	Huai	Ho-fei, Anhwei	An original follower of Li. Served in Ming-chün. Recommended as provincial commander in chief

See footnotes at end of table.

Name	Army	Place of Origin	Career
T'ang Ting-k'uei[55]	Huai	Ho-fei, Anhwei	An original follower of Li. Led Ming-chün and Wu-chün cavalry. Became provincial commander in chief
Teng Wan-lin[56]	Hsiang, Huai	Hunan	Recommended for provincial commander in chief
Ting Ju-ch'ang[57]	Huai, Pei-yang navy	Lu-chiang, Anhwei	Originally in the Ming-chün; commanded water forces. Korean campaign in 1882. Tientsin defenses. First commander and organizer of Pei-yang navy
Ts'ai Chin-chang[58]	Huai	Anhwei	Recommended for post of provincial commander in chief
Tsao K'e-chung[59]	Hsiang, Huai	Tientsin	Served in Hsiang-chün in Anhwei. Huai-chün after 1871. Commanded Huai forces in Chihli; later relieved of command and retired. Recalled to defend Tientsin in 1894
Tsao Te-ch'ing[60]	Huai	Anhwei	Local corps. Followed Li to Shanghai. Served in Nien camp. Recommended for brigadier general
Tso Pao-kuei[61]	Kiangnan, Shantung, lien	Shantung	Fought in Kiangnan army under Hsüeh Huan. Joined Li; trained lien-chün. Served under Li in Chihli commanding own Shantung forces

See footnotes at end of table.

TABLE 18, continued

Name	Army	Place of Origin	Career
Tuan Ch'i-jui[62]	Huai	Ho-fei, Anhwei	Grandfather in Huai Army as officer. Father at Huai camp at Weihaiwei. Joined father at camp as clerk; grew up at camp. Passed examination at age of twenty; entered first class at Li's new Tientsin military academy. Artillery expert. Sent to Germany by Li for further study. Assigned to Pei-yang defense bureau. Taught at Weihaiwei Academy. In 1896 assigned to new army. In 1898 joined command of Yüan Shih-k'ai. Provisional Chief Executive, 1924-26
Tung Ch'üan-sheng[63]	Huai, Lien	Kiangsu	Original follower of Li cavalry. Nien campaign. Assigned to command lien-chün. Recommended for brigadier general
Tung Li-kao[64]	Huai	Ho-fei, Anhwei	An original follower. Served in local corps, Taiping and Nien campaigns. Joined Yüan Shih-k'ai's new lien-Pei-yang army in 1899
Wang K'o-sheng[65]	Huai, lien	Unknown	Commanded cavalry in Nien campaign. Assigned by Li to command lien-chün in Chihli
Wang Te-pang[66]	Hsiang, Huai, Pei-yang	Hunan	Under Liu Ming-ch'uan. Transferred north for Pei-yang defense

See footnotes at end of table.

TABLE 18, continued

Name	Army	Place of Origin	Career
Wang Yung-sheng[67]	Hsiang, Huai	Unknown	First served under Hsiang-Huai command in Kiangsu. Transferred by Li to Pei-yang coastal defense under Sung Ch'ing. Under Yüan Shih-kai in Korea in 1885. Recommended for restoration of rank by Li
Wei Ju-ch'eng[68]	Huai	Ho-fei, Anhwei	Younger brother of Wei Ju-kuei. Brigadier general of cavalry and foot soldiers in Sino-Japanese war. Killed in action
Wei Ju-kuei[69]	Huai	Ho-fei, Anhwei	Followed Sheng-chün in Nien campaign. Appointed by Li to assist in Pei-yang defense affairs. A principal Huai commander in the north
Wu An-k'ang[70]	Southern naval commander	Unknown	Served in various southern provincial navies. Recommended for restoration of rank
Wu Ch'ang-ch'ing[71]	Huai	Lu-chiang, Anhwei	Local corps. Original Li follower. Water forces. Garrisoned Kiangsu and Korea. Pei-yang defense commander. A principal commander under Li
Wu Ch'ang-lu[72]	Huai	Ho-fei, Anhwei	Recommended for brigadier general
Wu Tien-yüan[73]	Huai	Ho-fei, Anhwei	Recommended for provincial commander in chief. In 1894 commanded Tientsin volunteers. Brigadier general

See footnotes at end of table.

TABLE 18, continued

Name	Army	Place of Origin	Career
Wu Yü-fen[74]	Huai	Ho-fei, Anhwei	Civil. Military commander from beginning; Taiping and Nien campaign. Specialized in likin affairs
Wu Yü-lan[75]	Huai	Ho-fei, Anhwei	Civil. Local corps; an original follower of Li. Rose to prefectural post. Coastal defense command; waterworks and naval supply. Recommended for circuit intendant
Yang Ch'i-chen[76]	Huai	Anhwei	Recommended for provincial commander in chief
Yang Ting-hsun[77]	Huai, others	Szechwan	Joined Liu Ming-ch'uan in early 1850's. Served in Pao Ch'ao's Szechwan-Hsiang army. Joined Li and Huai Army. Fought Nien in Honan. Transferred to Tientsin. Became provincial commander in chief. A principal commander
Yeh Chih-ch'ao[78]	Huai	Ho-fei, Anhwei	Steady Huai Army follower. After Nien campaign transferred to Pei-yang defense. In charge of lien-chün. Provincial commander in chief of Chihli in 1889. Fought in Korea in Sino-Japanese War

See footnotes at end of table.

TABLE 18, continued

Name	Army	Place of Origin	Career
Yüan Chia-san[79]	Hsiang	Honan	Originally commanded both Li and Li's father. Later co-operated fully with Huai-chün. Had own army, partially supported by Li. His relatives joined Huai-chün and Li (Yüan Pao-heng, Yüan Pao-ling, and Yüan Shih-k'ai). Important transitional figure, though not Huai-chün member. Had civil degree
Yüan Chiu-kao[80]	Southern	Unknown	Commanded southern fleet at Taku during Sino-Japanese war. Not closely connected, but recommended for provincial rank
Yüan Pao-heng[81]	Huai	Honan (Anhwei border)	A favorite of Li's. After he was demoted by others, Li attached him to his own headquarters as deputy. Li's representative in combined campaign with Tso against Moslems. Promoted by Li after he broke with Tso. Uncle of Yüan Shih-k'ai; nephew of Yüan Chia-san
Yüan Pao-ling[82]	Huai, Pei-yang water forces	Honan	Civil. Assisted Li in Tientsin and Pei-yang coastal defense. Naval affairs. Rose to circuit intendant of Chihli. Son of Yüan Chia-san, brother of Yüan Pao-heng, uncle of Yüan Shih-k'ai

See footnotes at end of table.

TABLE 18, continued

Name	Place of Origin	Army	Career
Yüan Ping-fu[83]	Probably Anhwei	Huai	An original follower of Li. Transferred to Pei-yang coastal defense. Became lien-chün commander. Recommended for provincial commander in chief
Yüan Shih-k'ai[84]	Honan	Huai	Civil. Purchased degree. Managed military and commercial affairs. Served in Korea. Later succeeded Li in command of Pei-yang defense. First President of Chinese Republic

1 *LWCK Memorials*, 33:50a-51b, KH 4/12/19.
2 *CSK*, 459.9b.
3 *LWCK Memorials*, 71:40a ff., KH 17/4/1.
4 *Ch'ing-shih lieh-chuan* (Shanghai, 1928), 51:25b.
5 *Ibid.*, 54:13a ff.; *Lu-chou chih*, 58:10a-11b; *LWCK Memorials*, 57:30a-31a, KH 12/6/20.
6 *LWCK Memorials*, 75:7a-b, KH 18/7/21.
7 *Ibid.*, 75:7a-8a, KH 18/7/21.
8 *Ibid.*, 56:11a, KH 12/2/9.
9 *Ibid.*, 33:50a-51b, KH 4/12/19.
10 *Ibid.*; Ts'ai Kuan-lo, *Ch'ing-tai ch'i-pai ming-jen chuan* (Shanghai, 1937), II, 1177-78.
11 *LWCK Memorials*, 33:50a-51b, KH 4/12/19.
12 Hummel, *Eminent Chinese*, p. 115.
13 *LWCK Memorials*, 33:50a-51b, KH 4/12/19.
14 *Ibid.*, 68:14a-15a, KH 16/5/22; *Ch'ing-shih lieh-chuan*, 26:23b.
15 *LWCK Memorials*, 54:26a-b, KH 11/7/6; 60:34a-b, KH 13/8/30; *Ch'ing-shih lieh-chuan*, 65:22a.
16 *LWCK Memorials*, 49:30a-b, KH 10/3/17.
17 *CSK*, 459:9a.
18 *LWCK Memorials*, 75:7a-8a, KH 18/7/12.

19 *Ibid.*, 33:50a-51b, KH 4/12/19; *CSK*, 461:2b.
20 *LWCK Memorials*, 74:21a, KH 18/3/30.
21 *Ibid.*, 33:50a-51b, KH 4/12/19.
22 *CSK*, 415:1a.
23 *LWCK Memorials*, 75:7a-8a ff., KH 18/7/21.
24 *Ibid.*, 37:14a-15b, KH 6/4/26.
25 *CSK*, 431:2a-b.
26 *Ibid.*, 433:5a; *Lu-chou chih, chüan* 48, *wu-kung*, pp. 3b-5b.
27 *CSK*, 433:4b-5a.
28 *Ibid.*, 457:2a-b.
29 *LWCK Memorials*, 69:27a-28b, KH 16/10/29.
30 *CSK*, 457:2b.
31 *LWCK Memorials*, 79:13a-b, KH 20/9/7.
32 *Ibid.*, 79:33a ff., KH 20/10/26.
33 *Ibid.*, 33:50a-b, KH 4/12/19.
34 *Ch'ing-shih lieh-chuan*, 59:50a ff.
35 *CSK*, 447:56-66.; Ts'ai Kuan-lo, *Ch'ing-tai ch'i-pai ming-jen chuan*, pp. 1181-84.
36 *LWCK Memorials*, 33:50a-b ff., KH 4/12/19.
37 *Ibid.*, 20:16a ff., TC 11/9/26; 35:13a-b, KH 5/9/2.
38 *Ibid.*, 37:29a-b, KH 6/5/13.

TABLE 18, footnotes continued

39 *Ibid.*, 22:6a-7b, TC 12/6/10.

40 *Ibid.*, 33:50a-b, KH 4/12/19; *CSK*, 467:3a-b.

41 *LWCK Memorials*, 75:7a-8b ff., KH 18/7/21; *CSK*, 461:2a-b.

42 *LWCK Memorials*, 69:3a-b, KH 16/8/10.

43 *LWCK Memorials*, 79:30a-31b, KH 20/10/26.

44 *Ibid.*, 29:23a-25a, KH 3/5/28; *CSK*, 457:5b-6a.

45 *LWCK Memorials*, 75:7a-8b ff., KH 18/7/21; 80:84a, KH 27/8/22; *CSK*, 461:3a; Hummel, *Eminent Chinese*, p. 688; Ts'ai Kuan-lo, *Ch'ing-tai ch'i-pai ming-jen chuan*, pp. 1094-95.

46 *LWCK Memorials*, 75:7a-8b ff., KH 18/7/21.

47 *Ibid.*, 33:50a-b, KH 4/12/19; *CSK*, 467:2a.

48 *Ch'ing-shih lieh-chuan*, 55:26b; *LWCK Memorials*, 75:41a-b, KH 18/12/2; 63:30a-32a, KH 14/9/13.

49 Hummel, *Eminent Chinese*, pp. 609-10.

50 *CSK*, 459:9b.

51 *LWCK Memorials*, 33:50a-b ff., KH 4/12/19; 75:7a-8b ff., KH 18/7/21.

52 Hummel, *Eminent Chinese*, pp. 686-88.

53 *LWCK Memorials*, 49:30a-31b, KH 10/3/17.

54 *Ibid.*, 13:24a-25a, TC 7/2/29; *Ch'ing-shih lieh-chuan*, 51:30a-b; *CSK*, 431:4a.

55 *LWCK Memorials*, 59:42a-43b, KH 13/4/7.

56 *Ibid.*, 33:50a ff., KH 4/12/19.

57 *CSK*, 462:1a; *LWCK Memorials*, 35:24a ff., KH 5/10/16; 42:22a ff., KH 7/10/11; 44:48a ff., KH 8/8/29; Hummel, *Eminent Chinese*, pp. 467-68, 950.

58 *LWCK Memorials*, 33:50a-51b ff., KH 4/12/19.

59 *Ibid.*, 19:80a ff., TC 11/8/2; *CSK*, 430:2b-3a.

60 *CSK*, 457:5a-b.

61 *LWCK Memorials*, 79:10a-b, KH 20/9/7; *CSK*, 460:1a-2a; Ts'ai Kuan-lo, *Ch'ing-tai ch'i-pai ming-jen chuan*, pp. 1073-74.

62 Wu T'ing-hsieh, *Ho-fei chih-cheng nien-p'u* (*chu-kao*), pp. 1a-4a.

63 *CSK*, 457:3b-4a.

64 *Ibid.*, 457:3a-b.

65 *LWCK Memorials*, 18:1a, TC 10/1/12; 51:33a ff., KH 10/9/4.

66 *CSK*, 459:5b-6b.

67 *LWCK Memorials*, 57:7a-b, KH 12/4/10; 56:13a-b, KH 12/2/9.

68 *CSK*, 462:2a; *LWCK Memorials*, 75:7a-8b, KH 18/7/21.

69 *CSK*, 462:2a; *LWCK Memorials*, 33:50a-51b ff., KH 4/12/19; 71:23a-24a, KH 17/2/26.

70 *LWCK Memorials*, 69:19a-22a, KH 16/8/29.

71 *Ch'ing-shih lieh-chuan*, 56:19a; *LWCK Memorials*, 50:26a-28b, KH 19/6/2.

72 *LWCK Memorials*, 33:50a-51b ff., KH 4/12/19.

73 *Ibid.*

74 *Ibid.*, 74:5a-6a, KH 18/2/9; 72:43a-45a, KH 17/8/19.

75 *CSK*, 433:5a.

76 *LWCK Memorials*, 33:50a-b, KH 4/12/19.

77 *Ibid.*, 23:34a-b, TC 13/6/16; *CSK*, 431:3a-b.

78 *CSK*, 462:2b-3a; *LWCK Memorials*, 33:50a-51b ff., KH 4/12/19.

79 Hummel, *Eminent Chinese*, pp. 949-50.

80 *LWCK Memorials*, 78:13a, KH 20/4/25.

81 *Ibid.*, 14:27a ff., TC 7/7/8; *CSK*, 418:4b.

82 *LWCK Memorials*, 66:3a-4a, KH 15/8/5.

83 *Ibid.*, 67:17a-b, KH 16/2/12.

84 Hummel, *Eminent Chinese*, pp. 950-53; *LWCK Memorials*, 75:26a-b, KH 18/10/22; 76:30a ff., KH 19/4/15.

armies. Nevertheless, his brother, son, and nephew all joined the Huai-chün and served Li with distinction. From this group came Yüan Shih-k'ai who later succeeded Li to the command of the Pei-yang armies.

Sung Ch'ing and Pao Ch'ao were not members of the Huai-chün itself, but commanded armies of their own fellow provincials in frequent and close contact with Li's forces. Sung Ch'ing, whose forces were recruited in Shantung, worked closely with Li's Huai and lien troops, and Li repaid this allegiance by making Sung his assistant in northern defense. Sung Ch'ing remained a major military figure after the Sino-Japanese War, leading one branch of the new northern army. His forces apparently were poorly equipped and drilled, and in this respect were different from those of Li, and later of Yüan Shih-k'ai.[49] Li Hung-chang's close connections with Sung Ch'ing, Pao Ch'ao, and a few other independent commanders provided an important reserve for the Huai-chün, helping Li to fill gaps in defense lines at times of emergency.

Li's relations with his regular Huai-chün commanders were usually closer than with his auxiliary commanders. In most cases local-corps leaders had joined Li with their forces intact and had retained command of these forces from the very inception of the Huai-chün. This basic form of organization did not change through the years. Thus, for example, the various Huai-chün divisions in the north directly under Li still retained the names of their old commanders, and the command was generally passed from brother to brother. Li Hung-chang's position was therefore that of patron, overseer, and arbitrator of a number of commanders who were from his native province and largely from his home district. If he depended entirely on the continuing loyalty of these commanders, he in turn gave them an importance through unity and organization which they probably never could have otherwise acquired. This was especially true of those who were strictly military officers and whose opportunities to rise were limited by lack of either civil or military degrees.

Excluding Pao Ch'ao, Yüan Chia-san, and Sung Ch'ing, who were not strictly classified within the Huai-chün ranks, the great majority of these men rose either as local-corps leaders in the early days of the Taiping and Nien rebellions, or rose from the ranks to the position of brigadier general or provincial commander in chief.

---

[49] Hummel, *Eminent Chinese,* pp. 686-88.

Comparison of Li's Civil and Military Followers

In comparison with those who rose entirely upon their merits as military commanders, the subordinates of Li who were civilians but were concerned with military affairs were far more diverse in background and career. Of all the civilians mentioned above only thirteen came from Anhwei. Thirteen came from Kiangsu, twelve from Kwangtung, and two from Chekiang. The origins of twenty-three men could not be determined. But even this small and hardly satisfactory sampling indicates how many of the new bureaucrats came from the coastal provinces. Well over half of Li's bureaucratic followers dealt with one or another aspect of Western affairs, and it was in the treaty ports, where commercial and missionary influence prevailed, that these men received the most important part of their education—knowledge of the West.

Almost half of Li's civil assistants came to him through military routes, either as local-corps organizers or as civilian administrators at Li's and Tseng's military headquarters. Most of those who started their careers in the personal secretariats had regular civil degrees, although in some cases exceptional military merit or Western knowledge was the decisive factor that led Li to employ them.[50] Study of the functions of Li's bureaucratic assistants shows that the interplay between military and economic activity (financial, commercial, and industrial) was tremendous. Because of this, the men who dealt with military problems, even when they were actually in the field with the troops, had a broader background and wider perspective than the regular army commanders. They were, indeed, more like Li Hung-chang than the regular commanders with whom they worked. But both types were important for China's future.

---

[50] Li Hung-chang was a champion of those who received "military merit" (*chun-kung, wu-kung*), and strongly urged the throne to give recognition and office to those who served faithfully and with distinction in the armies, particularly his own. *Peking Gazette:* Trans. in *NCH*, March 13, 1872. Interesting comments on the advantages of a feudal system over Li Hung-chang's type of nepotism are found in Alexander Michie, *The Englishman in China*, II, 399. A survey by British Intelligence, after observation of the Huai-chün and lien-chün in various places over a period of years (1876-82), concluded: "The commander of a regiment is appointed by the Viceroy of Pi-chih-li and 'Commissioner of Defence, North China' (Li), to whom he is alone responsible. This and all other grades are obtained by family and court influence chiefly. As regards promotion in the regiment, the Viceroy gives to a friend any rank that he chooses.... Besides a few personal aides-de-camp attached to the Viceroy as secretaries, no army administrative staff in the European sense exists." Bell, *China*, II, 58-59.

Emergence of New Leaders

Li Hung-chang's bureaucratic machine, both civil and military, provided a good number of the outstanding political leaders of the latter nineteenth century. His original Huai-chün commanders rose to high rank. Chang Shu-sheng became governor of Kwangtung, acting governor-general of Liang-Chiang and later governor-general of Liang-Kuang. P'an Ting-hsin rose to be governor of Kwangsi. Liu Ping-chang came to serve as governor-general of Szechwan. All three were natives of Anhwei, and all were originally gentry leaders of local corps, possessing civil degrees. Others from Li's own province who joined the Huai-chün in lesser capacities and rose on the basis of civil degrees and military service were: Liu Jui-fen,[51] governor of Kwangtung, T'u Tsung-ying,[52] governor-general of Hu-kuang, and Chou Fu,[53] who became governor-general of Liang-Kuang. Among these Anhwei men, the most spectacular rise to high office was made by Liu Ming-ch'uan. He had started as a bandit, then organized local corps, and on the basis of outstanding military merit crossed from the military to the civil bureaucracy, finally becoming governor of the new province of Taiwan.

Ting Jih-ch'ang, who began as an expert in Western manufacture, also was indebted to Li for his promotion to high provincial office.

---

[51] *CSK,* 446:9a; *LWCK Memorials,* 74:41a-43a, KH 18/6/4. Liu had formerly served as a customs intendant in charge of telegraphs. When British officials in 1883 expressed doubt to Li about his agreements with them in connection with the construction of the Shanghai-Chinkiang-Canton Telegraph because of Tso Tsung-t'ang's opposition, Li, then at Chihli, assured them that Liu Jiu-fen, the Shanghai customs intendant, "would obey Li's orders." (From notes on an interview with Li Hung-chang, sent by the British consul at Tientsin, Brenan, to Minister Grosvenor, Feb. 26, 1883; British Foreign Office, F. O. 17/1009.) This despite the fact that Tso, not Li, was Liu's superior as governor-general of Liang-Chiang.

[52] T'u Tsung-ying was a *chü-jen* from Liu-an, Anhwei. He was summoned to Kiangsu by Li after the fall of Nanking. He became circuit intendant in Liang-Chiang, and later assisted Li in diplomatic negotiations. He was appointed by Li as financial commissioner of Hunan and later rose to be governor-general. See *Shanghai-hsü hsien-chih,* 15:2b; *LWCK Memorials,* 9:22a, TC 4/7/22. T'u succeeded Li Hung-chang in that post. *CSK,* 200 (Table 4):13a-23a.

[53] Chou Fu was a native of Chien-te, Anhwei. He joined Li's camp at an early age during the Taiping Rebellion. His talent was brought to the notice of Li, who had him educated at the Huai camp. Later he served in Li's headquarters staff. There he managed Li's records. He rose to the civilian rank of candidate for prefectural magistrate. Later he dealt with military finance, defense, telegraphs, and railroads, holding the office of customs intendant. See *CSK,* 449:3a; *LWCK Memorials,* 59:31a, KH 13/3/26. At the turn of the century he became governor-general of Chihli, succeeding to the post formerly held so long by his patron. See also Ralph L. Powell, *The Rise of Chinese Military Power, 1895-1912* (Princeton: Princeton University Press, 1955), p. 232.

Ting was a native of Kwangtung and possessed a *hsiu-ts'ai* degree. Li characterized him as "an expert on foreign weapons, a man who loves to study, loves thinking, and has paid special attention to Western affairs."[54] In his years as governor of Kiangsu and later of Fukien, and as Nan-yang defense commissioner, Ting was of great value in helping Li to establish many of his basic enterprises.[55] The eighth of Li's followers to rise to a governorship was Wang K'ai-t'ai, whom Li brought to Shanghai in 1863. Li promoted him and recommended him highly. In 1870 Wang became acting governor of Fukien, serving there, with a brief interruption, until 1874, when he was replaced by Ting Jih-ch'ang.[56]

Li and His Heirs

The final stage of the transition in leadership was reached in two personalities who represented the militaristic trend that led China directly into the warlordism of the early twentieth century. The first of these was Yüan Shih-k'ai, who succeeded Li in control of the Pei-yang defense forces. He had been helped along in this early career largely because of Li's close personal relationship with the Yüan family. Unlike the majority of Li's followers who achieved the rank of governor-general, Yüan Shih-k'ai had not obtained his degree by passing the government examinations but had purchased it and had then advanced by displaying uncommon efficiency in handling military supplies. Yüan continued Li's tradition in so far as he attempted to remodel the armies of northern China, making them a personal, regional force under the guise of reorganizing the national defense. His real grasp on power, which was eventually decisive in his successful bid for the presidency of the Republic of China, was his control over the military academy of the Pei-yang army, the school in which many of the later warlords received their early military training.[57]

The second man who bridged Li Hung-chang's organization and the warlord period was Tuan Ch'i-jui. He had grown up in the Huai-chün camps, and had been selected by Li to attend the newly founded Tientsin Military Academy. After studying artillery technique in

---

[54] *LWCK Memorials,* 10:24a, TC 5/9/7.

[55] *Ibid.,* 25:27a, KH 1/6/11. See also *CSK,* 448:1a.

[56] *CSK,* 204 (Table 8) :16a-18a.

[57] Powell, *The Rise of Chinese Military Power, passim.* Compare this with Li's control of the Tientsin Academy and Chiang Kai-shek's later control of the Whampoa Academy. Professor Franz Michael in his manuscript "Regional Forces and the Decline of China's Last Dynastic Government" has strongly emphasized the role of the military academies in shaping the leadership of modern China.

Germany under Li's auspices, he returned to China to teach at Li's academies in the north. Around him gathered a new group of young officers. Tuan supported Yüan, and after Yüan's death even served for a time as the chief executive of China.[58]

The followers and successors of Yüan and Tuan were the *t'u-chün,* or military governors—warlords like Feng Yu-hsiang, Wang Shih-chen, and a score of others, whose personal *ti-fang* (regional) armies became the looters of China and the substitute for orderly government for more than two decades of Chinese history. Yet Yüan was as much the legacy of Li as the warlords were the heritage of Yüan.

In the context of their times the failures of both Yüan and Li were inevitable. Yüan had arisen in a period of near collapse, when the central government of China had been greatly weakened and the unifying forces of tradition and culture had given way to a struggle for power through violence. When Yüan emerged there was no way of going back, and the future held only the prospect of anarchy.

Li, too, was driven on by forces and events over which he had little control. It is true that from the beginning he had accepted the idea that military force was the real basis for political ascendancy and survival, but in an era when invasion and rebellion threatened to upset the dynastic order and the Manchu dynasty itself gave little security to its officialdom, Li's course was, so far as he was concerned, well chosen. Li's astute understanding of the processes of power-building and of the need for fundamental changes was best applied in the development of new military forces, the establishment of arsenals, and the introduction of modern machine techniques for production and communication. He acquired great skill in diplomatic negotiations and trained a corps of experts to succeed him in this field. But his quest for reform was limited. He perpetuated in his military forces a spirit of narrow personal loyalty which served to check any tendency toward the development of a national system of military defense. He filled the managerial posts of his economic enterprises with profit-seeking bureaucrats. He overprotected and at the same time over-exploited the weak merchant class. Having thus denied to his "Westernized" institutions the independent spirit which gave such institutions life and growth in the West, he attempted to impose them upon China. But even here he limited his efforts to those regions which

[58] Wu T'ing-hsieh, *Ho-fei chih-cheng nien-p'u, chu-kao,* pp. 1a-4a; Powell, *The Rise of Chinese Military Power,* p. 79. Feng Yu-hsiang, the "Christian General" of the 1920's, 30's, and 40's, also grew up in the Huai-chün camps.

served him and his army alone. In doing all this he paved the way
for the new China by undermining the institutions which had given
China strength in the past. Though Yüan Shih-k'ai and Sun Yat-sen
and their adherents may have been responsible for the final downfall
of the Manchu dynasty, it was Li Hung-chang and leaders like him
who were first to give expression to the fundamental forces which
destroyed not only a dynasty but an entire way of life.

Reign Periods of the Ch'ing Dynasty

Shun-chih	1644-1661
K'ang-hsi	1662-1722
Yung-cheng	1723-1735
Ch'ien-lung	1736-1795
Chia-ch'ing	1796-1820
Tao-kuang	1821-1850
Hsien-feng	1851-1861
T'ung-chih	1862-1874
Kuang-hsü	1875-1908
Hsüan-t'ung	1909-1912 (February)

Glossary of Characters

Names of Persons

Chang Chih-mou	張之某
Chang Chih-tung	張之洞
Chang Chih-yin	張之蔭
Chang Chung-yüan	張仲遠
Chang Hai-lung	張海龍
Chang Hung-chün	章鴻鈞
Chang Kao-yüan	章高元
Chang Kuo-liang	張國樑
Chang Shao-k'an	張紹堪
Chang Shao-t'ang	張紹棠
Chang Shih-heng	張士珩
Chang Shu-p'ing	張樹屏
Chang Shu-shan	張樹珊
Chang Shu-sheng	張樹聲
Chang Tsung-yü	張總愚
Chang Wen-hsüan	張文宣
Chang Yin-huan	張蔭桓
Chao Huai-yeh	趙懷業
Ch'en Chi-tung	陳季同
Ch'en Ch'in	陳欽
Ch'en Fu-hsün	陳福勳
Ch'en Hung-chü	陳鬻擧
Ch'en Lan-pin	陳蘭彬
Ch'en Nai	陳鼐

Ch'en Pen-jung	陳本榮
Ch'en Shih-chieh	陳士杰
Ch'en Shu-t'ang	陳樹棠
Ch'en Yü-ch'eng	陳玉成
Ch'en Yün-i	陳允頤
Cheng Kuo-k'uei	鄭國魁
Cheng Kuo-pang	鄭國榜
Cheng Tsao-ju	鄭藻如
Ch'eng Hsüeh-ch'i	程學啟
Chia Ch'i-sheng	賈起勝
Chiang Chung-yüan	江忠源
Ch'ien Ting-ming	錢鼎銘
Chin Hung-pao	金鴻保
Chin Hung-pin	金鴻賓
Ch'ing Ch'in Wang (Prince)	慶親王
Chou Fu	周馥
Chou Sheng-ch'uan	周盛傳
Chou Sheng-po	周盛波
Chou Shou-ch'ang	周壽昌
Chu Ch'i-ang	朱其昂
Chu Ch'i-chao	朱其詔
Chu Huan-ming	朱煥明
Ch'un Ch'in Wang (Prince)	醇親王
Chung Wang	忠王
Ch'ung-hou	崇厚
Feng Chün-kuang	馮焌光
Feng Kuei-fen	馮桂芬
Feng Tzu-ts'ai	馮子材
Fu-chi	福濟
Fu T'ang	黼堂
Han Chao-ch'i	韓照琦
Han Tien-chia	韓殿甲
Ho Ch'un	和春
Hsieh (" the Fourth Tiger ")	謝
Hsieh Chia-fu	謝家福
Hsü Jun	徐潤
Hsü Pang-tao	徐邦道
Hsü Tao-k'uei	徐道奎
Hsü Wen-ta	徐文達
Hsüeh Fu-ch'eng	薛福成

Hsüeh Huan	薛 煥
Huang Chin-chih	黃 金 志
Huang Chung-yüan	黃 中 元
Huang Fang	
(also Huang Ho-ting)	黃 芳
Huang I-sheng	黃 翼 升
Huang Shih-lin	黃 仕 林
Hung Hsiu-ch'üan	洪 秀 全
Jung Hung	
(also Yung Wing)	容 閎
Ku Chao-hsi	顧 肇 熙
Ku Wen-pin	顧 文 彬
Kung Chao-yü	龔 照 澳
Kung Ch'in Wang (Prince)	恭 親 王
Kuo Sung-lin	郭 松 林
Kuo Sung-tao	郭 嵩 燾
Li Ch'ang-lo	李 長 樂
Li Chao-ch'ing	李 昭 慶
Li Chao-t'ang	黎 兆 棠
Li Chin-yung	李 金 鏞
Li Feng-pao	李 鳳 苞
Li Han-chang	李 瀚 章
Li Ho-chang	李 鶴 章
Li Hsing-jui	李 興 銳
Li Hsing-yüan	李 星 沅
Li Hsiu-ch'eng	李 秀 成
Li Huan	李 桓
Li Hung-chang	李 鴻 章
Li Nan-hua	李 南 華
Li Shan-lan	李 善 蘭
Li Sheng	李 勝
Li Shu-ch'ang	黎 庶 昌
Li Te-sheng	李 得 勝
Li Tsung-hsi	李 宗 羲
Li Wen-an	李 文 安
Li Yüan-hua	李 元 華
Li Yüan-tu	李 元 度
Liang Ch'i-ch'ao	梁 啟 超
Lin Kuo-hsiang	林 國 祥
Lin T'ai-tseng	林 泰 曾

Lin Tse-hsü	林 則 徐
Ling Huan	凌 煥
Liu Ch'i	劉 祺
Liu Ch'i-hsiang	劉 其 祥
Liu Chieh	劉 傑
Liu Han-fang	劉 含 芳
Liu Jui-fen	劉 瑞 芬
Liu K'un-i	劉 坤 一
Liu Ming-ch'uan	劉 銘 傳
Liu Ping-chang	劉 秉 璋
Liu Sheng-hsiu	劉 盛 休
Liu Sheng-tsao	劉 盛 藻
Liu Shih-ch'i	劉 士 奇
Liu Yü-lung	劉 玉 龍
Lo Feng-lu	羅 豐 祿
Lo Jung-kuang	羅 榮 光
Lo Kuo-chung	駱 國 忠
Lo Ping-chang	駱 秉 章
Lo Tse-nan	羅 澤 南
Lung Tien-yang	龍 殿 楊
Lü Hsien-chi	呂 賢 基
Lü Pen-yüan	呂 本 元
Lü Wen-ching	呂 文 經
Ma Chien-chung	馬 建 忠
Ma Fu-chen	馬 復 震
Ma Hsin-i	馬 新 貽
Ma Yü-k'un	馬 玉 崑
Mei Tung-i	梅 東 益
Nieh Shih-ch'eng	聶 士 成
Ou E-liang	區 諤 良
P'an Fu	潘 馥
P'an Ting-hsin	潘 鼎 新
P'an Tseng-wei	潘 曾 瑋
P'ang Chung-lu	龐 鍾 璐
Pao Ch'ao	鮑 超
P'eng Yü-lin	彭 玉 鱗
Seng-ko-lin-ch'in	僧 格 林 沁
Shan Ch'ing	善 慶
She Ch'ang-yü	佘 昌 宇
Shen Pao-chen	沈 葆 楨

Shen Pao-ching	沈保靖
Shen Ping-ch'eng	沈秉成
Sheng Hsüan-huai	盛宣懷
Su Te-sheng	蘇得勝
Sun Hsien-yin	孫顯寅
Sun Yu-ch'eng	孫有誠
Sung Ch'ing	宋慶
Tai Tsung-ch'ien	戴宗騫
T'ang Jen-lien	唐仁廉
T'ang Tien-k'uei	唐殿魁
T'ang Ting-k'uei	唐定奎
T'ang T'ing-shu	唐廷樞
Teng Wan-lin	鄧萬林
Ting Jih-ch'ang	丁日昌
Ting Ju-ch'ang	丁汝昌
Ting Shou-ch'ang	丁壽昌
Ts'ai Chin-chang	蔡金章
Ts'ao Jen-mei	曹仁美
Ts'ao K'e-chung	曹克忠
Ts'ao Te-ch'ing	曹德慶
Ts'ao Tsai-ch'un	曹載春
Tseng Chi-tse	曾紀澤
Tseng Kuo-ch'üan	曾國荃
Tseng Kuo-fan	曾國藩
Tso Pao-kuei	左寶貴
Tso Tsung-t'ang	左宗棠
Tu-hsing-a	
(Tohsinga, Toshinga)	都興阿
T'u Tsung-ying	涂宗瀛
Tuan Ch'i-jui	段祺瑞
Tung Ch'üan-sheng	董全勝
Tung Chün-han	董儁翰
Tung Li-kao	董履高
Wang Ch'ien-ping	王乾炳
Wang K'o-sheng	王可陞
Wang Te-pang	王德榜
Wang Te-sheng	王德勝
Wang Yung-sheng	王永勝
Wei Ju-ch'eng	衛汝成
Wei Ju-kuei	衛汝貴

Wei Yüan	魏 源
Weng Hsin-ts'un	翁 心 存
Weng T'ung-ho	翁 同 龢
Wu An-k'ang	吳 安 康
Wu Ch'ang-ch'ing	吳 長 慶
Wu Ch'ang-lu	吳 長 璐
Wu Chia-shan	吳 嘉 善
Wu Chih-ch'ang	吳 熾 昌
Wu Chung-hsiang	吳 仲 翔
Wu Hsü	吳 煦
Wu Ju-lun	吳 汝 綸
Wu T'ang	吳 棠
Wu Tien-yüan	吳 殿 元
Wu T'ing-fang	伍 廷 芳
Wu Tsan-ch'eng	吳 贊 誠
Wu Yü-fen	吳 毓 芬
Wu Yü-lan	吳 毓 蘭
Wu Yüan-ping	吳 元 炳
Wu Yün	吳 雲
Yang Ch'i-chen	楊 岐 珍
Yang Chieh	楊 楫
Yang Fang	楊 昉
Yang Shou-mei	楊 壽 楣
Yang Ting-hsün	楊 鼎 勳
Yang Tsung-lien	楊 宗 濂
Yang Yüeh-pin	楊 岳 斌
Yeh Chih-ch'ao	葉 志 超
Yeh T'ing-chüan	葉 廷 眷
Ying Pao-shih	應 寶 時
Yung Wing	
(also Jung Hung)	容 閎
Yü Tsai-pang	余 在 榜
Yüan Chia-san	袁 甲 三
Yüan Chiu-kao	袁 九 皋
Yüan Pao-heng	袁 保 恒
Yüan Pao-ling	袁 保 齡
Yüan Ping-fu	阮 炳 福
Yüan Shih-k'ai	袁 世 凱
Yüan Ta-hua	袁 大 化

Terms and Names Other Than Those of Persons

an-ch'a-shih	按察使
chang-fu	長夫
chang-lung	長龍
Chao Shang Chü	招商局
chen lien-chün	鎮練軍
Chen-tzu-ying	震字營
cheng-shao-kuan	正哨官
Ch'i-tzu-ying	奇字營
Chiang-wai	江外
chien-sheng	監生
chin-shih	進士
ch'in-ping	親兵
Ch'ing-tzu-ying	慶字營
Ch'u-chün	楚軍
Chung-p'o-ying	忠樸營
fu-shao-kuan	副哨官
Hai-chün	海軍
Hai-chün t'i-tu	海軍提督
Hai-chün ya-men	海軍衙門
Hsiang-chün	湘軍
hsiao-ch'iang	小槍
Hsing-ying	行營
hsiu-ts'ai	秀才
Hsün-chün	勳軍
Hsün-tzu-ying	勳字營
hu-chün	護軍
hu-wei	護衛
hu-yung	護勇
Hua-tzu-ying	華字營
Huai-chün	淮軍
Huai-yung	淮勇
huo-yung	火勇
I-ho	怡和
Jen-chün	仁軍
k'ai-hua-p'ao	開花砲
K'ai-tzu-ying	開字營
Ko-kuo shih-wu ta-ch'en	各國事務大臣
Kuei-tzu-ying	桂字營

K'uei-tzu-ying	魁字營
lao-Hsiang-chün	老湘軍
liang (tael)	兩
lien-chün	練軍
lien-Hsiang-chün	練湘軍
lü-ying	綠營
Ming-chün	銘軍
Ming-tzu-ying	銘字營
mu-fu	幕府
mu-yu	幕友
Nei-ko Hsüeh-shih	內閣學士
Ning-ch'uan	寧船
pa-kung	拔貢
pang-pan	幫辦
p'ao-tui	砲隊
Pei-yang ta-ch'en	北洋大臣
p'eng	棚
p'i-kao	批稿
p'i-shan-p'ao	劈山砲
pien-hsiu	編修
pu-cheng-shih	布政使
Sha-ch'uan	沙船
shan-nei	山內
shao	哨
shao-chang	哨長
shao-kuan	哨官
Sheng-chün	盛軍
Sheng-tzu-ying	盛字營
sheng-yüan	生員
shih-chang	什長
shu-chi	書記
Shu-chün	樹軍
Shu-tzu-ying	樹字營
Ta-t'ung Chao-shang-chü	大同招商局
t'ai-ch'iang	抬槍
T'ai-ku	太古
Ting-tzu-ying	鼎字營
tou	斗
Tsai-hsiang Ho-fei	
T'ien-hsia shou	宰相合肥天下瘦

tsou-kao	奏稿
t'uan-lien	團練
tui	隊
t'ung-ling	統領
t'ung-nien	同年
t'ung-shuai	統帥
tzu-shih	字識
wu-kung	武功
Wu-I	武毅
ying	營
ying-kuan	營官
yung	勇

Bibliography

BOOKS AND ARTICLES IN CHINESE

Chang Po-ch'u 張伯初. "Shanghai ping-kung-ch'ang chih shih-mo" 上海兵工廠之始末 *Jen-wen yüeh-k'an* 人文月刊, V, No. 5 (June 15, 1934), 1–14.

Chang Shou-yung 張壽鏞. *Huang-ch'ao chang-ku hui-pien* 皇朝掌故彙編. 1902.

Chao Feng-t'ien 趙豐田. *Wan-Ch'ing wu-shih-nien ching-chi ssu-hsiang shih* 晚清五十年經濟思想史. Yenching Journal of Chinese Studies, Monograph Series No. 18. Peiping, 1939.

Ch'eng Yen-sheng 程演生. *T'ai-p'ing t'ien-kuo shih-liao, ti-i-chi* 太平天國史料第一集. Peiping, 1926.

Chiang Chung-yüan 江忠源. *Chiang Chung-lieh kung i-chi* 江忠烈公遺集. 1873.

Ch'ien Hsü 錢勖. *Wu-chung p'ing-k'ou chi* 吳中平寇記. Shanghai, 1875.

Ch'ien Ting-ming 錢鼎銘. *Ch'ien Min-su kung tsou-shu* 錢敏肅公奏疏. 1878.

Ch'ing (Huang)-ch'ao hsü-wen-hsien t'ung-k'ao 清(皇)朝續文献通考. Compiled by Liu Chin-tsao 劉錦藻. Shanghai, 1936.

Ch'ing-ch'ao yeh-shih ta-kuan 清朝野史大觀. Shanghai, 1916.

Ch'ing-shih kao 清史稿. Compiled by Chao Erh-sun 趙爾巽 and others. Mukden, 1937.

Ch'ing-shih-lu. See *Ta-Ch'ing li-ch'ao shih-lu.*

Ch'ing-shih lieh-chuan 清史列傳. Compiled by the Ch'ing Shih Kuan.

Shanghai, 1928.

Chou Shih-ch'eng 周世澄. *Huai-chün p'ing-nien chi* 淮軍平捻記. Shanghai, 1877.

Ch'üan Han-sheng 全漢昇. " Ch'ing-chi ti Chiang-nan chih-tsao chü " 清季的江南製造局, in *Bulletin of the Institute of History and Philology,* Academia Sinica (Taipei, 1951), XXIII, Pt. 1, 145–60.

Chung-kuo chin-pai-nien shih tzu-liao, ch'u-pien. See Tso Shun-sheng.

Chung-kuo jen-ming ta-tz'u-tien 中國人名大辭典. Compiled by Tsang Li-ho 臧勵龢. Shanghai, 1934.

Fang Hao 方豪. " Ming-mo hsi-yang huo-ch'i liu-ju wo-kuo chih shih-liao " 明末西洋火器流入我國之史料, *Tung-fang tsa-chih* 東方雜誌, XL, No. 1 (January, 1944), 49–54.

Feng Kuei-fen 馮桂芬. *Hsien-chih-t'ang kao* 顯志堂稿. 1877.

Hsiao I-shan 蕭一山. *Tseng Kuo-fan* 曾國藩. Shanghai and Nanking, 1946.

Hsüeh Fu-ch'eng 薛福成. *Yung-an ch'üan-chi* 庸盦全集. 1901.

———. *Yung-an pi-chi* 庸盦筆記. 1898.

Huang-ch'ao ching-shih-wen t'ung-pien 皇朝經世文統編. Compiled by Shao Chih-t'ang 邵之棠, 1901.

Kuo Sung-tao 郭嵩燾. *Yang-chih shu-wu ch'üan-chi* 養知書屋全集. 1892.

Li Chien-nung 李劍農. *Chung-kuo chin-pai-nien cheng-chih shih* 中國近百年政治史. Commercial Press, 1942.

Li Han-chang 李瀚章. *Ho-fei Li Ch'in-k'o kung cheng-shu* 合肥李勤恪公政書. Compiled by Li Ching-yü 李經畬, n. d.

Li Hung-chang 李鴻章. *Li Wen-chung kung ch'üan-chi* 李文忠公全集. Compiled by Wu Ju-lun 吳汝綸, 1908.

———. *Li Wen-chung kung i-chi* 李文忠公遺集, in *Ho-fei Li-shih san-shih i-chi* 合肥李氏三世遺集, compiled by Li Kuo-chieh 李國杰, 1904.

Li Shu-ch'un 李書春. " Li Wen-chung kung Hung-chang nien-p'u " 李文忠公鴻章年譜, *Shih-hsüeh nien-pao* 史學年報, I (1929), 97–124.

Liang Ch'i-ch'ao 梁啟超. *Chung-kuo ssu-shih nien-lai ta-shih-chi, I ming Li Hung-chang* 中國四十年來大事記 (一名李鴻章), in *Yin-ping shih ho-chi* 飲冰室合集, *chuan-chi san,* Shanghai, 1936.

Liang Ssu-kuang 梁思光. *Li Hung-chang mai-kuo shih* 李鴻章賣國史. Tientsin, 1951.

Lo Erh-kang 羅爾綱. *Hsiang-chün hsin-chih* 湘軍新志. Hong Kong, 1929; 2d printing, 1949. (I did not have a printed copy of this book but used instead a handwritten copy made by Dr. Lo and presented to the Far Eastern and Russian Institute. —S.S.)

Lo Yü-tung 羅玉東. *Chung-kuo li-chin shih* 中國釐金史, Kuo-li chung-yang yen-chiu-yüan she-hui k'o-hsüeh yen-chiu-so ts'ung-k'an, No. 6 國立中央研究院社會科學研究所叢刊. Shanghai: Commercial Press, 1936. 2 vols.

Hsü-hsiu Lu-chou fu-chih 續修廬州府志. 1885.

Miao Ch'üan-sun 繆荃孫, compiler. *Hsü pei-chuan chi* 續碑傳集. 1910.

Pai Shou-i 白壽彝. *Chung-kuo chiao-t'ung shih* 中國交通史. In the series *Chung-kuo wen-hua shih ts'ung-shu* 中國文化史叢書, edited by Wang Yün-wu 王雲五. Shanghai: Commercial Press, 1937.

Shanghai-hsien-chih 上海縣志. 1872.

Shanghai-hsien hsü-chih 上海縣續志. 1918.

Shanghai-shih t'ung-chih-kuan ch'i-k'an 上海市通志舘期刊. Shanghai, 1933.

Shen Pao-chen 沈葆楨. *Shen Wen-su kung cheng-shu* 沈文肅公政書. 1880.

Sung-chiang-fu hsü-chih 松江府續志. 1884.

Ta-Ch'ing li-ch'ao shih-lu 大清歷朝實錄. Compiled by the Man-chou ti-kuo kuo-wu-yüan. Tokyo, 1937.

Tientsin fu-chih 天津府志. 1899.

Hsü Tientsin-hsien-chih 續天津縣志. 1870.

Ting Fu-pao 丁福保, and others. *Hsi-chin yu-hsiang t'ung-jen tzu-shu hui-k'an* 錫金游庠同人自述彙刊. 1931.

Ts'ai Kuan-lo 蔡冠洛. *Ch'ing-tai ch'i-pai ming-jen chuan* 清代七百名人傳. Shanghai, 1937.

Tseng Kuo-ch'üan 曾國荃. *Tseng Chung-hsiang kung ch'üan-chi* 曾忠襄公全集 (including *nien-p'u*). 1903.

Tseng Kuo-fan 曾國藩. *Tseng Wen-cheng kung ch'üan-chi* 曾文正公全集. Compiled by Li Han-chang 李瀚章 and others. 1876.

———. *Tseng Wen-cheng kung shu-cha* 曾文正公書札. 1945. (All letters by Tseng quoted in this study are taken from this source and not from *Tseng Wen-cheng kung ch'üan-chi,* which also contains his letters.)

Tso Shun-sheng 左舜生 (ed.). *Chung-kuo chin-pai-nien shih tzu-liao ch'u-pien* 中國近百年史資料初編. Shanghai, 1930.

Tso Tsung-t'ang 左宗棠. *Tso Wen-hsiang kung tsou-kao* 左文襄公奏稿, in *Tso Wen-hsiang kung ch'üan-chi* 左文襄公全集, 1888–97.

Wang Hsien-ch'ien 王先謙. *Shih-i-ch'ao Tung-hua lu* 十一朝東華錄. 1899.

Wei Hsi-yü 韋息予. *Li Hung-chang* 李鴻章. Shanghai, 1931.

Wei Yüan 魏源. *Hai-kuo t'u-chih* 海國圖志. 1849.

Wen-ch'ing 文慶, Chia Chen 賈楨, and others. *Ch'ou-pan i-wu shih-mo* 籌辦夷務始末. Peiping, 1929–30.

Wu T'ing-hsieh 吳廷燮. *Ho-fei chih-cheng nien-p'u (ch'u-kao)* 合肥執政年譜(初稿). 1938.

Books and Articles in English

Allen, Bernard M. *Gordon in China.* London: Macmillan, 1933.

Bell, Mark S. *China. Being a Military Report on the Northeastern Portions of the Provinces of Chihli and Shantung; Nanking and Its Approaches; Canton and Its Approaches; etc.* 2 vols. Simla: Government Central Branch Press, 1884.

Bland, John O. P. *Li Hung-chang.* London: Constable, 1917.

Boulger, Demetrius. *The Life of Sir Halliday Macartney.* London and New York: John Lane, 1908.

British Foreign Office. Papers Relating to Telegraphs in China, F. O. 17/380 and 1009–11. Public Record Office, London.

Brunnert, H. S. and V. V. Hagelstrom. *Present Day Political Organization of China.* Translated by A. Beltchenko and E. E. Moran. Shanghai: Kelly and Walsh, 1912.

Chang, Chung-li. *The Chinese Gentry: Studies on Their Role in Nineteenth-Century Chinese Society.* Seattle: University of Washington Press, 1955.

Chang, Chung-li and Stanley Spector (eds.). *Guide to the Memorials of Seven Leading Officials of Nineteenth-Century China.* Seattle: University of Washington Press, 1955.

Ch'en, Ch'i-t'ien (Gideon Chen). *Lin Tse-hsü, Pioneer Promoter of the Adoption of Western Means of Maritime Defense in China.* Peiping: Department of Economics, Yenching University, 1934.

————. (Review of) "First Edition of Drafts of Sheng Hsüan-huai," *Yenching Journal of Social Studies* (English ed.), Vol. III, No. 2 (August, 1941).

————. *Tseng Kuo-fan, Pioneer Promoter of the Steamship in China.* Peiping: Department of Economics, Yenching University, 1935.

Cheng, J. C. "Some Aspects of the Taiping Rebellion in China, 1850–1864." Unpublished Ph. D. dissertation, Cambridge University, England, 1950.

Chiang, Siang-tseh. *The Nien Rebellion.* Seattle : University of Washington Press, 1954.

China. Board of Revenue. " Summary of Various Cases Under Consideration by the Board of Revenue." An unpublished translation by Chung-li Chang of a photostat of a handwritten manuscript in the Peking National Library entitled " Hu-pu hsien-pan ko-an chieh-yao " 戶部現辦各案節要.

China. The Maritime Customs. Decennial Reports on the Trade, Industries, etc., of the Ports Open to Foreign Commerce, and on the Condition and Development of the Treaty Port Provinces, 1922–1931. Statistical Series No. 6. Fifth issue. 2 vols. Shanghai : Inspectorate General of Customs, 1933.

Douglas, Robert K. *Li Hungchang.* London : Bliss, Sands and Foster, 1895.

Hinton, Harold C. " Grain Transport Via the Grand Canal, 1845–1901." *Papers on China* (Mimeographed for private distribution by the East Asia Program of the Committee on Regional Studies, Harvard University), Vol. IV (1950).

Hou, Wai-lu. " Hung Hsiu-ch'üan and Hung Jen-kan, Ideologists of the Taiping Rebellion " (translated from *Hsin Chien She,* April, 1952), *Soviet Press Translations,* VII (1952), 329.

Hsiao, Kung-chuan. " Weng T'ung-ho and the Reform Movement of 1898," *Tsing Hua Journal of Chinese Studies,* N. S., I (1957), 111–245.

Hummel, Arthur W. (ed.). *Eminent Chinese of the Ch'ing Period.* 2 vols. Washington, D. C.: Govt. Print. Off., 1943–44.

Jansen, Marius. *The Japanese and Sun Yat-sen.* Cambridge : Harvard University Press, 1954.

Little, Alicia H. (Mrs. Archibald). *Intimate China.* London and Philadelphia : J. B. Lippincott, 1899.

————. *Li Hung Chang : His Life and Times.* London, etc : Cassell, 1903.

Mayers, William Frederick. *The Chinese Government, A Manual of Chinese Titles.* 2d ed. Shanghai : Kelly & Walsh, 1886.

Menne, Bernhard. *Blood and Steel : The Rise of the House of Krupp.* New York : L. Furman, 1938.

Michael, Franz H. " Regional Forces and the Decline of China's Last Dynastic Government." Unpublished manuscript.

————. " The Chinese Military Tradition," *Far Eastern Survey,* XV (1946), 65–69, 84–87.

————. " Military Organization and Power Structure of China During the Taiping Rebellion," *Pacific Historical Review,* XVIII (1949), 469–83.

————. " State and Society in Nineteenth-Century China," *World Politics,* VII (1955), 419–33.

Michael, Franz and George E. Taylor. *The Far East in the Modern World.* New York : Henry Holt, 1956.

Michie, Alexander. *The Englishman in China During the Victorian Era.* 2 vols. Edinburgh and London : W. Blackwood, 1900.

Miller, James Martin. *China : Ancient and Modern* (also published under the title *China : The Yellow Peril, At War with the World*). Chicago : Monarch Book Co., 1900.

Montalto de Jesus, C. A. *Historic Shanghai.* Shanghai : The Shanghai Mercury, 1909.

Morse, Hosea Ballou. *In the Days of the Taipings.* Salem, Mass.: The Essex Institute, 1927.

————. *The Trade and Administration of the Chinese Empire.* London, New York, etc.: Longmans, Green, 1908.

Mossman, Samuel. *General Gordon's Private Diary of His Exploits in China.* London, 1885.

The North China Herald and Supreme Court and Consular Gazette, Shanghai, weekly.

Powell, Ralph. *The Rise of Chinese Military Power, 1895–1912.* Princeton, N. J.: Princeton University Press, 1955.

Shih, Vincent Y. C. " The Ideology of the Taiping T'ien Kuo," *Sinologica,* III (1951), 1–5.

Teng, Ssu-yü, John K. Fairbank, and others. *China's Response to the West, A Documentary Survey, 1839–1923.* Cambridge : Harvard University Press, 1954.

United States Congress. 45 Cong., 2 sess., House Miscellaneous Document No. 31, pt. 2. Washington, 1878.

United States Department of State. *Despatches from United States Consuls in Chinkiang, 1865–1902,* generally referred to as *Consular Despatches, Chinkiang.* (A part of Record Group 59, General Records of the Department of State, National Archives.) Microfilm : *File Microcopies of Records in the National Archives,* No. 103. Washington : National Archives, 1947.

————. *Despatches from United States Consuls in Shanghai, 1847–1906,* generally referred to as *Consular Despatches, Shanghai.* (A part of Record Group 59, General Records of the Department of State, Na-

.tional Archives.)   Microfilm : *File Microcopies of Records in the National Archives,* No. 112. Washington : National Archives, 1947.

————. *Despatches from United States Consuls in Tientsin, 1868–1906,* generally referred to as *Consular Despatches, Tientsin.* (A part of Record Group 59, General Records of the Department of State, National Archives.) Microfilm : *File Microcopies of Records in the National Archives,* No. 114. Washington : National Archives, 1947.

————. *Despatches from United States Ministers to China,* generally referred to as *Diplomatic Despatches, China.* (A part of Record Group 59, General Records of the Department of State, National Archives.) Microfilm : *File Microcopies of Records in the National Archives,* No. 92.   Washington : National Archives, 1946.

Wilhelm, Hellmut. " The Background of Tseng Kuo-fan's Ideology," *Asiatische Studien,* III (1949), 91–100.

————.   " The Problem of Within and Without, A Confucian Attempt in Syncretism," *Journal of the History of Ideas,* XII (1951), 48–60.

Williams, Samuel Wells.   *Chinese Commercial Guide.*   5th ed. Hong Kong : A. Shortrede, 1863.

Wilson, Andrew.   *The Ever Victorious Army.*   London : W. Blackwood, 1868.

Wilson, James Harrison.   *China : Travels and Investigations in the Middle Kingdom.*   3d ed. New York : D. Appleton, 1901.

Wright, Mary Clabaugh.   *The Last Stand of Chinese Conservatism : The T'ung-chih Restoration, 1862–1874.*   Stanford : Stanford University Press, 1957.

Wright, Stanley F. *Hart and the Chinese Customs.*   Belfast : Wm. Mullan, 1950.

Wu, James T. K.   " Impact of the Taiping Rebellion on the Manchu Fiscal System," *Pacific Historical Review,* Vol. XIX, No. 3 (August, 1950).

Yung, Wing.   *My Life in China and America.*   New York : Henry Holt, 1909.

Index

Acculturation: in nineteenth-century China, viii

Advisers: to Li Hung-chang, 278-84

Allied Expeditionary Force: Boxer expedition, 267

Admiralty. *See* Naval Board

America. *See* United States of America

American Association of Shanghai: attacks Li Hung-chang, 268n

American: mercenary soldiers in China, 30; steamers, purchased by Tseng Kuo-fan, 172; shipping, decline of, at Tientsin, 243; officials, difficulty in distinguishing central and provincial authority, 276

Amoy, Fukien: port opened, vii; mentioned, 27

Anhwei troops: Tseng Kuo-fan's opinion of, 38, 39. *See also* Huai Army

Anking, Anhwei: captured by Tseng Kuo-fan (1861), 24, 25; arsenal, 154. *See also* Arms; Arsenals; Munitions

Annam War [Sino-French War]: contribution bureau established for military support, 224. *See also* Sino-French War

Anti-Christian outbreaks, in Szechwan and Kweichow, 129

Appointments: of officials, xxiv; of revenue collectors at Shanghai by Li Hung-chang, 63-65. *See also* Bureaucracy; Bureaucratic machine

Arbitration: role of gentry in, xxv, xxvi

Arms: prohibition of right to carry, xxiv; production, 162, 163, 166. *See also* Arsenals; Munitions; Weapons

Army: corruption, xxxii; as source of government authority, xxxii; control as power factor, xxxv; of central government, equipment, 161; political importance of, 167. *See also* Banner armies; Hsiang Army; Huai Army; Lien-chün; Lü-ying; Military

Arrow War, 177

Arsenals: 180, 234; development, production, control of, 154-58, 160, 161, 162; as purchasing agencies, 164

—Foochow: 149n, 157, 173, 176; described as central government controlled, 174

—Kiangnan: 156, 157, 173, 174; revenues and expenditures, 174; purposes, 236

—Kuang-chou [Canton]: 157

—Nanking: 156, 165, 166, 234

—Shanghai: 155, 234

—Soochow: 155

—Tientsin: 138, 160-63 *passim*, 180, 182; accounts, 162, 163; supported by Chao Shang Chü taxes, 245. *See also* Arms production; Shipbuilding; Steamships; Tientsin Machinery Bureau; Weapons

Banner armies: bureaucratic administration within, xxxii; development of, xxxii; decline of, xxxiii-xxxv *passim;* fleet disbanded, 182

Bean-shippers, 116n

Blockade, 179

Board of Civil Offices: Tseng Kuo-fan evades regulations of, 19

Board of Foreign Affairs. *See* Tsung-li Yamen

Board of Naval Affairs. *See* Naval Board

Board of Posts and Communications, 244n

Board of Revenue: fails to enforce payments of due revenues to provinces, 71-

341

74; demands reduction of Huai Army, 146; subsidy schedule, 198; competition with Li Hung-chang, 219; mentioned, 90, 178. *See also* Revenue

Boat merchants: organize China Merchants' Steam Navigation Company, 238, 239. *See also* Chao Shang Chü

Bookkeeping: difficulties in, 201

Boxer Uprising, 266-67

British: forces in Shanghai, 30; forces impress Li Hung-chang, 83-84; Military Intelligence, survey of Chinese army, 165; consul at Chinkiang observes Huai Army in Kiangsu, 210

Bureau for Summoning Merchants. *See* Chao Shang Chü

Bureaucracy: defense, tax, trade functions of, viii; services to Manchu state and gentry, viii; civil and military power of, x; literary orientation of, x; types of careers in, xxix, xxx; displacement of old members in Shanghai, 51, 52; reorganized in Tientsin by Li Hung-chang, 136-39; personnel reform discussed, 179; control over, 259; factionalism within, 260; development of technician group in, 276; beginnings of changes within, 277; delineation of civil and military, 285. *See also* Central government; Government; Officials

Bureaucratic capitalism, 254-57 *passim*

Bureaucratic machine: created by Li Hung-chang in Shanghai, 60-67 *passim*, 132-33; personal loyalty of, 227; as basis of Li Hung-chang's strength, 260-61; origins, functions, and careers of members of, 285-96; gentry functions of, 286; members categorized, 286; mobility of career in, 317. *See also* Chao Shang Chü; Regional organization; Regionalism

Burgevine, Henry A.: assumes command of Ever Victorious Army, 59; dismissed, 95

Camels, 135n

Canada: toured by Li Hung-chang, 264

Canton: opened to trade, vii; supplanted by Shanghai, 27; likin from, 55; customs revenues of, withheld, 71; arsenal at, 157

Cantonese: in Li Hung-chang's employment, 133

Capitalists: foreign, take over Chinese enterprises, 248

Carles, Vice-consul: describes Huai Army, 211-12

Cassini, Count: Russian minister, 264

Cavalry: of Nien Army, 102; of Huai Army, 121, 122; of Ch'ing Army, 213

Central government: dependence upon emperor, xxx; control system as cause of decline, xxxi, xxxii; control of local administration by, xxxii; decisive role of army for, xxxv; power conflicts of, with local interests, xxxvii; fears Tseng Kuo-fan, 103; assigns revenue quotas, 216. *See also* Bureaucracy; Ch'ing dynasty; Manchu dynasty

Chang Chao-t'ang: troops of, 123

Chang Chih-mou: organizes local forces in Ho-fei, 8

Chang Chih-tung: ideas anticipated by Li Hung-chang, 237, 278; promotes industry, 266; opposes anti-foreign outbreaks, 267; employs Sheng Hsüan-huai, 279

Chang Chih-yin: supports Anhwei local forces, 9

Chang Chung-yüan: impeaches Shanghai officials, 56

Chang Hai-lung: origin and career of, 301

Chang Ho-ts'ai: Huai Army commander, 211

Chang Hung-chün: background, function, and career of, 288

Chang Kao-yüan: origin and career of, 301

Chang Shao-k'an: supports Anhwei local defense, 8

Chang Shih-heng: background, function, and career of, 288

Chang Shu-p'ing: origin and career of, 301

Chang Shu-shan: early Anhwei local corps leader, 41; origin and career of, 301. *See also* Shu-tzu-ying

Chang Shu-sheng: organizes Shu-tzu-ying, 41; campaigns in Kiangsu, 91, 92; ordered not to attack Nanking, 94; ordered to fight Nien, 107; troops of, 123; emerges from Li Hung-chang's group, 199n; subsidy request to, 209n; Commissioner for Southern Ports, 241; requested to supervise Chao Shang Chü, 242; origin and career of, 301; achieves high office, 317

Chang Tsung-yü: suicide of, 127

Chang Wen-hsüan: origin and career of, 301

Chang Yin-huan: background, function, and career of, 288

Chang-ching [Secretaries of Grand Council] : summoned by Li Hung-chang, 260n

Chang-fu: laborers and porters in Huai Army, 44, 122

Chang-lung boats : in Huai Army fleet, 182

Ch'ang-chou, Kiangsu: falls to Taipings, 25; gentry of, in Shanghai, 30; importance of, 45; attacked, 91

Ch'ang-hsing, Kiangsu: falls to Huai Army, 92

Ch'ang-lu: surtax on salt of, 218, 219; salt merchants of, protected, 219, 220

Chao Huai-yeh: origin and career of, 301

Chao Shang Chü [China Merchants' Steam Navigation Company] : study of, by Feuerwerker, xiii; sets pattern 238-57 *passim;* competes with foreign companies, 243; raises loans, 244; buys out competition, 244; corruption of, 244; under Communists, 244n; sells fleet, 244-45 *passim;* distribution of profits, 245; ratio of investment in, 245; special tax of, 245, 246; and navy, 246; fiscal operations of, 246-47; shares unsold, 274; as training ground for Li Hung-chang's bureaucratic machine, 297. *See also* Bureaucratic machine; Grain tribute; Sheng Hsüan-huai; Steamships

Chao-hsien, 10

Chekiang: gentry of, in Shanghai, 30; merchants of, concern for Shanghai, 30; corruption in clique of, 57; revenue contributions of, 208. *See also* Ch'en Fu-hsün; Tso Tsung-t'ang; Wu Hsü; Yang Fang; Ying Pao-shih

Chen-lien-chün, 217-18. *See also Lien-chün*

Ch'en Chi-tung: origin and career of, 301

Ch'en Ch'in: assists in reorganizing Tientsin customs administration, 137, 138 *passim;* background, function, and career of, 288

Ch'en Fu-hsün, 288. *See also* Chekiang

Ch'en Hung-chü, 288

Ch'en Lan-pin, 288

Ch'en Nai: and Li Hung-chang, 18; career of, 286

Ch'en Pen-jung, 301

Ch'en Shih-chieh: ordered to take over Shanghai, 47

Ch'en Shu-t'ang, 289

Ch'en Yü-ch'eng: defeated by Li Wen-an, 40; attacked by Liu Ming-ch'uan, 42

Ch'en Yün-i, 289

Cheng Kuo-k'uei, 301

Cheng Kuo-pang, 302

Cheng Tsao-ju, 289

Cheng-shao-kuan, 121

Ch'eng Hsüeh-ch'i: deserts Taipings, joins Tseng Kuo-fan, 20; joins Li Hung-chang, 83; reluctant to learn Western techniques, 84; campaigns of, 86, 91, 94, 95; career of, 302

Ch'i Chi-kuang: militia organizer of Ming dynasty, 16

Chia Ch'i-sheng, 302

Chia-ch'ing reign (1796-1820) : organization of local corps during, 7

Chia-ting, Kiangsu: attacked by Huai Army, 86

Chi-ning: supply depot for army at, 149

Chiang Chung-yüan: as governor of Anhwei, directs local corps organization, 9; as local Hunan leader, 13; requested to employ Li Hung-chang, 16

Chiang Kai-shek: controls Whampoa Academy, 318n

Chiang-pei, 117

Chiang-wai Revenue Office: established, 124; income figures of, 125

Chien-sheng: designation, defined, 9

Ch'ien Hung-pin: early local defense leader in Anhwei, 9

Ch'ien Ting-ming: local corps leader, 32; and Huai Army expedition, 33, 34, 45, 48; official biography of, 35n-36n; joins Li Hung-chang's staff, 63; as fund raiser, 97; governor, 199n; services of, as gentry, 286

Chihli, Metropolitan Province: governor-general of, 133-36, 172; military command of, 169; revenues of, 196-99; provides funds for lien-chün, 217-18 *passim*

Chin-chan-wei: Huai Army victory at, 86

Chinchow: army units at, 43

Ching Fu-tseng: career of, 286

Chin Hung-pao, 58

Chinkiang [Chen-chiang], Kiangsu: Li Hung-chang visits, 10; importance of, 26; Huai Army dispatched to, 86; customs revenue of, 196

Chin-ling [Nanking], Kiangsu: revenue office, 124. *See also* Nanking

Chin-shan: Huai Army victory at, 86

Chin-shih: degree, description of, 4

Ch'in-ping: Huai Army unit, 43, 44, 121

China Merchants' Steam Navigation Company. *See* Chao Shang Chü

China Shipping Company, 242n

Chinese companies: mortgaged to foreigners, 248

Chinese National Telegraph Administration: Sheng Hsüan-huai as manager of, 298

Chinese Navy. *See* Naval Board; Navy, Chinese

Chinese ruling group: conflicts within, ix

Chinese society: relationship of, to state, xxii; bureaucratic nature of, xxii

Chinese stockholders: investment of, in foreign companies, 258n

Ching-te-chen, Kiangsi, 22

Ch'ing dynasty: and decline of administrative and military organization, xxi; internal crises of, xxi; loss of control by, xxxi; reliance of, upon gentry, xliii; cavalry of, 213; "Veritable Records" of, and Kiangsu campaign, 45. *See also* Central government; Government; Manchu dynasty

Ch'ing-p'u, Kiangsu: attack upon, ordered, 46; Huai Army offensive against, 86

Ch'ing-tzu-ying [Ch'ing Battalion], 41, 144. *See also* Wu Ch'ang-ch'ing

Chou Fu: rises from Li Hung-chang's group, 199n; achieves high office, 317

Chou Sheng-ch'uan: his Sheng-tzu-ying reorganized, 42; transfer of his army to Shensi, 144; appointment of, to command in Chihli, 169; career of, 302

Chou Sheng-po, 42, 144, 169, 302

Chou Shou-ch'ang, 302

Chu Ch'i-ang, 239-41 *passim*, 289

Chu Ch'i-chao, 289, 297, 298

Chu Huan-ming, 302

Ch'u Army: component of Huai Army, 213

Ch'u-yung: organized as local force in Hunan, 13. *See also* Chiang Chun-yüan

Chung How's Corps, 136. *See also* Ch'ung-hou

Chung Wang [Li Hsiu-ch'eng], 103n. *See also* Li Hsiu-ch'eng; Taiping Rebellion

Ch'ung-hou: as Commissioner of Trade for Northern Ports, negotiates with French, 129; forces of, impress foreigners, 135; troops of, 136. *See also* Chung How's Corps

Circuit intendant: role of, in reporting upon officials, xxx; of Tientsin Customs, significance of, 137-39 *passim*

Civil bureaucracy. *See* Bureaucracy

Civil machine. *See* Bureaucratic machine

Civil officials: comparison of, with military officials under Li Hung-chang, 316

Civil service: violations of regulations of, 67

Coal mines: development of, 234. *See also* Mines

Coastal defense: collection of revenue for, 162; requirements for, 172; ideas of Li Hung-chang on, 175-79; organization of navy for, 181. *See also* Lien-chün; Northern Coastal Defense Bureau; Pei-yang defense

Copper mines: opened at P'ing-ch'uan, 234

Commercial activity: advocated, 178

Commercial licenses: as source of revenue, 68, 69

Commercial privileges: extended to boat merchants, 238

Commercial steam fleet. *See* Chao Shang chü

Commissioner for Northern Coastal Defense, 181. *See* Superintendent of trade for Northern Ports

Commissioner of Trade for Northern Ports: conflict of, with governor-general of Chihli, 134-36; office at Tientsin abolished, 135n, 136, 137. *See also* Commissioner for Northern Coastal Defense; Superintendent of Trade for Northern Ports

Communist movement in China, 270

Conflicts of interest: of class, group, and individual, ix; between central and regional officialdom, ix; as check on abuse of power, xxix; effects of, upon government, xxix

Confucian social order, xxii

Confucian classics: education of gentry in, xxiii

Confucian moral code: support of, by criminal code, xxiv

Conservatism: in traditional China, viii

Contributions: collection offices for, 15; coercion used in obtaining of, 58; special bureau for, in Chihli, 224. *See also* Revenue

Corruption: in dynastic decline, xxi; in Lü-ying, xxxiv; in Shanghai bureaucracy, 56; among Huai Army officers, 212; in Chao Shang Chü, 224; charged against Li Hung-chang, 263

Court: attempt of, to direct military campaign in Kiangsu, 46

Cruisers: of Pei-yang Navy, 192, 193

Customs: revenues from, 55, 178, 196, 197, 215, 216, 223, 224; administration of, by Li Hung-chang in Shanghai, 63; taxes from, related to likin, 108; struggle for income from, 108, 109; withheld by Li Hung-chang, 108, 109; regulations for, drafted in Tientsin, 137; revenues of, support Kiangnan Arsenal, 178; as largest source of Huai Army income, 215; quotas for, assigned by central government, 216; imposition of dues on foreign goods, 213-16 *passim*. *See also* Amoy; Chinkiang; Fukien; Hankow; Hsiang Army; Huai Army; *Lien-chün;* Navy, Chinese; Pei-yang defense; Opium; Revenue; Shanghai; Shanhaikuan; Shantung; Tax; Tientsin

Cyclical crises: in Chinese dynastic history, xxiii

Dairen: Huai Army units at, 143
Danish technicians: instructors at Telegraph School, 277
Defense areas: discussion by officials concerning, 178, 179
Defense corps: conflict of, with provincial troops in Shanghai, 37
Defense organization, 181
Defense sectors: China divided into, 180-81
Deficit financing: Le Hung-chang's system of, for army, 109
Degree-holders: in Li Hung-chang's bureaucratic machine, 286-87
Dockyards. *See* Arsenals
Dunn, J. G.: official of Eastern Extension Telegraph Company, 252n
Dynastic history: instability of, xxiii
Dynastic state: activities and limitations of, xxiv

Eastern Extension Telegraph Company, 252n
Economic development: views of Li Hung-chang on, 25
Economic enterprises: as source of regional power, 254
Education: of gentry, xxii, xxiii; proposed reform of, 179
Educational commissioners: responsibilities of, xxx
Electrical mines and torpedoes, 163
Elite: education and characteristics of, xxii. *See also* Bureaucracy; Gentry; Officials
Enterprises: value of Western type of, 277. *See also* Chao Shang Chü; Mines; Railroads; Sheng Hsüan-huai; Telegraphs
Empress Dowager, Tzu-hsi: naval funds misspent by, 228; *coup d'état* by, 266
England, 183

European studies: schools for, proposed, 179
Europeans: as mercenary soldiers, 30
Ever Victorious Army: success of, 30; failure to advance, 59; partial demobilization of, 75; size and costs of, 78; impression on Li Hung-chang of, 83; as model, 84; campaign of, 86; expenditures for, 101. *See also* Burgevine, Henry A.; Gordon, Colonel Charles "China"; Ward, Frederick Townsend; Wu Hsü; Yang Fang
Examination System: role of, in dynastic government, xxiii; degrees and gentry status through, xxix; preparation for examinations, 4; reform of, proposed by Li Hung-chang, 179; views of Li Hung-chang on, 272-73. *See also* Bureaucracy; Gentry; Officials

Factionalism: within bureaucracy, 260
Farmers: as future suppliers of capital, 236, 237
Feng Chün-kuang: importance of, in Li Hung-chang's foreign interests, 133; background and career of, 289; in bureaucratic machine, 298
Feng Kuei-fen: as adviser, 28, 29, 279-81 *passim;* on Shanghai local defense, 31-34 *passim;* his account of Huai Army expedition, 48; appointment of, 63; land-tax reform proposals of, 87-88; on steamship operation, 238; mentioned, 260n, 286
Feng Tzu-ts'ai, 54
Feng Yu-hsiang: in Huai Army, 319
Feng-hsien: victory of Huai Army at, 86
Fengtien: garrisons at, 218
Filipino seamen: in Ever Victorious Army, 30
Financial accounts: of Li Hung-chang, 69, 70, 100, 101, 148, 149, 199-207; system of, 100, 201. *See also* Customs; Likin; Revenue; Subsidies
Financial administration: of Shanghai, 52; of Kiangsu, 67-74 *passim*
Financial commissioners, xxx
Firearm production: government monopoly of, 236-37. *See also* Arsenals; Munitions; Weapons
Fleet: of Banner force, demobilized, 183
Fontanier, French consul, 129
Foochow: opening of, vii; surpassed by Shanghai, 27; Li Hung-chang withholds customs due to, 71; shipyards at, 180; naval forces of, 181

Foochow Arsenal. *See* Arsenals; Shen Pao-chen; Ting Jih-ch'ang; Tso Tsung-t'ang

Foreign affairs: and Tseng Kuo-fan's *mu-fu*, 19; jurisdiction of, 138, 139

Foreign customs: military revenues from, 70, 125, 126; duties on commodities, 196

Foreign machines: production of, planned, 156. *See also* Arsenals

Foreign merchants: rental of steamers to Huai Army by, 33

Foreign military instructors, 170

Foreign military threat, 185

Foreign steamship companies: control of trade by, 242

Foreign Studies Bureau [*Yang Hsüeh Chü*], 272

Foreign trade: growth of, viii, 197; role of Shanghai officials and merchants in, 57; as new source of local strength, 217

Foreign troops: expenditures by Li Hung-chang on, 75, 76; campaigns of, around Shanghai, 86

Foreign weapons: use of, by Tseng Kuo-fan, 95, 154; adoption of, by Huai Army, 122. *See also* Arsenals; Western ideas

"Fourth Tiger Hsieh": local bully in Anhwei, 9

France: negotiations by, with China, 129; dispute of, with China over Annam, 150; mentioned, 192

French forces: and protection of Shanghai, 30

Fu T'ang. *See* Li Huan

Fu-chi, governor of Anhwei, 10

Fu-shao-kuan [Assistant company commander], 121

Fukien province: rebellion in, following Taiping collapse, 102

Fund-raising: and corruption in bureaus, 56-57; for military forces, 178, *See also* Revenue

Gentry: and dynasty, viii, ix, xlii; privileges of viii, xxiii; in bureaucracy, viii, 4; militarism of, ix, x, xxxviii-xxxix; relations with officialdom, ix, xxvi, xxvii; roles and functions of xxiii-xxvi *passim*, 5; and political divisions of state, xxv; services of, and property, xxv; size of, xxv; educational and ideological authority of, xxv, xxviii; social autonomy of, xxvi; assumption of official roles during rebellion, xxvii; controls on, xxviii, xxix;

resistance of, to Taipings, xxviii, xxix, 6, 7, 12; "bad gentry," xxxvi; local government rebuilt by, xlii; and Anhwei defense, 8, 9; and Shanghai defense, 29-31; and Huai Army expedition, 47, 48; Tso Tsung-t'ang demands contributions by, 79-82 *passim*; conflict of, with Li Hung-chang, 113; failure of, to invest in railroads, 253. *See also* Bureaucracy; Elite; Local forces

German language, 276

Germany, 183

Gill, Captain: report of, on Huai Army, 171-72 *passim*

Goodnow, American consul: opposes Li Hung-chang, 268n

Gordon, Colonel Charles "China": brings Ever Victorious Army reknown, 30; dispute of, with Li Hung-chang at Soochow, 87; attacks I-hsing, 91; and Li Hung-chang, 283. *See also* Ever Victorious Army

Government: official staff of, xxiv, xxv; rights and powers of, xxiv, xxxi; tax controls of, xxiv, xxxi; checks on power within, xxix; responsibilities of, xxx; controls army and bureaucracy, xxxi; appoints regional leaders as governors, xl; supervision of commerce by, 240, 244, 255-57. *See also* Board of Revenue; Bureaucracy; Ch'ing dynasty; Manchu dynasty; Naval Board

Grain tribute: sea transportation of, 26; in Kiangsu, 68; protected by Huai Army, 144; shipments of, 209; role of Chao Shang Chü in transport of, 240; allocation of shipments of, 243. *See also* Chao Shang Chü; Land tax

Grand Canal: importance of, to Manchus, 26, 27; control of, by Huai armies, 210

Granville, Earl, 252n

Gunboats: purchase and production of, 183, 192-93. *See also* Navy, Chinese; Pei-yang defense

Gunpowder, 157. *See also* Arsenals; Munitions

Hai-chün t'i-tu [Admiral], 190

Hai-chün Yamen [Ministry of Navy], 190. *See* Naval Board

Han Chao-ch'i, 302

Han dynasty: and Confucian scholars, xxi

Han Tien-chia, 155, 156

Hangchow: relief of, 46

Hankow customs: appropriated by Li Hung-chang, 70, 71; and Chao Shang

Chü tax, 245, 246. *See also* Customs

Han-lin, 18

Han-lin Academy, 128, 279

Han-yang arsenal, 157

Hart, Sir Robert: proposal for opium tax, 91; trusted by Li Hung-chang, 227; attitude toward Li Hung-chang, 228; criticism of Pei-yang Navy, 228; mentioned, 283

Heilungchiang: garrisons in, 218

Ho Shen, xxxv

Ho Shen-hsiu, 286

Ho-fei, Anhwei: native place of Li Hung-chang, 3; local defense activity in, 8, 9; lawlessness of its people, 106

Honan: mounted rebels in, 102

Hong Kong: ceded to Great Britain, vii, viii

Hope, Admiral Sir James: and Shanghai gentry defense plan, 33

Horses: in Huai cavalry, 122

Hospital: founded by Li Hung-chang, 277

Hou Wai-lu: discusses Tseng Kuo-fan, 104n

Hsi-yung [foot soldiers], 121

Hsiang Army: as model for provincial armies, xxix; organizational pattern of, xxxix, xl; as model for Huai Army, 12; origins, 13, 14; early revenue sources of, 14-16; origins, careers, and ranks of officers of, 20, 21; deterioration and demobilization problems of, 39; organization of, compared with Huai Army, 44, 45; receives subsidies from Li Hung-chang, 77-79; battalions in Shanghai, 83; and ration shortages, 92-93; demobilization of, 97, 104; elements allied with Huai Army, 98; decline of morale in, 105; diet problems of, 120; cavalry components of, in Huai Army, 123; remnants in Kiangsu disbanded, 145; attempts at revival and modernization, 158; reliance on arsenals, 164. *See also* Regionalism; Revenue; Tseng Kuo-fan

Hsiang-chün. *See* Hsiang Army

Hsiang-yung [Hunan "Braves"], 13

Hsiao-ch'iang [small-arms] platoons in Huai Army, 43, 44

Hsiao-hu [small families], 88

Hsieh Chia-fu, 289

Hsieh clan, 9

Hsing-ying revenue office, 124, 125

Hsiung-nu ["Huns"], 51

Hsü Ch'ang, 170n

Hsü Jen, 289

Hsü Pang-tao, 302

Hsü Tao-k'uei: cavalry of, 144; mentioned, 303

Hsü Wen-ta, 290

Hsü-chou, Kiangsu: and Huai Army recruits, 119; banditry in, 120; natives in Huai Army, 123; Huai Army garrisons at, 144, 145

Hsüeh Fu-ch'eng: records experiences of Li Hung-chang, 18; recounts Huai Army expedition to Shanghai, 34; sends funds to Li Hung-chang, 227; as secretary to Li Hung-chang, 281; discusses economic development, examination reform, westernization, 282

Hsüeh Huan, governor of Kiangsu: provincial forces of, 30; opposes reinforcement of Shanghai, 32, 33; described by Tseng Kuo-fan, 36; conduct watched by Court, 45; attempts to block Huai Army expedition, 47, 48; position in Shanghai, 51-53, 59; as Commissioner of Foreign Trade in Shanghai, 60

Hsüeh Shih-yü: on Li Hung-chang's staff, 64

Hsüeh Shu-t'ang, 87

Hu Lin-i, governor of Hupeh, 61

Hu-yung, company guards, 43, 44

Huai Army: ordered by Tseng Kuo-fan, 24; early history of, 40, 41; original units of, 41, 42; and Hsiang Army, 42, 42n, 44, 45, 107; structure of, 42, 43, 44; size of, 42, 44, 45, 76, 79, 123, 124, 146, 147, 150, 207, 211; company organization of, 42-45; personal guard units of, 43, 44; and preparations for expedition to Shanghai, 47-50; Tseng Kuo-fan's memorial on expedition to Shanghai, 48, 49; expenses of, 70; Huai-yang "water troops" of, 83, 175; victories in 1862-63, 86; Huai-yang water troops attack of, 92; accused of sacking Nanking, 96n; reorganization following fall of Nanking, 98-100; composition, in 1865, 99; income and expenditures of, 1863-64, 100-101; expenditures on "foreign items," 101; revenues of, 101, 108, 109, 210; and Tseng Kuo-fan, 105, 106-7, 110; demobilization planned, 106; paid with certificates to official titles, 109; not subject to outside control, 110; regional character discussed, 112; dependence upon Kiangsu, 112-13; income, souces of, 117, 125, 126, 208-9, 213; diet problems, 120, 121; cavalry organization and size, 121, 122, 123;

changes in, during Nien campaign, 122-24; revenue offices for, 124, 125; revenues during Nien rebellion, 125, 126; role in Nien campaign, 127; dispatched to Chihli, 130; Moslem campaign, 142; location and distribution of, 142, 143, 146, 147; troop movements after 1870, 144, 145, 146; supply and procurement, 144, 149, 164; garrisons, 145, 146, 209-11 *passim;* and memorial by Li Hung-chang, 146, 147; in Shantung, 147, 148; financial accounts, 148, 149, 200-208 *passim;* and *lien-chün,* 169, 170, 217, 220; fleet, 181-83 *passim,* 252; regional character maintained, 200; manpower and income losses, 207; and Li's control over Southern units, 207; protection of grain tribute shipments, 209, 210; corruption in, 212; officers described, 212; income sources by type, 213-17; overturned, 262; backgrounds and careers of commanders, 300-314; local corps origins of commanders, 315; career achievements of commanders, 317. *See also* Regionalism; Revenue

Huang Chin-chih, 303

Huang Fang: employed by Li Hung-chang, 60, 65; as revenue collector, 87

Huang I-sheng: departs for Shanghai, 49; as commander of Huai-yang "water troops," 55, 83; origin and career of, 303

Huang Shih-lin, 303

Hunan: local corps and militia leaders, 13; as revenue source, 208, 209

Hunan Army. *See* Hsiang Army

Hundred Days of Reform, 1898: effect on Li Hung-chang, 238; as attempt to centralize power, 265

Hung Fu, Taiping King, 104

Hung Hsiu-ch'üan, 95, 104. *See also* Taiping Rebellion

Hung Jen-kan, xxxiv

Huo-yung [army cook], 43, 44

Hupeh: as revenue source, 208, 209

I'hsien, Shantung: coal mines opened at, 234

I-hsing: captured, 91

I-i chih-i ["Use barbarians to control barbarians"]: policy of Li Hung-chang, 261

Ili territory: dispute over, 148

Imperial Chinese Maritime Customs Administration, 69. *See also* Hart, Sir Robert

Imports and exports: unfavorable balance of, 250

Indemnities: paid to French and British, 72

Industrial development: regional limitations of, 251-54, *passim*

Industrial Revolution: studied by Li Hung-chang, 251. *See also* Western ideas

Industry: development of, 249-50

Inland waterways: guarded by Huai Army, 209

Iron mines: development of, 234

Ironclad vessels of war, 183, 192, 193

Japanese: agreement on withdrawal of Huai troops from Korea, 143; navy, 184, 185, 227-28 *passim;* influence on China's modernization, 238; in Korea, 261; mentioned, 192

Jen Army, 213

Jen-Ho Insurance Company, 257n

Judicial Commissioners: responsibilities of, xxx

Jung Hung (Yung Wing): background, function, and career of, 290; mentioned, 19, 156

Jung-lu, Manchu general: overthrows Reformists, 266

Kaiping mines: tax on coal exported from, 249; railroad built at, 250, 251; role of Sheng Hsüan-huai in development of, 299

K'ang Yu-wei: reforms mentioned, xlii; seeks power centralization, 261n; and dismissal of Li Hung-chang, 265; reform proposals of, 278

Kansu: rebellion in, 102

Kao T'i: recommended by Li Hung-chang, 286-87

Ke-kuo shih-wu ta-ch'en [Minister for Foreign Affairs], 187

Kiangnan Arsenal. *See* Arsenals

Kiangsu: likin revenues of, 113, 197; customs revenues of, 197; subsidies from, 215

Kiangsu gentry: and Huai Army expedition, 29-37 *passim;* interests in Shanghai, 30, 31; as revenue collectors, 63, 64. *See also* Bureaucratic machine; Gentry

Kiukiang, Kiangsi: customs revenues of, 196

Korea: transfer of Huai Army units to, 143, 213; hostilities over, 262

Kowshing: transport ship, sunk by Japanese, 262

Ku Chao-hsi, 290

Ku Wen-pin, 31, 32, 45

K'uai Te-mo, 287

Kuang-chou Arsenal [Canton Arsenal]. *See* Arsenals

Kuang-hsü emperor: and Li Hung-chang, 261n, 265

Kung Chao-yü, 290

Kuo Sung-lin: military follower of Tseng Kuo-fan, 20; reluctance of, to learn foreign military techniques, 84; campaigns of, 91, 96, 144; and Huai Army, 100; as provincial commander-in-chief of Chihli, 169; origin and career of, 303

Kuo Sung-tao: and development of likin tax, 15; in Tseng Kuo-fan's *mu-fu,* 19; career of, 61-63; on naval affairs, 185, 186; and Li Hung-chang, 199n, 279-81; end of career, 280

Kwangtung: likin revenues of, 197; Li Hung-chang as governor-general of, 266, 267

Landownership: not basis of power, xxv

Land tax: as source of revenue in Kiangsu, 68; reforms in Kiangsu, 87-89. *See also* Grain tribute; Revenue; Tax

Lang, Captain: Pei-yang naval commander, 194

Lao Hsiang-chün ["old" Hsiang Army], 160. *See also* Hsiang Army

Li Ch'ang-lo: origin and career of, 303; mentioned, 169

Li Chao-ch'ing: biography of, 99n; troops of, 123; origin and career of, 303; mentioned, 18, 111

Li Chao-t'ang, 290

Li Ch'ao-pin: commander of T'ai Lake Corps, 92

Li Chin-yung, 290

Li Ch'ing-ts'u: appointment canceled, 260-61n

Li family: as connection between Tseng Kuo-fan and Huai Army, 111

Li Feng-pao: background, function, and career of, 291; mentioned, 183

Li Han-chang: as local corps leader under Lo Ping-chang, 17; rises to high offices, 18; manages Hsiang Army likin, 22; appointed governor of Kiangsu, 110; son of, dismissed from office, 260-61n; mentioned, 20, 142, 160, 199n

Li Ho-chang: biography of, 100; origin and career of, 303; mentioned, 18, 20, 111

Li Hsing-jui, 291

Li Hsing-yüan, 23n

Li Hsiu-ch'eng, Taiping commander: campaigns of, 86, 94

Li Hsü-i, governor of Anhwei, 61

Li Huan, 23n

Li Hung-chang: as suppresser of rebellions, ix; as modernizer, ix, 234-38 *passim,* 257; rise as regional leader, x; regional armies defeat Taipings, xxxix; and dynastic crisis, xliii; poem "On Entering the Capital," 3; attains *chin-shih* degree, 6; and local corps leadership, 7, 10; and Yüan family, 10; poem, "On Leaving to Join Tseng," 16; enters Tseng Kuo-fan's *mu-fu,* 18-20; as circuit intendant, 22; dismissed by Tseng Kuo-fan, 22; rejoins Tseng Kuo-fan, 24; role in Huai Army expedition to Shanghai, 34-38; assigned eastern Kiangsu military sector, 38; his account of origin of Huai Army, 40, 41; ordered to Chinkiang, 47; appointed acting governor of Kiangsu, 50; arrives at Shanghai, 50; his *mu-fu,* 65; avoids participation in Nanking campaign, 93, 93n, 94-96; supports Tseng Kuo-fan, 105; declines to support Tso Tsung-t'ang's troops, 108; as principal regional leader, 111, 112; declines to leave Nanking, 112; impeached for corruption, 113; appointed to command Nien campaign, 117; missions to Szechwan and Kweichow, 129; appointed governor-general of Chihli, 130, 131, 133; attitude of foreigners toward, 130, 131; and concept of self-strengthening, 153; views on navy, 184, 185; and Naval Board, 188, 226-27; scope of powers, 189, 190; opposes military campaigns in western regions, 199n; as military financier, 201, 207; controls regional revenues, 210; control over officer corps, 212; finances *lien-chün,* 217-20; and Board of Revenue, 219, 233; as Commissioner of Defense of the Northern Coast, 220-26; and Sir Robert Hart, 228n; as paramount military leader, 230; appraisal of China's military situation, 233n; cultural ideas of, 237; attitude toward political reform, 238; on shipbuilding, 239; and Chao Shang Chü, 240-41, 244n, 246-47; resists foreign encroachment, 248, 249,

250; investments in weaving factory, 254; violation of bureaucratic control regulations, 260-61; illegal appointments by, 260n; decline of his power, 261, 262; negotiates Treaty of Shimonoseki, 263-64; travels to Russia, Europe, and America, 264, 265; last years of, 264-69 *passim;* appointed to Board of Foreign Affairs, 265; appointed governor-general at Canton, 266; supervises water conservancy, 266; summoned to north, 267; and United States, 267; negotiates Boxer Settlement, 268, 269; death of, 268-69; final order to Huai Army, 269; his heritage, 271; ideology of, 271-75 *passim;* examination reforms advocated by, 272; letter to Kuo Sung-tao, 273-74; described educated class, 275; relationship with Kuo Sung-tao, 280; regional nature of his command, 300, 315; nepotism of, 316n; legacy of, 318-20

Li Nan-hua, 303

Li Shan-lan: in Tseng Kuo-fan's *mu-fu,* 19, 20n

Li Sheng, 304

Li Shu-ch'ang, 291

Li Te-sheng, 304

Li Tsung-hsi, 181

Li Wen-an: father of Li Hung-chang, 4; organizes local corps, 7, 8; association with Yüan Chia-san, 13; death of, 17

Li Yüan-hua, 291

Li Yüan-tu: in Tseng Kuo-fan's secretariat, 19; impeached by Tseng Kuo-fan, 20n

Li-chia: as system of control, xxvii

Liang, currency unit, 212

Liang Ch'i-ch'ao: on Li Hung-chang and Tseng Kuo-fan, 11; on Sino-Japanese War, 184; on Li Hung-chang's enterprises, 257

Liang Ssu-kuang: views on Li Hung-chang, 275n

Liang-chiang: payment of subsidies, 198; provision of revenues, 209. *See also* Huai Army

Liang-Huai region: salt revenues to Huai Army, 215

Liaotung Peninsula: stationing of Huai troops in, 143

Lien-chün [modernized forces]: in area around capital, 137; origins of, 158, 159; adopted by Li Hung-chang, 167; command of, 169; organization of, 170; as extension of Huai Army, 217, 218;

finances of, 217-20 *passim; chen-lien-chün* and *hai-fang lien-chün,* 218; commanded by Huai officers in Chihli, 218; size of, 218; operates Mo-ho gold mines, 252. *See also* Coastal defense

Lien Hsiang-chün ["modernized" Hsiang Army], 160. *See also* Hsiang Army

Likin [*li-chin*]: origin of system, 15; commodity tribute, 58; administration in Shanghai under Li Hung-chang, 63; collections, 68, 69; importance of, 75; collected by local forces, 75, 76; bureaus reformed by Li Hung-chang, 76; new sources of, 76; kept by local and regional officials, 89; increases reported, 90; and Tseng Kuo-fan, 92-93, 97; reductions sought by gentry, 98; corruption in administration of, 113; collections, stations, articles subject to, 114; revenues from, 114, 125, 197, 213, 214, 215; on opium, 213, 214, 218; revenues for Pei-yang defense, 223, 224; discontinuation sought, 273. *See also* Opium; Revenue; Tax

Lin Chih-wang, 135n

Lin Kuo-hsiang, 304

Lin T'ai-tseng, 304

Lin Tse-hsü: and westernization, 153, 154, 172, 235

Ling Huan, 291

Literati, 12

Liu Ch'ang-yu: and *lien-chün* development, 158, 168

Liu Ch'i, 304

Liu Ch'i-hsiang, 291

Liu Chieh, 129

Liu Han-fang, 291

Liu Hsün-kao, 53

Liu Ju-i, 291

Liu Jui-fen: appointed to Su-Sung-t'ai circuit intendancy, 133; achieves high office, 317

Liu K'un-i: military leader under Tseng Kuo-fan, 20; becomes Liang-Chiang governor-general, 181; cooperates with Li Hung-chang, 199n; and subsidies to Huai Army, 209n; recommends Li Hung-chang's nephew, 260n

Liu Li-pin, 9

Liu Ming-ch'uan: early bandit career of, 42; interest in foreign military technique, 84; campaigns, 86, 91-97 *passim;* and Nien campaign, 107; cavalry of, 123; commands troops in Shensi, 135n, 144; recommended as director of proposed railroad, 253; origin and career of, 304; spectacular rise of, 317. *See*

also Ming Army; Railroads
Liu Ping-chang: rebuked in decree, 259n-60n; and Li Hung-chang, 260n, 272; origin and career of, 304; achieves high office, 317
Liu Sheng-hsiu, 304
Liu Sheng-tsao, 304
Liu Shih-ch'i: origin and career of, 305; mentioned, 92
Liu Yü-lung: artillery battalion of, 144
Liuchiu Islands: dispute over, 184
Lo Erh-kang: work cited, 20, 21n
Lo Feng-lu, 291
Lo Jung-kuang, 305
Lo Kuo-chung, 305
Lo Ping-chang, 17
Lo Tse-nan, 13
Lo Yü-tung, 197
Local bandits, xxxvi
Local "bullies," xxxvi
Local corps [*t'uan-lien*]: distinguished from bandits, xxxvi; employed by Tseng Kuo-fan, xxxix; formation of, 7; in Anhwei, 8, 9; leadership of, by Li Hung-chang, 10; as basis of Huai Army, 40-42 *passim*
Local forces: in early Ch'ing period, xxxv, xxxvi
Local gentry: and land tax, 89
Local military organizations, xxxvi. *See also* Local corps; Local volunteers
Local officials: in Shanghai, establish China Merchants' Steam Navigation Company, 238, 239
Local volunteers: in Kiangsu, 145
Lu-chou, Anhwei, 7, 8
Lü Hsien-chi: organizes local corps, 7; death of, 10
Lü Pen-yüan, 305
Lü Wen-ching, 305
Lü Yao-tou, 135n
Lü-ying: organization, composition, and command of, xxxii-xxxiii; decline and corruption of, xxxiii-xxxiv; later development of, 167, 168, 185
Luan-chou, Chihli: coal and iron mines, 234
Lung Tien-yang, 305

Ma Chien-chung: secretary to Li Hung-chang, 281; description and career of, 283
Ma Fu-chen, 305
Ma Hsin-i, 159
Ma Yü-k'un: forces of, defeated, 262; ordered to lead Huai Army to Tientsin, 269; origin and career of, 306

Macartney, Dr. Halliday, 155, 165, 283
Manchu Banners, xxxii, 167, 168
Manchu dynasty: dissolution of, vii; conflict of, with gentry and regional officials, viii, x; and gentry, viii, x; as alien dynasty, xxix; as conquest dynasty, xxxii; military forces of, xxxii; power of, protected, 259. *See also* Ch'ing dynasty
Manchuria: Huai Army in, 143; Japan blocked in, 263; concessions to Russia over, 264
Mandate of heaven, xxii
Mannick, Major, 163
Manufacturing, 178. *See also* Arsenals
Maritime customs: revenues of, 178; quotas and revenues of, 196, 197. *See also* Customs
Medhurst, British consul, 33
Medical school, 277
Mei Tung-i, 306
Meiji Restoration, 261
Merchants: from Chekiang in Shanghai, 30; complaints of, 90; as potential capitalists, 236-37; exploitation of, 255-57; suspicion of, by government, 257; failure of, to invest, 274. *See also* Chao Shang Chü; Commercial privileges
Miao P'ei-lin, xxxvi
Military academies: Tientsin Academy, founded, 234; instruction at, 276; provide training for Li's machine, 276, 277; and creation of new leaders, 318n
Military finance: and expenses of foreign weapons and ships, 73, 76; subsidies for, 80, 198, 209; and pay systems of Huai and Hsiang armies, 108, 109; in north China, 195; as part of national budget, 195, 196; and Pei-yang defense, 222; and income of Li Hung-chang (1873-91), 230-32. *See also* Contributions; Customs; Likin; Opium; Salt
Military organization: leadership of, by gentry, x; control of, as basis of bureaucratic administration, xxxv; and tax power, xxxv; of Tseng Kuo-fan, 20-21; of Li Hung-chang, 41-45; and foreign military strength, 84; and resistance to foreign techniques, 84; and Li Hung-chang's views on defense, 175-79 *passim;* need for competence in, 178; and national wealth, 242; weaknesses in, 262; characteristics of leadership of, 300-314 *passim. See also* Ever Victorious Army; Hsiang Army; Huai Army; Lien-chün; Local corps; Local

forces; Lü-ying; Manchu Banners; Navy, Chinese; Pei-yang defense

Militia, 13, 68. *See also* Local corps; Local forces

Min Tsao, 58

Mines: modernization of, 176, 177, 178, 234; importance of, 248; and arsenals, 251; and navy, 251; opened in Hu-kuang by Sheng Hsüan-huai, 299

Ming Army: campaigns of, 82, 96, 107, 111, 213; ordered to guard telegraph lines, 252. *See also* Liu Ming-ch'uan; Ming-tzu-ying

Ming-chün. *See* Ming Army

Ming-tzu-ying: local corps, organized by Liu Ming-ch'uan, 41, 42. *See also* Ming Army

Ministry of Communications, 244n

Ministry of Defense: administration of Lü-ying by, xxxiii

Ministry of Navy. *See* Naval Board

Ministry of Revenue. *See* Board of Revenue

Modernization: effects of, on Chinese bureaucracy, 276

Modernizers: in Tseng Kuo-fan's *mu-fu*, 19

Mo-ho gold mines, 234

Morse, Hosea Ballou: on China's financial system, 201

Moslem [Hui] Rebellion: origin of, xxxvii; campaigns for suppression of, 102, 144

Mu-fu [secretariat]: of Tseng Kuo-fan, 19; of Li Hung-chang, 65

Mu-yu: members of *mu-fu*, 19; of Li Hung-chang, 270-300 *passim*

Mukden: Huai Army units at, 143; subsidies to, 198

Munitions: production of, 162, 163; furnished to Chihli forces, 215; purchase and production of, 222. *See also* Arsenals; Tientsin Machinery Bureau; Weapons

Nan-ch'ang, Kiangsi, 17

Nanking: as Taiping capital, 6, 25; siege of, 93-94; fall of, 94-96; as source of loot, 95, 96; rehabilitation of, 97

Nanking Arsenal. *See* Arsenals

Nan-yang: regional command sector, 178; fleet of, 183, 184; coastal defense, 187

Nan-yang navy, 178, 183, 184. *See also* Navy, Chinese

National defense. *See* Military organization

Nationalist movement, 270

Native goods: taxes on, 72, 74

Naval Board: origins of, 186-87; misuse of, by court, 193; financial problems of, 223-27 *passim;* and the Pei-yang fleet, 228, 229. *See also* Pei-yang defense; Regionalism

Navy, Chinese: role of, 179-80; staff of, 181; purchase of modern vessels for, 183; reform of, 183; ship construction for, 184; limitations on development of, 185; provincial rivalry within, 191; organizational conflicts concerning, 192; before Sino-Japanese War, 192-93; expenditure reports for, 222; decrease of funds for, 223-24; vessels compared with Japan's, 229; medicine taught for, 277. *See also* Nan-yang navy; Pei-yang navy; Steamships

Newchwang: customs revenues of, withheld by Li Hung-chang, 71

Nieh Shih-ch'eng: killed during Boxer campaign, 267; origin and career of, 306

Nien Rebellion: origins of, xxxvii; connection of, with Ho-fei "bullies," 9; Hsiang Army campaigns for suppression of, 109; failure of government campaigns against, 110; final campaigns and collapse of, 126, 127; mentioned, 98, 102, 107

Ning-ch'uan [Ning-po boats], 239-40

Ningpo: opening of, vii; mentioned, 27

Northern Coastal Defense Bureau, 181, 183, 184. *See also* Coastal defense; Pei-yang Defense Bureau; Tientsin coastal defense

Offices: sales of, 57-58; in Chihli, 134-36

Official titles: sale of, 15, 57-58

Officials: limitations upon service of, xxx; classes of, 285. *See also* Bureaucracy

Opium: taxes upon, used for military revenues, 73; license tax on, opposed, 90, 91; military revenues from, 125; likin on, 197, 198; likin on, supports coastal defense, 218; traded privately by Li Hung-chang, 247; and Huai Army income, 245n. *See also* Customs; Likin; Tax

Opium War: local Chinese forces in, xxxix; capture by British of Chinkiang, during, 26, 27; mentioned, vii, 153, 177

Ou E-liang, 292

Pa-kung [senior licentiate], 17

P'an Ting-hsin: local corps leader in

Anhwei, 41; origin and career of, 306; achievements of, 317; mentioned, 92, 97. *See also* Ting-tzu-ying

P'an Tseng-wei: as gentry leader in Shanghai, 31, 32

Pang-pan [manager]: of cavalry, in Huai Army, 121

P'ang Chung-lu: commissioner of local militia in Shanghai, 31; influence of, 45-48 *passim*

Pao Ch'ao: mutinies in army of, 39n, 79; origin and career of, 306, 315

Pao-chia: system of local control, xxvi

Pao-shan, Kiangsu: occupied by Huai Army, 83

Pao-ting, Chihli: as residence of governor-general, 130

Parker, E. H.: tax expert on China, 201

Pawn merchants: of Chekiang, borrow government funds, 219

Pawnshops: of Li Hung-chang's family, 115

Peasants: as rebels, xxxvii

Peasant rebellions, xxxvii

Pei-yang Academy, 318

Pei-yang defense: financial accounts for (1875-91), 222-23; income sources for, by category, 223, 224; income sources for, by region, 225, 226; income for, and Li Hung-chang, 230. *See also* Coastal defense; Naval Board; Revenue

Pei-yang Defense Bureau: managed by Li Hung-chang, 188; provides *lien-chün* funds, 217; mentioned, 181, 183, 184. *See also* Northern Coastal Defense Bureau; Pei-yang defense

Pei-yang fleet. *See* Pei-yang navy

Pei-yang forces: command of, 178; accounts of, 220, 222; in Sino-Japanese War, 262; backgrounds and careers of commanders of, 300-314

Pei-yang navy: acquires gunboats, 183; modern vessels of, 184; formation of, under Li Hung-chang, 188; weakness of, 191; components of, 192, 193; and *Pei-yang ta-ch'en*, 200; accounts of, 222; quota assigned for, 224, 226; disputes over funds for, 226-27; reactions to sinking of, 228; value of, 277. *See also* Navy, Chinese

Pei-yang ta ch'en. See Commissioner of Northern Coastal Defense; Commissioner of Trade for Northern Ports; Superintendent of Trade for Northern Ports

Peking Field Force, 219

Pender, John, 252n

P'eng: military organization unit, 121

P'eng Yü-lin, 20

People's Republic of China, vii

Pethick, William: American secretary of Li Hung-chang, 284

P'i-shan-p'ao [cannon] platoons, 43, 44

Pien-hsiu [compiler], 31n

Political authority: government spheres of, xxiv

Political machine: of Li Hung-chang, installed in Shanghai, 60-67 *passim*

Political power: and landownership, xxv

Political reform: obstacles to, 238

Political reorganization: and social continuity, xxii

Power struggles: and changes in military revenue system, 217

Prince Ch'ing (I-k'uang): and Naval Board, 188

Prince Ch'un (Tsai-feng): director of Naval Board, 188, 193; fails to prevent misuse of funds, 228

Prince Kung (I-hsin): interest of, in modernization and strengthening of China, 155, 185, 273

Provincial commander-in-chief: responsibilities of, xxx

Provincial Hong Kong and Macao Steamship Corporation, 242n

Provincial revenues: as source of Huai Army income, 215; provided by treasuries, 213, 214. *See also* Revenue.

Public works: management of, by gentry, xxv, xxvi

Railroads: constructed at Kaiping mines, 234; proclamation ordering construction of, 235n; and military needs, 250; advantages described by Li Hung-chang, 253; reasons proposals fail, 253, 253n. *See also* Liu Ming-ch'uan; Sheng Hsüan-huai

Rebellion: Taiping, Nien, Hui, ix; composition of forces, xxxvii; traditional type described, xxxvii, xxxviii; following Taiping collapse, 102. *See also* Moslem Rebellion; Nien Rebellion; Taiping Rebellion

Reform: of land tax, in Kiangsu, 87-89

Regional organization: conflicts among leaders of, x; and autonomous power, xxi; leaders of, fill power void, xxi; and growth of regional armies, xxi; and formation of governments by gentry, xxvii; as basis of leadership after Taiping rebellion, xli; machines as part of official bureaucracy, xli, xlii; officials withhold revenues, 74-75; forces needed by central government, 102; as basis of military organization, 111; control of, maintained by Li Hung-chang, 113; power limitations of, 128; forces given preference over Naval Board, 229; interregional ties, 242; structure broken from outside, 261; armies of warlords, 319. *See also* Bureaucratic machine

Regionalism: development of concept, vii; defined, xxi; interpreted, xl; versus centralism in naval development, 193, 194, 226-27; effect on industrialization, 251-54 *passim. See also* Bureaucratic machine; Hsiang Army; Huai Army; Li Hung-chang; Naval Board; Navy, Chinese; Regional organization; Tseng Kuo-fan

Revenue: struggle by military for, 54; distribution in Kiangsu, 54, 55; supplied by Li Hung-chang to Tseng Kuo-fan, 54, 55; collection offices in Kiangsu acquired by Li Hung-chang, 63; Kiangsu as a source of, 68, 69; from salt, 69; misappropriations of, by Li Hung-chang, 70-74; competition for, 98; offices for collection to supply Huai Army in Nien campaign, 124, 125; for coastal defense, 162; of provinces, for defense, 178; Chihli as source of, 196-99 *passim;* quotas set by central government, 196, 197; likin, 197; struggle for, 199n. *See also* Board of Revenue; Contributions; Customs; Hsiang Army; Huai Army; Land tax; Likin; Pei-yang defense; Salt; Shanghai; Tientsin

Rice contributions: demanded by court, 74; demanded by Li Hung-chang, 79

"Root and branch" theory, 237

Russia: tension with China over Ili, 148; intervention following Sino-Japanese War, 263; and Li Hung-chang, 264; influence on Li Hung-chang feared by British and Japanese, 268

Russell and Company, 242n, 245

Salt: responsibilities of intendants of, xxx; Ch'ang-lu merchants, 7, 219, 220; tax on, 69; likin on, 69, 93, 125; merchants, 69, 220; offices controlling, 92, 93; income from, in Liang-Huai, 93; distribution of revenues from, 93, 118; government's demand for revenues from, 117; protection of shipments of, 210; as Huai Army revenue source,

213-15; production of, as source of local strength, 217; surtaxes on, 218; licenses, 219, 223, 224. *See also* Revenue; Tax

Sampans, 183

Secret societies, xxxvi

"Self-strengthening," 152

Seng-ko-lin-ch'in, 109, 110

Seward, George: United States consul at Shanghai, 68

Sha-ch'uan boats: inability of, to compete with foreign steamships, 239

Sha-men: customs revenues of, withheld, 71

Shan-ch'ing, 188

Shan-nei Revenue office, 124, 125

Shan-t'ou: customs revenues of, withheld, 71

Shanghai, Kiangsu: opening of, vii; foreign trade of, 27-29; strategic value of, 27, 82; defense corps in, 30; gentry at, 37, 45; officials at, 51-53, 55-60 *passim;* revenues of, 54, 69-70, 75, 108, 196, 210; remains important for Huai Army, 216; customs income of, supports *lien-chün,* 219. *See also* Revenue

Shanghai Arsenal. *See* Arsenals

Shanghai-Canton Telegraph, 252n

Shanghai Steam Navigation Company, 243

Shanghai Weaving Mills: opening and reconstruction of, 234; and Sheng Hsüan-huai, 299

Shanghai-Woosung Railway: destruction of, 298

Shanhaikuan: Huai Army units at, 143; revenues of, 196; revenues of, support *lien-chün,* 245

Shantung: revenue of, 208; customs revenues support coastal defense, 218

Shao-chang, Shao-kuan [company and assistant company commanders], 42-44 *passim*

She Ch'ang-yü: background, function, and career of, 292

Shen Pao-chen: in Tseng Kuo-fan's *mu-fu,* 19; considered for governorship of Kiangsu, 38; ordered to report to Tseng Kuo-fan, 45n; needs Huai Army, 145-46; discusses Kiangnan Arsenal, 164n; takes over Foochow Arsenal and dockyards, 173; achievements at Foochow Arsenal, 176; as governor-general of Liang-Chiang, 181; receives gunboats from Li Hung-chang, 183; and Taiwan defense, 187; on support of Huai Army, 210; reliance of, on

Huai Army, 211; cooperation with Li Hung-chang, 199n

Shen Pao-ch'ing: recommended and promoted, 137, 138; described by Li Hung-chang, 162; background and career of, 292

Shen Ping-ch'eng: appointed salt controller in Liang-huai, 133

Sheng Hsüan-huai: describes Li Hung-chang's role in planning Shanghai expedition, 34, 35n; reorganizes Chao Shang Chü, 244n; appointed by Li Hung-chang, 260n; survives collapse of bureaucratic machine, 263; promotes Hupeh enterprises, 266; background, function, and career of, 292; discussion of career of, 297-99. See also Railroads

Sheng-chün [Sheng Army], 111, 144, 213

Sheng-yüan: defined, 8n

Shensi: Huai Army in, 144

Shih-chang [sergeant], 121

Shih-chiao relationship, 10

Shipbuilding industry: development of, 177

Shu-chün, 111

Shu-tzu-ying [Shu battalion]: organized by Chang Shu-sheng, Chang Shu-shan, 41

Sian, Shensi, 267

Silk tax: appropriation of, 73; at Shanghai, 109. See also Tax

Sinkiang: military subsidies, 198; garrisons in, 218

Sino-French War (1885), 224

Sino-Japanese War, 248, 262

Social order: Confucian, xviii; continuity of, xviii, xx

Soldiers: pay of, 212. See also Huai Army; Military finance

Soochow: falls to Taipings, 25; gentry of, in Shanghai, 31; gentry of, at court, 36; importance of, to economy, 45; falls to Huai Army, 86; likin bureau, 210. See also Arsenals

Steamships: rented by Shanghai gentry for Huai Army, 33, 47; transport Huai Army to Shanghai, 49-50; expenditures by Huai Army on, 100; production of, 157, 173; purchased from England, 177; foreign companies in China, 242. See also Chao Shang Chü; Navy, Chinese

Special contributions: as Huai Army income source, 213, 214

State: and society relationship, xli

Strategic defense areas of China, 177

Student missions abroad, 222, 275

Students, overseas-trained: in bureaucracy, 277

Su Te-sheng, 306

Su-S'ung-t'ai: circuit intendancy, 133

Subsidies: military, 198; as major Huai Army revenue source, 213-15 passim

Sun Hsien-yin, 307

Sun Yat-sen: correspondence of, with Li Hung-chang, 268n; mentioned, 320

Sun Yu-ch'eng, 9

Sung Ch'ing: defeat of his forces, 262; origin and career of, 307; army of, 315

Sung dynasty: education, examinations, and development of elite, xxiii

Sung-tzu-chün [Sung Army]: as part of Huai organization, numbers, 100; mentioned, 82

Superintendent of Trade for Northern Ports: position described, 129; post consolidated with governor-generalship of Chihli, 137-40 passim. See also Ch'ung-hou; Commissioner of Trade for Northern Ports; Pei-yang

Szechwan: troops of, in Huai Army, 83; revenue contributions of, 208; subsidies to Huai Army from, 215

Sung-chiang: Huai Army victory at, 86

Sung-tzu-ying. See Sung-tzu-chün

Ta-hu [large families], 88

Tai Tsung-ch'ien, 292

T'ai Lake Corps: attack Ch'ang-hsing, 92

T'ai-ch'iang [firearm] platoons: in Huai Army, 43, 44

T'ai-ku Company (British), 242n

T'ai-ts'ang gentry: in Shanghai, 30, 31

Taiping Rebellion: crushed by regional forces, xxix; origin of, xxxvii; ideology, revolutionary content of, xxxviii; attempt to create new elite, xxxviii; gentry resistance to, xxxviii, xxxix; rebel forces capture Nanking, 6; threatens gentry, 12; victories in Kiangsu, 25; blockade of Yangtze River, 33; deserters employed as provincial troops, lawless activities described, 36; leaders at Soochow executed by Li Hung-chang, 87; collapse of, 96

Taiwan: stationing of Huai troops in, 142-43; naval vessels at, 184; defense of, 187

"Takee." See Yang Fang

T'ang Jen-lien, 307

T'ang Tien-k'uei, 307

T'ang Ting-kuei: location of forces of, 144, 145; origin and career of, 308

T'ang T'ing-shu: background, function,

and career, of, 293; variety of duties of, 297

Tao-mao [sword and spear] platoons: in Huai Army, 43, 44

Tax: right to impose and collect, xiv; reduction in Kiangsu, 88, 89; in Liang-chiang, by Li Hung-chang, 106; and conflicts involving gentry, 113; quotas, 196; sources, 213-17. See also Customs; Land tax; Likin; Opium; Salt; Silk tax

Tea merchants, 116n

Technicians: training of, 174

Technology: library on, maintained by Li Hung-chang, 284

Telegraph: lines guarded by Huai Army, 213; lines established, 234; and military security, 249-51 passim; school established at Tientsin, 277

Teng Chün-han, Censor: attacks Li Hung-chang's companies, 256

Teng Wan-lin, 308

Teng-chou: customs revenues withheld, 71

Textile mills: opening in Shanghai proposed, 249-50

Ti-fang chün [regional armies], 319

Tientsin: customs revenues withheld, 71; circuit intendancy of customs, 137-39; effects of Li Hung-chang's residence upon, 139; dockyards at, 180; strategic location of, 187; revenues of, 196; customs house supplies defense forces, 218, 219. See also Arsenals; Customs; Revenue; Tientsin Coastal Defense; Tientsin Machinery Bureau; Tientsin Military Academy; Tientsin Naval Academy

Tientsin coastal defense: reports of Contribution Bureau (1872-93), 220, 221; reports of lien-chün, 220, 221. See also Northern Coastal Defense Bureau; Pei-yang defense

Tientsin Machinery Bureau: accounts of, 162, 163. See also Arsenals; Tientsin Arsenal

"Tientsin Massacre," 129, 135n

Tientsin Military Academy: trains leaders of twentieth-century China, 11, 163, 234, 318n

Tientsin Naval Academy, 276, 277

Ting Jih-ch'ang: mu-yu of Tseng Kuo-fan, 19; career under Tseng Kuo-fan and Li Hung-chang, 131, 132; on defense, 178-80 passim; proposes use of steamships for tribute shipment, 238; achieves high office, 317, 318; mentioned, 97, 118, 155, 156, 162, 173, 174, 181, 183, 199n

Ting Ju-ch'ang, Huai Army water force commander: dispatched to England, 183, 184; dismissed from admiral post, 229; defeat, suicide of, 263; origin and career of, 308; mentioned, 190, 191, 194, 228

Ting Shou-ch'ang, 293

Ting-tzu-ying [Ting battalion]: commanded by P'an Ting-hsin, 41. See also P'an Ting-hsin

Torpedo and Electrical School, 163, 235

Torpedoes: production of, 177

Trade: replaces agriculture as source of wealth, 101

Tradition: manifestations of, viii

"Trained armies" [Lien-chün]: development of, 200. See also Lien-chün

Training: of military and naval officers, 276, 277

Transportation: tax as source of revenue, 69; protected by Huai Army, 144

Transit dues: appropriated by Li Hung-chang, 72-74

Treaty: opening of ports, vii; First Treaty Settlement (1842-44), viii; of Nanking, 27; of Shimonoseki 248n; for Boxer settlement, negotiated by Li Hung-chang, 268-69

Troops. See Army; Hsiang Army; Huai Army; Lien-chün; Local Corps; Lü-ying

Trotter, Captain, of Royal Engineers, 165, 211

Ts'ai Chin-chang, 308

Tsao K'e-chung, 308

Tsao Te-ch'ing, 308

Tsao-piao [grain transport troops], 210

Ts'ao Tsai-ch'un: on exploitation of merchants, 256-57

Tseng Chi-tse, 187

Tseng Kuo-ch'üan: younger brother of Tseng Kuo-fan, 20; assigned to capture Nanking, 38; compares importance of Shanghai and Nanking, 46; ordered to take Shanghai and Soochow, 46, 47; opens siege of Nanking, 86, 91; captures Nanking, 94-96 passim; needs Nanking loot for army, 96, 97; retirement forced by court, 104

Tseng Kuo-fan: and regional armies, xxi; as mentor of Li Hung-chang, xxi; his appeals to gentry, xxxviii, xxxix; on Taiping ideological attack, xxxix; as organizer of regional army, xxxix;

relationship with Li Wen-an, 6; and
Li Hung-chang, 11, 16, 38, 40; native of
Hsiang-hsiang, as a Confucianist, 13;
organizes Hsiang Army, 13, 14, 15;
his *Mu-fu* or "brain trust," 19; as
governor-general of Liang-chiang, 28;
strategic problems of, 31-38 *passim;*
Shanghai gentry opinion of, 32; negotiations with Shanghai gentry, 33;
strategy against Taipings, 37, 38; states
reasons for creating Huai Army, 39,
40; memorial describing strategy in
Kiangsu, 46; memorial reporting Huai
Army Shanghai expedition, 48, 49; on
impeachment of Wu Hsü, 56; opinion
of pro-foreign officials, 60; relationship
with Kuo Sung-tao, 61; financial assistance sought from Li Hung-chang,
77-79, 92, 93; land tax reforms in Kiangsu, 87-89; strategy for Nanking capture, 93-96; discusses suspicions against
him, 103; instructions on military command to Li Hung-chang, 106; assumes
command of Nien campaign, 109; succeeded by Li Hung-chang, 112; reappointed governor-general of Liang-
chiang, 119, 159; provides rations for
Huai Army, 124-27; modernization attempts of, 158-60; regional outlook of,
160; and *lien-chün,* 168, 169, 217; and
navy, 172, 173; classified as "civil" official, 285. *See also* Hsiang Army
Tso Pao-kuei, 308
Tso Tsung-t'ang: regional army defeats
Taipings, xxxix; in Tseng Kuo-fan's
organization, 20; role in Taiping campaign (1862), 37; armies mentioned,
45; demands rice contributions, 79;
rivalry with Li Hung-chang, 79-82 *passim,* 199n; memorial denouncing Yang
Fang, 80-82; governor-general of Liang-chiang, 149; develops gunpowder
works, 166; retains control of Fukien-
Chekiang region, 180; northwest campaign of, 199n; depends on subsidies,
209n; and Foochow shipyard, 239; and
telegraph rivalry, 252n; classification
of, 285. *See also* Chekiang
Tsungli Yamen [Board of Foreign Af-
fairs], 137, 139, 178, 187, 264
Tu-hsing-a, Manchu commander: seizure
of revenues by, 54
T'u Tsung-ying: appointed salt controller
of Liang-Huai, 133; achieves high office, 317
T'u-chün [military governors], 319. *See
also* Warlords

Tuan Ch'i-jui: role during Republic, 11;
origin and career of, 309; significance
of, 318-19. *See also* Warlords
T'uan-lien. See Local corps
Tui [military platoon]: organization of,
in Huai Army, 42, 43
Tung Chüan-sheng, 309
Tung Li-kao: troops of, 123; origin and
career of, 309
Tung-hai: customs revenues, 196
Tung-yang, defense zone, 180
T'ung-chih Restoration: discussed, xlii
T'ung-ling [detachment commander]: in
Huai Army organization, 44
T'ung-nien relationship: of Li Wen-an
and Tseng Kuo-fan, 18; defined, 18;
of Li Hung-chang and Kuo Sung-tao,
280
Tzu-shih [official in Huai cavalry], 121

United Defense Bureau: in Shanghai, 33
United States: Archives of, possess muster roll of Ever Victorious Army, 78;
consul of, at Tientsin, 135, 136; Li
Hung-chang's visit to, 264-65; military
and naval academies requested to accept Chinese cadets, 275

Wade, Thomas, 252n
Wang Hsiao-feng: attack on Li Hung-
chang, 273
Wang Hsüeh-mo, 65
Wang K'ai-t'ai: appointed to Li Hung-
chang's staff, 64; achieves high office,
318; mentioned, 260n
Wang Kan-ping, 9
Wang K'o-sheng, 309
Wang Shih-chen, 319
Wang Ta-ching: appointed to Li Hung-
chang's staff, 64; mentioned, 287
Wang Te-pang, 309
Wang Wen-shao: replaces Li Hung-
chang at Tientsin, 264
Wang Yung-sheng: troops of, 123; or-
igin and career of, 310; mentioned, 92
War Party: in Sino-Japanese War, 262
Ward, Frederick Townsend: commander
of Ever Victorious Army, 30; killed,
59
Warlordism: and deterioration of re-
gional organization, xli
Warlords: and Tuan Ch'i-jui, Yüan Shih-
k'ai, 318, 319
Water mines, 162, 163, 176
Water troops, 83. *See also* Huai Army
Weapons: of Chinese compared with

European weapons, 84; supply control, 161. *See also* Arms; Arsenals; Munitions

Wei Ju-ch'eng, 310

Wei Ju-kuei, 310

Wei Yüan: historian and geographer, 154

Welfare activity: role of gentry in, xxv, xxvi

Wen ["civil" officials], 285

Wen Hsiang, Grand Councilor, 273

Wen-tsung, Emperor: orders Li Wen-an to lead local forces, 40

Weng Hsin-ts'un: imperial tutor, his influence on military strategy in Kiangsu, 47

Weng T'ung-ho: antagonism toward Li Hung-chang, 261n

Western ideas: on military technology and economic development, ix; and military techniques introduced to Huai Army, 84; and weapons, Li Hungchang's views on, 154, 155; introduced to China, 234; and studies in China, 272, 273; Li Hung-chang's views on influence of, 272-74 *passim;* influence advisers to Li Hung-chang, 283, 284; and functionaries in Le Hung-chang's machine, 287-96 *passim*

Western merchants: in Shanghai, neutrality of, 32; rent ships to Huai Army, 47

Western military forces: in Shanghai, 30

Western powers: protect Shanghai, 28; intervene in settlement with Japan, 263

Whampoa Academy: control of, 318n

World market: China drawn into, viii

Wu ["military" official], 285

Wu An-k'ang, 310

Wu Ch'ang-ch'ing: local corps commander in Anhwei, commander of *Ch'ing-tzuying,* 41; transferred to Korea, 213; origin and career of, 310; mentioned, 144, 211. *See also Ch'ing-tzu-ying*

Wu Ch'ang-lu, 310

Wu Chia-shan, 293

Wu Chih-ch'ang, 293

Wu Chung-hsiang, 293

Wu Hsü: position of, in Shanghai, 32, 33, 51, 52; agrees to gentry defense plans, 33; undermined by Li Hungchang, 55-56, 59; involved in scandal, 72-73; mentioned, 48, 109, 219n. *See also* Chekiang; Ever Victorious Army

Wu Ju-lun: in Tseng Kuo-fan's *mu-fu,* 19; secretary to Li Hung-chang, compiler of his papers, 281; background, function, and career of, 293

Wu Tien-yüan, 310

Wu T'ing-fang: background, function, and career of, 293; varied functions of, 297

Wu Tsang-ch'eng, 294

Wu Yü-fen, 311

Wu Yü-lan, 311

Wu-ch'ang, Hunan, 119; supply depot, 149

Wu-I Army ["Resolute Army"]: organized by Li Chao-ch'ing, 123; in Shensi campaign, 144; reorganized, combats Boxers, 267

Wu-I-chün. *See* Wu-I Army

Wu-kung ["military merit"], 316n

Yang Ch'i-chen, 311

Yang, Chieh, 294

Yang Fang: manages finances of Shanghai defense corps, 30; heads Chekiang clique, 51; corruption of, 57; and Burgevine, 59-60; denounced by Tso Tsung-t'ang, 80-82; mentioned, 219n. *See also* Chekiang

Yang Hsiu-ch'ing, xxxviii

Yang Sou-mei, 294

Yang Ting-hsün: commander of Szechwan troops of Huai organization, 83, 92, 122, 311

Yang Tsung-lien: background and career of, 294; varied functions of, 297

Yang Yüeh-pin, 108

Yang-chow: supply depot at, 149

Yeh Chih-ch'ao, 311

Yeh T'ing-chuan, 294

Yellow River Conservancy: Li Hungchang as commissioner for, 266

Yen Wei: appointed to Li Hung-chang's staff, 64

Yin-ts'ao, Anhwei: early local corps service of Li Hung-chang at, 10

Ying [battalion], 42

Ying Han, Governor-general: personal power limited by government, 260n

Ying Pao-shih: negotiates with foreigners at Shanghai, 33; hires steamers, 47; appointed by Li Hung-chang, 64; promoted, 132, 133; career of, 295. *See also* Chekiang

Ying-k'ou, 170

Ying-kuan [battalion commander], 42

Yü Lien-fang: attack by, upon Le Hungchang, 273

Yü Ping: plot of, in Shanghai, 58